Political Networks and Social Movements

POLITICAL NETWORKS AND SOCIAL MOVEMENTS

Bolivian State–Society Relations under Evo Morales, 2006–2016

Soledad Valdivia Rivera

berghahn
NEW YORK · OXFORD
www.berghahnbooks.com

First published in 2019 by
Berghahn Books
www.berghahnbooks.com

Library of Congress Cataloging-in-Publication Data
Names: Valdivia Rivera, Soledad, author.
Title: Political networks and social movements : Bolivian state-society
  relations under Evo Morales, 2006-2016 / Soledad Valdivia Rivera.
Description: New York : Berghahn Books, 2019. | Series: Cedla Latin America
  studies ; Volume 106 | Includes bibliographical references and index.
Identifiers: LCCN 2019006551 (print) | LCCN 2019009042 (ebook) | ISBN
  9781789202205 (ebook) | ISBN 9781789202199 (hardback : alk. paper)
Subjects: LCSH: Political participation--Bolivia. | Democracy--Bolivia. |
  Social movements--Political aspects--Bolivia. | Policy networks--Bolivia. |
  Morales Ayma, Evo, 1959- | Movimiento al Socialismo (Bolivia) |
  Bolivia--Politics and government--2006-
Classification: LCC JL2281 (ebook) | LCC JL2281 .V34 2019 (print) | DDC
  306.20984/0901512--dc23
LC record available at https://lccn.loc.gov/2019006551

British Library Cataloguing in Publication Data
A catalogue record for this book is available from the British Library

ISBN 978-1-78920-219-9 hardback
ISBN 978-1-78920-220-5 ebook

Contents

Illustrations

Figures

Table

Introduction

The presidential elections in December 2005 in Bolivia represented a milestone in the country's history, with social leader Evo Morales being chosen as the first president of indigenous origin. The uniqueness of this situation was also reinforced by the absolute majority the Movement towards Socialism (MAS) – a left-wing coalition of social movements that had chosen the coca farmer as their leader – won in the vote. Since Morales came to power in January 2006, the country has been the scene of a series of reforms that have substantially transformed the relationship between state and society. Equally important is the fact that, since then, the MAS and Evo Morales have managed to consolidate a regime that has lasted for more than ten years. During this period, Bolivia has experienced significant economic growth, together with political transformations such as the formulation of a new state constitution, the implementation of redistributive policies and the nationalisation of strategic sectors. At the same time, serious questions have been raised about corruption, deficiencies in the justice system and authoritarianism.

Despite this, the MAS's staying in power has equalled economic and political stability. This is important, since Morales' electoral victory occurred after a period marked by an insurgence of strong social movements and a legitimacy crisis in the political system. Between 2000 and 2005, there were several episodes of social unrest, in which an increasingly structured set of social movements opposed the state, forcing U-turns in state policies as well as the resignation of two constitutional presidents on more than one occasion. The socio-political crisis in this period resulted in a scenario of 'ungovernability' that posed serious questions to the state of democracy, twenty years after it had been reinstalled in the Andean country. The first years of the Morales government were marked by social unrest but, after the new constitution was passed, although social conflict has been pervasive, the political impasse seems to have been overcome. The high number of votes won by the MAS and its leader in the re-elections reflect the confidence the Bolivian population has in the regime – and particularly in Morales – as carriers and guarantors of continuity. In effect, his charismatic leadership is identified as being key to the MAS administration, and to some it is even deemed 'indispensable'.

More recently, however, there have been signs of change. On 21 February 2016, a referendum was held asking the population whether Morales should stand in the 2019 elections. The referendum proposed a reform of the new constitution concerning the article that prohibits a second re-election. The reformation of that article would potentially prolong Morales' power for two decades. Previous electoral victories gave confidence to Morales and the MAS on the referendum but a nip majority of the Bolivian people voted against the governmental plan. In that way, the referendum put an expiry date on Morales' leadership, posing the question of how a political project that had grown so dependent on its political leader could continue without him. The uncertainty surrounding the stability and governability of the country as a result of the leadership vacuum Morales would leave behind was short lived: in December 2017 the Constitutional Court ruled that re-postulating as presidential candidate is an inalienable right of all citizens 'to elect and to be elected', enshrined by the Pact of San José of Costa Rica. By this means the ban on term limits has been lifted, paving the way for Morales' candidacy at upcoming elections, while at the same time raising once again serious questions about the state of democracy in the country.

This book analyses the changing relationship between state and society, and its effect on democratisation processes in the last decade. More specifically, this study analyses the relation between the social movements and the state, particularly the 'indigenous' social movements, as the most important actors in starring and influencing the state–society relation in current Bolivian politics. The analysis aims to part from traditional conceptualisations that place social movements in opposition to the state and institutional politics, building on more recent studies and debates that question the conceptualisation of state and society as two separate spheres. Indeed, the rise to power of Morales and the MAS constitutes perhaps the clearest example in the region of the penetration of social movements into state structures. Thus, the Bolivian case is in need of a theoretical framework allowing us to make sense of a scenario in which the lines that divide state agents from social actors are blurred.

With social movements at centre stage, the arguable convergence between state and society is characterised as 'state–society interface' (Long 2001; Dagnino et al. 2006; Isunza Vera 2005, 2006a, 2006b. Subsequently, the analysis utilises the concepts of 'political networks' and 'network governance' (Kenis and Schneider 1991; Börzel 1997; Zurbriggen 2003; Sørensen and Torfing 2005a, 2005b; Kahler et al. 2009) to grasp the dynamics of the interaction of different socio-political actors who enact processes of decision-making, formulation and implementation of public policies. These concepts not only allow us to solve some of the contradictions and incoherence emerging in more traditional analysis of the state–social movements relation in

Bolivia (for example in terms of 'autonomy' and 'co-optation'); it also makes visible and conceptualises the role of other actors who appear as highly influential on the state–social movements' relation in Bolivia – that is to say, NGOs and the (new) media, and their impact on the process of democratisation.

The state–social movements' relation and its impact on democratisation situate this book outside the bulk of the literature on social movements. As della Porta and Diani (2006) point out: 'with few exceptions ..., the literature on social movements has traditionally shown little interest in democratization processes' (quoted in Rossi and della Porta 2015: 15). The New Social Movements debate dominated the last quarter of the twentieth century, emphasising the 'a-political' (Brandt 1986) or 'anti-political' nature of the 'new social movements'. Authors such as Proietto maintained that new social movements embodied a conflictive socio-cultural project whose aim was to transform everyday life and so could not be captured by the state. In that way, strictly speaking, the social movement was not a 'political actor' (1995: 370–71). Similarly, Melucci (1980) stated that the potential of new social movements lies in their concern about conquering the autonomous and independent arena of political power and of the institutional state system. In this way, Offe proposed that social movements' opportunities for action essentially exist in 'non-institutional politics' (1985: 826), which are not recognised in the doctrines and practices of liberal democracy or the welfare state. Since then, this strand of the debate has been the object of much criticism and has suffered various adaptions. Particularly the 'contentious politics' debate (McAdam, Tarrow and Tilly 2001) was important in bringing the political aspects and effects on social movements back to debate, questioning the 'a-political' conceptualisation.

However, the opposition to the state structure – and the political arena in general – has been emphatic in Latin America, particularly because of the unique socio-historic context from which social movements emerge. The wave of authoritarian regimes during the 1960s and 1970s propitiated the articulation of civil society; in other words, a large number of social movements in this period emerged in order to resist state repression and to regain democracy. During and after the democratic transition – from the beginning of the 1980s onwards – the new civil governments were not able to deal with civil society's demands for the creation of institutional instruments to ensure effective participation. Instead, the majority of the new democratic regimes adopted a top-down and technocratic model, which was combined with the implementation of severe neoliberal economic reforms. In the same way, corruption became systemic in the political class, contributing to a rapid drop in people's trust of political parties (Philip 2003), in particular in the groups most affected by the negative impact of state policies involving structural adjustments. Thus, the recent historical developments set important precedents that explain why the relationship between state and society in Latin America continues to be marked by distrust, tension and hostility, especially in Andean countries (Lagos 2001; Gibbs 2004; Drake and Hershberg 2006; Booth and Seligson 2009; Carreras 2012).

This particular socio-historical context serves to explain why the study of social movements in opposition to the state has been endemic in the region. Studies of social movements in Latin America from the 1960s onwards (feminist movements, human rights' activists, those demanding basic services, indigenous movements and environmental movements, for example), studied under the concept of 'new social movements' (Slater et al. 1985), have predominantly characterised them by their manifest opposition to the state, understood as the main source of repression and manipulation of the interests of marginalised sectors of society. For this reason, a large part of the academic discussion on social movements in Latin America has been preoccupied with the distance that should be maintained from state institutions, underlying the importance of autonomy to avoid practices of co-optation (Eckstein and Garretón1989; Escobar and Alvarez 1992; Bacallao-Pino 2016; Lopes De Souza 2016; Peña and Davies 2017).

This study aims to move beyond traditional approaches of 'autonomy' and 'co-optation'. By looking at the state–society relation, in which social movements take centre stage, and inquiring about the processes of democratisation, the book aims to contribute to filling the gap in the literature about the impact of social movements on democratisation processes (Tilly 2004; Klandermans and van Stralen 2015). In that way, the book is embedded within the academic debate on social movements and democratic construction in Latin America (see Foweraker 1995; Alvarez et al. 1998a; Lievesley 2009; Gutmann et al. 2004; Dagnino et al. 2006; Stahler-Sholk et al. 2008; Domike et al. 2008), particularly the studies that have been acknowledging and studying the growing convergence between the state and social movements, and the impact on democracy (Klandermans and van Stralen 2015; Rubin and Bennet 2015; Wolford 2015; Wickham-Crowley and Eckstein 2015; Gago and Mezzadra 2017; Fuentes-Nieva and Nelli Feroci 2017).

After the dictatorships and under neoliberalism, Latin America saw the emergence of important social movements. Perhaps the most important one towards the end of the twentieth century was the Zapatista movement in Mexico, not only because of its influence but also because it incorporated an indigenous element into the resistance against neoliberalism. Indigenous social movements were also visible in the region from the 1980s onwards. Their degree of importance was seen when Rigoberta Menchú, leader of the indigenous movement in Guatemala, won the Nobel Peace Prize. At the turn of the century, social movements were important actors in several different scenarios: the Movimiento sin Tierra in Brazil, the popular movements in

Venezuela that upheld Chavism, the Piquetero movement in Argentina, indigenous social movements in the form of the CONAIE in Ecuador and the MAS in Bolivia, and the student movement in Chile. Most recently, the region shows how 'social movements' are evolving with the use of technology, in particular social networks, with clear examples in the #YoSoy132 movement in Mexico and the more regional #NiUnaMenos. The recent removal of President Rousseff in Brazil was certainly not caused by the social movements, but the wide range of demonstrations did contribute to gaining support for the impeachment. Thus social movements, far from being on the political margins, are at the centre of the region's politics, exerting notable influence in the way democracy is practised.

Social movements in Bolivia – in particular indigenous movements – and their impact on politics and democratisation processes should be understood as part of this theoretical framework and the historical and regional context. The relevance of the MAS, and their leader Evo Morales, coming to power is explained in four parts. Firstly, through the MAS, Bolivian social movements effectively managed to penetrate state structures, demonstrating a clear political orientation while questioning the anti-state nature of social movements, diverging significantly from conceptualisations that place them in the arena of the social or of 'non-institutional politics'. What at the time was called the 'government of the social movements' is the expression and cause of the redefinition of state–society relations. The MAS and Morales' more than ten years in power have characteristics that cannot be explained by the dominant academic debate and, at the same time, they have posed and continue to pose great challenges for the Bolivian political system.

On the one hand, the Bolivian state has had to face the task of establishing (institutional) mechanisms that allow for society's demands, articulated in a wide variety of movements, to be channelled and organised. On the other, social movements have played a leading role in qualitative changes on the political scene. Being themselves the result of severe and uncompromising confrontations with the governments of the traditional political elite, who marginalised and repressed them, social movements under the Morales administration have redefined their relation with the state, transforming their traditional understanding of the state as the 'enemy' and coming to recognise it as a partner and a vehicle for emancipating reforms. In the same way, their involvement in political institutions has demanded a vision of the 'common good' that tensions with social movements' particularistic interests.

Secondly, the electoral triumph of Evo Morales, an indigenous movement leader, has been key to their further political articulation and evolvement in domestic politics, effectively challenging the position of the traditional white mestizo elite. Taking control of the executive and legislative powers suggests a re-accommodation of social structures, as well as a transformation of the political culture, as exemplified by the constituent process (2006–2009) and the new political constitution (in place since January 2009). Therefore, the recent Bolivian political process not only indicates transformations within the socio-political structure – a new social pact – but impacts on the democratic functioning of the political system.

By becoming the main vehicles for mediation between the state and society, social movements have taken on a role traditionally performed by political parties. On the one hand, the MAS is understood as a coalition of social movements with a structure that is different to that of other parties, but which participates as a political party in the electoral process and in the state structure. On the other hand, as will be seen, the political impact of the social movements does not occur exclusively by means of the political party MAS but it is embodied in a series of changing relations with the state and other important socio-political actors. This study conceptualises such relation in terms of 'political networks' that embody the 'state–society interface', bringing together various types of socio-political actors and so effectively questioning the state–society dichotomy. The more explicit political role that social movements have adopted needs to be understood in relation to the fact that, like many of its regional counterparts, the Bolivian political party system has suffered from a severe legitimacy crisis from which, arguably, it has still not been able to recover. In the same vein, aside from internal factors, the weakness of the political opposition is an external factor that accounts for the hegemonic nature of the MAS regime. In this study both social movements are understood as vehicles for political participation and representation, and so special attention is paid to the relation between the two, and its impact on the practice of democracy.

Thirdly, the state–society relationship under Morales' government presents unique characteristics that this study proposes to conceptualise as 'political networks' and 'network governance'. Whereas President Morales' first term was thrown into turmoil by the constituent process, after the approval of the new constitution and aided by economic prosperity, a relatively more stable political scenario has emerged in which a network governance dynamic can be observed. The political networks approach allows one to understand the central role of social movements in the state–society interface, while at the same time making visible the important part played by other actors, particularly national NGOs and the (new) media, in affecting the political process and the state–society relation.

Finally, the study identifies leadership as a significant factor in the state–society relationship, particularly in regard to social movements as they link up in political networks. The leaders of indigenous social movements act as joining points in the state–society relation, right at the centre of the state–society interface. Through the MAS, indigenous leaders have made their way into the state to occupy political offices, where they have encountered much tension and many contradictions. Still accountable to their grass-roots constituencies while having to act from a logic of the 'common good', social leaders stand at a seemingly impossible intersection. That position has generally been ignored by academics – the only exception, to my knowledge, being the work of Donna Lee Van Cott (2008). The importance of the issue of leadership becomes evident in the figure of Evo Morales. Morales' leadership started with the *cocalero* movement, then became the indigenous movements leadership, adopting finally the leadership of (popular) social movements. Assuming the presidency, his leadership has grown increasingly pivotal to the political process, and to the MAS project of *proceso de cambio* (process of change). Although the positive economic situation is certainly a factor, Morales' charismatic leadership has been key to his continuous electoral victories, and paradoxically, it also constitutes the main factor explaining his first defeat at the polls in the referendum held in February 2016. A significant number of his public supporters have come to regard him as 'indispensable', but there are also growing concerns about anti-democratic features, such as an alleged concentration of power and a recent, very controversial ruling by the Constitutional Court that has lifted the bans on re-election, annulling the results of the referendum that had rejected his presidential candidacy for the upcoming 2019 elections. In this way, understanding Morales' simultaneous leadership of social movements and the Bolivian government is an important element of analysis, as it addresses issues of the quality of political institutions, the judicialisation of politics, populism, the rotation of power, and their impact on democracy.

Methodology

This book is the result of qualitative research based on an 'actor-oriented approach' (Long 1999, 2001; Bigs and Matsaert 1999). This perspective explores how social actors, both 'local' and 'external' to a unique power, are continuously connected through struggles over resources, meanings and control, and institutional legitimacy. Therefore, social actors are involved in a constant process of training and transforming society, of network dynamics and of producing multiple realities, whether personal, interpersonal or collective. In this sense, society becomes 'provisional' and is never complete, but constantly in construction. The concept of an 'interface' is important in this methodological approach, since it describes where a range of actors are to be found in the processes of accommodation and conflict when generating new forms of organisation and understanding (Long 2001). The actor-oriented approach thus emphasises the effect of social actors on social structures, assigning a greater impact to the first.

This approach is particularly apt for the case study. It can be argued that, in the recent Bolivian history that preceded Morales' coming to power, social structures – in the form of state and political institutions – were not capable of capturing or reflecting the social dynamic. In this context, from a conceptual division between state and society, social movements as 'local' actors in the dominion of society have become more intertwined with other actors of the 'political institutional' domain that are understood as 'external' to society. By emphasising social actors above any kind of structure, this type of analysis makes the point of intersection – the interface – visible as an opportunity for conflict and negotiation, and in which multiple social realities are constructed. It is worth noting that the result of these encounters does not necessarily respond to what is planned or projected by these actors and may have unexpected results.

The 'interface' is made up of a series of actors who act according to a network dynamic. This aspect of the actor-orientated approach particularly stands out in this research, since it corresponds to the type of analysis that is gaining terrain in the study of the state–society relationship (Kenis and Schneider 1991; Zurbriggen 2003; Sørensen and Torfing 2005a and 2005b). The network perspective in political theory emerges from a proliferation of the concept in sociology. According to this, social organisations are the result of individual actors' planned interaction in a continuous exchange of information and other important resources, which is why society stops being exclusively controlled by a central intelligence (for example, the state). In a network analysis, modern political decision making can no longer be interpreted as being based only on formal political-institutional functions, as it is understood that such processes occur within the framework of a complex constellation of actors and of the interdependence of resources that escape the reach of formal institutions. According to Börzel (1997), network analysis has the advantage of allowing for a more detailed representation of sectorial and sub-sectorial differences, of the role of public and private actors, and of their formal and informal relations.

Taking into account these aspects of the methodology, this book considers the results of research that started in 2009. Between 2010 and 2012, two extensive research visits were carried out in the country's most important cities – La Paz, Cochabamba and Santa Cruz de la Sierra. During this seven-month period, more than fifty interviews were carried out with representatives from the MAS government, from social movements and from support institutions, as well as with intellectuals and academics working at think tanks and academic institutions. Later, the study was complemented by shorter stays in 2014 and 2016, when more than ten interviews were carried out and new material for analysis gathered. The research thus includes the analysis of a wide body of printed material. Apart from the relevant academic literature, government publications and political programmes, MAS documents and printed material from the different social movements, as well as archives from the Bolivian and international press, were studied. From 2009 onwards, different types of event were attended (in Bolivia, Chile, Europe and the United States), as well as political meetings, workshops, book launches, conferences and congresses, in which diverse types of information were collected.

Theoretical Approach

This book can be situated within the rich and ongoing debate on social movements in Latin America. At the same time, it aims to move beyond more traditional conceptualisations that emphasise the confrontation with the state, to build on more recent studies that aim to explore how current social movements – in their interaction with the state – affect the process of democratisation. In that way, the study finds embedding in the regional research agenda on the quality of democracy.

In consideration of the above, this study sees a close relationship between the academic debate on 'democratic transition' in Latin America and the antagonism or opposition that has characterised the state–social movements relationship in the dominant literature on the region. The source of the tension that marks the state–society divide is found in the real regional experiences with authoritarian and repressive regimes (although arguably the origin could be traced to the legacy of colonialism and its impact on state formation). This opposition found continuation after the transition to democracy, where the characteristic institutional weakness of the state and the failure of the neoliberal reforms to deliver citizens' expectations served to reinforce the characteristic hostility and distrust of state–society relations.

During the transition, Schumpeterian or minimalist interpretations of the practice of democracy, that emphasized the existence of political parties and electoral practices as conditions of democracy, were dominant. This placed social movements' actions at the margins of institutional politics as 'undesirable' for the establishment and consolidation of democracy: social movements had the potential to undermine and destabilise the still fragile 'democratic' institutions (political party system and elections). Later, minimalist concepts of democracy gave way to a research agenda concerned about the *quality* of democracy. As it became evident that the new civilian governments were not capable of responding to their people's most urgent needs, the return to democracy was soon encountered by increasing disillusion and citizen discontent. This stimulated the rejection of the definitions of procedures that impeded a qualitative appreciation of the democratic regime, opening the way for a more positive valuation of the role for social movements in democracy, understanding them as the empiric expression of that rejection. In opposing to the state, using pressure and protecting their autonomy, social movements played a 'democratising' role, forcing the state to be more responsive to society's needs and demands. In this way, two opposing views on the role of social movements can be distinguished. Yet, whether destabilising the democratic regime or making it more democratic, social movements are in both views understood to be in conflict with institutional politics and the state structure, reproducing or reinforcing the state–society dichotomy.

As stated before, this study aims to move beyond this opposition, to account for the visible collaborations between state and social movements, and their impact on the process of democratisation. For that reason, it is important to define democracy as a type of relationship between the state and society. The definitions of 'democracy' and 'democratisation' formulated by Charles Tilly (2007) are useful. Tilly defines democracy as a type of relationship between the state and citizens in which the state acts according to the will of the people. According to this definition, Tilly understands that 'democratisation' occurs when there is an increase in the level of correspondence between state politics and the will of the people. As a result, if this goes down, a 'de-democratisation' process is observed. Thus, Tilly offers a way of appreciating the democratic quality of a regime that has previously been qualified as (minimally) democratic, such as the case of Bolivia since the beginning of the 1980s. This definition of democracy allows us to understand how changes in the relationship between the state and social movements in particular – and the state and society in general – affect the 'democratisation' (and the 'de-democratisation') process in Bolivia.

The joint responsibility of the state and society that Tilly's definition suggests is in line with the most recent studies on social movements, in which the practice of these kinds of actor has caused the state–society dichotomy to be questioned. The dichotomy assumes a homogeneity in both spheres and thus produces a qualitative division between 'institutionalised politics' (party politics) and 'non-institutionalised politics' (e.g. social movements). However, such homogeneity does not seem to find empiric support. On the one hand, critics argue that conceptualising the state as a single body with extraordinary faculties in an elevated sphere, that exercises tutorage on citizens in a vertical relationship, minimalises and trivialises 'the rich negotiations, interaction and resistance that occurs between multiple systems of rules in human society' (Migdal 2001: 15). Dagnino et al. (2006) explain that, in the Latin American context, the state has been conceptualised as a homogenous entity that has come to embody all the vices of politics, but that this conceptualisation has failed to acknowledge the diversity of the practices and interactions that can be observed in different political acts and in different periods. On the other hand, Goldstone et al. (2003: 2) propose that social movements make up an essential element of normal politics in modern societies, questioning the dominant vision that places social movements in the domain of the 'non-institutionalised'. This view has found support in important authors (Costain and McFarland 1998; McAdam, Tarrow and Tilly 2001). In as far as it challenges a qualitative separation between political parties and social movements, this line of analysis appears particularly relevant, allowing us to make sense of the MAS party as a coalition of social movements.

These questions and propositions are congruent with the recent academic debate on the construction of democracy in Latin America, which states that in order to improve the quality of the democratic practice it is key to recognise plurality as characteristic of modern societies. Social movements have played an important role in this sense, emphasising pluralism and tolerance, pushing democracy to be constructed in a context of a multiplicity of subjects and spaces, and mutual recognition of the difference (Fals Borda 1992). Cannon and Kirby have proposed the need to conceive the state–society relationship as 'dialectic' (2012: 7) – in a process of mutual shaping and constitution – to gain a deeper understanding of the region's democratisation process. Along the same lines, Dagnino et al. (2006) suggest understanding the democratisation process as links, coordination and movement between civil society and the state, under the premise that both actors are historically mutually constitutive.

Thus, building on the aforementioned academic debates, this study sets out with the idea that the state–society dichotomy obstructs rather than facilitates the analysis of the state–social movements' relationship in Bolivia. With the aim of moving beyond a dichotomist vision, this research introduces an alternative view, making use of the concepts of 'state–society interface', 'political networks' and 'network governance'. The concepts are particularly useful since they make explicit reference to the crossroad – the connections between different actors that are dominantly understood as coming from either the sphere of the state of from the sphere of society. By laying the focus on the points of interaction, where the borders are blurred, from this approach actors are more accurately labelled as 'socio-political'.

The network approach is initially presented as a tool that helps to visualise the complexity in the state–society relationship. However, considering the theoretical debate surrounding the concept, 'political networks' also suggests a new type of governance that responds to the nature of modern societies. The so-called 'network governance' entails a more flexible and complex kind of governance, in which socio-political actors form different alliances and collaborations, according to the specific matters they are involved in. The network approach seems more capable of dealing with the diversity, conflict and complexity characteristic of modern societies, while considering their democratising potential (Börzel 1997; E. Sørensen 2002).

Finally, the concept of 'network governance' implies a more explicit political role for organisations in society – the social movements in this particular case study – which poses the question about the effect of a state and social movements network dynamic on the democratisation process. For this reason, the study also registers – though in a limited way – the debate on 'governability' (Revilla 1994; Camou 2000; Prats 2001; Silva and Rojas Aravena 2013), since this allows for an analysis of the functionality of the state–society/social movements relationship, without losing sight of its regulatory component.

Academic and Social Justifications

In theoretical terms, Latin American social movements have long appeared as social actors – that is to say, beyond or on the margins of institutional politics – who have organised according to particular interests with the aim of pressuring the state and gaining attention for their demands. In this model, questions about autonomy and co-optation take on a central role, since they define a social movement's capacity to influence the state. More specifically, social movements' autonomy in relation to the state and political institutions is highly valued as the expression of the democratic values and citizen participation that oppose and challenge the vices of the political system. By avoiding manipulative co-optation by the state, social movements can effectively pressure formal political institutions, making these more responsive to the needs of sectors of society that have remained voiceless in formal channels. In this way, social movements, while maintaining a tense distance from the state, provide a significant contribution to consolidating or strengthening democracy.

The inclusion of indigenous social movements in formal politics in Bolivia, and their capicity to effectively influence national politics, is a very recent political phenomenon. As such, the rise to power of the MAS – as a coalition of social movements – has characteristics that do not fit well with the dominant model described above. In Bolivia, the social movements have taken on a very central political role as they have effectively entered the state structure. In this sense, the Bolivian political scenario under Evo Morales' government offers an excellent opportunity to explore both the possibilities and the contradictions of a growing convergence between state institutions and social movements organisations.

In the same way, the overlapping in the interaction reinforces the questioning of the state–society dichotomy and points towards the need to complement the debate on social movements and the construction of democracy in Latin America with a theoretical perspective that allows for a more reliable appreciation of the complex relationship and the challenges to governance that modern scenarios present. In this sense, a network analysis is advantageous, since it allows for a wider and more dynamic vision of socio-political actors in a 'state–society interface', where social movements play a central role, and where other decisive actors become visible: NGOs and the media.

As far as social relevance is concerned, Bolivia has historically been one of the region's most politically unstable countries, and the country's prior experiences with democratic regimes shows that these were not viable over long periods of time. Although the period 2006–2016 has been characterised as one of relative political stability and economic development, clashes with indigenous movements, and current developments surrounding the extended presidency of Evo Morales, have given way to the questioning of the democratic quality of the regime. Social movements have undoubtedly been the main actors in Bolivian politics in the last few years, and it can be argued that they have always played a significant role in domestic politics in the country's modern history. The relationship between the state and social movements seems to have changed substantially under Morales, with the country embarking on a reform of the state–society relationship, and on the basis of this study, it is expected to continue be a key aspect of Bolivian politics. For these reasons, it is important to question how this type of relationship, characterised by a greater convergence between social actors and politicians, has affected the Bolivian process of democratic consolidation. Indeed, the study argues that only by understanding the complexity of the state–society relationship can the regime's democratic quality and its process of consolidation be appreciated.

Likewise, it should be considered that the Bolivian case is highly linked to its regional context. Countries such as Mexico, Guatemala, Peru and, in particular, Ecuador have active indigenous social movements in politics that see Bolivia as an important regional reference as far as the emancipation of indigenous populations is concerned. More generally, despite the economic boom in Latin America in the last decade, levels of inequality have remained high. This inequality inevitably translates into the exclusion of groups in society, pointing to the need to study the institutional experiments and innovations that underpin a more democratic relationship between the state and society, as well as the more inclusive political decision-making processes. The political reforms carried out in Bolivia in this sense during Morales' administration are a clear opportunity for this.

Lastly, after a wave of leftist regimes that justified terms such as 'the pink tide' and the 'turn to the left', progressive regimes seem to have lost their impetus: the election of Macri in Argentina put an end to ten years of the Kirschners' rule; Brazil had serious difficulties in overcoming the political crisis that led to the removal of Dilma Rousseff while we await the impact of the recently elected extreme right candidate Jair Bolsonaro; and the rapid deterioration of Maduro's regime in Venezuela all question the left's position in Latin America. After a period of consistent economic growth, these regimes seem to have experienced serious difficulties when dealing with the increasing demands of a growing middle class, particularly in the recent economic downturn. Morales' re-election in Bolivia in 2014 and the real possibility a new re-election in 2019 shows that Bolivia is somehow resisting the regional tendency, which immediately leads to questions of 'how?' and 'for how long?'.

Structure of the Book

After this Introduction, Chapter 1 presents a theoretical framework on the state–social movement relationship and its effect on democracy. Firstly, it looks at how the relationship was understood by academics during and after the 'democratic transition' within a specific conceptualisation of 'democracy' in direct relation to the socio-historic context. This debate is identified as key to understanding the dominant antagonistic vision of the relationship and the reification of the state–society dichotomy. The discussion is followed by an overview of the different roles that have been ascribed to social movements in the construction of democracy, and that have been embedded in the division between 'institutionalised politics' and 'non-institutionalised politics'. At this point, views that make a case for a more integrated vision of state and society are introduced. The concepts of 'state–society interface' and 'political networks' are put forward as they contribute to a more accurate appreciation of the state–society relation in general, and the state–social movements relation in particular. Finally, the concept of 'governability' is briefly discussed with the aim of including in the analysis the element of *viability* of state–society relations. Indeed, if we can recognize that there is a more integrated relation between state and society actors, then it is necessary to pose questions about the impact of this for the political model. In other words, it is not sufficient to look at how democratic the relationship is, but also at how feasible the model or political system is in terms of governability.

Chapter 2 analyses the socio-historic context, tracing the development of social movements from marginal social actors to central political agents. The most significant facts from after the return to democracy at the beginning of the 1980s are collected, following the trajectory of the political articulation of social movements. Covering the period between 1980 and 2005, it is seen how, after the transition to democracy, a Marxist analysis and the centrality of the Bolivian Workers' Centre (COB) are gradually replaced by a culture-based discourse on indigenous identity and indigenous social movements. This is expressed in the growing importance of Katarist political thought, as well as through the creation and rise of what would come to be known as the Unified Syndical Confederation of Peasant Workers of Bolivia (CSUTCB), to the detriment of the Bolivian Workers' Centre.

Taking this into consideration, the chapter continues by tracing the beginnings of the Movement towards Socialism. The creation of the 'political instrument of the social movements' answers to the political articulation and further coordination of indigenous social movements, as well as to their interaction with the neoliberal state. The severe policies that were adopted during the US-led 'war on drugs' were particularly repressive of coca peasants, resulting in the formation of the *cocalero* social movement. At the same time, decentralisation policies and a growing distrust of the *democracia pactada* that characterised the political party system, created a scenario in which the *cocalero* movement would gain more national importance. By projecting itself as a national popular movement against the imperialism of the United States, and by gaining a more national profile as a popular struggle, at the same time as taking advantage of recently created institutional opportunities for participation with their own alternative 'instrument', the movement will gain national recognition and profile, forming the bases for the consolidation of the Movement towards Socialism.

Interaction between the state (in the form of public policies), the *democracia pactada* of political parties and rebel social movements amounted to a governability crisis, known as *el ciclo de las movilizaciones* (the cycle of mobilizations), between 2000 and 2005. Social movements became more visible and influential, with clear episodes in the 'Water War' (2000) and the 'Gas War' (2003). At the same time, the various indigenous movements progressed in the organisation and coordination of strategies, gaining more political influence, and leading to the creation of the *Pacto de Unidad* (Unity Pact) – an expression of the empowerment of the indigenous movement. That development would be seen as a determining factor when explaining the victory of the MAS and its leader, Evo Morales, in the December 2005 presidential elections.

The following chapters embark on an analysis of the political scenario during the Morales government. Chapter 3 analyses the Bolivian constituent process (2006–2009) as 'state–society interface' (Dagnino et al. 2006). The interaction between state and society, which is identified as key in understanding the political articulation of the social movements, continues and becomes more explicit during the first few years of the Morales administration, where the mutual and continuous reshaping between and state and society actors is observed. The demand for a constituent assembly had served as a container for the plethora of demands and reforms demanded by the different sectors of society, and so it had been one of the main features of the MAS electoral campaign. The chapter first analyses the constituent process as part of 'the judicialisation of politics' and 'the new Latin American constitutionality' in which legal structures and a language of rights acquires greater importance. Thereafter, the concept of 'state–society interface' is used to analyse the conflicts, contradictions and negotiations that characterised the period. This concept allows for the analysis to be extended beyond the institutional body of the constituent assembly to consider the influence of events and processes that took place in 'non-institutional' spaces. Here a defining role for social movements – especially indigenous movement organisations and civic movements – is once again observed, in which the confrontations on the streets were just as or even more important to the result of the constituent process than what happened within the confines of the Constituent Assembly.

The chapter continues by describing the participation of social movements in 'political networks'. This analysis shows how social movements, while maintaining their political activism in the form of social mobilisation, also connected with state agents and institutions (through the MAS), as well as with other decisive actors such as NGOs (or support institutions) and the media. In this way, the limits between formal decision-making opportunities and those involving social struggle and society are challenged – or blurred, at the very least. During this period, the social movements' 'format' is still the most effective form of political participation, although the connection with other types of actor emerges as key to understanding their impact in the political arena and on decision making.

Chapter 4 analyses the network dynamic in the state–society relationship during the post-constituent period. The political scenario was in turmoil until 2009, with important confrontations between the MAS government and the political opposition. By contrast, the following term of Morales' government was characterised by *relative* stability, combining the consolidation of the MAS hegemony and strong economic growth. During this period the relationship between social movements and the state acquires a more diverse content, varying over time and frequently contradictory, at least in the traditional analytical terms of 'autonomy' and 'co-optation'. The chapter draws a more complex scenario of changing alliances and oppositions, one that also involves other 'socio-political' actors. This is seen in the analysis of the most noteworthy socio-political conflicts between 2010 and 2016, in which, next to the centre state of social movements, NGOs and the media continue to exert considerable influence in politics. Finally, the analysis locates the Movement towards Socialism at the crossroads between state and society, and considering the shortcomings of alternative conceptualisations as 'political party', 'social movement' and other hybrids such as 'movement party', suggests a conceptualisation as a 'political network'.

The characterisation of the Bolivian political scenario as a 'state–society interface' embodied by political networks, leading to a network governance, may give the impression that they dynamics are relatively horizontal, but the salient role of political leadership in the figure of Evo Morales shows they are not. The last chapter focuses on the topic of political leadership to analyse this factor, which has been identified as a gap in the literature on social movements. The study sees social political leadership standing at the crossroads between state and society, playing a key role in mediation – an extremely difficult position to occupy, full of contradictions and conflict. The most striking example is that of Evo Morales, whose leadership has been key to the political process of the last two decades, and who seems to be indispensable to its future. A network analysis once again helps to discern the central role of political leadership in the state–social movements relationship. As the analysis show, articulating and entering on particular political networks is for a significant part the result of the leaders' agency. Morales appears as a successful leader in a context of network governance precisely because of his capacity to orchestrate and consolidate political networks, despite divergent interests and actors (also international ones).

In that way, the network perspective serves to explain the predominance of Morales' leadership. Subsequently, the chapter reflects on the impact of political leadership in a context of network governance on the process of democratisation. In order to do so, an analysis is presented of the events around the referendum in February 2016, through which Morales aimed to secure his candidature for the elections in 2019. The network analysis shows the involvement of socio-political actors in 'political networks', with a starring role for the media and the new social media, as illustrative of how different political interests act and react in modern political scenarios. More specifically, it analyses the issue of re-election, as the topical materialization of the role of leader in the construction of democracy.

To end, the Conclusion presents a summary of the research's results, as it reflects on the significance of the 'network governance' in understanding changes to the state–social movements' relationship in particular, and the state–society one in general. By suggesting that there is a much more interconnected and dynamic relationship between socio-political actors of different types, the concept of 'network governance' seems apt to describe the characteristics of the Bolivian political process. Likewise, it suggests that Morales' government and the centrality of social movements in the political arena are not quite unique or extraordinary, but rather it presents the Bolivian experience with a type of diverse and complex governance that is characteristic of modern societies.

Lastly, the Conclusion deals with the concept of 'governability'. The central role of social movements and their connection with a state structure that attempts to be more responsive to the needs of society suggests a greater correspondence between the political projects embodied by society and those enacted by the state as key to strengthening democracy. However, the central role of an actor characterised by activism, aggressiveness and conflict, plus the complexity of the relationship between socio-political actors and the importance of a quite unpredictable factor like the political leader, all suggest at the very least cautious optimism about the governability of this model.

1

Social Movements, the State and Political Networks in the Construction of Democracy in Latin America

The study of social movements in Latin America has generally portrayed a hostile relationship vis-à-vis the state, that finds embeddedness in the state–society dichotomy. Social movements have been conceptualised in the sphere of society where they assume one of two positions: either, maintaining a certain distance from the state, which allows them to achieve their aims exactly because they stand on the borders of formal politics; or, by enacting collective action and pressurising the state that seems ever reluctant to deal with their demands. In the Latin American context, the origin of the antagonistic character of the relation can be traced to the emergence of Latin American social movements in a scenario of authoritarianism and state repression, as discussed in the academic debate on 'democratic transition'. This discussion has built on a conceptualisation of state and society as two separate spheres of actions, which has subsequently been pervasive in the study of Latin American social movements.

Firstly, the theoretical discussion about the social movement phenomenon and, more specifically, the debate on 'new' social movements should be tackled. This concept emerged in the 1960s from movements in Europe and North America, serving as a reference for the study of this phenomenon in the Latin American region. This implied a certain adaptation of the concept, not least because of the need to adjust to a different context, in which social movements' greatest concern was the recovery, not the consolidation, of democracy. In its subsequent conceptualisations in Latin America, the constant division between state and society is seen, characterised by a relationship that is a somewhat hostile on both sides. This occurs, to a great extent, due to the specific experience with the authoritarian regimes that repressed the actors in society, which persisted in post-transition contexts in the political projects identified in the region.

However, the state–society dichotomy has been called into question by the more recent debates on social movements as well as other academic debates. Central to this discussion are the porosity or blurring of the limits that separate the state from society, making visible the limitations of the dichotomy. This is why the concept of political networks is resorted to, since, in a more fragmented vision both of the state and society, it makes explicit reference to the interaction of different actors when these paths cross. In this way, in this study the 'political networks' are understood to embody the 'state–society interface' that has been observed in the Latin American debate regarding the construction of democracy. This perspective not only proposes a different vision of the state and society with its more positive relationship, but also a new type of governance that emerges from the nature and needs of modern societies, whose characteristics bury democratising power. Although 'democratic', the question arises as to how *feasible* this type of 'network governance' is, since it implies a much more central role for social actors – in this research, social movements. For this reason, the concept of 'governability' is finally and briefly introduced, as it offers an appraisal in terms of functionality without losing sight of the regulatory component.

Thus, this chapter firstly characterises the predominant conceptualisation of social movements in opposition to the state, particularly in the Latin American context and within the debate on the construction of democracy. Thereafter, following recent debates, it questions the state–society dichotomy that conceives state and society actors as moving in separate spheres of action. This questioning justifies the following introduction of the network approach as a feasible conceptualisation that moves beyond the traditional categories ('conflict/autonomy vs. co-optation', 'institutionalised vs. non-institutionalised politics', 'representative vs. participatory democracy', 'the social vs. the political'), as it not only solves the contradictions and incoherence emerging from more traditional conceptualisations, but it also allows for a more complex scenario in which the role of other socio-political actors becomes visible.

'New' Social Movements in the Construction of Democracy in Latin America

Theories dealing with social movements in Latin America have been developed referring to the existing literature on social movements in Europe and North America. McAdam, McCarthy and Zald (1996) generally conclude that the vast production of theories emerging from the turbulent 1960s is concentrated on three broad combinations of factors that analyse the emergence and development of social movements. McAdam et al. maintain that the majority of social movements are caused by social changes that make the established political order more vulnerable or receptive to change (*political opportunity theories*). However, these 'political opportunities' are only a precondition for action. If there is not sufficient (either formal or informal) organisation, these opportunities run the risk of not being taken advantage of (*resource mobilisation theories*). With the aim of interceding between the structures that provide opportunities and the organisation itself, a combination of shared definitions and meanings must emerge (*frame theories*). Once the social movement has appeared, the opportunities and limitations stop being independent of the movement's actions. In other words, the structure of political opportunities stops being a reflection of the changes that occur in the environment and becomes a product of the movement's interaction with this environment.

Along these same lines, Thompson and Tapscott (2010) identify three main questions for the study of social movements: (1) what motivates groups or communities to take collective action; (2) how social movements come together in different forms of collective action; and (3) who exactly gets involved in social movements. Thus, Thompson and Tapscott identify three main threads. The first refers to the view that emphasises the role of mobilising resources and structures of opportunity in either more or less formal types of social movement action. The second unites the views that emphasise the importance of collective interpretation (*framing processes*) and the creation of collective identities. The third underlines the importance of putting the social movement into a historical and country context.

Together with these main concerns of the study of social movements, theories have been developed since the 1960s on 'new social movements', such as the feminist, environmental, pacifist and anti-nuclear ones. These theories, developed in Europe and North America, identify three constituting elements to justify the adjective 'new'. The first refers to the emergence of new forms of struggle as a response to new forms of modern capitalist society subordination and oppression, characterised by bureaucracy, the transformation of things into commodities and mass consumption. The second component breaks away from the idea of the economy as a determining factor of structuralist and Marxist currents. New social movements are characterised by the empowerment of various positions of the political subject, the absence of a previously constituted scheme to historically situate the position of the subject, and the dissolution of the representation of 'interests', in which everything is more dependent on the articulation of demands and specific social concerns in different discourses. Thus, a clear difference emerges between the now 'old' and the 'new' social movements in a post-material or post-industrial context, making the latter fundamentally different to the industrial period's working-class movements. This explains the changes to the leading demands of industrialism on topics such as quality of life that are a response to post-materialism (Pichardo 1997: 412). The third refers to 'democratic' values in which higher levels of participation in decision making, cooperation and the socio-cultural 'meaning' of interpersonal relations are granted importance. These components mark a difference, and are the basis for understanding the newness of the 'new social movements' (Tilly 1978; McAdam 1982; Tarrow 1983; Kriesi 1989; Joppke 1991; Kriesi et al. 1995).

However, the debates on the phenomena observed in Europe and North America were developed without knowledge of social movements in other regions of the world (Foweraker 1995), while also being used as a reference for studying social movements in other regional contexts. Thus, several differences and adjustments had to be cleared up. Thompson and Tapscott (2010) posed a series of questions differentiating the social movements 'of the south', therefore making it necessary to adopt a theory 'of the north'. Summarising a group of authors, Thompson and Tapscott emphasise that many of the southern movements were originally concerned with the struggle against colonisation, which effectively implied an internal struggle on access to state structures. At the same time, these movements can be understood as new actors in the political arena who do not aim to take power, but rather to create an open arena in which a democratic society can emerge. The southern social movements can also be understood to have prepared a future society in which the authenticity of the original movements leads democratic 'window dressing' into true democracy.

According to the publication quoted, southern social movements should not be conceptualised as anti-state organisations either (although some of them actually are). Social movements present new forms for citizens to relate to the state, looking to replace deficient institutional channels. Demonstrations and social protests form an integral part of the political landscape in many southern states, coexisting and in some cases replacing institutional channels. In these contexts, social movements become the conventional vehicle for an increasing number of citizens, especially the poor, to obtain democratic rights. In addition, although resources and political opportunities cannot be ignored, the struggles of collective action in the South are different in that they are usually more connected to struggles for basic socio-economic rights, which were resolved long ago in more developed states.

In the same way, in their book on social movements in Latin America in 1985, David Slater et al. (1985) underlined the need for Latin America to reflect on the universality of social movements' theory produced in North America and Europe. Social movements emerged in the region during the second half of the twentieth century, sharing many of the characteristics of their European and North American counterparts, and were understood to be part of the 'new social movements' phenomenon. As opposed to experiences in the North however, the state played a much more central role in theories on social movements in Latin America.

Among the most important differences, Slater (1985) highlighted the fact that the struggle against new forms of subordination and oppression was related to the state crisis, as well as to an even more intense feeling of alienation. In Latin American societies, generalising the structural relationship between capital and paid work is much more limited. The state crisis is related to bureaucratisation processes, but, as opposed to Western Europe, the involvement of the state in civil society has been much less effective in Latin America.

Slater identified three focal points of protest in Latin American social movements. The first was opposition to the state model because of the excessive centralisation of decision-making powers, combined with an increasing and acute administrative incapacity. The second focal point was related to the state's inability to provide adequate services in the area of so-called 'collective means of consumption', such as water, electricity, health and transport. Finally, the constant erosion of state legitimacy accompanied by increasing scepticism towards established political parties led to the articulation of social demands through channels beyond the existing incorporation and control ones. The latter is not exclusive to Latin America, since some of the new social movements in Europe have also looked to maintain their distance from the political system to various degrees.

Another important difference indicated by Slater was that social movements in Europe were mainly concerned with 'democratising democracy', while in Latin America they had emerged during the struggle to recuperate democracy. The Central American region in particular stood out because the struggle was fought against a highly repressive state and against a considerable level of institutionalised violence, which meant that, in many cases, social movements were armed. Thus, Latin American social movements resorted to forms of political action that were effective under the specific military dictatorship in which they emerged. In this respect, both the state and authoritarian regimes are crucial to conceptualising the relationship between state and society.

Social Movements in 'Transitional' Debates in Latin America

The authoritarian regimes that emerged from the 1960s onwards caused the closure of institutional channels to social demands through the repression of political parties, labour unions and other working-class organisations. As a result, new forms of collective action emerged in the region during the 1970s and 1980s. During this period, civil society was formed as an arena for organising resistance towards the state, creating real opposition between the two.

A period known as 'the transition to democracy'[1] began in the region in 1978, with military regimes being replaced by elected governments on numerous occasions. It is difficult to say exactly what the role of resistance movements was in this process, and it is even more difficult to generalise about the many types of Latin American transitions. However, the transitional literature agrees that social movements played an important role in the demand for democratisation. Although Alfred Stepan (1986) argued, in terms of theoretical reflection at least, that it was difficult to conceive that a process of democratisation could be consummated by collective action – such isolated activities could, at the most, cause the abolition of a regime, without it necessarily being replaced by a democratic one – the authors of the transition (Stepan included) recognised the frequently crucial and in some cases indispensable role of civil society in the democratisation process.

Despite the relative success of dictatorial relationships in taking apart and depoliticising civil society, the beginning of a transition to a democratic government was frequently accompanied by social or working-class uprisings, in which different groups of civil society, such as labour and trade unions, base movements, intellectuals, artists, the defenders of human rights and professional associations joined together in the name of democracy and under the political name of 'the people'. Their importance was credited to continued confrontation with the state, which contributed to the breaking down and discrediting of authoritarian regimes. At the same time, their capacity for creating and channelling social processes was crucial for successful negotiations, especially for the democratisation processes that began within authoritarian regimes – through civil leadership or dissident leaders in the military governments (Stepan 1986).

The significant role of civil society during the transition produced an air of optimism regarding the democratising role of social movements, and led to a 'rediscovery' or 'uprising' of civil society. Social movements were initially celebrated for their putative resemblance to institutional politics, their defence of autonomy and the emphasis they put on a type of direct democracy. However, this enthusiasm was short lived, and these exact qualities were quickly considered unfavourable or downright damaging to the democratic regime's consolidation.

The wave of transitions in Latin America was particularly extensive in a relatively short period of time (between 1978 and 1990), which led to the widespread creation of theories that sought to resolve questions such as why some countries went through transitions while others did not, and why some democracies were more stable than others. The studies concentrated on the formulation of the characteristics or principles that distinguish democratic regimes from non-democratic ones, as well as on the conditions that are important for the transition to democracy and its stability.

The distinction between democratic and non-democratic regimes was made through a slightly minimalist conceptualisation of democracy, in which Schumpeterian definitions were common. According to the vision of Joseph Schumpeter (1943), democracy gives citizens the opportunity to choose between rival political leaders who compete for their votes and can be ousted in the next election. Even in more recent studies, democracy understood as a minimum number of conditions is the norm. In these, at least three basic principles can be identified: (1) the existence of open and hard-fought elections that allow for the possibility of a change in power; (2) the inclusion of the majority of the adult population in the electorate; and (3) a basic guarantee of certain civil rights, such as freedom of expression, freedom of association and the right to procedural equity (see, for example, Shugart and Mainwaring 1997, or Hagopian and Mainwaring 2005). Along these same lines, the facilitation and celebration of competition between political parties is emphasised, as well as the uncertainty that exists surrounding the distribution of political forces. In other words, political parties should be able to believe they have a fair shot at getting into government, and that the citizens' vote will be respected by politicians.

For authors such as Guillermo O'Donnell, the installation of an 'elected' government did not constitute a process of democratisation, which is why he spoke of the need to conceptualise the election process as one of 'two transitions' (O'Donnell 1992, 1993). The first transition refers to the change from an authoritarian regime to a democratic government, and the second to the transition of that government to a consolidated democracy, understood as the effective functioning of the democratic regime. The basis for this distinction is the concern that existed at the time about a possible fall back to an authoritarian regime. This return could occur either through a new coup d'état ('sudden death') or through a 'slow death', with a regression in the arenas in which civil power is exercised and in the efficiency of the classic guarantees of liberal constitutionalism. According to O'Donnell, democratic actors faced avoiding such a fall back at the same time as pushing ahead with the process of democratic consolidation.

Concerns about a possible regression amounted to a kind of understanding of the relationship between the state and civil society, in which the role of social movements in the democratic transition needed to be treated with much more caution. The precariousness that was a characteristic of the transition period meant that the democratisation process was painstaking and gradual, and civil society had to allow for a certain 'peacefulness' for the newly elected government in order to create better conditions for democratic consolidation (O'Donnell et al. 1986). With the aim of improving the possibilities of democratic longevity, civil society was encouraged not to look to maximise ideals, and new governments frequently looked to break up demonstrations and prevent their interests becoming political, all to avoid the worst possible result for everyone: a coup d'état.

With the latent threat of regression, emphasis shifted to political institutions that assured stability and the consolidation of democracy. Social movements and civil society organisations were delegated only a secondary role, and were expected to contain their struggles so as not to overwhelm a new government's capacity. The very characteristics of the social movements that in the beginning had been celebrated were quickly considered problematic. Collective action and protest in particular, and the rejection of institutional policies in general, came to be understood as an obstacle for the effective articulation of demands and interests in formal political arenas. Other authors indicated that the fragmented and 'one issue' orientation of social movements made them incapable of transcending local issues in order to get involved in national politics, which was seen as necessary to consolidate democracy (Alvarez et al. 1998a). The short-term nature of social movement's demands and the tendency to re-structure relationships within the patronage system were pointed as the difficulties that social movements experienced in adapting to new forms of political representation (Assies et al. 2005).

In this way, both under authoritarian regimes as well as in periods of transition, social movements and civil society were described as opposing the political regime, reinforcing a conceptual division between state and society. The opposition had already been created between the authoritarian state and repressed society but persisted under the new democracies, in as much as civil society was pushed to the margin of institutional politics in order to allow the democratic regime to consolidate.

In the post-transitional Latin American context, a theoretical discussion on the meaning of democracy developed, reflecting on the quality of the relationship between the state and society. In the light of the installation and the endurance of elected governments in Latin America, at the end of the 1980s a branch of academia focused on the processes that came after the transition, including studies with a variety of aims but that can be grouped together under the common denominator 'democratic consolidation'. Authors such as Marcelo Cavarozzi (1992) argued that Latin America was already beyond the transition to democracy. In this respect, Gerardo L. Munck (2004) identified the emergence of two important research agendas: the first took the stability of the democratic regime as its main focus, and the second focused on the quality of such governments. Research into democratic stability was the most direct continuation of the transition research agenda, basically concentrating on the sustainability and durability of democracies, and the constant threat of the democratic regime's collapse, which in itself emanated from the experiences of former transitions in Europe, as well as the Latin American region itself.[2]

The agenda on democratic quality involved a deeper understanding of democracy, derived from the observation that many regimes wearing the label 'democratic' showed in fact persistent practices of corruption, patronage systems, and large differences in social inequality and exclusion. In this sense,

O'Donnell coined the term 'delegated democracies' (1999). The agenda on democratic quality proposed the formulation of a wider concept of democracy that complemented the principles of competition and participation with that of accountability, in which political leaders and elected representatives were understood as 'agents' of their constitutions and were thus obliged to justify their actions and decisions to maintain their positions of power (Smith 2005: 7). Robert Dahl (1989) asked for such participation to be analysed to consider how the distribution of economic resources directly affected the opportunities to participate in political processes. David Held (2006) emphasised the equality of rights and obligations, which should be free and equal in the deliberation and determination of living conditions.

Along these lines, the analysis of Sebastián L. Mazzuca (2007) is particularly interesting because of its direct allusion to democracy as a relationship between the state and civil society. Mazzuca argues that, in societies where means of coercion are concentrated on the state, state offices become crucial sources of power, creating two types of relationship between the state and civil society. In the first, from civil society towards the state (bottom-up), groups in society make an effort to gain control of state offices: the 'accessibility' side of politics. The second, from the state towards civil society (bottom-down), refers to the use of political power to align the behaviour of social groups with that of the order established by the state: the 'exercising' side of politics.

In summary, the central point that emerges from a research agenda on the quality of democracy is that Schumpeterian definitions, characteristic of the theoretical production of the 'transition', are limited when applied to a wider analysis of the post-transitional period. Such definitions concentrate on aspects related to obtaining power, ignoring those concerned with the exercising of power, resulting in an inability to capture the variations that exist within democratic norms. This book is located along the line of study that argues a wider definition of democracy as a kind of relationship between the state and society, understanding that the changes related to the state and actors in civilian society (in this case, social movements) are part of this variation and are therefore indicators of change to the quality of democracy.

In this respect, the definition of democracy provided by Charles Tilly (2007) in his classic book on the topic is useful. Even though Tilly does not consider a specific geographical region or experience but rather looks towards a more abstract definition in the study of modern democracies in general, its conceptualisation coincides with an attempt to widen the meaning of democracy, paralleling the aim of the research agenda on the quality of democracy in the Latin American debate. Democratisation is conceived as being the extent to which the conformity of citizens increases (or decreases, in which case Tilly speaks of a process of 'de-democratisation'). The connection between state policy and the citizens' will, as a democratic quality, also appears in Robert Dahl's critique (1989) of the Schumpeterian concept of democracy. In the same vein, Dirk Berg-Schlosser (2004) underlies the importance of clarifying 'democratic' workings, understood as political systems' capacity for response, their ability to produce effective mechanisms to respond to the articulated and aggregated interests of large segments of the population, and the capacity to satisfy their demands and expectations to a great extent in the long term. In this way, these authors provide the tools for understanding (de-) democratisation processes, which are needed to appreciate the quality of a regime within a system that has previously been classified as 'democratic' (as in the case of Bolivia in this study).

Due to their complexity, democratisation and de-democratisation processes continually take place, without the guarantee of finality in either direction. On this point, Tilly agrees with the analysis of Laurence Whitehead (2002), which emphasises the complexity of a great majority of contemporary democratisation processes, since these are the result of different amassed histories, which means that democratisation processes can only occur through a long process of social construction that is condemned to an uncertain end.

The Role of Social Movements in the Construction of Democracy

Taking into account the previous discussion on the theorising about the relationship between state and society in general, it can be concluded that there are two positions on the role that social movements play in the construction of democracy: one that sees them as a threat to the consolidation of democracy and one that gives social movements a democratising role. To understand these two very different positions, the model proposed by Craig Jenkins and Klandermans (1995) is useful, in which the relationship between the state and social movements is conceived as part of the interaction between citizens, social movements, the political representation system and the state.

In modern democracies, political parties ideally serve as vehicles to represent different groups in society, organising them and regulating access to state power. The party works as a channel at the same time as it articulates interests, giving more to some than to others, which directly affects governmental and democratic stability, and contributes to a structure of accountability. The political system thus turns into a group of institutionalised organisations that aim to represent the various social interest groups (Mainwaring and Scully 1995).

Social movements represent groups of citizens who question this system and, as such, in their struggle to restructure the relationship between the state and society, form a potential rival to the political system of representation.[3] In this way, the legitimacy crisis of political parties in Latin America is frequently linked to the emergence of social movements. The extent to which a party system is institutionalised, capable of transmitting the demands of society to the state and seeing them carried out, contributes to democratic consolidation, preventing or constraining the space for the collective action of social movements.

The importance of a high degree of institutionalisation of the system lies in the fact that the lack of it has negative consequences for democracy. A weak party system does not structure to the political process, producing policies that are less institutionalised and therefore more unpredictable. Democratic policies become more erratic, legitimacy is harder to achieve and governing is more complicated. Political parties contribute to the structure of account-ability, and a lack of solidity can therefore lead to paternal practices and weak legislation. Although maximising levels of institutionalisation is not neces-sarily optimum (that is up for debate), lower levels inevitably cause problems for stability and the workings of democracy (Mainwaring and Scully 1995). As a result, strong social movements are not only indicative of a deficiency in the functioning of democratic institutions, but they also have the effect of weakening the political party system to the detriment of the consolidation of democracy. This is exactly the argument that was used in the democratic transition period to reduce the role of social organisations and to limit political demands.

In the theoretical sphere, the 'apolitical' (Brandt 1986) or 'anti-political' (Berger 1979) nature of the 'new social movements' were one of its most distinctive features. Following Touraine's line of analysis, Proietto explains that, when talking about social movements that are understood, above all, as 'self-reflexive' actors, it is necessary to emphasise what is 'social' more than the 'movement' itself. 'Social' designates the type of action that is being carried out, while 'movement' designates the object through which this is made possible. In this way, participants in social movements are in a per-manent state of 'self-education', in which their opponents are not so much their enemies but rather the 'co-participants' of a conflictive socio-cultural project whose aim is the transformation of the daily social arena. Therefore, the aim of the social movement cannot be captured by the state, and thus the social movement is not, strictly speaking, a 'political actor' (Proietto 1995: 370–71).

Melucci adopts a similar stance, indicating that new social movements are not focused on the political system and that their aim is not to gain political power or the state, but rather control of the autonomous space and inde-pendence relating to this system. According to the author, although social movements have instrumental aims and look to take advantage of the politi-cal system, these are secondary to the search for solidarity and the expression of the relationships they embody (Melucci 1980: 220).

For Claus Offe, the opportunity for social movements to take action lies in non-institutional politics (Offe 1985: 826), which are not recognised in the doctrines and practices of liberal democracy and the welfare state. Offe indicates that this is related to the fact that social movements do not interact with their opponents in terms of negotiation, but rather in terms of conflicts, thus inhibiting a practice of political exchange or gradual tactics. Since they do not have anything to give in exchange for granting their demands, their inability to negotiate appears as one of the distinctive features of new social movements (Offe 1985: 830) and as the reason why their nature is essentially 'pre-political' (Proietto 1995: 380).

These are the features of the 'new social movements' that received the most severe criticism. According to Boggs, 'new social movements' opted to operate at a distance from the political system, which was an obstacle to the achievement of their aims. This failure results in the gradual but inevitable disillusionment of activists and followers, in the form of withdrawal, escapism or spiritualism, as well as a cultural introversion centred on building a community and even terrorism (Boggs 1986: 75). For Kauffman, this type of 'anti-politics of identity' produces apolitical introspection, with an emphasis on politically correct lifestyles, in which political activity ends up being substituted by personal transformation (Kauffman 1990).

Another feature that inhibits the political impact of the 'new social movements' is that their ideals are generally defined in terms of denial. In other words, although post-modern, the new social movements reject both liberal and Marxist traditions, but are much less convinced about what they *do* want. Thus, they are characterised by the absence of an exhaustive vision or institutional theory for a new type of society (Handler 1992: 720). This lack of ideology not only separates them from 'old' social movements but also makes them more likely to be absorbed by the dominant political system, forcing them to form coalitions with traditional parties, with only partial or reformatory results (Offe 1985). Based on this, a debate emerges on the tension that exists between the social movements' overly autonomous position (which prevents them from having a real political impact) and the danger of co-optation that inevitably appears when they come too close to formal political institutions . In opposing the initiatives or policies of a more powerful political institution, social movements may have different outcomes: institutionalisation of the movement, social control, co-optation, a change of policies, or a mixture of these. The institutionalisation of a social movement can produce recognised disadvantages such as co-optation or demobilisation (Coy and Hedeen 2005: 406–7).

Summarising a series of authors, Doowon indicates that the professionalisation and bureaucratisation of social movements run the risk of civil society being manipulated by corporate intermediaries that serve the interests of political parties or other state actors, or being directly incorporated by them. Social movements need to constantly mobilise collective action so as to confront the political elite in an effective way. From this perspective, institutionalisation restricts the potential of social movements to achieve social transformation (Doowon 2006: 116–17).

Thus, autonomy in relation to the state and in relation to groups that operate through state power (political parties and unions) is central to the study of social movements. Understood as the capacity to say 'no' to the existing forms of power and domination, the autonomy aims towards the deconstruction of the state (Holloway 2002; Böhm et al. 2010: 18–21). As Melucci explains, the potential of social movements lies in the fact that they look to transcend the political system by opening new channels to express political demands, pushing for participation beyond the limits predicted by state institutionality (Melucci 1980: 203). Along the same lines, Scott argues that the 'the autonomy of the struggle' is one of the main aspects of the new social movements' ideology, referring to social movements' insistence on pursuing their aims without their demands being interfered with by, or subordinated to, external interests (Scott 1990: 20).

In the study of new social movements, the preoccupation with autonomy has produced a kind of romanticism that presupposes that the nature of politics in the state field is basically elitist and repressive, and so the autonomy of the new social movements is needed to counterbalance alienation and authoritarianism (Steyn 2012: 332). Thus, the strategies employed by civil society to intervene in politics are more complex than those implied by the literature on new social movements (Doowon 2006: 177). In the Latin American context, and in the case of Chile specifically, Garretón demonstrated that negotiations were indispensable both for the transition itself and for democratic consolidation, and so resulted in the need for some degree of institutionalisation of collective action (Garretón 1989).

The maximisation of the autonomy of the social movement becomes undesirable when considering the achievement of their objectives. Coy and Hedeen indicate that, although it is practically impossible to distinguish between cooperation and co-optation in relationships framed by an imbalance of power, the social movement should maintain a fluctuating position relating to state power, however difficult this may be, in order to achieve its aims (Coy and Hedeen 2005: 426–27). In the same vein, when analysing the case of the Workers' Party in Brazil, Earle concludes that the interaction between the social movement and the state requires a 'delicate balance' in order to maximise the benefits of collaboration and avoid accusations of co-optation (Earle 2013: 67).

A more extreme point of view suggests that 'autonomy' is impossible for the social movement. Social movements are always found in the context of the social, economic, cultural and political relations from which they cannot escape. Such a historical understanding questions 'autonomy' as a positive quality and as the negation of state power (Böhm et al. 2010: 28). Similarly, Steyn argues that the infatuation with autonomy in the academic debate on new social movements could involuntarily legitimise the pillaging of neoliberal capitalism. Even more importantly, the author indicates that the relationship between the state and new social movements is dialectic and fluid, with struggles that take place transversally in institutional and non-institutional arenas. In this way, autonomy can only partially be achieved and, because of its heterogeneous nature, the degree of autonomous operation in relation to the state varies considerably from movement to movement (Steyn 2012).

In summary, the theory that sees social movements as a threat to democratic consolidation is formulated on the basis of the need for strong democratic institutions. From this point of view, because of their 'apolitical' or 'pre-political' nature, social movements do not seem to be the right bodies to consolidate democratic practices – and certainly not in relation to the state. The tension surrounding their autonomy places social movements in a paradox from which it is very hard to escape: in relation to political power, too much autonomy makes it incapable of fulfilling its aims, whereas becoming close to the institutions that exercise power increases their chance of success but also risks manipulation, a patronage system and co-optation, inevitably compromising their interests and ideals.

From a post-modernist perspective, the emancipatory potential of social movements lies in their capacity to conquer arenas outside the state as an institution and removed from political power. In this way, social movements are situated at the margins of institutional politics and the state, which could make it difficult to pursue their main or practical interests, even if these are regarded as 'secondary'.

On the other hand, it can be observed that when social movements have drawn closer to institutional politics, in particular in their orientation towards the state (with a greater or lesser degree of autonomy), their impact on the construction of democracy has given these actors a more explicitly political role. Particularly in the academic debate on Latin American social movements, a more positive role for social movements emerges in relation to democratic consolidation and the deepening of democracy.

In their paradigmatic book, Alvarez et al. (1998a) present us with the concepts of 'cultural politics' and 'political culture'. This focus is based on the post-structural understanding of 'culture', formed from anthropology's insistence on analysing the production and significance of meanings and practices as simultaneous and inextricable aspects of social reality. The definition of 'cultural politics' proposed by Álvarez et al. is the one formulated by Weedon:

The legitimation of social relations of inequality, and the struggle to transform them, are central concerns of CULTURAL POLITICS. Cultural politics fundamentally determine the meanings of social practices and, moreover, which groups and individuals have the power to define these meanings. Cultural politics are also concerned with subjectivity and identity, since culture plays a central role in constituting our sense of ourselves ... The forms of subjectivity that we inhabit play a crucial part in determining whether we accept or contest existing power relations. Also, for marginalised and oppressed groups, the construction of new and resistant identities is a key dimension of a wider political struggle to transform society.[4]

Considering this definition, Latin American social movements constitute another example of the enactment of 'cultural politics'. When social movements intervene in the political debate, they actually embark in an attempt to give new meaning to dominant cultural interpretations of politics, contesting prevalent political practices. Social movements' cultural resistance and contestation should be understood as central aspects of a struggle to redefine the meaning and limits of the political system. In this sense, culture is political if it aims to redefine social power, either explicitly or implicitly.

The movements' cultural politics involve an analysis of their effect on the 'political culture'. Álvarez et al. define 'political culture' as 'the particular social construction in every society of what counts as "political"' (1998b: 8). Each society is marked by a dominant political culture that delimitates the dominion of those practices and institutions that historically have come to be considered as properly 'political', such as the state. In essence, social movements' cultural politics seek beyond material and institutional achievements to redefine the limits of political and cultural representation and social practices. In doing so, they uphold a struggle to transform the political culture in which they move and in which they need to become social actors with political aspirations. In this sense, this understanding of politics is no longer limited to state structures but extends to areas that have previously been culturally defined as 'private', 'social', 'economic' or 'cultural'. This implies a decentralised vision of politics in which power does not have structural blocks or mechanisms to impose order from top to bottom, but is rather a social relationship that expands into various areas of social reality.

This understanding of the mutual creation of 'what is political' and 'what is cultural' – in other words, the struggle of social movements to transform political culture; for example, the transformation of the state and the democratisation of social reality – has a series of consequences that help us to understand the role of social movements in the democratisation process. From this perspective, social movements have collective systems of reciprocal recognition, expressing new and old identities with important cultural and symbolic components. At the same time, they form non-party political intermediaries that take people's unarticulated needs and demands from the public arena to the state institutions. The expression of demands and interests as well as social recognition in the construction of new collective identities is understood as being essential to democratic vitality. In this way, the inability of political parties or formal institutions to co-opt these movements is not an indication of weak or deficient democratic institutions – on the contrary, social movements, like other non-party actors, become a way of guaranteeing a dynamic democracy (Jelin 1998).

Evelina Dagnino (1998) thus identifies a clear role for social movements in the construction of a more democratic 'political culture', underpinning an understanding of democracy that transcends the limits of current political institutions and thus looks to expand and consolidate democracy. This is expressed in the struggle to democratise the whole of society and not only the political regime, including the cultural practices that embody the social relations of exclusion and inequality. This struggle, however, does not imply the rejection of the political institutions or the state, but rather a radical demand for their transformation. In this way, social movements' cultural politics could be included in the formal arenas of political representation.

The struggle to transform the state is related to the legitimacy crisis that has befallen this institution, certainly in the Latin American region. As a result of structural adjustment reforms and neoliberal policies, levels of inequality and poverty increased among vast segments of the Latin American population in the 1980s and 1990s. The governments' inability to respond to the population's expectations, plus the systematic expansion of corruption in the political class, contributed to the evaporation of confidence in state structures and institutions (Philip 2003). The state crisis materialised in the loss of legitimacy of institutional representation channels,[5] and was therefore concerned with redefining the institutionalised political system, in which social movements looked to set up a regime of rights again through transforming the means of social representation. Social movements not only expected to update citizens' social and political rights (for example, participation in mechanisms of decision making), but also to create a space for institutional conflict in which their demands could be legitimately expressed (Calderón, Piscitelli and Reyna 1992).

The most recent Latin American debate on social movements thus identifies a much more positive role to social movements as actors in democratic construction or consolidation. Through the creation of autonomous spaces of contestation, social movements are capable of democratising not only political institutions, but also the 'political culture', understood as the daily social practices that embody the social relations of exclusion and inequality. Despite their differences, for both positions to a greater or lesser extent there persists a division between the state and political parties (institutions) on the one hand and social movements and citizens on the other. This division stems from the conceptual division between state and society. Whether seeing social movements as a threat to the consolidation of democratic institutions or as actors that encourage a deepening of democracy, both stances project an antagonistic relation between social movements and the state that reifies the state–society dichotomy.

The State–Society Relationship in Latin America

Evelina Dagnino et al. (2006) identify three political projects for the Latin American continent, following on from the wave of dictatorships that battered the region from the beginning of the 1960s until their experiences with neoliberal development models. This characterisation generally coincides with the development of the relationship between the state and social movements. In this section, these three political projects are taken as a starting point, while they are expanded to include a more detailed characterisation of the state–society relationship in general and the state–social movements relationship in particular. The political projects are (1) the authoritarian project, (2) the neoliberal project, and (3) the participatory democracy project.

The authoritarian project generally coincides with the 1960s and 1970s, when the relationship between the state and civil society organisations was characterised by a vertical system, patronage, a mixture of repression and co-optation and a complete absence of or total inefficiency of the instances of citizen participation. Under the dictatorships, civil society was practically disregarded by an organic-cooperative model of the state that did not distinguish the state from civil society. The dictatorships witnessed a proliferation of relatively informal base movements, the majority organised around relatively limited social spaces (such as the neighbourhood or the parish). The atomisation policies of the authoritarian regime, the destruction of representation networks and the emphasis on centralised and technocratic public policies created the context for the emergence of this type of organisation. As O'Donnell and Schmitter (1986) underline, the emergence of these organisations was important for democratisation processes. Their proliferation forced regimes to pay attention and increase their resources to deal with the specific problems of urban life that, until then, had been ignored.

Considering this period, what should be highlighted is that the organisations and social movements in civil society in the second half of the twentieth century occurred in direct response to the repression being exercised by authoritarian regimes, thus effectively opposing the state. As such, they were repressed and manipulated by authoritarian states. Despite their important role in driving forward the democratisation process, after a brief period of revival in the first democratic openings, these organisations were soon ignored and/or marginalised by the new democratic governments, thus maintaining the division between the state and civil society organisations that had originated under repressive regimes well into the transition period.

Authoritarianism was generally accompanied by the introduction of neoliberal reforms. In the first part of the democratisation process, some of the social movements that had emerged in opposition to the authoritarian regimes stopped playing a central role and, in many cases, disintegrated altogether. The instauration of the political arena and parliamentary debate reduced the opportunity for social mobilisation, leading to a reduced role for social movements and confining them to alternative arenas.

Although the neoliberal model is, above all, an economic one, different analyses have demonstrated its significance beyond economic reforms, with important implications for both society and politics in the region. It is difficult to appreciate the consequences of the structural adjustments and the implementation of neoliberalism for social movements. Various authors have indicated that the negative economic situation should be the basis for understanding social activity in the 1980s and 1990s. The data on poverty and exclusion in Latin America in this period is well documented, as well as the portrayal of the 1980s as the 'lost decade' (Jelin 1998; Assies 2005). Civil society, however, played a different role. Civil society organisations had to provide authorised information on social demands, as well as providing the necessary capabilities to carry out the public policies aimed at fulfilling these demands. This new role of civil society in a context of increasing social inequality, as explained by Elizabeth Jelin (1997), shows the contradictory nature and double meaning of the democratic discourse: a discourse of participation and a non-discourse of economic exclusion. Along the same lines, George Yúdice (1998) underpins the double impact of neoliberal reforms and economic adjustments on civil society. On the one hand, civil society needed to respond to the neoliberal state's need for stability and political legitimacy. On the other hand, civil society constituted the ground for the development of base movements as a survival strategy to confront social and economic deterioration – examples are the movements surrounding the assembly-line workers in the *maquiladora* industry and the large numbers of economic emigrants (Torre 1997; Díaz 1997).

Nevertheless, the neoliberal model involves a series of obstacles that, while not hampering it completely, make the articulation and mobilisation of these new social movements and groups more difficult. In the first place, understanding public administration as an extension of private administration brings with it a technical – or, more precisely, a 'technocratic' – focus on the problems, leading to their depoliticisation (Silva 2006). This implies that, in the new role of civil society, different sectors must adapt and develop their 'technical' capacities to comply with the functions conferred on them by the state. The consequence of this was the exclusion of those social actors that were too politicised or too (technically) incapable of responding to the demands of the neoliberal state. In this way, social movements' characteristics made them unfit for the neoliberal project.

This exclusion is also linked to the second obstacle presented by neoliberalism: the issue of social participation. Participation is instrumentally defined to achieve the structural adjustment reforms. To compensate for the shrinking of the state, society's participation is called upon in the name of 'solidarity', a concept that becomes essential for redefining participation. Under the veil of 'solidarity', participation is stripped from its political and collective significance and confined to a private and more moral terrain, becoming more and more understood in terms of voluntary work and 'social responsibility' from a private and individualistic perspective. As Dagnino et al. (2006) explain, 'at the heart of this reformulation is the dissolution of exactly that which makes up the nucleus of what is understood as citizenship, the idea of universal rights'. The neoliberal meanings of citizenship, of civil society and of participation thus express a minimalist view of politics. Poverty and inequality are withdrawn from the (political) public arena and moved to the moral and private area of solidarity and charity.

Although the neoliberal model restricted political activity in several ways, favouring the marginalisation of social movements, it did not manage to eliminate these actors. On the contrary, citizen demands were forced to open up alternative space for their contestation. For example, under neoliberalism organisations defending consumer rights emerged, which, although they did not have specifically political aims, served as opportunities for citizen participation (Taylor 2005). On the other hand, as Elizabeth Jelin (1997) explains, there was an expansion of NGO activity in the 1990s as a consequence of public cuts in social policy. NGOs frequently acted as intermediaries between those who were deprived and the state, occupying the vacuum that had originated from the state's contraction.

Many social movements were institutionalised as NGOs or looked to create alliances with them. NGOs adopted a role of representation for those 'without a voice', whether to attract resources or to defend democracy. The increasing social and economic deterioration of vast working-class sectors and the limited space for NGO participation created the opportunity for social movements to look for alternative actions. In particular, the movements that were developed on the basis of collective identity defended their autonomy in relation to the state. In the same way, the lack of state interest in specific everyday problems encouraged the local and autonomous organisation of certain sectors of the population.

In parallel, next to authoritarianism and neoliberalism, a third political project can be identified. Emerging in Brazil in the 1980s, the participatory democracy project only began to expand and be implemented in the rest of the Latin American continent in the new millennium, with Ecuador and Bolivia as the most recent national examples. The participatory democracy project looked to consolidate and radicalise democracy, questioning the limits imposed by representative liberal democracy, which had dominated the relationship between the state and society. In this project, the participation of society in the decision-making process enhances democratisation, being understood as an instrument to build greater equality. Democratic innovation is achieved through the principles of participation and social control, and is brought about in several forms, such as participatory budgets, citizen councils, governors, decision-making mechanisms and roundtables, depending on the national context.

In particular, the concept of accountability has a central role, connecting with other forms of citizen participation orientated at guaranteeing rights and ensuring social control of that which is public. Dagnino et al. (2006) distinguish three models of accountability: (1) the actions of groups from civil society who take on the surveillance of a state body or political process; (2) the creation of institutions within the state, whose function is to guarantee the right to information or to help citizens to monitor how the government is run; and (3) the creation of internal control offices of the state, which operate as autonomous entities. In this way, civil society forms an environment for the construction of public and/or societal spaces in which conflict, discussion and deliberation mingle. These spaces are considered to allow the effective implementation of participation, so that even in societal spaces marked by diversity and fragmentation, adequate terrain is found for conflicts to appear, and for public matters to be discussed, articulated and negotiated.

This model also launches a redefinition of citizenship as 'the right to have rights', which attempts to articulate the struggle of social movements regarding specific demands (such as health, housing, education, and the rights of minorities) within the wider struggle of the construction of democracy. In reality, this model recognises new forms of enacting politics in social movements' activities. These are understood as new political subjects in a process in which transformations towards a more participatory democracy are actually the state's institutional reply to the specific demands of social movements. This explains why the implementation of this model is expanded and intensified at the beginning of the twenty-first century, since, in this period, the neoliberal model's crisis became more explicit. Specific demands were formulated in terms of citizen rights, the right to have rights, and the right to political participation. In this way, social movements implied a more active state role (as opposed to a shrinking neoliberal state), but which had to be democratised through citizen participation and social control.

Despite the important differences between these three political projects, the prevalence of opposition between state institutions and society – to which social movements belong – can still be observed. Even in the participatory democracy project, which gives an explicitly political role to civil society actors, a sense of *struggle* in society to advance in the democratisation of the state permeates, falling back to the state–society dichotomy. However, the reification of the dichotomy has been subject to increasing criticism, based on analyses that show that the limits that distinguish the state sphere from the social one are becoming increasingly hazy.

Questioning the State–Society Dichotomy

The recognition of a more explicit political role for social movements contests a conceptualisation of the state and society as two separate arenas. The state–society dichotomy suggests two well-defined entities, which can easily be distinguished, particularly in a situation in which they are found to be in opposition. However, the homogeneity that is assumed in both arenas is at least problematic.

The Homogeneity of State and Society

Probably one of the most decisive thinkers regarding the modern understanding of the state is the German, Max Weber. Weber defines the state as an association of rule that adopts an institutional form and that has successfully monopolised the legitimate use of violence as its means of domination within a given territory. According to Weber, the state should be considered as more than a 'government' and rather as a continuous administrative, legal, bureaucratic and coercive system, which not only tries to structure relations between civil society and the public authority, but also many of the crucial relations within civil society (Stepan 1978: 10). At the beginning of the 1980s, after a short period in which 'world systems' and dependence theories (which emphasised the importance of international relations) dominated the debate, the state as a source of power for imposing social order returned once again as an object of study (Evans et al. 1985). These state-orientated academics largely based their ideas on Weber's understanding of the state as an autonomous organisation with extraordinary means of domination (Migdal 2001: 8).

In his book *State in Society*, and taking Weber's viewpoint as a starting point, Joel S. Migdal proposes that a type of ideal state is created, providing a uniform and continuous concept. This idea is reinforced every day in both the press and colloquial language, where the state is always presented as a coherent and integrated entity. The theoretical output about society almost always implies the existence of a state, more specifically a nation-state. In effect, the national territory often constitutes the framework of reference for studies on a variety of topics. Authors such as Kymlicka and Straehle (2001) have indicated the dominance of the nation-state paradigm, which assumes that political regulations are always applied within a nation-state, which is perceived as an integrated 'society'. The prevalence of the supposition explains why these theories have often been found unnecessary to explicitly justify the use of the concept.

The prevalence of this paradigm is not strange when one considers that the great thinkers who created the basis for modern thought on the state also sowed the seeds of the idea of the nation-state. Hobbes underlined the idea of a social contract in which individuals form an agreement to make up a Commonwealth. Locke, on his part, conceived an 'original compact' where a number of men would form a community or government in which the majority had the right to act and decide on behalf of the rest. Later, Rousseau talked of a number of men establishing the state through a social compact (Van Dyke 1995). Rustow (1970) proposed 'the national unit' as a condition for democratic transition. In this way, these initial theoretical reflections on the state proposed the constitution of a kind of unit – a type of integrated community – that would develop within the more complex concept of the nation-state as theoretical political thinking progressed.

In this respect, two important trends in the West in the last two centuries can be observed. On the one hand, the political arena has been almost universally reorganised into a system of nation-states, leaving behind the confusing group of empires, kingdoms, city-states, protectorates and colonies. On the other, the political arena has almost universally excluded forms of pre-liberal or anti-democratic government, at least formally, showing a clear preference for liberal democratic systems. Thus, there seems to exist a correlation between nation-states and liberal democracy. Indeed, according to liberal nationalist authors, it is not a coincidence that the nation-state has emerged as the most common form of government. Some of them even maintain that the implementation of liberal democratic principles is only possible within this form of government.

In effect, liberal democratic states have been consciously concerned with constructing the 'nation' during their history: states have encouraged and sometimes forced the integration of their subjects (within the territory) into common public institutions that operate in a single language. In Western states, institutional and linguistic integration has been achieved through a series of strategies: for example, laws of citizenship and naturalisation, laws on education and linguistics, military service and the national press. In general, these policies have been aimed at different kinds of minorities (Kymlicka 2001). All these strategies have been used as legitimate means to help the state and the nation better resemble each other (Kymlicka and Straehle 2001). Why is such resemblance considered necessary?

Theories on democracy confirm that a certain degree of social justice and the possibility of carrying out (deliberative) dialogue are essential for the functioning of a democratic regime. Social justice is only possible through the sacrifice of 'a few anonymous people' for 'other anonymous people': members of a community are expected to carry out sacrifices for other members of this community. The demand for sacrifices is complicated by the nature of the 'national community', in which most of its members will never get to know one another and in which members' ethnicity, lifestyle and/or religion may vary. In the same way, in democratic dialogue, different opinions must be understood and considered when making decisions. This is why there is not only the need for a common language but also for a sense of belonging and trust between members who do not know each other. The importance of creating a sense of 'national community' thus derives from the need to legitimise sacrifices as sacrifices made 'for one of ours', and the results of democratic dialogue as a dialogue 'among ourselves'.

The archetype of the 'national community' as united and integrated, with a state that embodies the unity of the nation, has led to the conclusion that variations in the form and functioning of real states are understood as 'deviations' from the standard. George Sørensen (2008), on describing the state as 'weak' for example, identified the lack of a coherent national community as a large 'deficiency', implying that the diversity of social groups in society is problematic for the state and therefore for democracy. Considering that there are between five thousand and eight thousand ethno-cultural groups in the world but only around two hundred states, simple maths allows the conclusion that the majority of the states are shared by one or more different social groups that could be seen as nations. In other words, on the basis of the archetype of the 'national community', the vast majority of the nation-states in the modern world present deficiencies that hinder democratisation.

In that regard, when looking at the Latin American states it is necessary to consider their history. Undoubtedly, the colonial experience is one of the most decisive historical factors for Latin American societies. After independence, in the majority of the new countries, the state was constructed based on the structures of Spanish governments, and the image of the nation-state – in other words, the idea of a 'national community' – was also built around a 'criollo' identity. The native populations that were not exterminated in the colonies were submitted to a process of assimilation that, as is known, was not completely successful, resulting in the coexistence of (hybrid) cultures and traditions, and diverse identities. Many of the social problems and struggles embodied by social movements are the result of social differences and injustices that coincide with different social groups. For example, it is well known that poverty in Latin America is greater among indigenous populations than in other social groups.

At the same time the state continues to be projected as a united and coherent entity with special faculties in an 'elevated' sphere of society. As Migdal (2001: 15) explains:

> The assumption that only the state does, or should, create rules, and that only it does, or should, maintain the violent means to bend people to obey those rules minimises and trivialises the rich negotiation, interaction and resistance that occur in every human society among multiple systems of rules.

Migdal conceives society as a mixture of social organisations, including the idea of the state[6] that offers strategies for personal survival and, for some, an improvement in their social position. Although the state projects the image of a unit, its practices show that it is made up of different branches, which maintain diverse and changing relationships with society's social organisations. Understood in this way, the state is part of a conflictive environment in which its very parts fight amongst themselves.

Along these lines and in the Latin American context, Dagnino et al. (2006) explain that the state has been understood both as homogenous and as the same as the incarnation of all the vices of politics in a struggle for power. This understanding does not recognise the diversity of state practices, nor how state interactions have been shaped in different political functions and periods. The state shows much structural diversity within, in the form of ministries and institutions at both national and local level, which have formed various and changing alliances and pacts with different groups in society.

The State, Political Parties and Social Movements

If, at a certain time and specifically in the academic debate on 'new' social movements, these actors were distinguished by their 'apolitical' nature or by placing them in different arenas to those of institutional politics, this characterisation has been questioned in the most recent literature on social movements. Under the term 'contentious politics' (Tarrow 1998; Tilly and Tarrow 2007; Seferiades and Johnston 2012), social movements are now frequently studies as part of the practice of politics, based on the understanding that social movements account for more popular or less elitist ways of enacting politics (Johnston 2011: 1).

Goldstone explains that in the vast study of the interaction between the state and social movements, there is a persistent tendency to consider the practices of social movements as different to institutionalised politics, which are understood as the act of voting, political parties, the legislature, courts and elected leaders. The author argues that social movements are an essential element of normal politics in modern societies, and that there is only a vague and permeable frontier between institutionalised politics and 'non-institutionalised' politics (Goldstone et al. 2003: 1–3). Both the state and political parties intertwine with civil society, in a continuous and mutual remodelling of socio-political actors.[7] The interaction between such actors changes constantly, meaning that it is impossible to define which actors are part of institutional politics and which are not (Goldstone 2003: 9).

To conceive social movements as opposing the state not only overshadows socio-political interactions but also limits our understanding of the scope of social movements. Seen as adversaries, social movements can only have two types of relationship with the state: they are either repressed or influenced by it, to the detriment of their will or interests. However, according to Goldstone, the range of relationships between the state and social movements is much wider, especially if heterogeneity within the state institutions is recognised. In this way, it must be acknowledged that social movements influence political parties, produce political parties and/or cooperate with them, without their degree of influence depending on fixed variables (Pelletier and Guérin 1998; Goldstone 2003: 24).

Social movements and political parties actually share the same historical roots that date back to the construction of the state in Western Europe and the United States at the beginning of the eighteenth century and in the nineteenth century, when the principle that citizens are worthy of consultation was availed. The arrival of the state turned the national government into the main body to which citizen demands could be directed, and also encouraged the formation of group (movement) coalitions that, until then, had remained separate or opposed. Thus, the growth and consolidation of the state was accompanied by the need to consider the popular will (Tarrow 1998). An initial 'mandate' model, in which the fusion of protests with votes was encouraged and in which representatives acted according to the orders of citizens was gradually replaced by a 'trustee' model. This formed the basis of the concept of the modern bourgeois republic, in which protest is separated from the act of voting, following the requirement that citizens withdraw once voting is carried out, trusting administration of the state to the political elite (political parties). Later, in the twentieth century, this model gave way to the 'elite' or pluralist theory of liberal democracy, in which direct voices and protests ended up being considered as dysfunctional in democratic regimes (Aminzade 1995), ultimately relegating social movements to a marginal position in politics.

From this model of 'elite politics', social movement emerges as different to a political party, with the latter being an institutional organisation that forms part of the formal practice of politics. As Desai explains, focusing solely on the organisational characteristics of political parties and thus separating them from their roots in social movements creates blind spots. Even more importantly, in societies where political parties have recently emerged from social movements, studying them exclusively as organisations or institutions reflects a prejudice based on the model of more established Western democracies, in which political parties have long left behind their roots in social movements (Desai 2003: 171–72).

There are, therefore, various studies that have not only tried to elucidate on the porosity or permeability of the barrier that divides social movements from political parties but have also made an effort to explain what occurs when a movement becomes a political party – and later, a government (Schönwälder 1997; Roberts 1998; Glenn 2003; Desai 2003; Deonandan et al. 2007; Van Cott 2005, 2008; Dufour 2008; Anria 2013). These authors agree that these sort of actors – 'movement parties' (Kitschelt 2006) or 'organic parties' (Roberts 1998) – face a series of difficulties and strains that complicate their standing as far as the social base they represent is concerned, as well as the political power through which they intend to achieve their aims.

One of the most important problems is certainly that described by Michels (1911). His classic 'iron law' maintains that mass movements are inevitably processed into formal – democratic – organisations that favour an elite oligarchy instead of the masses. Thus, Michels suggests that it is impossible for representative democracy to comply with its official aim of eliminating political elitist power. In relation to social movements, this risk of becoming absorbed by elite interests has been formulated in the terms 'bureaucratisation' or 'co-optation', practices that unavoidably compromise the aims of the social base that the movement represents. Van Cott maintains that the social movement that looks for political power needs first to overcome the obstacles presented by the powerful elite, who look to control divergent movements and exclude 'challengers'. Once inclusion has been achieved and on entering formal institutions, representatives of social movements are subject to the same pressures and incentives as their predecessors (Van Cott 2008: 95).

In spite of all its complications, the transition from movement to party seems less unusual and less problematic from the point of view that nuances the division between institutionalised and non-institutionalised politics and the implicit state–society divide. From this perspective, the state, political parties, social movements and citizens all appear to belong to the same system – they do not move in different arenas – and, as such, they are subject to a constant process of mutual influence and reshaping.

Social Movements vs. Social Movement Organizations: Actors or Processes?

Up until now the theoretical discussion of this chapter has evolved without an explicit definition of 'social movement'. At this point it is necessary to clarify how this study will conceptualise social movements. The academic discussion on social movements is very large and at least unequivocal when it comes to defining its very object of study. In the words of Tilly (2004: 6–7): 'Inflation of the term [social movement] to include all sorts of popular collective action past and present, conflation of the movement with its supporting population, networks, or organizations, and treatment of movements as unitary actors ... badly handicap any effort to describe and explain how social movements actually work'.

In an attempt to organise the discussion, both 'social movement' and 'social movement organization' (SMO) have been understood as forms of collective action that are 'moralistic and idealistic' and 'marginal/excluded' (Lofland 1996: 7). The difference between 'social movement' and SMO follows differences in scale, continuity and level of organisation. Social movements are characterised by considerable scale, continuity and organisation. The organisation of the social movement is marked by the participation of several 'associations', that are understood to be part of the 'movement'. Those associations differ from the larger social movement in that they are smaller in scale but stronger in continuity and organisation, and usually have an office, a phone, and suchlike (ibid.: 7–12). As Lofland points out, because of these characteristics, it is possible to talk to or visit an SMO but it is not possible to do so with a social movement, since it cannot be located in a single place. In order to assess the social movement, it is necessary to speak to the movement's SMO. It is for these reasons that the terms 'social movement' and 'social movement organization' often appear to be used inconsistently and interchangeably, and are perhaps above all analytical categories.

To alleviate the potential confusion, this study finds support in the discussion that proposes to understand social movements as processes instead of as actors (de Bakker, den Hond and Laamanen 2017), to find the middle way between a narrowly defined, structured and formal 'social movement organization' and the more 'inflated' or loosely defined 'collective action' or 'contentious politics'. More recent experiences have shown that social movements are finding new ways to organise, connect and enact their collective action, mainly in relation to technological and communicational innovations. This points to the necessity to distinguish between the act of *organising* collective action (planning, coordination, etc.) and the social movement organizations as separate *entities* characterised by some level of formal and bureaucratic organization. Reflecting on a considerable body of literature, de Bakker, den Hond and Laamanen argue that organisation in social movements is often incomplete and heterogeneous, existing between fluidity and stability. Particularly in view of the more volatile forms of organising observed in recent examples of social movements, it is necessary to pay attention to the fluidity of social movement participation, and move the investigation more towards the ways in which participants 'interpret and enact the various opportunities to organize that are available to them' – in other words, to see organising more as an 'ongoing process' instead of as a static snapshot of 'the organisation' (ibid.: 224).

Considering the above, the distinction between 'social movement' and 'social movement organisation' is understood to be above all theoretical. While it helps to justify speaking to and observing the SMOs as proxy of the social movement, this study acknowledges the fluidity and continuation between these two analytical categories captured by the concept of 'organising'. This fits well with the focus of the study on the *relations* between social movements and other actors, particularly the state, and the effect of this relationship for the construction of democracy. Since its ultimate aim is to contribute to the larger debate on state–society relations and its impact on democracy, the focus of the book is not so much on the social movements themselves, but more on the processes and relations in which they take centre stage.

Because they have taken centre stage in Bolivian politics, the book pays particular attention to the indigenous social movements (and organisations). For the purposes of this book, those are the actors who claim 'indigeneity' or who mobilise in pursuit of 'indigenous' interests. As Canessa (2014: 156) points out: 'There is an inherent tension between the universality of indigeneity as a powerful and enabling globalised concept and the fact that the discourse of indigeneity is one that lays claim to a cultural and temporal specificity'. Indeed, the 'indigenous' constitutes a fluid category that does not regard the 'indigenous movement' as one (Lucero 2008). Following Lucero, this book understands that given the changing, and often contradictory, meanings of 'indigenous', the movement organisations are crucial to analyse, to the extent to which they channel those meanings politically (ibid.: 8).

The political orientation is important, as it materialises the aim of political transformation and thus the connection to the state. Continuing the discussion of the previous section on the relation between social movements, political parties and the state, the centrality of the 'indigenous' claims brings us to the issue of representation, as pointed out by Lucero (2008: 5): 'what does "representation" mean when one does not talk of individual citizens, but socially constructed ethnic communities in polities where party systems are notoriously inchoate and unrepresentative?'. In that way, the focus of this study is not so much on how varying meanings define and separate the 'indigenous' movements from others and among themselves, but more on how these movements enact representation and participation in relation to the state in order to pursue their objectives, and on the impact of this on the exercise of democracy.

The State–Society Dichotomy and Democratisation in the Latin American Context

In the context of Latin America, this dichotomy has been questioned following the argument that the state–society division does not express a theoretical division but rather a distinction between two antagonistic political positions. The dichotomy has a concrete base in the case of a hostile relationship between the repressive authoritarian state and resources in civil society, from which resistance emerges. With the return of democracy, the division that projects a unitarian state and homogenous society begins to make less sense, unable to reflect the diversity observed in Latin America's modern societies. The contemporary regional scenario is constituted by different actors, multiple types of practices and projects, and various kinds of relationship with the state. This diversity is also expressed in political and cultural projects (some of which may even be non-civil or anti-democratic) deriving from the coexistence of different cultures and traditions within civil society (Dagnino et al. 2006).

Indeed, the homogeneity presumed in civil society is one of the elements that questions the dichotomy, as previously discussed. On this point, Escobar observes that the struggles of social movements have demonstrated the existence of a variety of groups within society, thus acknowledging modern Latin America as a highly heterogeneous and complex region. The economic and cultural differentiation in the modes of production, and the segmentation and transnationalisation of economic and cultural systems, presupposes and produces a mixture of pre- or non-modern, modern, post-modern and even anti-modern forms. For this reason, Latin American modernity is plural, contradictory and irregular (Escobar 1992).

Regarding the process of democratisation or democratic consolidation, there is an increasing awareness that plurality should be inherent to democracy, particularly to its deepening and consolidation. Social movements have successfully placed emphasis on pluralism and tolerance, obliging democracy to be created and constructed in the context of a multiplicity of subjects and spaces, as well as a mutual acknowledgement of their differences (Fals Borda 1992). Roxborough (1997) observed a closer relationship between the state and the social movements, arguing that Latin American states would look to expand their capacity to respond to the increasing (diversity of) society demands, and that social movements would acquire greater importance and/or become more institutionalised. The combination of these trends would result in an organisational density in the relationship between the state and civil society. According to Roxborough, this development could improve the possibilities of various forms of politics, contributing to the prevention of 'populist' demonstrations or elitist exclusion projects. In this scenario, the state provokes a response in civil society, both intentionally and non-intentionally. If the political parties and social movements accept this challenge, the creation of a kind of positive spiral is possible, in which both actors serve to strengthen each other.

More recently, Canon and Kirby (2012: 7) have argued the need to conceive the state–society relationship as 'dialectical' – in which both parts are formed and constituted mutually – in order to achieve a better understanding of the processes of democratisation in the region. In this sense, the concept of a 'state–society interface' presented by Dagnino et al. (2006) is particularly interesting. These authors suggest understanding processes of democratisation in the space of linkages, articulations and transit between civil society and the state, since, historically, both of these social actors are constructed simultaneously. To do so, it is proposed to study 'political society' as the set of actors and institutions that mediate relations between civil society and the state: the government apparatus and its institutional and legal frameworks, the political parties in government and parliament, and the local and regional governments. The crisis of representation of political parties that spread throughout the region (and beyond) means that their role as intermediaries has been weakened. The system is thus less and less capable of recognising and expressing social diversity, while becoming more informal by moving outside the institutional area to use informal networks and come to short-term agreements with ever-changing actors.

Dagnino et al. (2006) argue that, in order to have better chances of deepening and consolidation, it is necessary to increase the correspondence between the democratic projects of civil society and those of the political society. On that point, the concept of a 'state–society interface' gains importance as a space characterized by exchanges between societal and state subjects, conflict, incompatibility and negotiation, and as one where (asymmetric) relations occur. Whether individually or collectively, in the 'state–society interface' subjects are located in a place of confronting cultural paradigms characterised by a multiplicity of discourses, where the processes of knowledge are central and where power is understood to be a struggle for strategic relations and meaning. In the same way, the system of accountability is presented as the space where the state and civil society become intertwined (Gurza Lavalle and Insunza Vera 2010). According to this author, the state–society interface presents two options:

- The delegation of state responsibilities: a functional collaboration for politics to be carried out. This, however, implies a loss of sovereignty in social representation and, according to the author, is condemned to failure.
- Society adopts a critical and controlling function of the state apparatus, where both parts acknowledge each other's autonomy. In this case, it is about influencing and controlling the political process.

Thus, for a better consolidation of the democratic project, a higher degree of correspondence is needed between the democratic content of the political projects in both arenas of activity. The connection must look at the 'state–society interface' as a meeting place between social and state actors, in which the concepts of 'accountability' and 'social control' become particularly important. As previously discussed, in the political project identified by Dagnino et al. (2006) as a participatory democracy project, accountability and social control emerge as some of the model's most decisive components. That is also reflected in the more recent debate on the relation between accountability and the quality of democracy for the Latin American region (Jiménez 2012; Del Tronco 2013; López Pacheco and Hincapié Jiménez 2014; Gurza Lavalle and Insunza Vera 2015; Zaremberg et al. 2017).

Regarding the state–society relationship, Migdal maintains that the structure of society, especially the existence of several organisations that exert social control,[8] has had a decisive effect on state capabilities (Migdal 2001: 64). The strength of these organisations influences the priorities of state leaders and eventually the capacity of state agencies to implement laws and policies. This dependency leads to a need to manoeuvre, negotiate and accommodate, which produces what Migdal calls 'the paradox of the dilemma of state leaders'.[9] Social control of other organisations, obtained through the mobilisation of certain parts of the population, can form a threat for local state representatives. Without this local support, the state loses the political base needed to pursue policies that contest the existent distribution of power between different sectors of society. The lack of an adequate basis of support can also encourage the ambitions of power of other sectors with social control. For these reasons, the state is constantly interacting with other social formations in a continuous process of transformation. Thus, neither the state nor society is a set entity but rather they change their structure, aims, constitutions, rules and forms of social control as they interact.

For the reasons mentioned above, it is necessary to question the state–society dichotomy when studying the relationship between the state and social movements. This questioning is necessary not only because the dichotomy presupposes the homogeneity of both state and society arenas, but also because it dictates a qualitative distinction between institutionalised political practices and non-institutionalised ones. Even though for analytical purposes such a separation could be to a certain degree fruitful, it ends up being artificial when verified empirically.

In the Latin American context and in relation to social movements, many more intertwined relations have been observed, particularly in terms of 'cultural politics' and 'political culture', as well as by the concept of a 'state–society interface'. The struggles of social movements have raised questions about whether democracy is a mere exercising of political representation in the institutional arena of the state, demanding greater citizen participation as part of democratisation, and thus making the state–society separation problematic. And so, at least in the Latin American region, the state–society dichotomy could be obscuring the interrelations that exist between the different actors that make up these two spheres. In the last section, a network perspective will be introduced. At least as a methodological tool, the network perspective allows us to go beyond this dichotomy and the antagonistic vision of the state–society relationship, shedding more light on the state–society dynamics such as interaction, negotiation and conflict.

State and Social Movements in the Twenty-First Century: Political Networks and Governability

With the aim of offering a better appreciation of the current relationship between the state and social movements in Bolivia during the government of Evo Morales, this section introduces a discussion on networks. A network analysis presents considerable advantages when exploring the areas of interaction and intersection, as well as processes of mutual influencing and shaping between the categories 'state' and 'society'.

In the same way, the concept of governability is briefly discussed. As previously mentioned, this volume aims to rate the state–social movement relationship in terms of democratic construction or consolidation – in other words, to assess the democratic quality of the relationship. However, looking only at the democratic quality is not sufficient, especially if it is considered that a highly 'democratic' kind of relationship (or political project) is not necessarily 'feasible' or 'doable'. This is the reason why the study is complemented by an analysis of the 'governability' of the political project embodied in the changing relationship between the state and society in Bolivia. Camou's proposal that a functional concept of governability 'is capable of empirically explaining to us why a certain system becomes governable, irrespective of its moral quality' (2000: 183) can be inverted to maintain that a democratic relationship between the state and social movements (a moral valuation) does not necessarily coincide with functional governability.

The relations (negotiations, interactions and intersections) that are made visible between the state and social movements from a networks perspective will be valued for their democratic quality, for their effects on democratic consolidation – but this is not enough. Such assessment must be complemented by a rating of their quality in terms of governability.

The State–Society Relationship from a Networks Perspective

In their review on the topic, Kenis and Schneider (1991) indicate that, in public policy literature, the first observations on network configurations date from the end of the 1960s and beginning of the 1970s. Since then, more and more authors have looked to use the concept of networks in the study of modern politics. A revision of literature shows that there are a large variety of terms used to denominate how different political and social actors function together – for example, 'network governance', 'political networks', 'policy networks' and 'issue networks'. At the same time, no agreement is reached about whether each network concept refers to a metaphor, a methodology, an analytical tool or rather to a theory in itself.

The network perspective in political theory originates from the proliferation of the concept in sociology. In sociology, social organisation emerges from the deliberate interaction of individuals in a continuous exchange of information and other important resources, in which society stops being controlled exclusively by central intelligence (for example, the state). From a network point of view, modern political decision making can no longer be understood exclusively on the basis of formal political-institutional operations, because such processes occur within a framework of complex constellations of actors and interdependent resources that cannot be captured by formal institutions. This forms the basis of our interest in a 'networks' perspective, since it holds the potential to make the interrelations between the different actors, from both the state and civil society, visible.

To begin with, an initial distinction must be made between the *quantitative* and *qualitative* networks analysis, both of which begin with an understanding of networks as an analytical tool. The quantitative perspective considers the networks analysis in terms of social structure, making use, for example, of classifications, density tables and matrixes. The qualitative approach is more orientated towards processes – in other words, it is not so focused on the structure of interrelations but rather on their content, making use of interviews and discursive analysis. These methodological approaches are generally complementary.

In political theory, a second distinction is made between the network as a 'typology of mediation of interests', and the network as a 'specific form of governance'. In Anglo-Saxon (North American and English) literature, the study of the relationship between state and society has been characterised by an approach of interest mediation, dominated by different versions of pluralism. From the 1970s onwards, this theoretical current received strong criticism from those who defended a corporate theory model. The models produced a series of variants (for example, 'pluralism', 'post-pluralism', 'corporatism', 'neo-corporatism' and 'institutionalism') to refer to typologies of the state–society relationship. However, as Martínez Escamilla explains, these ended up being slightly confusing, as well as incapable of transcending what were increasingly being interpreted as theoretical and methodological rigidities in the study of political–social relationships (Martínez Escamilla 1996).

As an alternative, 'the network' was proposed as a generic concept in order to tackle the different types of relationship between the state and societal interests (Zurbriggen 2003; Sørensen and Torfing 2005a). The concept of 'policy networks' in interest mediation was applied above all in the study of the production of sectorial policies and, in general is understood as an analytical tool for examining the institutionalised relations of exchange between the state and civil society organisations. The advantage of this type of analysis is that it allows for a more detailed representation of sectorial and sub-sectorial differences, the role of public and private actors, and the formal and informal relationships between them (Börzel 1997).

The network understood as a specific form of governance is more recent and was developed in Europe. From the 1980s onwards, modern society was characterised more and more in terms of differentiation and complexity (Kahler et al. 2009), causing an 'overload' in political production and consequently putting governance under pressure. For this reason, governments became increasingly dependent on cooperation and mobilisation, together with the resources of actors located outside state hierarchy, allowing for the mobilisation of political resources in situations in which these were highly dispersed between public and private actors. The policy network thus included all the actors involved in the formulation and implementation of a policy in a specific political sector, mainly characterised by informal interactions between public and private actors, with different but interdependent interests that tried to resolve collective action problems at a central, non-hierarchal level. Thus, political networks facilitate the governance in modern societies by providing a framework of horizontal coordination for the interests of actors whose resources are mutually dependent (Kahler et al. 2009).

From an interest mediation approach, the network as an analytical tool is presented as one more typology in the state–society relationship that aims to transcend the confusion caused by different variants of the predominant models of pluralism and corporatism. The governance approach identifies the 'network' analytical tool as a model for analysing non-hierarchal forms of interaction between public and private actors in the production of policies, thus allowing sectorial and sub-sectorial variations in a disintegrated vision of both of state and society.

However, there are authors who see this concept as much more than an analytical tool, and confer on it a theoretical potential. Understood as a typology of interest mediation, it is indicated that the network structure affects both the process and the political result (Zurbriggen 2003: 5). In the network governance approach, the network stops being a model for simply reflecting the interactions between private and public actors, and is understood as a specific form of governance – network governance (Börzel 1997; Zurbriggen 2003).

Network Governance and Democracy

Network governance has received attention mainly in the European context, specifically as part of the study of the political functioning of the European Union. Network governance responds to society's increasing complexity and the diversity of political demands that emanate from it, and is carried out through so-called 'governance networks' (Sørensen and Torfing 2005b: 199). Theories on this type of network are largely based on those formulated around the previously mentioned concept of policy networks, which, when focusing on the interactions between the disaggregated actors in both society and the state, implies the blurring of the limits between these two spheres.

Governance networks are characterised by horizontal linkage of interdependent and relatively autonomous actors who interact through negotiations within a relatively institutionalised framework of rules, norms and knowledge. These networks are, to a certain extent, self-regulating and contribute to the creation of the common good through the formulation and implementation of public policies (Sørensen and Torfing 2005a, 2005b). Some authors have questioned the effect of this type of governance on the functioning of democratic rule, signalling possible advantages and disadvantages. Positive characteristics are found to be: the ability to identify new problems and provide negotiated answers that are flexible and real; the detailed and relevant knowledge for decision making that network actors generally count on; the capacity to establish a framework for reaching a consensus (or at least make conflict more civilised); and finally the capacity to reduce the risk of resistance to the policies implemented, since those affected are involved in the decision-making process (Sørensen and Torfing 2005a).

Among the possible threats to democratic principles, Eva Sørensen identifies four aspects of liberal democracy that are affected by the emergence of network governance (Sørensen 2002):

- 'the people' as a predetermined entity
- representation as the connection between 'the people' and decision makers

- administration as a non-player in democracy
- institutional separation between the political system and society.

As seen before, the notion of 'the people' as a unit is closely linked to the idea of a 'state-nation'. In modern societies, this political unit has been undermined by the creation of institutions such as the European Union, the United Nations and the International Monetary Fund on the one hand and by the increasing decentralisation of political and administrative policies in units of local government on the other. Therefore, understanding 'the people' as the sum of 'citizens' within a territory (the state-nation) – in other words, as a pre-political entity – is replaced by the idea that this entity is constructed within the process of decision making. The idea of 'the people' as a political construction also affects the concept of representation: the unity and political identity of 'the people' is constructed in and through their representation in the decision-making process. In this way, representation stops being a passive instrument in the hands of those it represents, since competition for the right to representation is no longer limited to the electoral process but rather occurs each time an actor – whether public or private – claims to represent someone. This undermines the notion of representation by mandate.

In the same way, governance networks affect the Weberian model of bureaucratic public administration as separated from politics (Bogason and Musso 2006). Although it can be argued that public administrators have always had a more influential role than that which Weber assigned them, network governance assigns them a more explicit and decisive role as coordinators and facilitators in a system characterised by horizontal, fragmented and negotiated processes of societal governance. For example, it is important to note that public administrators frequently exercise strong control over channels of communication between the actors involved (Sørensen 2002). Therefore, while a large part of the theory on democracy is concentrated on the relationship between citizens and politicians, a model of network governance stipulates that public administrators must also be considered.

A shift in the distribution of functions between the state, the market and civil society can also be added, as well as the emergence of institutional forms that cannot be classified using any of these categories. In this way, the debate on network governance is also one that has led to the questioning of the conventional separation between state and civil society, and that suggests that its corresponding representative democracy model is probably just one among various legitimate decision-making mechanisms.

For their part, in the aforementioned article, Bogason and Musso underline that, from a democratic point of view, the greatest dangers posed by governance networks arise from the topics of accountability and the abuse of power. There is a risk that interest groups and politicians in privileged positions may manipulate the system in favour of certain interests, at the cost of those who do not have the resources to organise themselves. For example, public administrators have more opportunities to take over power and resources than other actors who are subject to greater direct control. Sørensen and Torfing (2005a) see other risks, such as the possibility of co-optation, the lack of transparency in the government process, the atomisation and fragmentation of public governance, and a limitation of political protests through the development of strong hegemonic discourses.

However, these authors are not pessimistic about these emerging forms of governance and argue that, when complying with certain conditions, network governance has positive potential for the process of democratisation. The discussion on network governances proposes a 'metagovernance' to deal with the possible hurdles of network governance. This concept aims at the regulation of self-regulatory governance networks, and puts it in the hands of elected politicians. Metagovernance supposes first installing governance networks, by establishing an institutional framework that creates structures of societal interdependence in the desired manner. This would a better position from which politicians could monitor the networks, providing them with the ability to encourage or discourage the establishment and influence of certain networks.

Another important component of metagovernance is the active participation of elected politicians within a network. This participation provides direct knowledge of network activities, which facilitates direct political intervention and contributes to aligning governance network political decisions with the government's general aims. In this way, the image of governance networks as opportunities to mediate specific interests can be transformed into one of public decision-making opportunities that are subject to open public debate.

A third means of metagovernance refers to the articulation of governance networks within a framework of general political aims. Through a political, financial and discursive delivery, politicians can limit the area in which governance networks are self-governing – for example, deciding which questions are of general public interest and which can be delegated to the more detailed and particular decision making of governance networks.

Metagovernance thus aims to fulfil the democratising potential of governance networks, looking towards how more conventional democratic institutions complement the new forms of governance that emerge as a response to the complexity and diversity of political topics in modern societies.

A network governance model has consequences for how the state functions. As Sørensen and Torfing explain, governance networks are based on a pluricentric government system as opposed to the state's unicentric one (and the multicentric market system); they function on a rationality of negotiation as opposed to the substantial rationality that characterises the state (or the procedural rationale that governs commercial competition); and conformity within governance networks is achieved through trust and political obligation and not through the fear of legal sanctions from the state (or economic loss in the market). On the other hand, Atkinson and Coleman (1989) argue that this model brings with it a disintegrated vision of the state, and point to possible loss of autonomy that this political unit may suffer when infiltrated by groups with sectorial interests. In the worst cases, in a context of institutional weakness, the state may be reduced to a distillation of societal conflicts, dislocated by internal discord.

Manuel Castells ([1996] 2000) offers an interesting analysis of the effects of network systems on the state. He identifies the emergence of network mechanisms in a much wider context, responding to the transition of industrial societies to an information era, which affects the whole of society, not just the political arena. Regarding the state, Carnoy and Castells (2001) argue that this political entity is subject to a series of changes because of globalisation, and that although these undermine its position, they do not void it: the state does not disappear but rather is transformed.

Globalisation limits the state's sovereignty while redefining its social limits: the territory stops being the reference for determining a sense of community, and makes way for the emergence of identity policies that question whether citizens are the only source of political legitimacy. The modern state is obliged to respond to a series of cultural demands, which are often problematic in themselves, using a plurality of resources that surpass the individual citizen as the basis of political representation. The potential legitimacy crisis that results from this is counteracted by the reconfiguration of the state in two ways: through a decentralisation process and through the delegation of a series of functions to non-governmental organisations.[10] In this way, the state increases the chances of citizens By identifying with its institutions and participating in the political process, while transferring them greater responsibilities, it becomes transformed and re-enforced to respond to the needs of modern society, and ultimately recovers its legitimacy.

Given the loss of sovereignty in the global framework and the decentralisation within the state, a new kind of state emerges, constituted of shared institutions with constant and interactive negotiations between national governments, co-national governments, supranational entities, international institutions, regional governments, local governments, social movements and NGOs. Decision making and representation occur throughout this whole chain without necessarily following a prescribed hierarchal order. The state functions as a network, in which all points interact and are equally necessary to achieve state functions – the Network State.

Governance Networks in Latin America

The concepts of public policy networks or governance networks or the Network State do not (yet) seem to have gained sufficient importance in the study of Latin America. The majority of studies that use the network concept do so based on its initial meaning as a 'social network', regarding, above all, the problems of poverty in the region. However, a few publications look to introduce the network concept into political analysis and governance, indicating the gestation of networks in the production of public policies, although they limit their discussions to a theoretical revision of the concept with its possible advantages and disadvantages (see, for example, Moura 1996; Fleury 2002).

It is worth noting that, as opposed to Anglo-Saxon and European literature, the focus of studies in Latin America is on the implementation of social public policies (see Kliksberg 1998; Isuani 2005; Souto Maior Fontes et al. 2008), which reflect an increasing awareness that the success of public policies, aimed at dealing with the social problems of popular sectors, largely depends on the participation of their recipients in their formulation. This involves interaction between the different political and social actors, which can be better appreciated from a network perspective.

Martínez Escamilla explains that the political networks were initially considered as characteristic of democratically organised societies in the industrialised West, but are now being accepted as a much more common phenomenon (Martínez Escamilla 1996). In his talk at the 'Society and State Reform' seminar in Brazil, Castells (1996) argued that the evolution of the Network State was a global trend responding to current developments, and was therefore not limited to 'First World' states. The Network State is also being developed in the Latin American continent.

Dealing explicitly with the Latin American region, Douglas A. Chalmers et al. (1997) identify the emergence of what they call 'associative networks' as a kind of structure of representation (next to political parties), connecting state and societal actors. The diversification of the popular classes produces a changing ensemble of popular groups that struggle to form a set of organisations with the capacity to recognise, analyse, debate and make demands about specific matters. In this way, popular representation has become more and more dependent on the participation of societal and state actors in a changing ensemble of associative networks, which fuses or blurs the limits between activities of 'interest articulation', 'interest aggregation', 'formulation of demands' and 'formulation and implementation of public policies'.[11]

The representation structure is thus defined as a group of actors who are linked to decision-making centres through procedures and organisations in which cognitive and business exchanges take place, influencing the policies that these centres adopt. The networks developed around a particular topic involve the state authorities responsible for this matter, and the organised groups that exert pressure with demands and that encourage the debate. Therefore, these networks are not situated in civil society but rather in the arena that links civil society to the state.

In the context of the relationship between the state and social movements, the network concept becomes useful because of its specific reference to state–society connections, looking to make them more visible. As we have seen, this concept emerges from the deficiencies of the most traditional models of corporatism and pluralism, valuing the complexity, dynamism and connection that characterises the relationship in modern societies. The concept of 'public policy networks', understood as the changing configurations of societal and state actors around the formulation and implementation of a particular policy, is presented as a methodological tool that allows the state–social movement relationship to be assessed more accurately, by transcending a more traditional dichotomy and antagonistic vision.

At the same time, as has already been indicated, authors who have dealt with the concept have assigned it theoretical potential, which needs to be taken into account. 'Network governance' or 'the Network State' involves more than just making the structures that form the state–society relationship more visible. These concepts implicate a redefinition of the roles and functions of both actors, as well as the relationship between them. In this way, arguably such redefinitions have significant consequences for the theoretical understanding of the state, citizens/society (organisations), democracy, and the relationship between them all.

Governability and Social Movements

The analysis of the state–social movement relationship from a network perspective poses the question about whether the kind of relationship that exists between the state and society organisations in the modern context actually constitutes a different type of government, one that undermines the privileged position of the state as an (exclusive) body for decision making. In this way, a more integrated understanding that transcends the state–civil society dichotomy not only has implications for democracy – understood as a kind of state–society relationship – but it can also be expected to have a practical effect on how power is exercised.

The concept of governability is particularly appropriate when dealing with this kind of practical event, because of its explicit reference to the state–society relationship. Silva and Rojas Aravena maintain that the concept of governability should be understood in two dimensions: institutional efficiency and the articulation of social interests. The first refers to 'the capacity of the state to deal with and resolve social demands', while the second is linked to 'the group of mechanisms, processes and relations and institutions through which citizens and groups articulate their interests, exercise their rights and obligations, and mediate their differences' (Silva and Rojas Aravena 2013: 4). Along the same lines and related to governability, Torres-Rivas explains that 'there is a basic mutual relationship' between the state and civil society (1993: 10). Kooiman's view is that governability is the result of the interaction between the 'system being governed' and the two-way 'system of governance': 'participative interactions' and 'interactions that are a result of political administration' respectively (Kooiman 2008).

The concept of governability has received greater attention in academic debate in the region in the last few years, partly due to the negative impact of the economic reforms implemented from the 1980s onwards, and partly because of the gradual increase in the presence of actors from society in matters that were previously strictly of the state (Solheim 2013: 129–30). In this way, it can be concluded that governability is not a quality of governments themselves but rather of societies or social systems (Prats 2001: 120) – in other words, of the state–society relationship.

When observing the state–social movement relationship, the concept of governability is useful because it refers to both sides of the relationship. This study adopts Camou's definition of governability as 'a dynamic state of equilibrium between the level of societal demands and the capacity of the political system to respond to them in a legitimate and efficient way'.[12] Camou's definition thus allows for a more specific assessment of the state–social movement relationship.

It is necessary to point to a tension inherent to the concept of governability in the context of modern and complex societies like Latin American ones.[13] The emergence of a large number of new and different actors in societies is accompanied by the weakening of the centre that shapes social life (Camou and Castro 1997). In this way, preoccupations about the excesses of power – so present in the Latin American context – have given way to concerns about how to increase state power, thus reintroducing the old European debate of '*la raison d'État*' (Camou 2000: 174). This problem refers to the existing ambivalence regarding the need to satisfy social demands effectively – in other words, the tension between short- and long-term aims (Camou 2000: 174). The 'balance' in Camou's definition underpins the stability of the political system, in which the state's characteristic and necessary integral and long-term vision comes into conflict with achieving the societal actors' local and immediate aims, as well as the capacity of the state–society relationship (especially the state, but also society) to deal with that tension. This problem is particularly imminent for the state–social movement relationship because of the characteristics of social movements.

Looking specifically at social movements, Marisa Revilla asks whether the emergence of (new) social movements contributes to governability or rather damages it. The author puts the tensions down to different understandings of democracy. The concept of governability implies a representative democracy that puts emphasis on political parties as channels of participation. Social movements embody a concept of a more participatory democracy by introducing forms of participation that cause the regulated channels to overflow. The author concludes that, in order to allow for a meaningful contribution by social movements to governability, the supremacy of political representation must be abandoned. Only then does it become possible to consider an alternative understanding of democracy that sees the participation of society as necessary in the production of order. Only in this way can governability and social movements be considered as concepts that are complementary instead of oppositional (Revilla 1994).

In summary, governability prescribes an integral and mutually formed understanding of state and society. Governability is not only a functional concept that defines the quality of a political system in terms of effectiveness and stability. It also contains a regulatory element that considers the satisfaction of social demands and the stability of the regime, as well as the manner in which those aims are fulfilled, and so 'governability' seeks a kind of symbiosis between state and society. Thus, both sides are fundamental and complementary to the construction of governability. That is why the concept of governability is particularly useful for an assessment of the (anti-)democratic degree of the state–social movement relationship.

In the Latin American context, the state–society dichotomy – persistent in studies on social movements – responds more to the tension between two political positions than to the division between analytical categories. Under authoritarianism, actors in society were found to be in real opposition to the state by advocating a democratic political project. In the transition, the preoccupation with protecting the precarious democratic regime was reinforced by the very real danger that intense political intervention by societal actors posed to the consolidation of formal institutions. The obsession with institutionalising a representative and stable democracy prescribed that citizens would keep their distance from the political arena once they had voted, thus reinforcing the state–society divide.

Thus, this division persisted to various degrees in the political projects that followed the transition to democracy. In the most recent academic debate, however, it has been seriously questioned, particularly in the study of social movements. The criticism suggests that the state–society dichotomy obscures the complexity of the interactions, intersections and negotiations that can be observed in the relationship between different socio-political actors, questioning artificial distinctions between 'institutionalised' and 'non-institutionalised' politics, and arguing for a much more integral vision of the state and society, in which both are mutually constituted as one system. This vision not only allows for a better assessment of the socio-political dynamic, but also makes the potential for democratic construction more visible.

Following this line of critique, a network perspective is suggested to ana-lyse the state–social movements relationship, due to its potential to make the areas for intersection and negotiation more visible – in other words to visualise exactly where the conceptual dividing lines become blurry. Next to being a methodological tool, the concept of political networks has the theoretical potential to refer to a different type of emerging governance in modern societies, one in which political networks emerge as particularly apt for responding to the demands of democratic construction in diverse and complex societies.

Together with the possibilities of the network governance, its potential limits also need to be considered. The concept of governability allows for the democratic quality of the state–social movement relationship to be tackled in terms of its viability, including a regulatory element that draws a horizon of 'what is desired' while at the same time making clear reference to political stability. Thus, thinking in terms of feasibility, how doable or sustainable is a political project, however democratic that project is considered to be? More explicitly, regarding social movements, the 'satisfying demands in an effective way' component of the governability definition is placed behind the need to maintain a certain balance between satisfying short- and long-term aims (the stability and sustainability of a political project), and the real possibility of strain that might exist between them. In this way, the concept of govern-ability reintroduces the importance of the question of '*raison d'Etat*', which appears otherwise slightly obsolete or extremely weakened in the 'network governance' debate. This marks an important point of strain that is of special interest when analysing the relationship between the state and social move-ments in particular, and the state–society relation in general.

Notes

1. The phenomenon of the transition from authoritarian to democratic regimes is not exclusive to Latin America, and authors such as Adam Przeworski have tried to filter a transition to democracy logic by making comparisons to transitions in countries in Southern and Eastern Europe (Przeworski 1992).
2. The preoccupation with the 'stability' of the regime is of particular importance as it appears to be less likely in diverse societies and multinational states. This point will be further developed later in this study.
3. In this version, Craig Jenkins argues for the need to make a distinction between the 'state', the 'regime' and the 'government' to allow for differentiation between the social

movements that oppose the government and their policies, those that oppose the regime and its legitimising myths and those that adopt the most radical aim of reorganising the state and the political landscape (Craig Jenkins 1995).

4. Glenn Jordan and Chris Weedon (1995) quoted in Sonia E. Alvarez et al. (1998b): 5–6. This and all of the other quotes from texts originally in foreign languages in this volume have been translated by the author.

5. It is worth noting that the distance they maintained with political parties was not only due to their legitimacy crisis. Affiliation to a political party meant that social movements limited their capacity to move through various segments of society. Thus, the way in which social movements conduct their struggles provides a basis for the creation of new and more equal social identities, capable of overcoming pre-existing social hierarchies based on categories of race, class or gender (Thompson and Tapscott 2010).

6. In this model, the state is defined by Migdal (2001) as 'a field of power marked by the use and threat of violence, and shaped by (1) the image of a coherent and controlling organisation in a territory, which is a representation of the people bounded by that territory, and (2) the actual practices of its multiple parts' (ibid.: 15–16). The image of the state refers to the cultural fusion of the institution in whose name its members exercise authority, projecting the idea of a unique and dominant centre. This image prompts an integral perception of the state agencies that act in conjunction with each other. Migdal continues: 'The image of the state posits two sorts of boundaries: (1) territorial boundaries between the state and other states, and (2) social boundaries between the state – its (public) actors and agencies – and those subject to its rules (private)' (ibid.: 17). The practices refer to the performance or real functioning of actors and state agencies that can reinforce or weaken the state's image. This image involves morality, a standard and the correct way of doing things, while the practices denote the multiple ways it can function and possible contradictions about which way is the right one. Thus, for example, a state can adopt corrupt practices while endorsing legality (ibid.: 15–23).

7. For example, Burnstein and Linton point out that no real difference exists between political parties, social movements and interest groups, considering that all these have a substantial impact on the formulation of policies. Even more importantly, the authors conclude that this group of 'political organisations' only affect the production of public policies half of the time and to the same degree (Burstein and Linton 2002).

8. According to Migdal, the level of social control is reflected by three indicators: (1) conformity, in other words the extent to which the population conforms with state demands; (2) participation, understood as the organisation of the population for specialised tasks in the institutional components of state organisation; and (3) legitimacy, the acceptance of the symbolic order as true and correct, and as the symbolic order associated with the idea of the state as the people's own system of meaning (Migdal 2001: 52).

9. State leaders are in a situation in which they must reinforce state agencies to ensure their position before other states. On the one hand, reinforcing these agencies – in particular those with a coercive capacity – may put leaders who do not have widespread public support at risk. These agencies are needed to impose policies on the population. On the other, state leaders should be able to mobilise the support of the population directly, so that no state agency believes it has the capacity to overthrow them (for example, through a coup d'état). However, this political mobilisation cannot be achieved without channels running towards the population that induce mobilisation through a series of rewards, sanctions and symbols, exactly as strong state agencies do. This paradox is the dilemma of state leaders (Migdal 2001: 68–72).

10. Castells prefers to call these NGOs 'neo-governmental organisations', because the majority are subsidised or supported by (a certain) state and/or are created as important parties to oppose the production of policies.

11. As the authors explain, this model is different to pluralism. In pluralism, the interest groups make their interests known by putting pressure on the state. In associative networks however, the interaction between societal and state actors is characterised by cognitive processes (formulating, resisting and resolving competitive demands) that may lead to the negotiation of interests as well as to their definition.

12. Because of the specific focus of this research – the state–social movement relationship – slightly more complex definitions such as that of 'democratic governability' are left out, which includes, as well as the strengthening of institutional politics and socio-economic development and social integration, a third element promoting 'an international climate that favours the peaceful and negotiated resolution of conflicts' (Silva and Rojas Aravena 2013: 6).

13. See also Escobar (1992) and Larraín (2000).

2 Social Movements in the Neoliberal State

Evolution of the Social Movement into a Political Actor

Morales coming to power through a formal electoral process constituted the irruption of social movements in the institutional political field. From a historical perspective, the period from 1980 to 2000 presented the reformulation of a protest discourse in which a Marxist analysis and the centrality of the Bolivian Workers' Centre (COB) were replaced by a cultural analysis and an indigenous discourse that were adopted by several actors to formulate their claims. The leadership of this protest would end up being assumed by the indigenous social movements. Particularly between 2000 and 2005, in a time of crisis in the political system, social movements achieved a high level of political influence, becoming the most important actors in Bolivian politics and accounting for the election of the *cocalero* movement leader, Evo Morales, as president. In this chapter, this historical development is analysed through the 'dialectic' approach of the state–society relationship, in which both spheres of socio-political reality come together in an ongoing process of mutual reshaping. After the transition to democracy, new social movements emerged, undergoing a process of political evolution until becoming the main actors on the Bolivian political scene.

In the first section, the role of social movements – specifically the role of the Bolivian Workers' Centre at the heart of social articulation – is observed in the transition to democracy. Here, it can be seen how the Bolivian transition to democracy largely corresponds with the characterisation of that process for the Latin American region, marked by the quick marginalisation of social movements from politics in order to establish a new democratic regime. In the same way, this period sees the emergence of 'new social movements' characterised by 'cultural politics', specifically the political stream of Katarism and the consolidation of a unionised social organisation, although rural in nature, called the Unified Syndical Confederation of Rural Workers of Bolivia (CSUTCB).

In the second section, the role played by the *cocalero* movement is analysed as a new social movement that increasingly coordinated the social movements' foray into politics. The social vacuum left by a weakened COB, together with the violence that characterised the conflict between the *cocalero* movement and the state, are seen as important factors in the adoption of a more national profile of various 'new social movements' at a local level. The evolution into a movement of national range is observed in the creation of the 'political instrument' (the political party Movement towards Socialism), showing the neoliberal decentralisation reforms as a third important factor in understanding the political articulation of social movements.

The third section describes the irruption of the social movement into politics in the specific context of a legitimacy crisis involving political parties and the model of neoliberal development. The crisis resulted in important confrontations between the state and society, mainly featuring urban social movements that were increasingly influential and successful in opposing government plans. Between 2000 and 2005, the confrontations between the state and social movements resulted in real scenarios of ungovernability, particularly during the Water War in 2000 and the Gas War in 2003. As will be seen, the social insurgence that characterised this period is indicative of how social movements became legitimate channels for political participation and arbitration with the state.

The last section analyses the rather unexpected decision of social movements to opt for the formal electoral process to obtain political power. Up until then, Bolivian social movements had been more conventionally 'anti-state', opposed to the formal structures of politics. But at the decisive moment when social demonstrations occurred, they chose formal channels to compete for power, which was the means through which the MAS finally came to power. The last part of the chapter attempts to explain this apparent contradiction by using the approach that places social movements and political parties within the same system, thus questioning the distinction between 'institutionalised' and 'non-institutionalised' politics. The fact that political prominence passes from popular urban social movements to indigenous ones is also highlighted as being crucial to the understanding of Morales' victory at the beginning of December 2005.

New Social Movements and Structural Adjustment Policies: The COB, Katarism and the CSUTCB (1980–1990)

During García Meza's dictatorship, the COB, embodying the heart of social resistance, suffered great losses when its main leaders went into exile and/or were murdered. However, because of its important role fighting against dictatorial regimes, the COB became the dominant political actor in the transition to the democracy period, attaining a high level of legitimacy.

The Transition to Democracy: The UDP Government and the COB

The precariousness of the state during the transition to democracy is illustrated by the singularity of the dynamic that played out between the new civil government and the COB. The Popular Democratic Unity (UDP) government (1982–1985) was composed of a group of left-wing political parties, and was weak because of its tendency to form splinter groups, acting on more than one occasion in opposition rather than in support of the president (Morales 2010: 205). On the other hand, the explosion of demands from different sectors of society made the term of this first civil government considerably difficult, in a period characterised by a severe economic and social crisis, resulting in a call for elections one year earlier than planned.

Ibáñez Rojo (2000) argues convincingly that the UDP government's political and economic crisis was directly related to the organisation of the workers' movement. Given its role at the forefront of opposition to the authoritarian regime, the COB emerged in the transition to democracy as the only actor truly committed to democracy. This meant that the new government needed not only to collaborate with COB, but that there would be no legitimacy or governability unless agreement was found with the workers' movement.

This explains why, at the very beginning, President Siles Zuazo invited the COB to form a 'co-government'. Well aware of the frustration that exercising politics like this had caused in the *movimientista* state, the COB responded by demanding 'half plus one' of the seats in Parliament before beginning any kind of negotiations. This demand implied the immediate and full implementation of the economic plan drawn up by the COB. This proposal, which projected a great increase in public spending, was completely incompatible with the measures urgently needed for economic stabilisation. Although it can be assumed that the leaders of the COB were aware that their demands were irrational, their uncompromising attitude was due to the fact that the union organisation had no interest in a possible collaboration with the government. Siles Zuazo's political power was undermined by divisions within the UDP, which meant that sharing government with them simply represented a way of dealing with the political crisis without really obtaining more influence over economic policies.

A shift in the COB's base of representation constituted an additional problem. At one time, their main base was made up of miners with a strong collective consciousness, but this was eroded when very different types of worker (for example, public sector workers and oil rig workers without union experience) were incorporated. This development pushed COB leaders into maintaining unity through their historical strategy of opposition to the state, which, as the crisis got worse, led to bloodier confrontations with the government. The workers' movement refused to negotiate to find viable alternatives, effectively paralysing Siles Zuazo's government.

Given that it was impossible both to break off relations with the COB and to negotiate with them, Siles Zuazo's government was forced to give in to the demands. In the words of Ibáñez Rojo: 'The result of this interplay between a completely inflexible collective actor, tied to a maximalist pro-gramme of demands, which was simply the sum of all the zero-sum conflicts launched by the rank and file in different sectors and a government obliged to cooperate with it, was that Bolivia slid into the worst inflationary spiral ever seen in Latin America, and the labour movement suffered the worst legiti-macy crisis in its history' (2000: 205).

After these events, the COB's power decreased to the extent that neoliberal measures physically diminished its main base of social support: its backbone of miners. Following the fall of the UDP and faced with economic chaos, Víctor Paz Estenssoro was chosen as the new president in early-called elections. Paz Estenssoro immediately set in motion his plan for an economic restructura-tion, marking the beginning of what would be two decades of a neoliberal regime. Paz Estenssoro was relentlessly strict in his plans, in which there was no room for the COB. In this way, his policies were aimed at deconstructing the professional workers' unions, and undermining the protests held by the COB against his plans. The government responded to the social pressure with threats of sacking for strikers. At the same time, the government gained the support of the armed forces, declaring several states of emergency and facil-itating the detention and confinement of several leaders. Even so, in August 1986, the COB organised the 'March for Life and Peace' to resist the govern-ment's plan to close mining centres, relocate their workers, and disarticulate the national mining company COMIBOL. The government's response was to mobilise the army to contain the march. Finally, the union's leadership nego-tiated a peaceful retreat, but the agreement was rejected by the majority of its supporters and thus the COB experienced one of its biggest defeats.

The union organisation's gradual loss of legitimacy was also aggravated by the material and political deconstruction of the once-powerful Union Federation of Bolivian Mine Workers (FSTMB) and its mining unions, mean-ing that the COB lost both members and its impressive ability to mobilise people. In this way, from 1986, the COB was evermore reduced to 'a formal fact of Congresses and Executive Committees'.[1] However, the importance of the COB in collective historical memory must be underlined, since it con-tinues as a national reference point for social structure and mobilisation. As García Linera et al. (2010: 71) explain, the 'union structure that had existed before it, achieved in the form of the COB its most important organisational and political schooling on the collective experience of subordinate classes up until today'.

In this way, the transition to democracy in Bolivia coincides with the characterisation outlined in Chapter 1. As with many of the Latin American transitions, despite the success of dictatorial regimes in disassembling and depoliticising civil society, civil society actors played an important role in the transition. In the case of Bolivia, the resistance to a repressive state itself produced the coordination of a strong social actor like the COB. Enthusiasm for their democratising role was, however, short lived, giving way to a loss of legitimacy under the new formal democratic regime.

The Beginnings of a Cultural Analysis: From Katarism to the CSUTCB

The rural movement in Bolivia also has its origins in the unions. After the 1952 Revolution, peasants were organised into agricultural unions, using a model in which the Revolutionary Nationalist Movement (MNR) government party acted as mediator with the state. In 1953, the National Confederation of Peasant Workers of Bolivia (CNTCB), affiliated to the COB, was founded with the support of 'MNR commandos' (Albó 2008b: 29–32). Unions were first formed on ranches and then in Indian communes *ayllus*, coming to take the place of the 'community'. In this sense, the creation of peasant unions by the *movimientista* state meant the co-optation of the rural population through the creation of clientelistic networks.

When General René Barrientos Ortuño, whose successive terms of military dictatorship were in line with North American foreign policy, came to power, this relationship was changed by the so-called Military–Peasant Pact. This instrument was created as a way of confronting sectors of radicalised workers, and connecting para-state unionism with the armed forces. The latter took on a role as spokesperson before the state regarding the defence of what had been achieved in the Agricultural Reform. Peasant unions had already been domesticated sufficiently during the MNR government, and the figure of Barrientos was central to improving the clientelistic relationship. Because of his modest beginnings and charismatic personality, Barrientos won over the agricultural sector (to such a degree that the peasant movement recognised him as its leader), making the coercive policies of the Military–Peasant Pact possible. As a result of these military regimes, the agricultural movement went through several processes of construction and greater political coordination, growing more autonomous and involved in politics at a national level.

The first step occurred before the implementation of Barrientos's governmental plan to tax peasants' individual land. In opposition to the Military–Peasant Pact that supported the plan, the so-called Independent Peasant Bloc was formed, which quickly became affiliated to the COB. The anthropologist Silvia Cusicanqui adds two important processes to this first foray into autonomous coordination: the unionism of the 'colonisers' and the emergence of Indianist (Katarist) political currents. The 'colonisers' responded to the migrating populations of ex-miners in search of land, especially in the tropical zones in Santa Cruz, Alto Beni (La Paz) and Chapare (Cochabamba). Their members quickly became aware of the negative effects of capitalist policies on agricultural development (Rivera Cusicanqui, 1986: 176).[2] More autonomous forms of organisation emerged as a result of this awareness, constructed along the same lines as unions but disassociated from the official union apparatus and resulting in the formation of the National Confederation of Colonisers of Bolivia (CNCB), which will be referred to in more detail later.

The superiority of the Aymaran people in developing indigenous political awareness should be highlighted. Currently, the Aymaran group together a diverse number of populations unified by a common tongue, with the Spanish conquest being the event that has had the biggest impact on incorporation into this group (Makaran-Kubis 2009: 47). This is significant, since it shows the long road the indigenous movement has travelled. In effect, the formation of a common indigenous front had already been identified during the colonial period, with its maximum expression during the Indian uprisings of the 'Great Rebellion' between 1779 and 1781. The most important uprising was led by Túpac Katari in Bolivia,[3] who gave his name to the Katarist ideology and movement.

This political current began at the end of the 1960s and beginning of the 1970s. It was driven by an intellectual-unionist elite of Aymaran migrants in the city of La Paz, and its most important theories appear in the writings of the *indianista* Fausto Reynaga,[4] a theorist who advocated a return to the Inca empire's political organisation, production and government. The emergence of Katarism is, in part, due to the rural population's frustration with the fact that many of the promises regarding citizenship and equality in the 1952 Revolution were only partially carried out. The migration of young peasants to urban areas, particularly Aymara who went on to higher education in the city of La Paz, made the Indians' position as subordinates who were discriminated against more poignant, allowing for a growing awareness of indigenous identity that would serve as the basis of claims to culture and history.

As Albó (2008b) explains, the Katarist movement was able to expand rapidly because of its timely decision to become part of the predominant organisation of 'peasant union', even though this was under the tutelage of the Military–Peasant Pact. In only a matter of months, Katarist leaders gained access to the upper echelons of power. The brief democratic openings presented by the presidencies of Ovando and Torres (1969–1971) encouraged the renewal of the CNTCB's leadership with leaders who were more conscious of a peasant identity, producing Katarist leader Jenaro Flores as head of this organisation.

Despite Flores' efforts to connect peasant unionism to the workers' movement, the memory of the Military–Peasant Pact and Katarism's 'Indianist' discourse contributed to the workers' scepticism and distrust of the emerging political actor. As Hervé do Alto explained, Katarism not only questioned the main capital/work contradiction of Marxism but also maintained a discourse that could be interpreted as 'inverse racism' (*racismo al revés*) (quoted in Svampa et al. 2007: 20). That is why the different popular sectors could not form a working-class alliance during the brief opening to democracy that appeared at the beginning of the 1970s.

In 1971, when Hugo Bánzer Suárez came to power, Flores was exiled. Persecution of social organisations, leftist political parties, unions, and anything that opposed the dictatorship also ended up weakening the fledgling independent peasant organisation. However, as a response to repression, a stronger unionist peasant movement emerged, with more experience in politics. Flores secretly returned from exile in Chile in 1972, more aware of the importance of an alliance with the workers and determined to undertake the underground reorganisation of grass-root level unionism and the important job of training young union representatives (Hurtado 1986: 273). A decisive landmark in this process of strengthening a peasant organisation that was independent of the pact with the military was the 'Valley Massacre' in Cochabamba in 1974. This confrontation made it clear that the Banzerist regime's attempts to re-establish the Military–Peasant Pact were useless, since the independent peasant movement continued to get stronger. Thus, in 1977, the de facto leadership of the CNTCB was taken over by Jenaro Flores and others, in plain defiance of the government-recognised leadership.

The struggles of the rural Katarist movement were recognised by the COB in 1979, which allowed their incursion into the V Congress (despite opposition from some Marxist parties) and decided to call on rural unification. As a result of this initiative, the current Unified Syndical Confederation of Rural Workers of Bolivia (CSUTCB) emerged, unifying the different peasant organisations and putting a definitive end to the Military–Peasant Pact. From this moment on, the confederation became a high-level space for the organisation and mobilisation of the indigenous-peasant segment of society.

The process of political articulation of the peasant movement through a Katarist discourse could not have occurred without the decisive role played by their leader, Jenaro Flores. Although his political party[5] did not win enough votes outside its regional Aymaran base – giving it a limited role in institutional politics – Katarism was victorious in other, more important areas. Jenaro Flores began a campaign in favour of renewing the leadership for younger representatives, more independent from traditional co-optation, thus taking over the upper echelons of union organisations (from the CNTCB to the CSUTCB). As leader of the CSUTCB, he managed its consolidation as an independent peasant organisation, while recognising the importance of the workers' movement, thus achieving both real recognition by and an alliance with the COB.

From these national platforms, the Katarist movement came to exert a strong influence in the political arena, first resisting the dictatorship and contributing to the return of democracy, and then providing the indigenous movement with an initial, more integral and articulate insight into national politics. This also shows the relativity of the electoral failure of its parties, which had split into a dozen and obtained a low number of votes (Madrid 2008), showing again how in the different political scenarios in Bolivia (co-optation, dictatorship, a legitimacy crisis) the political parties do not constitute the efficient and/or real means of political participation.

The rise of the peasant movement was specifically expressed through the creation of the CSUTCB and its incorporation into the Bolivian Workers' Centre, as well as the fact that Jenaro Flores came to assume leadership of the COB at this time – during the important period of transition to democracy under García Meza's dictatorship – thus becoming the first indigenous leader to hold national leadership of this organisation. In this way, Katarism managed to reverse the dominant class analysis hawked by the COB – in which peasants only occupied a rearguard role – in order to project the peasant movement into a central role in national politics.

Despite being set up as independent, and presented as the most important peasant organisation in the country, the CSUTCB faced certain difficulties at the beginning. As Ströbele-Gregor explained, the CSUTCB did not manage to break free from the practices or rhetoric of the dominant political culture. The confederation's structure mirrored the COB, and was based on a pyramidal organisation that managed, at least until the mid-1980s, a top-down organisation of the indigenous population. This unionist hierarchy did not allow room for the different forms of local leadership linked to religious and social practices, making the CSUTCB an umbrella organisation that represented peasants mainly as an economic sector, that is to say as rural micro-producers and not strictly speaking as 'indigenous' (Ströbele-Gregor 1994; Hahn 1996).

However, the peasant movement continued its political articulation. As indicated, after the fall of the UDP, Víctor Paz Estenssoro was chosen as president of the MNR party. In a paradoxical turn of events, his government ended up completely reversing the reforms and achievements of the state of 1952, of which it had been the main inventor in the first MNR revolutionary government, specifically with the adoption of the famous 21060 decree. Aiming to achieve economic stability, the economy was privatised and the market opened up; state companies were closed (with the subsequent dismissal of thousands of workers) and given access to multinationals. The

New Economic Plan was successful in stabilising the economy, but it was a disaster, socially speaking, for the working-class sectors.

These changes not only noticeably diminished the number of salaried workers (to the detriment of the COB) but also encouraged the growth of the informal sector. The latter contributed to the emergence of a number of small urban organisations, mainly made up of rural migrants, characterised by the precarious nature of their work and a lack of access to basic services (Albó 2008b: 45). The importance of this group was expressed politically towards the end of the 1980s with the creation and quick rise of populist political parties, such as CONDEPA and UCS.[6] In summary, in the context of economic policies with a high social cost, the dismantling of the workers' movement and the discrediting of the traditional left during the UDP government created an 'ideological' (Ströbele-Gregor 1994: 112) or political vacuum, providing the indigenous movement with the chance to come onto the scene and offer an alternative.

In this way, the period between 1980 and 1990 meant the dismantling of the national working-class union organisation, the COB, in favour of 'new social movements' of a more local nature, in whose approach identity, particularly Katarism, began to play a more important role.

Neoliberalism and the Political Articulation of Social Movements: The Creation of the 'Political Instrument' (1990–2000)

The incursion of the indigenous movement into politics can be understood using the concept of 'cultural politics' (see Chapter 1), in which social movements' main struggles are understood as those redefining the meaning and limits of the political system itself. This section tracks the main role played by the *cocalero* movement in the political articulation at a national level of a number of social movements. The struggle in defence of the coca leaf was increasingly formulated as a cultural struggle, effectively enacting a 'politics of culture' by a 'new social movement'.

Towards Articulation at a National Level: The Cocalero Movement

The peasant movement also received a boost with the centrality the *cocalero* movement adopted towards the end of the 1980s. One of the effects of the austerity of Paz Estenssoro's neoliberal government was the resettlement of a large number of families in the Chapare area, who began to cultivate the highly profitable coca leaf; the majority of the families were those of miners who had been laid off. Notably, President Morales' family was among the displaced, having to move from the mining region of Oruro to the Chapare region. The boom in the drug industry during García Meza's 'narco-dictatorship' was related to an increasing demand for cocaine in the international markets of the Global North. Cultivating coca became the only real option for survival for many, as one of the free market principles extolled by Víctor Paz Estenssoro's brand new government was achieved.

The government's response to considerable expansion in the cultivation of the ancient leaf was the so-called 'Triennial Plan against Drug Trafficking' in 1986. Expansion was impeded by posting military personnel in the area to eradicate the coca plantations that were considered illegal (beyond the traditional areas where it was grown), as well as to control the market. The plan also involved implementing agricultural and livestock projects as substitute 'crops' to 'compensate for the eradication of coca plantations' (Gutiérrez Aguilar 2008: 179–81).

In 1988, the Law Regulating Coca and Controlled Substances, known as the '1008 Law' was passed; among its rulings, the legal atrocity that considered someone accused of drug trafficking guilty until proved innocent particularly stood out. The *cocalero* movement was involved in the struggle against these measures, which were particularly harsh on peasants. It set up unions – with the capacity for mobilisation and resistance – who defended their source of survival given that the alternatives were not real options. From then on, the movement focused on two subjects: fighting the eradication of the coca leaf and emphasising its 'sacred' nature as ancestral heritage. During the 1990s, the *cocalero* movement combined multiple strategies, discourses and organisational forms to constantly confront successive governments, consolidating itself as a social and political force that was different and autonomous (Gutiérrez Aguilar 2008: 383–89).

The structural organisation of the *cocalero* movement began with the creation of federations of unions from the 1960s onwards. After a series of divisions and processes involving reorganisation, six coca farmer federations were finally established. These organisations were not affiliated to the Unified Federation of Cochabamba but were linked directly to the national peasant organisations. Thus, four were affiliated to the Syndicalist Confederation of Colonisers of Bolivia (CSCB) and two to the CSUTCB. Towards the end of the 1980s, a series of committees were formed for coordination purposes. In 1992, the umbrella organisation of the Cochabamba Tropic's Six Federations was finally created. Gutiérrez Aguilar explains that the umbrella organisation 'takes advantage of the tradition and experience of peasant and mining unionism but is not exactly like the model of aggregation and organisation represented by the CSUTCB, particularly in the country's western region' (Gutiérrez Aguilar 2008: 188).

Based on this method of organisation, the *cocalero* movement gained ground in national-level organisations to become the most important social force within the indigenous-peasant movement, stripping Katarism of its leadership of the CSUTCB. From this position, the *cocalero* movement was able to expand its influence towards the Bolivian Workers' Centre, which, on repeated occasions, represented coca farmers' interests when making demands to the state.

The rise of the *cocalero* movement can be understood as the expression of a more cultural interpretation of social differences and the popular struggle. From a national platform, the *cocalero* movement was able to insert itself into the national political framework. First, coca was projected as a synonym for Andean culture, and it was argued that its eradication by external forces would be akin to destroying a way of life and a cultural legacy, inserting the struggle in anti-imperialism discourse. This interpretation gained the support of the Chuquisaca, Potosí and Oruro regions, where the tradition of chewing on coca (*acullico*) was widely practised.

Since growing coca put a roof over the heads of families and food in their mouths, its defence was expressed as being opposed to the negative effects of neoliberal policies. Also, the role of the United States government in the so-called 'fight against drug trafficking'[7] contributed to the emergence of a nationalist rhetoric in which the coca leaf came to be 'the symbol of the defence of national dignity and memory, as well as sovereignty before the United States, turning it into a topic of national importance' (Castillo Gallardo 2004: 5). From this point onwards, the discourse defending the coca leaf appealed to and raised awareness among other sectors, appealing to urban actors such as students and progressive professionals, and expanding its influence beyond the unions.

Social Movement Incursion into Politics: The Law of Popular Participation

The capacity of the *cocalero* movement to expand its discourse at a national level must also be understood within the framework of a series of political reforms that were carried out during the first of Gonzalo Sánchez de Lozada's governments (1993–1997); in particular, the Law of Popular Participation passed in 1994.[8] The importance of this law lies in the fact that it made political participation possible by making council authorities from provincial capitals eligible. In this sense, the legal and constitutional reforms of the 1990s can be understood as 'political opportunities' (McAdam et al. 1996), without which social movements' increased influence cannot be understood.

Despite the difficulties and all the delays to the Law[9] after 1994, many rural organisations began to participate in local elections. The coca farmers made the most systematic effort to construct a political organisation linked to the peasant and union structure, and were the most successful social force in occupying positions of local power, thus enabling them to project themselves towards national politics later on. This development would mark the beginning of the indigenous-peasant social movement's experiment with politics.

The context in which the Law for Popular Participation was passed was characterised by the convergence of international and internal processes that facilitated the indigenous movement's political articulation. Indigenous people from the lowlands began to enter the national arena, looking to occupy a place next to the more powerful indigenous organisations from the highlands. Towards the end of the 1970s, the Grand Guarani Captain, Mburuvichaguasu Bonifacio Barrientos Iyambae, also called the 'Big Shadow', began an initiative to unite the indigenous people in the lowlands. This process also received an important stimulus from NGOs and anthropologists, who supported the organisational process through which, with the return to democracy, the Western Bolivian Indigenous Confederation (CIDOB) was founded in 1982. At the beginning, the CIDOB grouped together five indigenous populations – the Guarani, Izoceños, Chiquitanos, Ayoreos and Guarayos. During the 1980s, the CIDOB represented the emerging and diverse organisations of indigenous people from the lowlands; among them, the Mojeño Indigenous Town Council Centre in Trinidad and the Centre for Indigenous Peoples of Beni, in a kind of umbrella organisation (Postero 2005: 274–75; Albó 2008b: 41–42; García Linera et al. 2010: 217–19).

The CIDOB began to position itself as an indigenous organisation on a national level when it held the 'March for Land and Dignity' in 1990. The march had been the initiative of the indigenous Beni people to defend their territory against the invasion of farmers and timber merchants. Beginning in the east of the country and heading towards the capital, the march mobilised some eight hundred people over thirty-four days, with widespread coverage in the media and gaining sympathy from urban sectors. This obliged the then president, Jaime Paz Zamora, to open a dialogue with them and concede to a series of demands. However, probably the most important achievements were that the march made the indigenous people of the lowlands visible at the national level, and that bonds were formed with their Andean counterpart, the CSUTCB, who organised a welcome reception for the *marchistas* in the capital. This process ended with preparatory meetings in the region on the eve of 12 October 1992, when the Latin American indigenous movement commemorated '500 Years of Resistance' as opposed to the '500th Anniversary of the Discovery of America' (Albó 2008b: 43).

During the 1990s, the indigenous movement continued to achieve political victories. An example was the fact that the vice-presidency of the republic was held by the Katarist indigenous leader, Víctor Hugo Cárdenas, from 1993 to 1997, as an expression of the growing political articulation within the indigenous movement. On the one hand, the fact that the MNR chose Cárdenas as its vice-presidential candidate – to form the binomial with Sánchez de Lozada – showed that the indigenous population was starting to be recognised in politics. The rapid rise of populist parties at the beginning of the 1990s, appealing to urban sectors with a strong component of Aymaran migrants, made it clear that the social costs of economic stabilisation particularly affected those segments of the population who increasingly identified with a specific ethnicity. In this sense, traditional parties saw the need to open up and make concessions to the indigenous movement. On the other hand, the Cárdenas candidacy was rejected both by Katarism and by the leaders of the political and unionist left – actors who had been working on the construction of a socialist movement based on the figure of this indigenous leader. For them, the candidacy not only meant cutting this project short but also the successful co-optation and dismantling of the Katarist movement by traditional politics (Laserna 1993). Either way, Cárdenas acceptance of the MNR's proposal made it clear that, at that time, the indigenous movement was not ready to make incursions into politics autonomously, once again adopting a secondary role behind a traditional party.

From his privileged position, Cárdenas helped to approve a series of reforms that favoured indigenous people. Thus, in 1994, through constitutional reform, the multi-ethnic and pluricultural nature of the country was recognised; at the same time, the figure of Indigenous Community Land (TCO) was also incorporated, with the attributes of indigenous territories set out as per Agreement 169 of the ILO. That same year, the Law for Educational Reform was also passed, which was important in integrating intercultural principles and bilingualism, leaving behind, once and for all, the previous policies of 'assimilation' and '*mestizaje*'. These policies and reforms need to be understood in a framework of the growing visibility of indigenous issues, partly due to the political achievements of indigenous organisations from the lowlands and partly following the regional trends.[10]

A third factor of the context in which the Law for Popular Participation was passed is the accelerated rhythm of 'neoliberal globalisation' (Scholte 2005) during the 1990s, of which Bolivia was no exception. Intercultural reforms formed part of a package of policies aimed at the establishment of a hegemonic neoliberal regime on a national scale. As Silva explains, neoliberalism in Latin America implied the depoliticisation of the economy and the restriction of the state to 'state matters', so that there would be no room for 'social matters'. Market orientation brought with it the understanding that, in democracy, decision making at a macro level would be delegated to a technocrat group of state administrators – on the same wavelength as their peers in multilateral proceedings – and that social policies would be submitted to a market logic (Silva 1999). Revising the case of Bolivia, Medeiros maintains that the 'democratisation' policy from 1985 onwards brought with it the tendency to separate what was social from what was political, as well as separating the struggle for ethnic recognition from that of economic redistribution (Medeiros 2001: 410).

Although these neoliberal policies produced positive rates of growth (especially in the early 1990s), the distribution of income became more and more unequal. A CEPAL study in 2003 on inequality in Latin America proved that inequality in Bolivia increased during the 1990s, and that if future economic development went unchanged, poverty would continue to increase (CEPAL 2003: 3). This is significant to the extent that it shows that economic stabilisation generally occurs at the cost of social development – at a time when the state was decreasing its involvement in social matters – while requesting social actors to cope themselves with the deterioration in their situation. In the Law of Popular Participation, this translated into a decentralisation of the state body by empowering the municipal level and conferring greater administrative independence and more economic resources to local governments. At the same time, as Medeiros explains, the law was framed around a specific discourse on 'civil society' that prescribed a certain type of state–society relationship, consistent with the neoliberal project (Madeiros 2001). In this relationship, citizens assumed a more active role through political participation at a local level.

The cultural component of the law was expressed through legal recognition of native communities, tackling the diversity of organisational structures under the generic grass-roots Native Territorial Organisations (OTBs). Before the 1994 constitutional reforms, indigenous communities were not recognised as such by the state, and the former legal framework did not recognise the indigenous people as having due authority. The state apparatus considered indigenous people as 'peasants' and, as a result, their 'legal status' under the Civil Code was given as a *rural* community, union or association. As this was the only way of achieving legal recognition, the need to possess 'legal status' meant that many indigenous communities were themselves classified as *rural* (productive) communities. Facing a lot of tension and obstacles, the LPP made it possible to rectify the classifications made according to cultural identities.[11]

As Albó explained, many grass-roots organisations initially regarded the law with certain distrust, fearing that the OTBs would turn into one more opportunity for the state to control them (Albó 2008b: 50–51). This was the case, for example, of the CSUTCB, which saw in the law an instrument to undermine peasant union organisations. This hypothesis was not far removed from reality considering that, when the Law was drawn up, the union organisation was excluded as a possible contender for OTB status. Certainly, the territorial reference was effective in excluding every organisation based on sectorial interests. Thus, the LPP involved a reorganisation of the geography, 'dividing up the associations and existing community and popular ties, and imposing forms of control and territorial management that were more manageable for technocrats and public and private administrators' (Gutiérrez Aguilar 2008: 193). In this way, the law was 'instrumental' (Gustafson 2002: 276) to the aim of neoliberal hegemony, to the extent that it not only depoliticised social demands but it also dismantled both local and national alternative spaces of indigenous-peasant participation.

However, for the *cocalero* movement in particular, the LPP meant political reinforcement. The criminalisation of their main economic activity and constant confrontations for more than ten years had helped them to accumulate great political experience that now found a 'recognised' field for action in the politics of local democratic governments. Unions that were organised into federations thus obtained even greater legitimacy when they started to occupy municipal governments in Chapare after the 1995 elections. Those who received the majority of votes in the region were the union leaders, for whom electoral participation was presented as another way of resisting the central government's anti-coca policies. The vote thus occurred in the midst of such policies being rejected, and meant that, with no exceptions, all the candidates for the following election came from coca unions (Kohl and Farthing 2007: 252; Gutiérrez Aguilar 2008: 196–97).

In this way, the 'instrumental' nature that had initially characterised the Law of Popular Participation, had the opposite effect in the long-run. Gradually, the law was welcomed because of its potential for direct political participation by local leaders of organisations such as the CSUTCB and the CIDOB in municipal proceedings. This meant that grass-roots organisations would temporarily lose their leaders, but, when they finally returned, they would have gained political experience. At this point, it is worth mentioning the more critical position of Patzi Paco, who sees in this process 'the broadening of state ideology at the same time as the emptying of indigenous ideology', by which indigenous political participation serves to 'reproduce the existing schemes of domination created by the dominant class', incorporating once again 'new forms of state domination' into the movement (Patzi Paco 1999).

However, this appears to be only a partial interpretation. Patzi Paco's position seems to presume an indigenousness or 'pure' indigenous ideology, from which certain patterns are taken by the state and manipulated, achieving 'the broadening of the state' and 'the emptying of indigenous ideology'. However, such a 'pure' indigenous ideology has arguably never existed, particularly considering the colonial experience by which native cultural forms have been in constant contact or interaction with other dominant logics. It is as part of this dialogue that different logics or discourses are continuously being redefined. In this particular case, the state is redefined, recognising the country's multi-ethnic and pluricultural nature – a redefinition of which the LPP forms a part – while the indigenous movement is redefined by assuming a more explicit and active political role.

On one hand, the LPP was successful in breaking down social resistance locally, but, on the other, it allowed for a weakened COB to be substituted for a series of rural social movements focused on the municipal struggle. Of these struggles, the *cocalero* movement is highlighted, which came to be the dynamo for demonstrations and for the articulation of diverse actors on a national level.

Political Articulation of Social Movements: The Creation of the 'Political Instrument'

Towards the end of the 1990s, social movements in Bolivia started to become more visible in the new political spaces created by the Law for Popular Participation, expressed in the electoral victories of the 'political instrument' and with a leading role for the *cocalero* movement as the most successful social organisation in the new formal political arena.

In the absence of the state in rural zones, the coca headquarters became the public authority with the greatest regional authority and legitimacy. The importance of this is that through these practices, the indigenous movement in general and the *cocalero* movement in particular actually became incorporated into formal politics. In this process, and from its local dominions, the *cocalero* movement began to orient itself politically towards the national arena – an idea that other social movements would later follow – resulting in the creation of the 'political instrument' and the MAS.

The notion of 'political instrument' of the social movements refers back to Katarism. This movement's experience, as previously described, shows that the indigenous movements' incursion into politics was not particularly new, with clear experiences in the creation and participation of parties such as MITKA and MRTK. It even had a precedent in the creation of Fausto Reynaga's indigenist party, although it was not very influential.

The Katarist trend influenced the union organisation of a great part of the peasant movement in the form of the national CSUTCB. As has been said before, because of the legacy of the workers' movement, during its first few years the Unionist Federation had difficulty connecting organically with its grass-roots supporters. However, towards the end of the 1980s, this organisation became more independent and had a greater capacity for action, as shown in its first Extraordinary Congress in 1988. On that occasion, the CSUTCB approved a political proposal[12] that was none other than the Katarist one, departing from Marxist class analysis and turning towards a more cultural and identity-based interpretation. The document presented a strong criticism of union behaviour and stressed the need to build 'communal power'. It discussed how that aim could be achieved, and the need for a 'political arm' that would allow the CSUTCB a greater field of action. At that time, the congress made the proposal to create an Assembly of Nationalities to take charge of constructing the 'political instrument'.

Regional trends contributed to greater visibility for the indigenous movement, related to the upcoming 500th anniversary of the arrival of Columbus in the Americas, which fed the development of these first proposals. In the IV CSUTCB Congress in 1980, the United Left proposed that the Assembly of Nationalities be inaugurated on 12 October 1992, rejecting the celebrations prepared by the government. In an effort to incorporate indigenous people from the east, an inter-institutional committee was created for the 500th anniversary of the Resistance to and Rejection of the Fifth Centenary, integrated by the CSUTCB, the CIDOB and the 'colonisers', as well as UNITAS and the Episcopal Commission.[13] In this sense, the March for Sovereignty and Dignity in 1990, previously mentioned, allowed the indigenous people of the east to meet the highlanders.

Although important, these first steps towards a national political presence for the indigenous movement still showed indecision and a lack of clear aims. The failure of the Assembly of Nationalities in October 1992 exemplified this; after its disorganised inauguration, it was cut short by disputes over its organisation and faculties. The event had brought together more than twenty thousand indigenous people in the capital, mostly grouped together to express their rejection of the celebrations of October 12th. As Patzi Paco explains, for part of the movement, the assembly was a mechanism for constructing a state that was 'pluri-national; others saw it as a mechanism for constructing a socialist state, while for the indigenous people of the east it was, above all, an opportunity to meet and talk with their counterparts from the highlands' (Patzi Paco 1999: 68). At the same time, the indigenous movement went through a change of leadership in which the Aymaran leaders were displaced by mainly native Quechua leaders from Cochabamba, which answered to the gradual rise of the *cocalero* movement at the national level.

Authors such as Felix Patzi Paco and Silvia Rivera maintain that the indigenous movement was harmed by this first attempt at political articulation, since disillusionment led to indigenous leaders opting to work for the state to implement reformist politics in the 1990s. However, seen from the perspective of a long process of political articulation, this episode does present positive qualities. The assembly constituted a parallel opportunity to visualise and channel the diversity of actors and demands that existed in society that could not be admitted by the unitarian institutional structures deployed by a homo-genising nation-state project. The mass presence of indigenous people, with the clear aim of change, showed that the indigenous issue was latently present in the country. In other words, the assembly made it clear that the model of building the nation through 'assimilation' and the 'mestizo' ideal had failed, and that there was a diversity of actors and demands that found no place in the nation-state institutional structures that aimed at standardisation.[14]

At the same time, towards the end of the 1980s, in the country's high-lands, a more radical movement was formed based on the indigenous people's cause of self-determination – the 'Ayllus Rojos', led by Felipe Quispe Huanca ('the Mallku'). An important characteristic of this group was that it adopted an armed struggle.[15] Both the right- and left-wing saw this organisation as a threat, since its recognition directly threatened the country's integrity and the nation's construction. For its part, the state quickly qualified the group as terrorists and ordered its leaders to be captured.

The importance of the Ayllus Rojos to the indigenous movement lies in the fact that it explicitly formulated one of the main points that would make up their agenda – the restoration of native forms of political organisation with complete self-determination. Until then, the demand for self-determination had not been so strongly emphasised, and action was more directed at the reformation of the state to better incorporate the indigenous population. In the same way, the radical nature of the group, expressed in its armed activity, once again revealed the lack of integration of the nations and, consequently, the illusory nature of the nation-state in Bolivia. According to Patzi Paco, this is why the state was forced to consider the pluri/multicultural proposal for coming to terms with the indigenous presence (Patzi Paco 1999: 84).

This forms the background for the constitutional reforms aimed at rec-ognising the ethnic and cultural diversity of the country approved under Gonzalo Sánchez de Lozada's first government. As previously mentioned, one of the most significant reforms of this period was decentralisation, imple-mented through the Law of Popular Participation. Together with the rise of the *cocalero* movement, the indigenous movement experienced a tran-sition from being a rebellious entity to the state to being one with greater participation in politics at a local level. In this process, the idea of the polit-ical instrument would reach maturation with the creation of the Assembly for Sovereignty of the People (ASP) in the CSTUCB Congress named the 'Land, Territory and Political Instrument', held in Santa Cruz in 1995. On this occasion, the participation of 'the instrument' in the recently created municipal elections was proposed for the first time.

The participation of indigenous organisations such as the 'Bartolina Sisa' National Federation of Peasant Women of Bolivia, the Syndical Confederation of Colonisers of Bolivia and the Western Indigenous Centre of Bolivia showed the beginnings of the construction of an indigenous-peasant political unit. At the same time, although participation in the political party system was proposed, indigenous organisations put special emphasis on not calling their new body a 'political party'. The attention paid to nomenclature should be understood in relation to the bad practices that indigenous organisations had experienced in former alliances with political parties – who generally manipulated and divided their organisations – as well as to the general legitimacy crisis of the whole political system, which was beginning to be felt both in the country and the region. The creation of the 'instrument' thus embodied the indigenous movement's desire to participate in politics directly – and not through representation – with something very different to a 'political party'.

The ASP faced a series of obstacles from the very beginning. On the one hand, as Raquel Gutiérrez explains, the ASP's request to join the National Electoral Court in order to participate in municipal elections was rejected twice.[16] On the other, the ASP had been created with the participation of a series of indigenous organisations under the leadership of a CSTUCB that felt the political ascendance of the *cocalero* movement occurring within the organisation. This is why, at the beginning, it was marked by strong internal contradictions, particularly because of the rivalry between the regional peasant leader, Alejo Véliz, and the executive secretary of the Cochabamba Tropic's Federation of Coca Farmers, Evo Morales.[17]

Although they persisted in achieving their own political acronym, the indigenous organisations under the influence of the *cocalero* movement decided to participate in the elections in alliance with registered political parties. In this way the ASP participated in the municipal and general elections of 1995 and 1997 under the name the United Left party. They gained considerable political participation in the coca region of Chapare in the 1995 elections, and in 1997 they gained four seats in Congress (of 130). Among these, Evo Morales was elected with more than 70 per cent of the vote in the district of Chapare, making him the uninominal representative with the most votes in Congress.

The geographical nature of these votes shows that the electoral results were more the success of the *cocalero* movement than of 'instrument' itself. As Moira Zuazo explains, the results of these elections were decisive to the instrument's consolidation in two respects. On the one hand, they demonstrated the feasibility and usefulness of the 'instrument' in the political arena, and in this way presented a convincing argument to those factions that still had reservations about political participation. On the other, it reinforced the position of the *cocalero* movement's leadership in the indigenous movement, and that of its leader, Evo Morales, with the struggles for the leadership of the 'instrument' being decided in his favour (Zuazo 2009: 39–40).

This decision was accompanied by a change of nomenclature. Alejo Véliz refused to hand over command of the ASP to Morales, which is why – with the support of a solid majority – the latter opted to break away from the ASP and continue being the 'political instrument' for the Sovereignty of the People (IPSP), aiming at participation in the 1999 municipal elections. In this respect, the CNE once again put obstacles in the way of their participation, not only rejecting the IPSP's inscription but also cancelling the United Left's licence. Thus, the IPSP once again opted to use the acronym of an existing, if practically lost-cause party, the Movement towards Socialism (MAS), which it would continue to use.[18] In the words of a CSUTCB leader: 'In the political commission [of the CSUTCB], the IPSP was founded in August 1995. That's where the IPSP was born; MAS came later. In 1999, Morales was elected, and by 2002 it was already the MAS-IPSP. The CSUTCB is the body, the MAS is its political arm.' (Belmonte 2012, personal interview)

The municipal elections in 1995 gave them convincing victories in the country's coca regions, although, with 3.2 per cent of the national total, they were still limited nationally. Locally, the leaders continued to gain political experience to be better prepared for the general elections in 2002, in which the MAS obtained a surprising second place, only a few points behind the MNR.

How can the victory of the MAS in the 2002 elections be explained? The reason for their electoral victory at a national level cannot only be found in indigenous-peasant organisations and their 'political instrument'. The structural and contingent socio-political context that formed the scenario for their political rise also needs be taken into account, as will be shown in the following section.

Prominence of the Social Movements as a New Political Actor: The Legitimacy Crisis of the Political System and the Cycle of Mobilisations

As has been seen, the indigenous-peasant movement went through a process of political articulation resulting in the creation of its 'political instrument' and its incursion into formal politics, first at a local level and expanding to national level. This increasing incursion into national politics is related to a structural and important socio-political context, namely the legitimacy crisis of the political system and the social insurgence that characterised the years from 2000 to 2005. As a result of these processes, social movements were able to obtain ever more political influence, becoming the main actor in Bolivian politics and paving the way for Evo Morales' election to president.

A Double Legitimacy Crisis: The Social Failure of the Neoliberal Model and 'Co-optation' of the Political Party System

The return to democracy in Latin America has been described as a double transition in the sense that, together with the restoration of democratic processes, a new economic model of development – neoliberalism – was implemented. The model had a significant effect on institutional legitimacy.

In an article on neoliberalism in Latin America, Kurt Weyland describes its effects on the democratic system as 'mixed'. The positive effects are related to countries participating in the global economy, with greater interaction with the international community supporting the consolidation of democratic regimes. Paradoxically, the negative effects are due to the growing influence of external actors, because of the pressure exercised on domestic politics that ends up limiting the actions of governments that have grown more and more dependent on foreign capital. This process thus restricts democratic options, weakening political parties and, therefore, formal political participation (Weyland 2004: 135–57).

Studying the specific case of Bolivia, John-Andrew McNeish (2006) argues similarly. Neoliberalism in Bolivia put greater emphasis on economic reforms, with the aim of attracting foreign capital, putting aside any efforts focused on social development or on political participation for society. In terms of institutional legitimacy, this translated into citizens perceiving that, in order to preserve (political and economic) stability, the interests of external actors took precedence over the (basic) needs of society. In the same way, external actors lent conditioned support to the local elite with the aim of maintaining favourable political and economic hegemony, in which social development was not considered. This process gradually deteriorated; the economic elite lacked the political will to launch actions that would provide a qualitative improvement in democracy, which ended up distorting the political system in general.

On the other hand, the way the party system worked after the transition was not optimal. In a study on Latin America, Mainwaring and Scully (1995) defined the institutionalisation of the political system as a stable inter-party competition, with political parties with roots in society, and in which parties and elections were accepted as legitimate institutions. After the transition in Bolivia, a relatively stable multi-party system was installed, built on the common understanding of the need to support representative democracy and the market economy. As René Antonio Mayorga (2004) explains, four factors influenced the creation of this system: the defeat of the traditional left, the appearance of more moderate positions within society, the implementation of structural adjustment economic policies and the adaptation of coalition governments.

However, (political and economic) stability was seemingly the only virtue of the model, since securing the subsequent democratic governments was not accompanied by social development or the creation of ties between political parties and society. The transition towards a market economy was accompanied by growth of the informal economy to the detriment of society's support for political parties, reinforced by that fact that these institutions remain incapable of meeting their electorate's demands and expectations. For these reasons, from 1979 onwards, the presidential elections showed a strong 'electoral volatility' (Mayorga 2004).

Governmental coalitions gradually turned into more of an agreement between the highest leaders in the party, making up a party triad structure, in which control of the coalition alternated between the MNR, MIR and the ADN, and in which new political groups (such as the CONDEPA and the UCS) were simply secondary or functional – the so-called 'pacted democracy'. Thus, a kind of 'hermetic', flexible style of politics was created, in which political parties turned into 'electoral machines and agencies that distributed public offices and appropriated resources' (Mayorga 2014), absorbed into state structures and lacking real connections with society. In the same way, the responsible practices of the opposition in Parliament were distorted, meaning that the institutional practices of the state could not be effectively controlled by political parties.

In summary, the party system was highly deficient. It could even be argued that such a system in Bolivia was historically rudimentary, selective and elitist (Van Cott 2000). It can therefore be concluded that, with the aim of maintaining a neoliberal economic model, the party representation system suffered a kind of co-optation by the economic elite, making it incapable of representing the demands and interests of society to the state, and in that way raising serious doubts regarding their democratic qualities in state–society mediation. This resulted in a serious legitimacy crisis for the system of political representation through political parties at the end of the century.

In a nutshell, the co-optation of political parties and the failure of the neoliberal model to bring the expected development and social well-being generated a double legitimacy crisis. To a certain extent, the growing political articulation of social movements occurred as a response to the deficient functioning of the political parties, and as a form of resistance to the negative effects of the development model implemented by the state. The difficulties faced by the representation system and the neoliberal model, as well as the growing political influence of the social movements, began to be more clearly visible between 2000 and 2005.

Building the 'Social Movement' Political Actor in Social Uprisings:
Urban Social Movements and the 'Wars' to Defend Natural Resources

The new millennium marked the end of 'pacted democracy', with the emergence of strong urban and indigenous social movements that gradually advanced their reactionary discourse against neoliberalism and the current political system. The general elections in 2002 marked a turning point that was followed by the social and political crisis that would lead to the ousting of two democratically elected presidents and the rise to power of a new political force.

The fact that the offensive by the new (indigenous) social movements had no influence over the coalition governments made the co-opted nature of political parties more and more notorious. Political parties became less important as counterparts to negotiation, which not only contributed to their erosion and delegitimisation, but also cleared the way for direct and more radical interpellation of the state by social movements.

To these structural factors, another important factor was added in the form of the economic standstill that was initiated in 1999. The international economic recession in this period had a greater influence on this country, since it was still subject to an economic model that was dominated by the export of raw materials. Because of economic restrictions, the capacity of state power to act and respond to the problems of unemployment, poverty and corruption was seriously questioned, creating a scenario that favoured the spreading of social conflict. The Bánzer government (1997–2001) was quickly involved in a harmful dynamic that entailed giving in to all kinds of demands and blackmail, making patrimonial use of state resources and leading to an intense cycle of demonstrations from 2000 to 2005.

From 2000 onwards, in the context of a growing economic and political crisis, the anti-system struggles of the *cocalero* movement were accompanied by a series of protests and social demonstrations throughout the country. The wave of demonstrations reached a head during the so-called 'Water War' in 2000 and the 'Gas War' in 2003. As Sven Harten explains, the general interpretation of this period is that it involved a process in which different local and 'one issue' demonstrations converged to coordinate collective actions with a national reach, aiming at political reforms at the national level (Harten 2011b: 118). Such demonstrations showed a certain continuation and reinforcement of the *cocalero* movement's strategy to insert a specific issue in wider discourse of national interest.

In my opinion, the presented account of this period is quite accurate. However, there is an alternative interpretation. The steps towards bringing together local and specific demands were accompanied by the intensification of a process that was perhaps even more important: the evolution of the 'social movement' as the main 'political subject' of the struggle for a new national popular project. This process would continue, as will be seen later, during Morales' first government, as it can also be argued that it continued on course during the second term of the MAS. From 2000 onwards, the social movement certainly made a considerable leap towards becoming a legitimate political actor in the Bolivian context through its struggles and successes, leaving behind its (marginal) role in society to take centre stage in politics.

The Water War began in the city of Cochabamba. As a precedent, in the framework of neoliberal policies, at the end of 1999 the Bánzer government handed over the concession of the city's drinking water and sewage system to the company Aguas del Tunari – a transnational consortium in the hands of Bechtel, based in the United States. Despite previous agreements, the bills that citizens received at the beginning of 2000 were up to 200 per cent higher, making the service unaffordable for the majority of the population. A series of spontaneous demonstrations followed almost immediately, accompanied by the creation of the Committee for the Defence of Water[19] and by the important Departmental Irrigation Users Federation of Cochabamba (FEDECOR).[20] The latter turned into the main vehicle for protests about the scarcity of water in the region.

The demonstrations quickly spread to involve other social organisations, including unions, who expressed their discontent through the new Coordinator for the Defence of Water and Life,[21] bringing together urban and rural actors and managing to radicalise the movement. Towards the end of March, thousands of participants gathered to resist state repression, with the resulting confrontation ending in one death and dozens injured.

The magnitude of the protests was such that they could not be contained by the government, and the contract with Aguas del Tunari was cancelled on 9 April. Administration of Aguas del Tunari returned to state hands and, more importantly, social movements were promised a greater level of control. That type of control could only be possible by a legislative amendment, turning the events in Cochabamba into ones of national significance (Assies 2003). In the same way, the Water War made it clear that social protests could be an effective measure to revert governmental policies that went against the interests of vast sectors of the population.

In a scenario of economic crisis, and with a legitimacy crisis for the politico-economic model, the Water War encouraged citizens to express their discontent and rejection through social protests. Therefore, the following years saw a proliferation of mobilised conflicts – such as the road blocks organised by the CSUTCB in Oruro in July 2001 – as well as the recurrent activism of the coca farmers.

In January 2002 in the locality of Sacaba, protests led by Evo Morales against governmental prohibition of the sale of coca in the local market resulted in the death of three peasants and two soldiers. This confrontation was important for two reasons. On the one hand, the social movement once again succeeded in achieving its aims, preventing the government from implementing greater restrictions on the leaf's sale. On the other, because of the conflict, Congress decided to expel Evo Morales (the representative with the most votes in the National Congress), accusing him of instigating social disorder and using dubious procedures.[22]

Morales' expulsion was interpreted by many sectors of the population as a humiliation that once again showed the 'pseudo-democratic' nature of the political class, in particular because Morales grew stronger is his role as leader of both the anti-establishment forces and the *cocalero* and indigenous movements. In response to these developments, the Fourth Indigenous March set out from the city of Santa Cruz in May 2002; its first demand was the creation of a Constituent Assembly,[23] a proposal that this time could count on higher levels of popular support since it had first been put forward during the first indigenous march in 1990.

These events were highly influential in the general election that was held only a month later on 30 June 2002. Against all expectations, Morales' Movement towards Socialism came second, as a result of growing dissatisfaction with the political system and the current development model. However, the traditional parties turned a blind eye to the clear message from society, and moved on to form a coalition as they had done in previous years. In this way, Gonzalo Sánchez de Lozada from the MNR party assumed control of the country for the second time. One of the first actions of the new president produced an episode that showed once again the social movements' prominence and influence.

Faced with an economic crisis, the MNR government tried to increase state income by raising the direct tax on salaries to 12.5 per cent. This measure severely affected the limited contingent of formal wage earners, especially teachers, doctors, nurses, the police and manufacturers.[24] The demonstrations against this mega tax erupted almost immediately (January–February 2003), with police mutiny at the heart. The conflict spiralled to such a level that the masses attacked government buildings and shopping centres, with a final death toll of thirty-three. The government once again had to give in to the demands of the demonstrators, and change its plans.

Social protest reached its apogee in the event known as the Gas War in October of the same year. The mega tax had an important effect on this, putting the low income the state received from its contracts with transnational companies (Gutiérrez Aguilar 2008: 227) at the forefront of public attention because of the privatisation of the state petroleum company, YPFB (Yacimientos Petrolíferos Fiscales Bolivianos) during the surge of capitalisation implemented by Sánchez de Lozada's first government. In 2003, there was a wave of almost continuous protests by social movements, carrying out locally based actions on specific demands that affected the whole country, especially rural areas. When the government began to make public their intention of selling the national reserves of gas and exporting them through Chile, Evo Morales, as leader of the opposition, immediately called on social movements to join the protests against the planned export of this natural resource.[25]

With the precedent of the Coordinator for the Defence of Water and Life, the National Coordinator for the Defence of Gas was created in mid-September 2013 to articulate and reinforce the protests and blockades. The slogan 'Not one molecule of gas to Chile' also galvanised public opinion, which was already sensitive to any anti-Chilean action as a result of the war the country had lost in the nineteenth century, which deprived Bolivia of sovereign access to the Pacific Ocean. The conflict began to worsen when government minister Sánchez Berzaín encouraged a military operation to rescue a group of tourists trapped by a blockade in the locality of Sorata. This military presence caused confrontations with those living in Warisata, resulting in seven deaths and seventeen injured (*El Diario*, 22 September 2003).[26] This event was baptised the 'Warisata Massacre' of Aymaran peasants, and the incident provided a new impetus for the wave of protests, meaning that more roadblocks were set up.

In the same way, in the locality of El Alto – a satellite city outside La Paz – a nucleus of protests against different government plans was created. The characteristics of this city, whose population was mainly made up of rural migrants of Aymaran origin, were decisive to the Gas War,[27] with the involvement of the Federation of Neighbourhood Councils in El Alto (FEJUVE-El Alto) particularly standing out. As Raquel Gutiérrez explains, '[t]hese groups are, to a certain extent, a kind of urban recreation of the traditional and/or union authorities of rural communities and, above all, in the neighbourhoods with a greater Aymaran presence, work in a similar way to the original peasant unions' (Gutiérrez Aguilar 2008: 246–47). The councils took advantage of their structures and practices for deliberation and mobilisation purposes during the collective actions of September and October 2003.

By early September, the demonstrations were ending in confrontations with the police. During these days, reference was also made to topics of national importance such as the Americas Free Trade Agreement and, even more significantly, the Law of Citizen Security. The latter, passed in August 2003, decreed blockades in streets and roads to be a crime that would result in imprisonment (Articles 213 and 214). Since this method was frequently used in social struggles in the country, the protests got worse – also gaining the support of the unionist Regional Workers Centre of El Alto (affiliated to the COB) – and thus contributing to the government and political parties' delegitimisation. The repercussion of heavy-handed state repression was a civil strike that left the city of La Paz cut off. From then onwards, the protests scattered, moving from El Alto to other regions of the country, and gaining the sympathy of urban workers who, through the COB, demanded a general strike and called for the president to resign. The government's decision to opt for repression made more actors join the protests, and the Gas War slogan became the common demand around which local and sectorial vindication was articulated in a complex manner. All this was promptly summarised in the 'Gas, constituent and resignation!' slogan.

The most serious point in the crisis was reached on 12 October 2003. After the government had passed the 'death decree',[28] arguing that they had to supply the city of La Paz with fuel, a convoy of tankers left a deposit in Senkata, located in the city of El Alto, guarded by military and police forces. The residents of El Alto fought the military for two days in a battle that would leave more than 250 injured and more than 60 dead. Thus, the Gas War left a tragic total of 80 dead and more than 400 injured (Perreault 2006).

The relentlessness of the events had an impact on the urban middle class, not only because of the degree of violence used against the population, but also because it revealed the seriousness of the crisis, in which the scenario of civil war became more and more likely. In the city of La Paz, segments of this class began to organise debates and gatherings, at the same time as the governmental cabinet collapsed, receiving minister resignations one by one. The number and scale of demonstrations and blockades increased. This would be the scenario that finally obliged President Gonzalo Sánchez de Lozada to resign and secretly flee the country on 17 October.

The Water War was initially a surprising incident in which organised citizens in the form of a social movement were capable of defeating the state and causing the government to backpedal, setting a precedent for a series of later episodes in which the mobilisation would prevail over the government's plans. Towards the end of 2003, the social movement appeared to become legitimate – at least in the eyes of citizens – as a highly effective means of political participation, to the extent that, through it, citizens' interests in the state were valued. In a socially convulsing state in institutional crisis, the social movement emerged as the most important political actor, exercising the de facto role of mediator between society and the state.

Taking stock, it can be concluded that the price of political and economic stability for more than fifteen years was high. The neoliberal economic model failed to bring social development, opening up the gap between rich and poor even further. In many cases, neoliberal policies harmed vast sectors of the population (for example, mining went offshore, the informal economy grew, the subsistence of the coca peasants was criminalised, and basic services for the population were privatised). This explains why the anti-neoliberal discourse gained so much force through social demonstrations, becoming more and more explicit as seen in the 'wars' over natural resources.

On the other hand, the party representation system suffered a kind of co-optation by the economic elite, weakening considerably its role as mediator between the state and society. As far as the effects of neoliberal politics can be felt, although the political parties were not capable of transmitting the population's demands and much less turning them into public policies, political parties were increasingly perceived by the population as instruments at the service of the capital. In a state–society relationship that appeared democratic – in the form of a stable competitive multiparty system – social movements revealed the serious deficiencies of the political structure. In this sense, the economic crisis appears only contingent to more structural problems. The crisis of legitimacy of political parties and of the performance of the government progressed into a total delegitimisation of the state institution.

The convergence between the political prominence acquired by social movements and the political system's legitimacy crisis raises the question of whether a causal relationship exists between the two. In this respect, George Gray Molina explains that it is not correct to explain the emergence of strong social movements by the political parties' legitimacy crisis or the state institution. In the same vein, it is incorrect to affirm that the emergence of new social actors – the new social movements – was the main cause of the legitimacy crisis of the political system in Bolivia. Gray Molina locates the truth somewhere in the middle, although, without saying as much, he also argues that it is necessary to take into account economic factors, both as a cause and as an effect, when analysing the relationship between social insurgence and institutional crises (Gray Molina 2004: 45–46).

Aiming to be specific, it can be argued that the political-social configuration in which the social movement became the most important actor in politics, assuming a role of mediation between the interests of society and the state, occurred as a result of the 'dialectic' interaction between state and society. This, for its part, responds to and is marked by a specific socio-political context, in a process of mutual formation and reformation. Thus, it is a causal but two-way and ongoing relationship that does not resolve 'the paradox of the chicken and the egg'.

Even more importantly, the growing prominence of social movements in Bolivia and the relationship of this development with the political party system stems from the debate presented in Chapter 1 on the distinction between 'institutionalised politics' and 'non-institutionalised politics'. The Bolivian scenario seems to support the idea that social movements are not essentially very different to political parties, but rather constitute one more channel in the state–society relationship, next to the most institutional form of the 'political party'. This idea can be effective in explaining why, on seeing a weakened channel (the loss of legitimacy of the political party system because of their co-optation), other channels (social movements) become more active. In this sense, and in particular between 2000 and 2005, it can be seen how the margins between 'institutional' and 'non-institutional' politics become blurry in Bolivia, questioning the state–society dichotomy from which such distinction derives.

Taking Political Power: The Arrival of Evo Morales as President

Up until now, the activity of social movements in Bolivia has been explained using the dominant vision that characterises them through their opposition vis-à-vis the state. Since the return to democracy, the gradual articulation of new social movements in Bolivia has resulted in resistance to state policies and pressure exerted through demands on the state. This 'anti-state' attitude was expressed with particular clarity from 2000 to 2005, when the struggle of social movements was linked to the legitimacy crisis suffered by this institution. As will be seen, the crisis led to a scenario of ungovernability due to the overturn of two constitutional presidents, which, at that time, raised serious doubts about the country's level of democratic consolidation. The fact that the legitimacy crisis found a solution in, and reached a democratic conclusion with, the election of Evo Morales as constitutional president is therefore rather surprising.

How can it be explained that social movements opted for the formal way of party elections at a time when the credibility of this institution was being seriously questioned, and when the political climate permitted people to imagine more radical scenarios? In considering social movements and political parties as part of the same system, this development seems less incoherent.

Social Movements' Choice for the Formal Political System

The Gas War caused widespread mobilisation within Bolivian society, highlighting urban activity. The escape of President Gonzalo Sánchez de Lozada emphasised the magnitude of the crisis, which was aggravated by a real threat of chaos and social disorder. In the same way, the strength of social actors, seen through their success at blocking government policies and expelling the state's highest authority, would dictate the course of politics.

The social insurgence was above all indicative of citizens' rejection of the current political system; however, a victorious society did not choose a way out that was the complete opposite of this system. On the contrary, the constitutional succession of the vice-president, accepted with practically no complaints, occurred exactly as prescribed by institutional formality. How can this contradiction be explained? In our opinion, the choice of a formal political system is related to three factors: the figure of the vice-president, the political strategy of Evo Morales and the MAS, and the absence of a unified political vision in the social force that brought down the government.

Carlos Mesa Gisbert, vice-president of the MNR government, was not someone immediately associated with 'the establishment'. Mesa's vice-presidency symbolised the first political incursion of a highly respected public figure. Before forming the binomial with Gonzalo Sánchez de Lozada, Mesa had been a journalist and historian, consolidating his status as a public figure in a high-level intellectual talk show ('De Cerca'). Despite the extent of social unrest, Mesa was able to assume the presidency on the basis of his background as a relatively neutral person, who was already generally accepted by society. In fact, in his inauguration speech, he highlighted his transitory role and promised decision-making power for citizens in future elections, something he was soon to forget.

A second factor that explains the choice of formal politics can be identified in Evo Morales' and the Movement towards Socialism's strategic calculations. It should be remembered that the MAS was the second political force in the 2002 elections, only a few points behind Gonzalo Sánchez de Lozada's MNR, making it a candidate with a real chance. As Gutiérrez explains, this situation took precedence in the Movement towards Socialism's decision to preserve the 'democratic process' (Gutiérrez Aguilar 2008: 265), expressed in Morales' initial support for Mesa's presidency. For their part, the same dominant classes understood the risks of social confrontation, which would be to the detriment of their own interests, leading them to accept Mesa's succession.

However, perhaps the most important reason why, after the events of the Gas War, there was no political transformation beyond the formal political system, with a starring role for those heavily involved in the social victory of October 2003 (in other words, social movements), is the fact that, at that time, the social movements had no unified vision of the country or political project that could be implemented. The main actors of the Gas War – the CSUTCB, the Coordinator and the coca farmers – had fundamental differences about how to deal with gas resources and the Constituent Assembly procedure, meaning that the so-called 'October agenda' – although resolute and explicit – did not present a project that entailed the reformulation of politics at the national level.

Thus, in October 2003, the rules of the current political system were respected and, at the same time, an important change was consolidated regarding where political decisions were made. Mesa had not assumed the presidency through the electoral process as such, but rather because the social forces expressed through social movements allowed it. In other words, he became president by the decision of social movements – or at least with their blessing. This is also expressed by the fact that Mesa assumed the presidency with a limited agenda that could count on backing from social movements: reversing the Hydrocarbons Law passed by Sánchez de Lozada in 1996, increasing royalties from 18 to 50 per cent, and calling a referendum to decide the destiny of hydrocarbons and the Constituent Assembly.

Political Empowerment of Indigenous Social Movements: The Unity Pact

The indigenous march in 2002 had managed to position the topic of the Constituent Assembly in the agendas of the indigenous organisations, laying the fundament for the collaboration of these organisations in the so-called Unity Pact.

Radicalised politics, together with the legitimacy crisis of the centralised political system, also had the effect of reviving politicised regionalism, mainly representing the country's economic elite. In mid-2004, the Civic Committee of Santa Cruz convened a 'First Council of Santa Cruz', whose aim was to neutralise the 'October agenda' in which President Mesa had proposed a referendum on hydrocarbons and the Constituent Assembly. In response, on 8–10 September of that year, different organisations from the indigenous territories of the highlands and lowlands attended a 'National Meeting of Indigenous, Peasant and Native Organisations' in Santa Cruz.[29] The Unity Pact was drawn up at this event, specifying the indigenous movement's intention of forming a single platform before the summons to the Constituent Assembly and, while guaranteeing this process. The pact, despite all its difficulties, would gradually replace the *cocalero* movement in leading the social struggle from 2004 onwards.

A precedent for the pact is found in the indigenous marches of the 1990s and the early 2000s, which were not only important because they presented indigenous demands to the state but also because they served as a meeting point and acknowledgement of the diversity of the country's indigenous people. It is worth highlighting that the CIDOB did not initially form part of the pact. However, the pact gradually became more stable and achieved recognition as the collaboration of five national original indigenous organisations who, together, represented practically all the indigenous peasant organisations in the country. These were:

- The CSUTCB
- The 'Bartolinas'
- The 'colonisers' (later the 'interculturals')

- CONAMAQ
- CIDOB

This conformation is revealing, not only because of its members, but also because of its timing, as it shows that from the very beginning the MAS was not just (or was more than) the sum of the indigenous social movements. In the same way, it could be said that the indigenous people, represented by the Unity Pact, had relative autonomy beyond the organic ties that united them to the MAS, and that there was no combined strategy of resistance to the opposing forces from other sectors of society. Alejandro Almaraz, who was involved in founding the MAS and was part of it until the first Morales administration, maintained:

> No one thought that the 'instrument' would have to have a different structure to the organisations. It was the organisations themselves who at the time made decisions and acted according to the politics of elections, and at that moment called themselves 'the instrument'. (Almaraz 2010, personal interview)

However, the Unity Pact seems to emerge beyond the 'instrument' itself:

> The NINA programme was an opportunity for organisations to come together; leaders came with their problems and found an identity based on the similarity of their programmes with those of other organisations, and they organised themselves to become a common force. Thus, the Unity Pact was constructed. The pact wasn't a declaration but was put together from the roots, in a long and difficult process. (Limache 2010, personal interview, 10 November)

> The Unity Pact was an organic opportunity for social movements ... The Unity Pact was a body of national organisations that broke away thanks to organic social groups at a regional level. (Taco 2010, personal interview)

> The government was one thing and the Unity Pact was something very different. The Unity Pact existed beyond the MAS and Evo Morales. (Mariaca 2010, personal interview)

This means that the social insurgence exceeded the capacity of the leadership of Morales and the Movement towards Socialism. As previously seen, gas was a topic that involved a series of demands from various social sectors whose diversity, complexity and internal conflict went beyond the reach of Morales and the Movement towards Socialism; it did not end with the reversal of the government's plans. It is indicative that, in the Gas War, the main role was not assumed by the 'instrument' but by the FEJUVE of El Alto, the

CSUTCB and, of course, the Coordinator, and followed by the social movements that emerged throughout the country in October. After the Gas War, this social energy would be channelled towards other arenas, including those created by the MAS. This constituted the context in which the Unity Pact was created.

It is also indicative that, despite the rise of the *cocalero* movement within the CSUTCB, its representative body, the Cochabamba Tropic's Six Federations (COCA TRÓPICO), did not join the Unity Pact, nor did FEJUVE or the Coordinator for Gas, or, for example, the COB. This emphasises a dynamism and plurality of demands within society that had not (yet) been unified behind a common agenda and, therefore, could not be embodied by a single entity, whether this be the 'instrument' or the Unity Pact.

The Unity Pact can be understood as the indigenous people's effort to talk with 'their own voice', understanding that, although they shared many demands with other sectors of society in the popular struggle, there existed more specifically 'indigenous' interests – the most important of which was the demand for a Constituent Assembly – which needed to be defended by their organisations through joint actions. In this respect:

> The Unity Pact is made up of five social organisations, with the aim of establishing a Constituent Assembly. These five organisations formed the pact where they enjoyed a good relationship, and there was also a good relationship between the pact and the government. (Becerra 2012, personal interview)

> Initially, the Unity Pact answered to the demands of the 'October agenda' – that a Constituent Assembly should be convened. This was one of its first aims. Foreseeing conflicts within the assembly, with potential sabotage by those who opposed this process, the Unity Pact of all the social organisations was created with the aim to press ahead and guarantee the Constituent Assembly. (Kochi 2010, personal interview)

> As a result of the Eastern Block, the Unity Pact was born, in which all national organisations – the confederations and their regional bodies – could be found to ensure that the Political Constitution of the State favoured all sectors of society. All of us, as an organisation, together. (Faldin 2010, personal interview)

Another important demand after the Gas War was the nationalisation of hydrocarbons. Although not a direct indigenous demand, it was grouped together with the demand for a Constituent Assembly, since it represented 'the search to reorganise the distribution of the country's colonial power, and to control attractive natural resources' (Garcés 2007: 232). On 5 November 2010, in a personal interview Mr E. Núñez explained: 'But the data showed that reality was different. It's here that everything that happened in October 2003 came into play, all the crises. Afterwards came what was called 'the October agenda', where the Constituent Assembly, nationalization and political change were to be found. That's where the Constituent Assembly comes in. Through this demand, the importance of the pact grew, ultimately allowing it to assume the role of representation of the social movements (Garcés 2010, personal interview) in the following period, particularly during the constituent process.

At this point the question arises of why indigenous organisations recurred to an indigenous coalition with political ends if they already had their own 'political instrument' in the MAS. As previously suggested, it seems that social energy exceeded the MAS's capabilities of containing and channelling demands in the political arena. The political and social instability that characterised the period between 2000 and 2005 contributed to the spontaneity that marked this process.

Of equal importance is the fact that, at least at the time of the Gas War and in the months following it, the MAS had mainly operated in the formal political arena, in a way more as a political party than as a social movement. Mesa's presidency was partly accepted in the political calculations of the MAS, which began to discern the possibility of obtaining power through an electoral process, and the MAS made skilled use of this position of power, managing to carry out politics both within the state structures that defended the political system as well as outside of it on the streets with social movements, thus maintaining its anti-establishment profile. However, this was perhaps exactly the reason why it became incapable of representing the popular struggle comprehensively. The spaces that the MAS was unable to fill would soon be occupied by the same social organisations in a more autonomous way. For example, it is indicative that, during the Gas War, the MAS followed a strategy that involved annulling Law 1689 and substituting it with one of its own design, based on a hike in corporate tax (a political solution). Within society, the popular demand was evermore clearly that of 'nationalising' hydrocarbons.

The Strength of Social Movements: The Arrival of Evo Morales to Power

The period between 2004 and 2005 was marked by the issue of hydrocarbons and the Constituent Assembly. President Mesa was granted a limited period to stabilise the country, a task which he was probably committed to, but in which he was unsuccessful due to pressure from the international community. As Gutiérrez explains, Mesa's strategy was to guarantee popular demands, showing political willingness but making much more modest progress by covering up his actions using tricks involving state processes.

Mesa defined the 'international order' and the 'obligations of the government before the community of nations' as the limit of his space of manoeuvre (Gutiérrez Aguilar 2008: 318), and therefore insisted on only partial adjustment of the Hydrocarbons Law, which was resisted both by the MAS (who insisted on their own law) and the people, who demanded the nationalisation of hydrocarbons.

On the other hand, Mesa's government was undermined by the activation of a politicised regionalism that began in Santa Cruz, coordinated by the Civic Committee of Santa Cruz, but which would soon expand into other regions (Beni, Tarija and Pando). In this way, an opposition bloc known as the Media Luna was formed. Openly challenging the central government, four regions decided to call for a referendum to decide on autonomy in May 2005, explicitly ignoring the president's calls for dialogue (*Europa Press – Servicio Latinoamericano*, 25 May 2005). These initiatives not only challenged presidential authority but also made social conflict worse, to the extent that indigenous and peasant organisations interpreted them as a strategy of the separatist 'oligarchy' to undermine the demand for a Constituent Assembly. From a legal point of view, autonomy did not figure in the Political Constitution, making it another topic that would need to be dealt with in the Constituent Assembly. Thus, politics were polarised into a band of indigenous and peasant social organisations – who praised the 'October agenda' and the demand for a Constituent Assembly – and the Media Luna, with their 'January agenda' and the demand for autonomous regions.[30]

The MAS and Morales continued as leaders of the opposition in the formal political arena and, although they maintained a level of activism on the streets through their organic ties, it was clear that they avoided the more radical popular demands, insisting on their own Law of Hydrocarbons and even defending Mesa's presidency when social protests began to demand his resignation (*Agence France Presse*, 8 March 2005). In this way, MAS left openings in the public space for the indigenous-peasant organisations to grow and become increasingly visible during the following waves of protest, on occasions even surpassing MAS leadership:

> If the government and Members of Parliament do not respond to our demands to convene a Constituent Assembly and nationalise hydrocarbons by Friday, May 2nd, they should watch out. They'll regret it because we, the national majorities, will radicalise the means of exerting pressure in the whole country.[31]

As the leader of the Movement towards Socialism, at the time Evo Morales did not lobby for the nationalisation of the energy industry like his former allies. On the contrary, he seemed to be content with the State sharing profits with foreign companies and administering how these resources were

commercialised. In reprisal to what they consider 'a betrayal of the prole-
tarian's cause', a small group from the Regional Confederation of Workers
(COR) blocked the roads to the *cocalero* leader's supporters when they
marched towards La Paz. (*El Mundo*, 18 May 2005)

In the following months, political decision-making power would return to
social demonstrations, which thus imposed themselves onto formal political
structures. Two important events led to this: faced with an increasing political
malaise regarding the gas matter, the topic of the nationalisation of hydrocarbons was imposed on Morales in mid-May 2005 at a council meeting in the
city of La Paz, forcing him to resign from his Law on Hydrocarbons; then,
at the beginning of June, with two-thirds of the country's motorways being
blocked, social movements demanded a 'triple resignation'.[32] The demonstrations resulted in a change to the Morales and MAS proposal on the mandate of nationalisation; furthermore, on 9 June, only days after the demand
was made, the triple resignation occurred. Eduardo Rodríguez Veltzé took
over as the new interim President of the Republic, at that time the high-
est-ranking representative of the judicial power and, therefore, designated in
the constitution as part of the presidential line of succession.

Rodríguez Veltzé's only task was to hold a general election, with the topic
of the Constituent Assembly being put on hold until a new government
was in place. During the electoral campaign, indigenous social movements
continued to pressure the political process by blocking roads and holding
protests, affecting both the election's content and results. The prominence
of the indigenous movement was also expressed through its position before
the Union Federation of Bolivian Mine Workers (the core of the COB), who,
in August 2005, proposed forming a 'front of fronts' that supported a single
candidate, eventually deciding to close ranks behind the MAS candidate. For
its part, Álvaro García Linera's proposal[33] of forming a single front was widely
accepted in El Alto (a locality that maintained strong political clout because
of its role in the Gas War), where both neighbourhood councils and the
Workers' Centre and peasants also decided to support Morales' candidature
(*Agencia Mexicana de Noticias NOTIMEX*, 9 August 2005).

The Movement towards Socialism gained an unprecedented victory in the
elections in December 2005, obtaining around 54 per cent of the votes (with
a turnout of 85 per cent). Although the electoral success certainly answered
to the circumstances and complexity of the political process, the common
interpretation seemed to assign a main role to Morales' political leadership
and his capacity to form alliances to widen his base of citizen support. In this
sense, his alliance with a recognised middle-class intellectual, Álvaro García
Linera, as candidate for the vice-presidency was actually of great importance. By opening up the Movement towards Socialism to these groups, a

bridge was formed between the indigenous movement and the intellectual left (Harten 2011b: 127–50).

Although the role of leadership is important – and will be taken up again later – the influence of social movements has not been fully recognised. It is notable that a large amount of academic literature concentrates on Morales' leadership, underestimating the political influence of indigenous social movements in this period. As mentioned previously, Morales and the MAS were practically obliged to adopt the same position as the social movements on the matter of gas (nationalisation) and the Constituent Assembly, the most important topics in the electoral campaign. The extent of social movements' pressure at that time is expressed even more clearly by the fact that the political parties who competed in the campaign also adopted this stance. Thus, the PODEMOS right-wing party promoted 'nationalising profits', while the National Unity centre party talked of nationalisation 'through shares'. In this way, social movements not only forced early elections but also effectively defined the political agenda around which the electoral campaign battle would be fought.

In a scenario of demonstrations, indigenous social movements gained ground over the MAS and, as John Crabtree explains, in the 2005 electoral process, the indigenous question became crucial to party identity (Crabtree 2011: 136). The formation of Morales' first ministerial cabinet showed a clear break with the past in favour of the participation of these sectors in formal politics: of the sixteen secretaries of state, only two were not of indigenous origin, and several of them were activists from within the peasant indigenous movement.[34]

Morales' coming to power was the result of social movements – in particular indigenous ones – adopting and recognising an explicit political role. After decades of opposition to state structures, when social movements were at their most powerful, they opted to take political power through these same structures. This breaks with the approach of social movements as 'anti-state' or 'a-political' actors, and supports the questioning of the relevance of the division between 'institutionalised' and 'non-institutionalised' politics.

The difficult transition to democracy was accompanied by the strict implementation of an economic neoliberal model aimed at stabilising the economic chaos of the UDP's government. With this aim, Víctor Paz Estenssoro's government took on the dismantling of a strong social movement, directly attacking their backbone through the mining clause. The subsequent 'resettlement' of large groups of miners to the inland areas was therefore accompanied by the transfer of the union mining experience to other regions, which undoubtedly helped the indigenous-peasant movement. In this way, a weakened COB was substituted for a series of new rural social movements who later found a focus in the new decentralised municipal governments, and who gradually came to occupy an important place at the national level in the form of organisations such as the CSUTCB and the *cocalero* movement.

Political and economic stability programmes negatively affected the popular sectors of the population, since they were implemented without an eye for social development, serving almost exclusively the interests of the economic elite. Historically discriminatory representation through political parties did not manage to create real ties with large segments of the population. Given that neoliberal hegemony did not allow for the interests of the people to be represented – above all in the context of the consequences of the economic crisis – it can be argued that political parties suffered a kind of 'co-optation' by the socio-economic elite, thus losing their role as mediators between the state and society, and gradually leading to a crisis of legitimacy.

For its part, cooperation among strong social movements – in particular indigenous peasants – during the 1980s and 1990s not only demonstrated the failure of the construction of nation-state based on 'assimilation' and the ideal of 'mestizos', but also rejected the development model and showed dissatisfaction with the political system in general. The Water War was a precedent for establishing the legitimacy and effectiveness of mobilised action as a means of effective political participation. Thus, between 2000 and 2005, the social movement became the main political actor, taking on the role of interlocutor with the state, and being consistently effective in asserting the interests of the people above and beyond governmental plans. In this way, when questioning the division between 'institutionalised' and 'non-institutionalised' politics, social movements and political parties can be understood to belong to the same system of mediation between the state and society, blurring the limits intended to separate them.

In a 'dialectic' relationship between the state and society, social movements go through a rapid process of political articulation, with important milestones in the *cocalero* movement and the creation of the 'political instrument' by which the MAS party went from being an actor with only local scope and sectorial interests to forming a political party at a national level in opposition to the government. At the same time, between 2000 and 2005, there was a certain complexity to this cooperation, since social movements did not only have an impact on the political arena through MAS, as demonstrated by the relative autonomy of indigenous organisations in the Unity Pact. Eventually, social movements opted for an institutional-democratic way out of the political impasse. The Gas War had left a political climate in which radical changes could be considered. However, even after the failure of Mesa's constitutional succession, and despite more radical actions, social movements opted to capture political power through a formal electoral process.

The evolution of the social movement as the most influential political actor was mirrored in the leadership of the popular struggle that the MAS would come to embody towards the end of 2005. Passing first through the *cocalero* movement in the 1990s, from which the political leadership of Evo Morales emerged, the popular struggle was then embodied by urban social movements that defended natural resources (the Water War and the Gas War), finally ending with the rise of the rural indigenous movement, shown through the importance that the topic of the Constituent Assembly would assume in their first government. In this sense, Morales' electoral victory, rather than being due the ability of the MAS and Morales to persuade indigenous social movements to close ranks behind him, was more a result of the determination of indigenous-peasant social movements – represented in the Unity Pact – to aim for political power through the electoral process.

The period from 2000 to 2005 can thus be understood as a 'cycle of social mobilisations' with a 'democratic conclusion' (Prada 2008: 142). In other words, the victory of Morales and the MAS in the elections was the direct result of popular struggles in which social movements played a leading role, showing the political power these actors have developed since the return of democracy. The social movements' victories gradually granted them greater legitimacy, creating a new dynamic in the state–society relationship in a process of mutual redefinition. Thus, the state was already redefined by the 1990s, recognising the multi-ethnic and pluricultural nature of the country while, in society, social movements – in particular the indigenous-peasant movement – took on a more explicit and active political role. A third factor was also added to the dynamic, namely the legitimacy crisis that the formal political representation system suffered because of the 'co-optation' of political parties.

In the following chapter, we will see how this process of redefinition continued. The social movements, whose actions were well known and embraced during the political struggle, played a leading role in the construction of a new social pact, and with it, the redefinition of state–society relations.

Notes

1. The reduced influence of the COB led to its factions negotiating separately. This produced an important change: the COB's union meetings stopped being an opportunity for mobilisation and decision making, and instead became an opportunity for different positions to be set forth. Thus, while the COB assembly's call for mobilisation had been effective in the past, from the mid-1980s onwards, their capacity to convene people notably diminished.

2. The increasing subordination of the rural family economy to monopolist market structures, and the creation of an agricultural semi working class that was poor in both land and resources, fed the growth of the corporate economy based on sugar cane, cotton, coca and soya, for example.

3. This concerns one of the main figures of the indigenous movements. Julián Apasa called himself Túpac Katari, taking his names from Túpac Amaru from Cusco – who led the insurrection there – and the Chayantan Tomás Katari – one of the first leaders of the uprisings in Alto Peru. Thus, his name symbolised the unity of the Andean indigenous movement. Túpac Katari was defeated and executed in 1781. His last words – 'You will kill me, but tomorrow I'll be back and I'll be millions' – took on a prophetic tone and have been adopted by current indigenous movements. Thus, it should be highlighted that the indigenous struggle has continued over time. During the republican period, the liberal reforms that favoured large estates once again inspired indigenous resistance from the Aymara, clearly seen in the uprising of Pablo Zárate Willka in 1899. The republic's policies aimed at integration, and thus managed to substitute a 'racialised cast' identity for that of a 'marginalised class' (Makaran-Kubis 2009: 48–50). As will be seen later on, the alienation of the ethnic component from 'rural' politics was one of the main causes of the National Revolution in 1952.

4. For a more detailed analysis of the school of thought of Fausto Reinaga on the most recent forms of Katarist expression, see Escárzaga (2012).

5. Since its beginnings, Katarism has been divided into two important trends: the first emphasised the indigenous aspect from a racial perspective, in the form of Indian struggle, repeating Fausto Reynaga's Indianist orthodox discourse; the second did not completely abandon the indigenist approach but rather formulated the rural problem using a national and class focus. Up until 1978, the difference between both trends got bigger, as did the need to make incursions to gain direct access to politics. Thus, taking advantage of the democratic opening announced by the Banzerist regime, the Túpac Katari Indian Movement (MITKA) was formed as the political party that represented the first trend, while Jenaro Flores the same year founded the Túpac Katari Revolutionary Movement (MRTK) party according to the second.

6. The Conscience of the Fatherland (CONDEPA) political party was founded in 1988, led by Carlos Palenque Avilés who had first made incursions into the public arena as a folklore musician and then as a television presenter. His programme 'La Tribuna Libre del Pueblo' turned him into well-known figure in popular sectors, as it paid direct and close attention to everyday problems and carried out a real, albeit limited, kind of social work. CONDEPA partly took possession of the inheritance of nationalism-revolutionism, but emphasised the value of popular culture at the same time as half-heartedly attacking the liberal economic model. Also, in 1988, the Solidarity Civic Unity (UCS) political party was founded, led by Max Fernández, who had worked in the beer business and accumulated a fortune, becoming the main shareholder in the Bolivian National Brewery. Using his position, he made incursions into social aid, marking a definite difference compared to the state's capacity to solve specific problems, for example, infrastructure. For this reason, he eventually decided to enter politics. Both parties have in common their prestige in urban sectors linked to the informal economy, in which the state does not participate, providing an alternative to more traditional forms of representation such as unions. They were also characterised by their pragmatism and subsequent focus on specific problems with simple solutions, as well as their condemnation of the harshness of neoliberal projects (Romero Ballivián 2003).

7. In this respect, special reference was made to the presence of the DEA (Drug Enforcement Agency) and its agents in Bolivia, to joint military operations, their meddling in the design of the anti-coca laws and the creation of UMOPAR (the Mobile Police Unit for Rural Areas). The UMOPAR was particularly problematic, since not only was it financed and led by the DEA, but also, on several occasions, the confrontations with the coca farmers ended in the excessive use of violence and torture, violating human rights (Healy 1991).

8. The Popular Participation Law (LPP) created local governments in rural areas and ordered the direct election of municipal officials, the redistribution of 20 per cent of national tax to municipalities and the creation of security and advice committees to design and control municipal spending. The law's aim was to increase the autonomy and political power of local governments, at the same time as it expanded municipal jurisdiction (until then restricted to urban areas) to the indigenous and rural populations in the hinterland and inland provinces. The law also established mechanisms for the participation of these sectors of the population, as well as a more effective 'social control' by grass-root-level organisations. The whole design, promotion and implementation of the law was carried out by academics, intellectuals and NGO activists, who praised the project as the legal framework for consolidating civil society and the prominence of active and responsible citizens. For many, it was considered the 'social' and friendly side of neoliberalism (Medeiros 2001).

9. Before the LPP, indigenous communities had no type of legal recognition from the state, and organising themselves through unions was the only way they could obtain legal status. Although the LPP proposed solving this problem by creating a legal status that was long-winded and costly, the process of certification caused conflicts of power between local groups, and the requests for procedures were often denied by local civil servants, since legal recognition conferred various rights, among which were land titles such as Native Community Lands (TCO) and indigenous lands.   In addition, the municipalities' processes for sets of laws implied the administrative rationing of space and population for the organisation, meaning politics was still subject to the logic of municipal planning. In this sense, Medeiros concluded that politics remained regulated by the economic development policies in which social problems were defined in technical terms and, therefore, received technical solutions. For this, effective participation was conditioned to the use of a vocabulary generally alien to indigenous and rural populations. Where social organisations were strong and had the technical support of NGOs, the experience was better, although for the large majority the economic development implied in the law served to maintain the outlines of exclusion. An even more severe critique argues that the LPP was no more than a 'social masquerade' to sell the (economic) model of neoliberalism (Medeiros 2001; Kohl and Farthing 2007: 235–37).

10. During the 1980s and 1990s, countries such as Ecuador, Colombia and Mexico implemented constitutional reforms recognising their indigenous populations (Gustafson 2002).

11. The recognition of indigenous organisations brought with it a series of rights, such as the legitimisation of the traditional structures of indigenous government, territorial rights and the transfer of 10 per cent of the general budget to them. For this reason, certification as an OTB was often hindered by authorities such as municipal governments and sub-prefectures, who could not reconcile the transfer of rights with their own territorial and budgetary interests. The certification process produced conflicts with local groups of power embedded in official agencies, which had the tendency to deny the existence of indigenous people because such credentials made the demand of Native Community Lands or Indigenous Land possible, as well as access to other rights established by law. In the same way, another difficulty that arose in relation to the existence of more than one type of traditional indigenous organisation – for example, the Ayllus and union organisations that functioned simultaneously – was the link between the size of the population and the resources available (either provoking or inciting territorial conflicts); and some organisations represented different sectors within the same physical space (Orellana Halkyyer 2008: 190; Calla 2008: 78–80).

12. It is important to note that this proposal was drawn up by José Enrique Pinelo, who was the director of the National Union of Workers for Social Action (UNITAS) at the time. Apparently, the influence of this organisation is still important nowadays, for example through the NINA programme, and its role in the drawing up of the proposal for the New

Constitution of the Pact of Unity. Patzi Paco explains that, during this period and faced with the weakening of the working class, left-wing intellectuals looked to take over the leadership of the indigenous movement, a process in which 'the indigenous lose the prominence that, at certain times, they have assumed and become participants in a movement that is subordinate to the interests of the left' (Patzi Paco 1999: 71).

13. Once again, the role of these leftist and ecclesiastical 'support organisations' can be seen, responding to the specific Latin American context in which progressive middle-class sectors, turned into 'civil society', form part of the resistance to the repression of authoritarian regimes. We will reflect on the relationship between these organisations and social indigenous movements later on.

14. The maturation of this idea is one of the indigenous movement's most important (if not the most important) contribution to the process of redefining the state, in what would later become the formula of the 'plurinational state' and the corresponding redefinitions for the state–society relationship. This will be dealt with in more detail in the following chapters.

15. The 'Ayllus Rojos' formed an alliance with a group of Bolivian and Mexican students. They had met in the Autonomous University in Mexico, first supporting the Salvadorian cause and then returning to Bolivia to fight for revolution from a Marxist perspective. Among them was Álvaro García Linera, who would later become vice-president to the Morales administration. The closing of the mines and the displacement of miners to rural areas obliged him to form an alliance with indigenous forces, in which the student group combined activism with the theoretical elaboration of Marxism to adapt to the indigenous issue in Latin America. The alliance with the 'Ayllus Rojos' group led to the creation of the Túpac Katari Guerrilla Army, which the state qualified as a terrorist body and accused of attacks against it, taking a large number of their leaders prisoner, such as Felipe Quispe, Álvaro García Linera and Raquel Gutiérrez Aguilar. The last two were imprisoned for five years without trial, and the charges dropped after they were let out (Escárzaga 2012).

16. This rejection is attributed to interference by the dominant political parties (ADN, MIR and MNR) in the National Electoral Court (Harten 2011b: 84).

17. The struggle for leadership of the 'instrument' was already visible in 1997 when Morales, together with other Quechua leaders, organised a Second Congress of the Political and Territorial Instrument, in which the Council of Native Power was set up – an organisation that did not end up having a significant role (Gutiérrez Aguilar 2008: 192).

18. There are people currently in the MAS who still remember the Falangist past of the party whose acronym they would later adopt, which is why it is important to mention this. The MAS was established in 1985 – paradoxically, as a leftist fragmentation of one of the oldest right-wing parties in Bolivia, the Bolivian Socialist Falange (FSB). Their historical leader was David Añez Pedraza, who would move towards left-wing politics, strongly influenced by the guerrilla Che Guevara and those from Teoponte. At the beginning of the 1990s, the failure of this project was seen in the limited number of permanent members (around twenty). The electoral court allowed the MAS to be transferred to Evo Morales, on the condition that none of the party attributes (name, symbols or colours) were changed (Harten 2011a: 85–86).

19. This organisation was created during the contract negotiations with Aguas del Tunari.

20. FEDECOR was formed in 1997. The regulatory and managerial structure of the water and sprinkler systems in the Cochabamba valleys dates back to colonial and even pre-colonial times, in the form of sprinkler associations. Although these did not enjoy a visible political prominence (peasant unions were the main players, of which the sprinkler associations made up only one component), they were always present and began to gain more political visibility from the 1990s onwards. Since then, the state has created policies directed at controlling, expropriating and regulating the water controlled by the inhabitants, forcing these local

organisations to take action, as seen in the so-called 'Well Wars' between 1994 and 1998. Thus, the autonomous articulation of these organisations led to the creation of FEDECOR. This organisation served as an umbrella for the associations, with members maintaining a wide margin of autonomy, and only certain tasks being coordinated. See also García Linera et al. (2010: 646–66).

21. The discourse of the umbrella organisation was based on national popular, anti-imperialist and anti-global rhetorical bases, protesting against the current development model. The umbrella organisation challenged the system that failed to defend popular interests. It also refused to become a formal organisation with official recognition, and preferred to continue as an informal network that connected different social actors (Assies 2003; Perreault 2006).

22. Morales was found guilty of 'abusing parliamentary immunity', despite complaints from fourteen indigenous and left-wing Parliament legislators.

23. This is the first time that the demand for a Constituent Assembly was so explicit and, as will be seen later on, it can be identified as the start of a Bolivian constituent process between 2006 and 2009.

24. In a revealing study on the relationships between the government and the FMI, Jim Schultz (2005) shows the pressure the FMI applied to try and reduce the fiscal deficit in a one-year period, so that it ended up at under 5.5 per cent. This was a requisite for access to long-term loans. This pressure divided the government into those who proposed reducing the deficit by increasing the tax on transnationals who exploited gas, and those who preferred a direct tax on salaries. Finally, the latter was chosen.

25. The conditions stipulated the following: operators would have to pay a bonus of 18 per cent for any new reserves that were discovered, to which a 12 per cent tax was added to the price of gas in ownership rights (that is to say, with no additional processing value), based on a price of only $0.50 cents per 1,000 BTU (British Thermal Units). From this price, already well below the market one, any transport and distribution costs could also be discounted (Harten 2011b: 120).

26. According to BBC reports, there were five deaths: one soldier and four civilians. 'La crisis paso a paso' (*BBC Mundo*, 18 October 2003).

27. The population of this locality grew considerably after the 1952 Revolution, when several different industries were set up there. A second surge in the population occurred from 1985 onwards because of the 'relocation' of mining families after neoliberal reforms had closed the mining centres. In 1985, turning El Alto into a municipality was approved, removing it from the control of the city of La Paz. Neighbourhoods were quickly formed, rapidly and almost entirely replicating rural communities and providing a notable homogeneity, with residents who maintained and still maintain strong ties to their places of origin. These characteristics formed the basis for a type of organisation from which the Neighbourhood Councils evolved.

28. This decree declared that the territory of the republic was in 'national emergency' and ordered the armed forces to take charge of transporting fuel in tankers. It also stipulated that '[a]ny damage to goods or people that may occur … was guaranteed compensation by the Bolivian State', understood as permission to kill. Supreme Decree 27209 of 11 October 2003, on the website of the Official Gazette of the Plurinational State of Bolivia: http://www.gacetaoficialdebolivia.gob.bo/edicions/view/2530 (last accessed November 2012).

29. The following organisations participated in this event: the Guarani People's Assembly (APG), the Confederation of Ethnicities of Santa Cruz (CPESC), the Landless Movement (MST), the National Association of Sprinklers and Community Systems of Drinking Water, the Cultural Movement of African Descent, the CSUTCB, the Bartolinas, CONAMAQ, the CPEMB, the BOCINAB, the CTDAC and the CSCB.

30. The 'January agenda' was made up of topics that emerged from the 'open councils' convened by the Civic Committee of Santa Cruz in January 2005, in which, through a seriously questioned process of signature collection, proposed autonomy for the regions.
31. Román Loayza, executive secretary of the CSUTCB, quoted in 'Crónica Bolivia – Mesa bets on dialogue on hydrocarbons and disregards the demonstrations that demand his resignation'. *Europa Press – Servicio Latinoamericano*, 25 May 2005.
32. With it, a political solution to the impasse was proposed, in which the resignation of President Mesa would be succeeded by the resignation of the President of the Chamber of Senators, Hormando Vaca Diez and by the President of the Chamber of Deputies, Mario Cossío (both associated with traditional neoliberal parties). A triple resignation implied that, following regulations, the presidency had to be assumed by the President of the Supreme Court as an emergency measure, with his sole function being to hold a general election within six months.
33. Álvaro García Linera was middle class and studied mathematics at the Autonomous University of Mexico between 1981 and 1985. On returning to Bolivia, he became affiliated with the indigenous cause, eventually participating in radicalised groups but mainly as an ideologist. In 1992, he was arrested on terrorism charges and, although he was never convicted, he was imprisoned for five years. During this period, he studied sociology (he claims to have read more than a thousand books) and received his degree when he was released in 1997. Afterwards, he worked as a university professor and newsreader, becoming a highly respected public figure, while continuing to dedicate his work as an intellectual and his academic opinion to union causes and indigenous movements in Latin America.
34. We can highlight the following ministries: Foreign Affairs, David Choquehuanca, with a long history of activism in the rural indigenous movement (among others, the CSUTCB) – he was also national coordinator of the NINA education and training programme of indigenous leaders; Economic Development, Celina Sosa Luna, leader of the Bartolina Sisa Federation of Rural Women; Education, Félix Patzi Paco, Aymaran sociologist and intellectual, ideologist of the indigenous movement; Employment, Santiago Gálvez Mamani, national leader of the Manufacturing Federation; Rural and Agricultural and Livestock Affairs, Hugo Salvatierra, from Chiquitania and with long-standing ties with social movements, and legal adviser to the Bolivian Workers' Centre and other union organisations; Mining and Metals: Wálter Villarroel, mining leader and president of the Mining Cooperatives Federation (Fencomin); Justice, Casimira Rodríguez, leader of the National Federation of Domestic Workers; Water, Abel Mamani, president of the Federation of Neighbourhood Councils in El Alto.

3

The 'State–Society Interface' and 'Political Networks'

Social Movements and the Bolivian Constituent Process, 2006–2009

From the point of view of authors such as Migdal, Goldstone and Johnston (see Chapter 1), there is a relationship of mutual and continuous formation between the state and actors in society which, in the Latin American context, has been referred to as 'dialectic' (Cannon and Kirby 2012). The coming to power of Evo Morales and the social movements' 'political instrument' can be understood as an expression of this type of relationship. As observed in the previous chapter, the neoliberal reforms implemented from the 1980s onwards in Bolivia had the effect of breaking up the national workers' movement into a group of relatively dispersed peasant ones. At the same time, the decentralisation policies that accompanied the implementation of the neoliberal model created opportunities for political participation at a local level that, in part, contributed to the political articulation of grass-root initiatives. The double legitimacy crisis – of both the neoliberal model and the institutional system in general – saw the emergence of strong social movements, articulated around an indigenist discourse and the rejection of the neoliberal development model. Political development from 2000 to 2005 and the MAS coming to power can therefore be understood as the result of a 'dialectic' relationship of the mutual and constant (re)formation between state and society.

One of the keys to the electoral victory was the incorporation of the demand for a Constituent Assembly in the political agenda. This was made up of a proposal that originated in the indigenous movement but which, in the 2000–2005 political context, acquired a wider political reach, becoming the vehicle through which a series of diverse demands from different sectors of society could be articulated. Thus, in August 2006, Evo Morales' government inaugurated the Constituent Assembly that, in a one-year period, had to produce a new social pact consisting of a profound transformation of the Bolivian state. The new constitutional text came into force in 2009, after a long and conflictive process involving many failures. In this chapter, the Bolivian constituent process from 2006 to 2009 will be analysed as the construction of a 'state–society interface', a concept proposed by Dagnino et al. (2006) and understood as a space for exchange between civil society and the state. In this scenario, 'political networks' entered into play to determine the course of the constituent process, and so the 'state–society interface' represented indeed the struggle to strengthen democracy, embodied by social movements.

This chapter analyses the role of indigenous social movements in the construction of the proposal of a new constitution, signalling the continuation of their prominence in the political process. The analysis highlights the modulation from social activism to proposal and negotiation, demonstrated by the fact that the indigenous movement was the only actor capable of formulating a complete proposal with an integral vision of the constitutional text. Such modulation is congruent with the concept of a 'state–society interface', which signals that the state and civil society are in a process of constant and mutual formation. In this case, by inserting themselves into a 'state–society interface', social movements experienced a qualitative transformation in how they carry out politics.

The insertion of social movements occurs in the form of 'political networks' that also involve other kinds of actor, in particular the so-called 'support institutions' (national NGOs). In the same way, it is shown how the 'format' of social movement is still the most effective method of politics in Bolivia during this period. This is particularly illustrated by the fact that opposition forces opted to make an impact on politics by making use of traditionally popular 'mobilisation repertoires'. It is also expressed by the fact that indigenous social movement organisations moved back and forth between proposition and mobilisation throughout the whole constituent process, with mobilisation and social movements and their articulation as 'political networks' having a greater impact on the assembly's results than what occurred inside this institution. This once again shows the 'state–society interface' nature of the constituent process, in which conflict, negotiation and political resolution occurred both in institutional and more informal spaces of action.

This chapter first analyses the apparent paradox that social movements – frequently understood as 'anti-state' – aimed at the achievement of their demands through an institutional formula (state transformation by Constituent Assembly). The preponderance that the demand for a Constituent Assembly assumed showed the appropriation of a discourse of rights, as well as the confidence placed in the Political Constitution of the State as a means to the realisation of rights. Reference is made to the academic debate on 'new Latin American constitutionalism' and the 'judicialisation of politics' to interpret this trend. This is followed by a more detailed discussion of the concept of the 'state–society interface', to depict the Bolivian constituent process (2006–2009) as a space of encounter and interaction between the state and civil society in a context of democratic construction.

New Latin American Constitutionalism and the 'State–Society Interface'

After an extensive and difficult constituent process, the new constitutional text came into effect in January 2009 during the government of Evo Morales. The new Bolivian political constitution follows a regional trend expressed in a number of constituent processes that gave way to the revision and reformulation of the social pacts of different countries. This was the case in Colombia in 1991, Ecuador in 1998 and 2008, and Venezuela in 1999.

These experiences have been discussed academically under the name of 'new Latin American constitutionalism' (Martínez Dalmau 2008; Gargarella and Courtins 2009; Nolte and Schilling-Vacaflor 2012). The discussion should be differentiated from the 'neo-constitutionalism' that, as the result of extensive academic theorisation, constitutes an elaborated doctrinal trend on the role of constitutions in modern democracies. On the other hand, as Viciano Pastor and Martínez Dalmau (2010) explain, the expressions of new Latin American constitutionalism – in which the experiences of Ecuador and Bolivia stand out – are the result of the acceptance and activity of social movements and, as such, do not involve a closed system of analysis or a proposal for a constitutional model.

The same authors identify a series of characteristics that differentiate the 'new Latin American constitutionalism' from other experiences. In general, the term refers to constituent processes with a greater level of social participation – that is to say, less elite and more democratic, and for those reasons enjoying a higher level of legitimacy. The constitutional texts are more extensive and use symbolic language that claims to represent a 'democratic rupture' with the past, characterised by linguistic simplicity in order to move past the typical elitism of the former constitutionalism, and promoting a popular version of it. The new constitutional texts are also characterised by 'principlism', in that the articulation of the will of the constituent is carried out through an abundance of principles. The texts highlight a constitutional rigidity that answers to the preoccupation that the modification of constitutions should only fall to the constituent power.

The prevalence of a discourse of rights and legal principles in the constitutional text allows for 'new Latin American constitutionalism' to be situated in the framework of the judicialisation of politics. Generally, the term is used to refer to the increasing importance the courts acquire in the political field (Couso 2004: 29), but in reality it points to a tendency in which 'the legitimacy of the political system is linked to the capacity of the modern democratic state to comply with its promises of the rule of law and the protection of citizens' rights, and to guarantee the principle of such process and the ways leaders are held accountable' (Domingo 2009: 37). Thus, the judicialisation of politics is linked to changes in the political culture regarding citizens' rights and the rule of law. In these changes, it is notable that there is a kind of 'discovery' of the discourse of rights by subordinate social spaces: in the case of Bolivia, by social movements.[1]

It is slightly paradoxical that social actors traditionally characterised as 'a-political' or 'anti-state' articulate their emancipatory struggles based on a discourse of political rights and of refounding state reforms – in other words, a new constitution. This is even more so if taking into account that, in the Latin American context, the rule of law has had very little legitimacy, and both laws and the judicial system have traditionally remained under the control of the economic, political and social elite in service of their interests (Domingo 2009: 39). In this way, the appropriation of the discourse of rights by social movements is both the cause and effect of changes in political and social power relations, in which a more explicit political role for social movements is revealed.

Thus, observing the diverse changes to citizen rights, Domingo indicates that, in the experience of the modern state, the conquests of rights 'supposes political conquests that bring changes to the political and social order' (Domingo 2009: 39). Along the same lines, Gargarella and Courtins maintain that the birth of constitutions in the Latin American region has usually occurred in moments of crisis, 'with the aim of resolving some kind of fundamental political-social drama' (2009: 10). In this way, the Bolivian constituent process that began in August 2006 can be understood as resulting from a legitimacy crisis of the political system and social order, through which it was hoped to reach a new equilibrium between the different political and social forces in society.

In this sense, the approval of a new constitutional text in January 2009, including an extensive list of rights and emancipatory principles, suggests social conquests and a new equilibrium. However, the 'transitory' nature of the constitutional texts of the 'new Latin American constitutionalism' must be emphasised which, more than defining or consolidating a type of state, expressed the desire for a model that is still being constructed. This was expressed by an extensive list of rights, together with 'mega-concepts' whose aim was to achieve the integration of marginalised sectors, as well as concerns for creating participation mechanisms to establish control and legitimacy. Thus, Domingo observes that the innovative and avant-garde nature of a constitutional text does not necessarily reflect the 'real' quality of the state–society relationship (Domingo 2009: 45). Although the conquest of rights says a lot about the emancipatory struggles that preceded them, it says little about the impact – the real effect – of regulatory and legal reforms on socio-political practices.

Regarding the democratisation processes or the strengthening of democracy, Fals Borda indicates that social movements have been successful in emphasising the need for pluralism and tolerance, so that democratisation occurs in a context of the mutual recognition of differences (Fals Borda 1992). In this sense, Roxborough observed that it was likely that state institutions would seek to expand their capacity to respond to the increasing diversity of demands from society, and that social movements would assume a more explicit role in politics. These developments entail a closer relationship between state actors and the actors from society (Roxborough 1997).

To analyse the relationship between state and society in the context described, the concept of a 'state–society interface' has been proposed in the debate on the construction of democracy in Latin America, initially formulated by Norman Long (1999) and Bryan Roberts (2001), and then elaborated further by Ernesto Insunza Vera, to whom we will refer in this section.

Insunza Vera conceives the state–society interface as an arena for exchange, characterised by conflict, in which the actors relate to each other intentionally, 'and where the projects, forces and strategies of the (state and societal) actors involved enter into play' (Insunza Vera 2005: 18). The subjects of the interface can be individual or collective and are understood as carriers of political-cultural projects that respond to their specific historicity, knowledge, norms and values (Gurza Lavalle and Isunza Vera 2010: 46), who, together with the public policy in which they are inserted, determine the structure of the state–society interface. Thus, the socio-state interface is conceived as a space in which different discourses both come together and interact.

According to Long, the interface has a series of characteristics: (1) it is an organised meeting of intentions, negotiations and interconnected relations; (2) it is a place for conflict, incompatibility and negotiation; (3) it implies a reality in which the processes of knowledge are central; (4) it is also constituted by power; (5) it is made up of multiple discourses; and (6) it can be an opportunity for planned intervention in the lives of individuals and collective social actors (Long 1999: 1–4). In the interface, two basic forms of exchange are identified for interaction between state and society. On the one hand, there is an exchange of information in agreements that are not of a binding nature. On the other, there are binding mechanisms in which the agreement forces certain actions.

For this study, the interfaces of a binding nature are relevant. In the first place, there is direct democratic relation and/or social control in which civil society controls, dominates or directs the state (*representative interfaces*). In concrete terms, this refers to referendums, plebiscites or citizen initiatives, social control and the election of authorities and legislators. Secondly, there are subrogated public policies and the transfer of policies (*transfer interfaces*), where the state controls, denominates or directs civil society. Examples of this type of interface are social development projects managed by civil society organisations, and other kinds of project carried out by social actors but financed using public resources. Finally, the *joint management interface* exists, in which civil society and the state carry out joint management.

As Insunza Vera explains, the notion of a state–society interface implies an intrinsic relational logic in each sub-system (state and civil society), which can be studied using a network analysis. This permits an analysis of the 'reticular structure' in which both actors and their relationships are understood as an exchange of, for example, material goods, information and prestige. In the same way, a network analysis shows that relations between subjects can be very different, based on the specific nature of the subject as well as the structure (network relationship) in which they are found (Isunza Vera 2005: 19–20).

Dagnino et al. (2006) make reference to the concept of a 'state–society interface' more specifically related to the construction of democracy and the role that social movements play in it. The authors maintain that the representation crisis of political parties has weakened their link with social sectors. The growing incapacity of formal channels of representation to express the diversity of what is social has had the effect of shifting politics to more informal networks. The construction of democracy requires a strong joint responsibility between the democratic project put forward by actors of civil society and those embodied in the state institution. This greater correspondence should be looked for in the state–society interface, in which individual or collective subjects meet at a site of confrontation of cultural paradigms, characterised by conflict, incompatibility and negotiation, and by asymmetric relations.

The remainder of the chapter will show how the Bolivian constituent process can effectively be understood as a 'state–society interface', responding to the characteristics presented here and characterised by the emergence of 'political networks' that link state and social actors.

From Protests to Proposals: Social Movements in the Formulation of a Draft Constitution

As seen in Chapter 2, social movements assumed a more central role in politics, ultimately articulating the 'instrument' that would bring Morales to power. Once in power, social movements turned into 'fully acknowledged political protagonists, and were addressed explicitly and directly by other political actors as if they were fully legitimate interlocutors in politics' (Salman 2011: 34). For the electoral victory of MAS at the end of 2005, the fact that the topic of the Constituent Assembly was adopted during their political campaign was vitally important (together with that of the nationalisation of hydrocarbons). Next, the history of this topic will be described to show how it was initially a demand of the indigenous movement but then came to assume importance at a national level.

The Constituent Assembly

The recurring indigenous marches in the 1990s formed an important mechanism for meetings between, and the articulation of, different indigenous organisations. In particular, they were central to encounters between organisations from the highlands and lowlands, as well as between trade union organisations with a longer trajectory (such as the CSUTCB) and younger indigenous organisations (like the CIDOB). Already in 1990, during the first indigenous march, the need for a process of this type was discussed, but it would only be in 2002 that the Constituent Assembly was explicitly presented as an indigenous demand, and triggered the debate on the need for a constituent process at a national level. It is worth remembering that, in this period, the nation was in the middle of a political and social crisis, availing the consideration of such radical measures.

The Fourth Indigenous March in 2002 became an important precedent of the constituent process. According to the official version, the march 'For Popular Sovereignty, Territory and Natural Resources' was convened by the CIDOB (despite their internal contradictions) and the Eastern Bloc – that is to say, by organisations of indigenous people from the lowlands. There seems to be consensus that the idea of a Constituent Assembly initially emerged from the indigenous population. In this respect, my interviews include different and even contradictory testimonies. However, what is important is that there were many claims to the authorship of the Constituent Assembly proposal from various indigenous organisations, demonstrating the value of the 2002 indigenous march in the collective memory. Even more importantly, the fact that different organisations identified the demand as their own reveals the degree of appropriation of the topic, and explains the level of commitment to it. The following extracts from my interviews with representatives of the indigenous social movements show this:

> More than fifty social organisations joined the countrywide march in 2002, demanding a Constituent Assembly. Why did social movements react? When they marched, they asked for an article of the law to be modified, then that of another law. Everyone said it couldn't be done. So they said: We're tired of marching for just one article. Why don't we call for a national mobilisation with everything, to make a constitutional reform? (Taco 2010, personal interview)

> In 2002, when a Constituent Assembly was proposed, the idea of a national march was born, requesting a Constituent Assembly from here, in the

CEPESC. It wasn't created in the CIDOB but in the CEPESC. (Faldín 2010, personal interview)

We are protagonists of the constitution, of the refounding of the state. I'm one of the legs of a chair. When we marched in 2002 with CONAMAQ, we arrived in La Paz, we said: 'We don't want to patch up the Political Constitution of the State, all that needs to be cancelled and given a new start using a new type of construction'. A new start, we understood that. The refounding of the state, the new constitution was a new starting point, and the foundation for us was the Constituent Assembly. The new CPE was already like a new house, and now we needed to think about how to furnish it. (Zacu 2010, personal interview)

We were the first agents to ask for a Constituent Assembly with the participation of the native indigenous population. Thus, the creation of the same Constituent Assembly was achieved, where the task was to draw up the new political constitution of the plurinational state with the participation of the people and rural indigenous organisations. (Choque 2016, personal interview)

In this way, even without firm indications of them being fulfilled, indigenous social organisations began to work together on this aim, with the result that, in 2004, the Unity Pact was created as a body representing the rural indigenous people, who would later put forward a proposal to the National Congress for a Law Convening the Constituent Assembly.

It is important to highlight that the demand for the Constituent Assembly was not adopted by the MAS from the very beginning, and the indigenous march of 2002 was not supported by the 'instrument'. When, on the way to La Paz, the march reached the region of Chapare, the coca federations did not join in but rather let it pass by. With the national elections being held only days later, it was understood, at least at that time, that the MAS bet more on the formal political process (participating in elections) than on its reform (not showing support for the matter of the Constituent Assembly). As previously discussed, as a second political force, the MAS continued their opposition both from within formal structures and from the streets through their organic links with social movements. In mobilising for the Constituent Assembly themselves, the indigenous organisations gave a warning to the MAS, demonstrating a de facto autonomy. As will be seen later on, the autonomy in relation to the MAS would be shown even more clearly in the relationship between the Unity Pact and the MAS during work on the Constituent Assembly.

In the period after the Gas War crisis, the Movement towards Socialism understood that the demand for an assembly had gained more and more resonance in society, going beyond the indigenous movement. Together with the topic of the nationalisation of hydrocarbons, the Constituent Assembly became a central issue in the MAS programme during the electoral political campaign at the end of 2005. On the way to the polls, the idea of a Constituent Assembly was being widely debated in society, as reflected by a series of events and publications dedicated to this topic.

How did the topic of the Constituent Assembly – originally a demand from the indigenous movement – came to assume so much importance in other sectors of society? Undoubtedly, the political context of the system's legitimacy crisis, which threatened to unleash anarchy, appears of importance as it pushed the possibility and even necessity of extraordinary solutions. In the same way, the proliferation of mobilisations and claims in different, diverse sectors, finally found a container in the demand for a Constituent Assembly. The disparity of demands (even those from the economic elite) could be dealt with in a constituent process, providing a way out of the political impasse.

For this reason, before it was set up and started functioning, the Constituent Assembly was predestined to be an opportunity for encounters, conflict and negotiation, with the meeting of different and contradictory logics of both state and society, and also of cultural paradigms and political ideologies. As such, it can be understood as an example of the 'state–society interface' as described by Dagnino et al. (2006), in which the incapacity of formal channels of political representation leads to strong social movements that, through their struggles, are capable of creating alternative opportunities for encounters with the state. In the case of Bolivia, the creation of the state–society interface was the result of the indigenous social movements struggles that were later assumed by wider sectors of society. Through this joint activism, Morales was elected president and the installation of this space in the form of a Constituent Assembly could be achieved.

In the following section, the role of the indigenous social movements is analysed, due to their critical role in the 'state–society interface' of the Constituent Assembly. As will be seen, from 2006 to 2009, social movements left the side lines of institutional politics and assumed a more explicit role mediating between the state and society as the main actors in the 'state–society interface'. This is particularly the case of the indigenous social movements that conformed the Unity Pact, a body that acquired the representation of the whole indigenous movement and which can be understood as a 'political network'. This fact is significant since it emphasises the relative capacity of the MAS to act as the social movements' 'political instrument'.

The 'Unity Pact' Political Network in the Constituent Process

The strength assumed by the demand of a Constituent Assembly had two important effects. Firstly, this indigenous demand, which would later be adopted by other sectors of society, led to the Unity Pact assuming the 'representation of the social movements'.[2] Formed by the five 'original' social organisations at the national level (CIDOB, CONAMAQ, CSTUCB, CSCIOB, CNMCIOB-BS) and understood as a political network, the Unity Pact represented the alliance of relatively diverse social forces. Thus, for example, the CSUTCB was a 'peasant' organisation from the highlands with a unionist tradition from the 1960s, and was linked to the Bolivian Workers' Centre. On the other hand, the CIDOB was formed at the beginning of the 1980s, bringing together the Amazon's indigenous populations, who gradually created their organisations with the support of anthropologists and NGOs. (Re)defining themselves more and more as indigenous social organisations and movements, the demand for a Constituent Assembly became an articulating demand of this political network. In the same way, the expectations for the constituent process reinforced the articulation of a regionalised right-wing opposition, which, for its part, contributed to the cohesion of indigenous organisations in the Unity Pact.

Secondly, it explains why, as a result of the MAS coming to power, the indigenous discourse assumed supremacy over the different political visions and currents that feed the MAS political project.[3] In other words, the Constituent Assembly project gave impetus to the indigenous movement, spreading their political articulation at the same time as conferring it centrality, even positioning itself as the force that sustained the MAS government against the opposition constructed from regional centres in the country.

The political process from the end of 2003 onwards was marked by the 'October agenda' – the nationalisation of hydrocarbons and the Constituent Assembly, which practically prescribed state reorganisation as a 'denial of neoliberalism' (de la Fuente Jeria 2010: 9). It can be said that this was the only common factor among multiple demands – in other words, of the demand of the Constituent Assembly converged with a desire to break with the past – but there was less consensus on how change should be formulated or carried out.

The role the 'Unity Pact' political network played during the constituent process should be understood in relation to the assembly's organisation. In the selection of candidates for constituents, the formal structures of party politics were once again chosen, establishing that the candidates would be chosen through political parties. This went against the direct representation being elected by customary means, initially proposed by the Unity Pact in their Convening Law proposal. Once more, respect for a certain level of formal and traditional institutionality was imposed, as was the case after the Gas War.

The Special Convening Law, passed in March 2006, emerged from Congress as the result of political negotiation between the official and opposition parties, resulting in many concessions (European Union 2006: 9) that were not all detrimental to the position of the MAS. In politically bipolar circumstances, the decision to participate through political parties left the indigenous organisations in particular, and popular actors in general, practically no other option than to look for representation in the assembly as part of the Movement towards Socialism. In this way, any form of autonomous representation that would diminish the position of the MAS vis-à-vis the opposition parties was avoided. Thus, just as in the period prior to the assembly and the elections, social movements imposed themselves on the MAS; at the time of the organisation of the Constituent Assembly, the MAS – moving from state structures and foreseeing the confrontation with the political opposition – imposed itself on the social movements as its political party, ensuring a greater presence within the assembly by monopolising the popular representation.

Less favourable was what Albó would call the 'arithmetic of the Convening Law', in which it was established that, of a total of 255 constituent members:

– 210 would be chosen in seventy local constituencies, with three members per constituency, two from the first majority and one from the second.
– 45 would be chosen by pluri-nominal district constituency, five per district, two from the first majority and one from the second, third and fourth positions.

This way of choosing assembly members had two important effects. First, given the bipolarity that characterised the time of the elections, a rather disproportionate distribution was produced: 'The fact that the system to turn votes into seats particularly favoured the second party was manifested by the electoral result of PODEMOS,[4] who maintained their status as the strongest opposition party. With 15.33 per cent of the total vote, PODEMOS earned sixty seats that represented 23.53 per cent of the total' (European Union 2006: 33). Secondly, this design fostered the right of the minorities to veto. As Garcés et al. (2010: 40) explain, 'even if the MAS-ISPS had won all the local constituencies and all the district ones, they would not have achieved the two-thirds set out by the Convening Law as needed to approve the constitutional text: they would have gained 158 assembly members of the 170 needed to make up the two-thirds'. Here, the tenacity of the political struggle is reflected. Congress, with a strong presence of right-wing opposition forces, thus aimed for a Constituent Assembly design that would not allow fundamental changes, and that would pave the way for a series of setbacks and delays that indeed came to characterise the whole constituent process. For their part, the MAS strategically accepted representation through the party structure, since otherwise a more autonomous opportunity for participation would have been created for other (indigenous) sectors outside it, particularly those that sided with the right (from the districts of Santa Cruz, Beni and Pando, for example) and to the detriment of the MAS capacity to influence the assembly.

The organisation of the Constituent Assembly based on the traditional design of political party representation, together with the particular mechanism of constituent election, once again shows the nature of the 'state–society interface' that marked the constituent process. Both demonstrate the constitution of the interface reflecting current power relations (Long 1994) and establishing 'asymmetric' relations within it (Dagnino et al. 2006). In characterising the constituent process as 'state–society interface', the aim is not to assess characteristics or developments as negative, but to express the dynamics that characterise the interaction between state and society.

The MAS obtained 50.7 per cent of the votes, obtaining 137 seats (53.73 per cent of the total) (European Union 2006: 33). The list of MAS assembly members included a considerable number of representatives named by indigenous organisations through their uses and customs. These entered the Constituent Assembly by mandate of their organisations and were subject to their control, which represented a diverse and less coherent presence within the MAS benches. These were called 'organic', differentiating them from the candidates from other sectors of society.

Once the Constituent Assembly had been set up, the articulating aim of the political network turned into the 'construction of a proposal for a new constitutional text from the indigenous movement'. Long before the inauguration of the Constituent Assembly on 6 August 2006 in the city of Sucre, the majority of indigenous organisations had already worked on their proposals, such as the Great National Assembly of Indigenous People in 2002, and the work involved in consulting on and formulating the CPESC proposals in 2004. From May 2006, much more intense work was carried out together with different organisations under the leadership of the Unity Pact, with the aim of presenting a single indigenous movement proposal. A series of unfocused deliberative events throughout the whole country converged in the formulation of a document that was presented to the assembly in May 2007. The process of constructing this proposal, characterised by complex and intense work involving advances, tensions and setbacks, has been well documented in the excellent work of Garcés et al. 2010 to which we refer. For this reason, the following discussion will deal only with those aspects that are most relevant to this analysis.

In the first place, it should be highlighted that the Unity Pact proposal was the result of an intense and deliberative work in which a real effort was made to collect information from different groups at a grass-root level and to come to an understanding in a single document. In the words of one leader:

'When I was leader in 2007, the Constituent Assembly was at its peak but there were still many workshops and meetings being held in the towns and communities to collect information for the new CPE proposals' (Taco 2010, personal interview).[5]

The Unity Pact was generally created as an alliance during the struggle of the indigenous people, later becoming stronger based around the topic of the Constituent Assembly and in response to the political opposition articulated in some of the country's regions. Constructing a proposal for the constituent text led to an even clearer and more comprehensive articulation in terms of the actors' participation, including indigenous and sectorial organisations at local levels, as well as the important participation of the so-called 'support institutions'. Thus, there was widespread participation among indigenous organisations that joined the original organisations of the Unity Pact. 'Support organisations'[6] were organisations with a history of cooperation and working together with the indigenous people and their organisations, which, at that time, were highly trusted by these actors. Organisations such as the Centre for Juridical Studies and Social Research (CEJIS), the Centre for Andean Communication and Development (CENDA) and the NINA Programme played a significant role in accompanying indigenous organisations and articulating their demands. During the constituent process, such institutions carried out an important job, providing technical support and organising the meetings and workshops carried out in towns and communities, and turning them into documents. In this way, it can be said that the Unity Pact's proposal constituted an organically constructed, genuine political resource from the Bolivian indigenous movement.

A second important element in the process of constructing the proposal of the constitutional text by the Unity Pact, which illustrates network dynamics, is the tension within the Unity Pact itself – in other words, in the relationship between social movements themselves and how social movements relate to the 'political instrument' MAS. The tension emanated from the dispute for 'prominence and leadership in the propositional context that the Constituent Assembly implied' (Garcés et al. 2010: 59). It could even be said that there were struggles for leadership of the political network, as indigenous movements and organisations were seen to be defining the constituent process.

The task of constructing a single indigenous movement proposal made the differences within this sector visible, because of those perceived to be between different organisations in the Unity Pact. Analytically – and, for that same reason, rather simplifying – it can be said that these differences were due to historical developments. They are also affected by a geographical factor, with indigenous people coming from the highlands and the lowlands, as well as by a factor of political articulation: those who respond to union-type

Table 3.1 Characterisation of the indigenous organisations of the Unity Pact.

	Highlands	Lowlands
Trade union organisation	CSTUCB, CNMCIOB-BS (Bartolinas)	CSCIB (Interculturals, before 'colonisers')
Community organisation	CONAMAQ	CIDOB

organisations (from rural areas) and those who responded to more native organisations – in other words, community-based (indigenous) ones.

From this perspective, the Unity Pact organisations can be described as per the table above.

Even though simplified, the table allows us to understand that the demands and interests of the different organisations can differ significantly among themselves. In that way, it can be argued that the Bolivian indigenous movement is not homogenous and that, therefore, its political articulation – whether through the 'political instrument' (MAS) or in the Unity Pact – has the potential for internal conflict. Indeed, the Unity Pact also suffered moments of internal weakness, for example between October 2006 and January 2007, when it did not manage to convene meetings among its members. As previously said, the articulation of a regionalised, right-wing opposition was perhaps a decisive factor for Unity Pact organisations in overcoming these setbacks and being able to act with a higher level of cohesion during the constituent process. Thus, the blocking of the Constituent Assembly by the actions of opposition groups in the streets and, in particular, the events of 11 January 2007 in Cochabamba,[7] once again motivated the Unity Pact to continue its task of constructing the organisations' proposal.

In the same way, it can be argued that the indigenous social movements that formed part of the Unity Pact did not have an easy relationship with the MAS during the constituent process. The fact that the Unity Pact opted to act on the fringes of the platforms created by the MAS, such as the Presidential Representation for the Constituent Assembly (REPAC) and the 'Group of 12', in order to construct their proposal are particularly illustrative.

According to official information, REPAC was created in March 2006,[8] 'in accordance with Supreme Decree 28627 as a body in charge of the organisation, coordination, diffusion and promotion of the constituent process, as well as having the aim of promoting public deliberation, diffusion, the nationalisation of information and the thematic strengthening of debates on the Constituent Assembly'. According to its official report, REPAC organised meetings between social and institutional organisations as opportunities for deliberation, debate and proposals, and took charge of the distribution of materials referring to the constituent process. Among its main tasks, the report highlights the 'collection of organic proposals from social organisations', the carrying out of 'thematic research into the main topics of conflict', and 'technical support for constituents who require it' (Vicepresidencia del Estado Plurinacional 2009: 7–8, 83). 'The Group of 12' answered to the presidential directive, announced in November 2006, that the MAS constitutional proposal would be drawn up by a team made up of four representatives from the Executive branch, four assembly members from the MAS benches and four from social organisations (Garcés et al. 2010: 60). The creation of this group should be understood as an attempt by the government's high command to group together, lead or otherwise 'control' the range of arenas of deliberation, debate and proposal that spread throughout the national territory.

It is difficult to mark the lines that divided the instances of the Unity Pact, the REPAC and the 'Group of 12' as separate institutional spheres from social ones, or social movements from the state apparatus. In this period, the limits between both fields appear to be particularly 'gaseous' or 'porous'. Through its 'organic' representatives in the Constituent Assembly, the social movements/organisations that made up the Unity Pact also formed part of the institutional fields of the MAS political party and the Constituent Assembly. In the same way, REPAC offered to coordinate with social organisations and civil society in order to collect together their proposals and organise them, while the 'Group of 12' explicitly represented social organisations. At the same time, the conflict and asymmetry of the 'state–society interface' were reflected in the failed meetings between these groups. The Unity Pact meeting on 19 January 2007 concluded: 'The groups supporting the assembly are widely dispersed; everyone has their own support group (the organisations, the government, the vice-presidency) but we have neglected to coordinate them, and this means that every effort is being carried out separately' (Garcés et al. 2010: 59).

The need to unify and coordinate the proposals of the different sectors of society, and in particular of the indigenous social organisations, was also perceived by the Unity Pact. In the meeting previously mentioned, it was also decided that there should only be one specialist team supporting the indigenous social organisations that would work on a single proposal. This team would be composed of representatives of the indigenous social organisations and their 'organic consultants' from the support institutions (national NGOs), representatives of the Executive branch consultants, representatives of REPAC, the assembly consultants and the assembly members themselves. Understanding that efforts needed to be unified and coordinated, the 'Group of 12' was reorganised and relaunched, made up of representatives from the Executive branch, representatives from REPAC and consultants from the organisations. However, this new form was short lived as it never even achieved a first meeting. Almost immediately there was a very limited participation from assembly members, in particular due to the refusal to admit members from the indigenous social organisations' team of specialists (specialists from the support institutions) (Garcés et al. 2010: 59–60). Quoted in Garcés et al., it is even maintained that the 'Group of 12' was created with the aim of taking control of what the Unity Pact had been developing. The fact that in the end it arrived at a kind of collaboration – albeit tense – between the 'Group of 12' and the Unity Pact shows that the aim was not achieved. As the leader of the CIDOB said:

> So that it wasn't an Eastern Bloc district proposal, we took it up to what is the Unity Pact (five confederations at a national level). We opened our doors to them so as to have a single proposal, but before that we had already fought with the government's 'Group of 12', because this group was drawing up a proposal that did not reflect the spirit of our people, our communities and much less our organisations. It was interesting that, once we joined the Unity Pact, we met at CIDOB Headquarters to do it [to bring together], the proposal of the 'government's 12' ['Group of 12'] and the proposal that was ours, of the social organisations, to discuss things among ourselves and thus have a single national proposal that could be presented to the assembly members from the Movement towards Socialism, so they [the MAS bench] could defend it in the Constituent Assembly. (Taco 2010, personal interview)

In March 2007, the Unity Pact approved the decision that the Eastern Bloc should present the Pact's proposal to the Territorial Assembly in Santa Cruz that was to be held by the Constituent Assembly. The collaboration with REPAC and the 'Group of 12' was extremely important since, from that moment onwards, the proposal took on a constitutional form and consensus was achieved, which allowed the Unity Pact's final document to be approved on 23 May 2007 (Garcés et al. 2010: 62). The final result of this joint effort was presented in the Constituent Assembly as the proposal of none other than the Unity Pact, which means that it was the indigenous-peasant social movements who managed to channel and direct the different forces emanating from sectors of society into one proposal to be inserted into the constituent process. In other words, in the scenario of a 'state–society interface' (marked by tension, conflict and negotiation), the 'Unity Pact' political network was successful in giving a voice to a series of actors with the aim of constructing a proposal for the country's new political constitution.

The fact that the Unity Pact managed to construct a complete proposal from the ideas of the indigenous movement, is significant. It shows that the different organisations had the capacity to heal differences and tension using a process of dialogue and consensus. As Walter Limache explains:

The organisations made a qualitative jump from interpellant to proposing answers. This was demanding for this sector; it required the capacity for construction and imagination, and the capacity to know the problem and the context for proposals to be made. It also demanded that these proposals were not merely based on sectorial interests but that they fundamentally aim for a collective interest, and be for the common good. (Limache 2010, personal interview, 10 November)

The organisations from the indigenous social movements thus show an effective modulation from voicing demands to propositions with a more integral vision. This is important since it tensions with definitions of social movements that characterise them as 'contentious' actors motivated only by a very limited number of specific/particularistic interests.

In the same way, the fact that the only comprehensive proposal for the constitutional text came from indigenous organisations is significant. Many sectors worked on proposals on specific topics of particularistic interest, and far removed from the degree of complexity and reality of the Pact's proposal. Integral proposals from other political parties were not seen either, since these opted for a reactionary attitude to distort the constituent process (as will be seen further on). Even more important is the fact that the indigenous organisations managed to force the MAS to adopt their proposal as the benches' official one, turning the Unity Pact's proposal to the single reference point on which negotiations were held, and on which the text for the new constitution was finally created. Thus, the Unity Pact's proposal proved the political role and centrality of social movements in one of the most important political moments in the history of modern Bolivia.

Social Movements and 'Political Networks' during the Constituent Process

Although the Constituent Assembly was organised within the formal and traditional political framework of the political parties – as opposed to what was projected by the social movements – the indigenous movement managed to maintain and defend this space of 'state–society interface' in a relatively successful way, ensuring that their demands and proposals were taken into account. The construction of an integral proposal for the constitutional text is indicative of the 'qualitative jump' that indigenous social movements made. In the form of the Unity Pact, they modulated from protest to proposition, demonstrating their capacity to be inserted in the formal political practices of deliberation, consensus and voting.

This modulation or insertion into formal political fields could question the appropriateness of talking about 'social movements'. However, social movements effectively maintained mobilisations during the constituent process. During the drawing-up of their proposal (not exactly an action of struggle or activism), the indigenous movement carried out autonomous political actions, operating beyond the spaces created and proposed by the MAS (the REPAC and the 'Group of 12'). At the same time, they sustained practices of collective action to ultimately push their proposal in the assembly, continuing with their starring role as social movements in politics. The social movement, as a format for participation within the 'state–society interface', is also expressed by the fact that the political opposition – i.e. the elites that were being displaced – also adopted popular proposals and decided to adopt practices of collective action. In this way, the political struggle that was being fought within the Constituent Assembly also took place outside the institutional structure – as clashes between social movements in the 'informal' are of the streets.

The Social Movement as a Participation Format of the 'State–Society Interface'

The first years of Morales' government were marked by a tie between the political forces of the economic elite who saw their power dwindle and a new force that had still not been consolidated. This 'disastrous tie', as Álvaro García Linera calls it, made the implementation of the reforms projected by government authorities considerably more difficult. Thus, from the very beginning, an intense struggle erupted within the assembly that, on many occasions, impeded the functioning of this body and even came to put its future at risk.[9] From its inauguration – on 6 August 2006 – there was conflict about the assembly's voting procedures. Headed by the main right-wing party, PODEMOS, the opposition defended the approval of each article by two-thirds (in line with the figure proposed by the Convening Law), while the MAS suggested that the articles should be approved by a simple majority and that only the final text should be subject to the approval of two-thirds of the assembly. In the same way, the MAS defended the 'original' nature of the assembly, completely empowered for the 'refounding' of the state, while the opposition announced the 'derived' quality of the body and said, therefore, that it was subject to existing institutional procedures.

The opposition's demand of the 'two-thirds' led the indigenous social movements, through the Unity Pact, to draw up a manifesto in which their organisations declared a 'state of emergency', since they understood the conflict as an attempt to sabotage the assembly's work. Everything seemed to indicate that, in the end, this was the opposition's strategy. In this way, the manifesto called for an immediate demonstration in the city of Sucre, and the forming of 'committees of defence of the assembly' (Garcés et al. 2010:

52–52). Towards November 2006, the different organisations coordinated to establish a constant 'vigil' of the assembly, with the installation of a head-quarters for these organisations in Sucre.

The controversy went on for months and the conflict became more and more political, with an agreement finally being reached using a mixed for-mula, in which both the commission's reports and the large-scale consti-tution project would be approved by an absolute majority, while detailed approval –article by article – required two-thirds of the votes (Paz Patiño 2007:166). This decision not only showed the strength of the opposition but was also the first major concession by the MAS. The decision was in total opposition to the Unity Pact, a body that had continuously rejected the two-thirds proposal. This situation made the relative autonomy of the MAS and the Unity Pact in relation to one another and the differences between the Unity Pact and the MAS on this point very poignant, at least at this stage.

It is worth highlighting the practical effect of this mixed formula. The opposition – with 39 per cent representation – could not approve any arti-cle by itself but did have sufficient votes to veto any proposal presented by other factions, since such veto required only 33 per cent of the votes (Webber 2011: 87). In other words, both how assembly members were elected and the voting regulations within the assembly favoured considerably (some would say disproportionately) the position of the right-wing minority, embodying once again the asymmetric relations characteristic of the 'state–society interface'.

The political struggle continued during 2007, forcing the postponement of the closing date of the assembly. In this period, 'civic' social movements had the greatest influence, managing to bring the assembly's sessions to a vir-tual standstill towards the middle of the year, galvanising the 'capital' issue.[10] This was a difficult topic for the government, since it caused internal division: the MAS had twelve representatives from Chuquisaca district who supported the return of the capital seat to the city of Sucre, as did the allied Movement for a Free Bolivia (MBL) party (Deheza 2008: 65).

The success of the opposition movements[11] obviously had repercus-sions for the indigenous and popular social movements who paralleled the construction of the draft proposal for the constitution with the collective actions considered necessary to defend it. Important examples are the Sixth Indigenous March that departed from Santa Cruz in July 2007, heading towards Sucre with the aim of defending indigenous recognition in the assembly, as well as the march of the coca growers in the Yungas region at the end of August. The polarisation of the country, observed both within the Constituent Assembly and in the confrontations between social movements, came to include an evermore racist content. In November 2007, univer-sity students from Sucre took over the headquarters of the Unity Pact and physically attacked the native assembly members. This violence prevented the sessions of the assembly from restarting, since the safety of the assembly members could not be guaranteed (*El País*, 9 November 2007). This once again caused the mobilisation of the indigenous social movements. The marches undertaken by the CIDOB and CONAMAQ heading to Sucre stand out; meanwhile, the opposition, through the 'civic' movements, encouraged the civil strikes throughout the whole country.

The assembly finally opted to transfer its sessions to the city of Oruro. In the auditorium at the city's technical university, and televised live, the new constitutional text was revised and approved in detail. Outside the university campus, peasant and mining organisations from Oruro and other districts held a peaceful vigil (Carrasco Alarrude and Albó 2008: 121). Finally, on 15 December, the new constitutional text was presented to the president in a large-scale celebratory event in the main square in the city of La Paz.

The initial and relative success of the government's political process, having created the Constituent Assembly and produced a new constitutional text, meant the opposition intensified their resistance to the political reforms ahead. Here, the autonomous discourse took centre stage, with an important role for the prefects and the 'civic committees' from the Media Luna districts – especially in the district of Santa Cruz – in what was understood as a movement to 'destabilise' Morales' government (Webber 2011: 124; Zegada et al. 2011: 237).[12]

As previously mentioned, in January 2005, the regional movement in Santa Cruz managed to take possession of the topic of autonomy in the national political agenda. Initially, this concept represented recognition of the indigenous people, and was understood as 'indigenous autonomous regions'. However, the regional economic elite provided different content for the proposal in the form of 'district autonomous regions', with a particular interest in gaining decision-making power over the existing natural resources in their regions, and directly capturing the economic benefits that these produced. With this discourse, new life was given to the old tension between the country's east and west, more specifically between *cambas* and *collas*, reinforcing, in particular, the racist content of such opposition.

Seeing themselves losing their traditional position of power in institutional structures at a national level, the local economic elite looked to fortify themselves in regional governments, strengthening their ties with local civil movements. From this perspective, the autonomous discourse was, to a great extent, instrumental. The election of constituent assembly members, held on 2 July 2006, was accompanied by a referendum that asked the population about the creation of autonomous *districts*.[13] Although the NO vote – supported by government authorities – obtained a modest victory of 57.6 per cent, the YES vote won by a considerable margin in the Media Luna districts, making the country's regional divisions visible. Anecdotally, it must be indicated that the topic of autonomy first appeared in the discourse of the MAS candidates in these districts, but a counter-order from La Paz forced a change of position which, a posteriori, was considered one of the most serious errors of perception of the MAS, since it passed the banner of autonomy to the right-wing opposition.

The autonomous movement once again came to prominence after the approval of the constitutional text in the assembly at the end of 2007. Ongoing negotiations with the government were blocked until February 2008, causing the autonomous prefects to come together unilaterally in a referendum on the autonomous statutes. The MAS response to this political act was that in a session in which the opposition representation was absent, Congress decided to call a referendum to approve the new constitutional text. However, both initiatives were rejected by the National Electoral Court.

The Media Luna prefects opted to carry out their referendums irrespective of what the Electoral Court had dictated, while the government accepted that the question of approval of the new constitution be postponed. The referendum was held in Santa Cruz in May 2008, and in June in the districts of Beni, Pando and Tarija, all showing rather ambiguous results. Although the statutes had a high level of approval (around 80 per cent), the number of people who did not vote (an estimated 62 per cent) suggested support for government authorities, who emphasised such referendums were illegal (Assies 2011: 109). These percentages were relative, given that there was no independent control nor any impartial international observers.

These referendums certainly served the political opposition to attain a degree of legitimacy based on the demand for autonomy, stimulating the continuation of their means of pressure. With a majority of district prefectures in their power, the opposition judged that the moment had arrived to hold a referendum to revoke the mandate of President Evo Morales. The recall referendum was actually a MAS legislative initiative that until then had been blocked in the Senate. Faced with increasing conflict, government authorities immediately responded by accepting the proposal for such referendum, on the condition that, together with the vice-president, the district prefects would also submit their terms to citizen consultation. From then onwards, social movements, the MAS and the government regained the political initiative, with strong campaigns both in favour of and against the relevant authorities and their opponents.

The recall referendum took place on 10 August 2008, with the participation of more than 80 per cent of the eligible population. Morales' presidency was ratified, with him winning 67.41 per cent of the vote, which was 10 points more than in the presidential elections in 2005. Of the eight[14] prefects involved in the referendum, those from Santa Cruz, Pando, Beni and Tarija (government opponents) were ratified; while the prefects from Cochabamba and La Paz (also from the opposition) lost their positions. This once again expressed the degree of division in the country but, at the same time, provided an undeniable legitimacy for Evo Morales and the Movement towards Socialism. In the event, the winnings were in plain sight, since the government authorities took over lost ground from the opposition and secured their advance, while the opposition saw their power dwindle.

These confrontations caused all the actors in society to mobilise, with each position looking to mobilise the most number of people. The country was the scene of multiple town council meetings, demonstrations, stoppages, strikes and marches, which took place in different locations and which often ended in violent confrontations. Thus, the question of autonomy served to define the division between the government's allies and the opposition (Deheza 2008: 62). The opponents of the government expanded their more conventional strategies – such as media campaigns – to include 'mobilisation repertoires' traditionally used by popular actors (Zegada et al. 2011: 237). For example, within the assembly, opposition representatives went on a hunger strike during the dispute over voting regulations, while more than two thousand people marched in Sucre in support of them. In the Media Luna districts, a series of town councils decided to form an autonomous board in December 2006, and in August 2007 an Institutional Committee decreed a civil strike and started a hunger strike to reject the resolution approved by the Constituent Assembly to end discussion about the topic of the 'capital'. In 2008, the Chamber of Industry and Commerce (CAINCO), made up of businessmen, approved a blockade of lorries, a measure that went on for a long time (Moldíz 2009: 140). This event presented a kind of co-optation of the local 'civic movements' by business leaders to defend economic interests.[15]

Paradoxically, it was precisely the use – or more specifically an overflow – of these measures that caused a 'breakthrough' among the political forces. The worsening of the conflict became visible in its evermore racist content, and the high levels of violence to which the autonomous movement recurred. This was perhaps the most decisive factor in the loss of legitimacy and the ultimate collapse of the opposition forces. The intensification of violent racism was seen in 2008 in particular. The events on 24 May of that year in Sucre stand out, when the indigenous people who had met up in this city to welcome the president were humiliated and attacked in the main square by 'civic' groups, leaving over twenty injured (*Agence France Presse*, 24 May 2008).

Another episode occurred when, after the recall referendum, President Morales called together the prefects from the Media Luna for dialogue on the topic of autonomy and the redistribution of the royalties from hydrocarbons.[16] These negotiations collapsed, setting off a series of mobilisations in the districts that were accompanied by attacks on state institutions, as well as on the offices of other non-governmental organisations in Santa Cruz and Pando. These events caused the first friction amongst the economic elite, who feared that the violence would affect the business environment (Assies 2011: 109–10).

The racist violence[17] observed in the confrontations between social movements culminated on 11 September with the so-called Porvenir Massacre. Rural inhabitants from different locations in the Pando district gathered to head to a meeting held by the Single Peasant Workers' Trade Union Federation of Pando (FSUTCP). According to supporters of the prefecture, the real aim of this mobilisation was to retake the offices of the National Institute of Agricultural Reform and ask for the resignation of the prefect at that time, Leopoldo Fernández. According to a United Nations report,[18] after an initial confrontation in the Tres Barracas neighbourhood, the situation got worse in El Porvenir. People arrived from Cobija, the district capital, with lorries from the prefecture dumping dozens of armed people there to fight the unarmed marchers. 'Wide-scale shootings',[19] as well as the persecution of individuals and the execution of some of the indigenous leaders, left at least eleven dead and fifty injured.[20]

In response, more than twenty thousand indigenous people and government sympathisers from other sectors marched towards the city of Santa Cruz, denouncing what had happened and protesting against the radicalisation of the 'process of change'. Once again showing their position, both within the government and in society, many MAS leaders made their support of the march public while, in his capacity as president, Morales called for the blockades to be lifted to begin negotiations with the right-wing in the city of Cochabamba under the auspices of UNASUR. The Union of South American Nations, under the presidency of the president of Chile, Michelle Bachelet, had already denounced what had happened in El Porvenir and condemned the secessionist violence used by the extreme right (UNASUR 2008a).

Condemnation from the international community severely affected the opposition's image, causing a great loss of their legitimacy in the eyes of the citizens, aggravated by a lack of willingness shown in the negotiations in Cochabamba. For their part, the social movements threatened to radicalise their forms of pressure if the autonomous right did not give signs of significant concessions, despite the call of the president for them to moderate their mobilisations. Thus, for example, the miners' federation (FSTMB), calling on the autonomy of the labour movement, expressed its open disagreement with the government's attempt to negotiate a way out with the right-wing.

A way out of the stalemate emerged in October 2008 and was due, to a large extent, to the willingness of Morales to open up a dialogue and come to an agreement with the opposition, accepting some of the main demands, and with the MAS making important concessions (Harten 2011b: 183; Webber 2011: 142). The most important agreements concerned autonomous powers, the process of reforms to the 'two-thirds' constitution, respect for private property, the limits to social control and the distribution of district income. However, perhaps the most important agreement – especially because it will later turn out to be so controversial – is that, during negotiations, the opposition demanded that the question about the presidential re-election be cleared up. The opposition feared interpretations of the 'only once continuously'[21] formulation that would allow Morales to extend his mandate until 2019. This is why it was agreed that re-election should consider the period of government prior to the new constitution. As is widely known, Morales cut short his constitutional period to take part in the elections of December 2009, thus carrying out what was understood as a continuous re-election, meaning he could not stand in the elections in 2014. However, the Constitutional Court ruled that Evo Morales could stand as a candidate in 2014, due to the fact that the agreement violated the constitutional principle that signalled the re-election of Evo Morales in the first election that the brand new Plurinational State of Bolivia, formerly known as the Republic of Bolivia, held.[22]

After these agreements, negotiations moved to Congress, where representatives from different parties revised the constitutional text and made several changes. The political agreement of 20 October 2008 defined changes to more than one hundred of the document's articles. Thus, as Gamboa Rocabado (2010: 168) explains: 'The constitution was rewritten several times due to the intense political negotiations between the government, prefects from all over the country and the opposition ..., since all the modifications and final agreements happened *outside the institutional framework* of the assembly.' These agreements made it possible for Congress set a date for the referendum on the new constitutional text. On 25 January 2009, the new constitution was approved with 61 per cent of the votes.

'Political Networks' and the Media

The political struggle was also particularly visible on the streets, where it often seemed to be a competition as to which side was capable of mobilising the most people. This can be observed in the press reports – generally controlled by the opposition – that hogged the headlines with either blown up or deflated numbers. Here, the economic elite's more traditional strategy of using the media can be observed; inasmuch as they can be considered an actor (Street 2001; Axford and Huggins 2001; Cook 2005; Chavero et al. 2013), they were a valuable ally within the opposition's political networks during the constituent process. This is illustrated by recognition of the need to respond to the media offensive of government authorities. In their official report, REPAC clarifies:

> We have resorted to the media, especially lately, conscious that one of the main battles has not changed, since our main job is to inform the population of the contents of the new Political Constitution of the State, despite the intensive campaign of disinformation coming from the sectors of the opposition, which looks to confuse and distort the country vision that the constituent process wants to put forward to the citizens.

The topic of the media as actors who participate in political networks with considerable influence will be dealt with in more detail in the upcoming chapters. Here, we will limit ourselves to the distinctive feature of the headlines to blow up or deflate the number of participants in the different social protests. In a context of the transition and reformation of the political system, the legitimacy of the different forces in conflict appears to be measured using the basic principles of democracy – that is to say, the number of individuals for and against, who are physically visible and who use the streets as a place of political struggle. Social movements – both those affiliated to the government and opposition ones – were the actors with the most influence in the 'state–society interface' constituted by the constituent process. Both 'sides' of the social movements moved within and outside the Constituent Assembly to achieve their political aims. In this sense, the 'informality' of many of the processes that determined the result of the constituent process should not be understood as 'deficiencies' or 'defects' of the formal process. The concept of a 'state–society interface' allows instead an understanding of such characteristics as part of the interaction between the state and society, particularly in a scenario in which social movements adopt a central role in the political arena.

In the same way, the concept of a 'state–society interface' allows for the dynamics of 'political networks' that had an impact on the constituent process being made visible. One of these networks can be seen in the Unity Pact as a body representing indigenous social movements. Its exact structure varied during the constituent process, with more and more indigenous organisations joining. At the same time, an important part of this body was the institution's 'specialists', who supported the organisation of events to discuss a proposal for the constitutional text and took charge of organising the different ideas into a single document. The relation the Unity Pact maintained with the MAS is also indicative of a dynamic of political network. As indicated, it is strange (if not contradictory) that a body representing indigenous social organisations with political aims would be articulated, when the 'political instrument of the social movements' already existed and was in power. At the same time, the 'political networks' dynamic was perceived in their slightly tense relationship with the MAS within the assembly, although they absolutely supported it outside of this, on the streets and in their opposition to civic movements.

Political networks are also observed in the dynamics that evolved around the seat of the capital, an issue that was effective in obstructing the workings of the Constituent Assembly. On the one hand, it involved a demand that fortified the opposition, looking to make the constituent process more difficult at the same time as it took advantage of the political environment to bring political power to Sucre. On the other, the MAS had twelve representatives from Chuquisaca district who supported the demand. Also, the Movement for a Free Bolivia (MBL), which in the election of constituents had allied itself with the MAS, favoured Sucre's demand. In this way, this 'political network' crossed the (informal) structures of the MAS, dividing it internally. With the same capacity to obstruct the Constituent Assembly, a third 'political network' was articulated under the banner of autonomy with the participation of a series of civic movements, social organisations and political actors (the Media Luna prefects) that had an influence on the constituent process.

Thus, once the Constituent Assembly's work was done producing a constitutional text, said result was subject to a series of revisions in different areas beyond the 'formal' procedures, before being submitted to citizen consultation. First, there were the negotiations between the government and the opposition in the city of Cochabamba. At this point, it is remarkable that the informal arena of the 'state–society interface' included an international actor: the international community, through UNASUR, had a significant intervention at that time. Later, the negotiations moved to the Senate which, although an institutional body, was 'informal' to or alien to the Constituent Assembly. It was here that substantial changes were made to the constitutional text, very much outside of the official 'constitutional power'.

The period 2006–2009 is thus understood as a time for interaction between the state and society, characterised by conflict, negotiation and asymmetrical relations. Regarding social movements, it can be seen that the MAS, in penetrating state structure, was obliged to adopt flexible positions to get out of the political impasse, making concessions to the opposition. Through the MAS, social movements were forced into positions of compromise. The influence they exerted on the constituent process in general and on the MAS in particular thus opened up a space in which the MAS achieved ascendency over social movements – only slightly over those of the opposition, but especially over those affiliated with the government – making a way out of the political stagnation possible.

The influence of social movements, both within the Constituent Assembly and outside of it, emphasises the centrality that this actor adopted in mediation between the state and society. At the same time, it justifies my assertion that the constituent process should be conceived as a 'state–society interface'. As Dagnino et al. (2006) explain, the incapacity of formal channels of political representation and participation (political parties) had the effect of making the political process 'more informal', with an important role for the social movements. This is exactly what the Bolivian case shows, where what occurred outside the institutional space of the Constituent Assembly had the same or even more impact on the final result: the new Constitution.

Initially a period of a year was established for the Constituent Assembly's work, but the formal sessions of this institution were extended for longer, and the constituent process as a whole only ended in January 2009. This delay was, to a large extent, due to the activities of the different social movements, and explains the great importance assigned to the new constitution by these actors. In this sense, the Bolivian constituent process can be understood within the framework of the judicialisation of politics and 'new Latin American constitutionalism', in which marginal social actors took over a discourse of rights and recognised them as vehicles for emancipation. Here, the Constituent Assembly was a proposal from the indigenous movement, and it only came into being due to the activism of the social movements. As Domingo explains, constitutionalism and citizen discourse are nothing new, since they have accompanied the history of independence. What is new is their 'social reach to sectors of society that were historically excluded de facto from citizen constitutional projects'. The appropriation of rights' discourses by subordinate actors is new to the region (Domingo 2009: 50), and the new Bolivian political constitution emerges as one of the clearest expressions of this tendency.

This chapter has proposed understanding the constituent process between 2006 and 2009 using the concept of a 'state–society interface' – in other words, as an arena for encounters and interaction between the state and society, as a response to the struggle of social movements, and characterised by conflict, negotiation, asymmetrical relationships and the influence of 'political networks'. These concepts allow the focus of the analysis to be widened beyond the formal sphere and proceedings of the Constituent Assembly, and to make more visible the events that occurred outside of institutionality, which were defining for the final result. Here, the role of social movements, articulated in 'political networks', stands out, emerging as the main actor for mediation between the state and society.

On the one hand, the important actions of the indigenous social movements are seen in the Unity Pact political network, which not only proposed the Constituent Assembly but also made a considerable effort to elaborate a proposal for a constitutional text. As was seen, this was the only social sector that had the capacity to transcend particularistic interests and adopt an integral vision of the state – a fact that, at least at that time, positioned the indigenous movement in the political vanguard. Equally significant is the fact that, through the Unity Pact, the indigenous social movements took a 'qualitative leap' from protest to proposal. The articulation of the Unity Pact thus questions the definitions of social movements as 'a-political' or 'anti-state' actors characterised by particularistic visions and activism. As the Unity Pact constitutional proposal shows, through its construction, the indigenous social movements demonstrated their capacity of embracing and creating awareness of topics that transcended their specific interests, as well as their ability to sit down to talks, negotiating and creating consensus. On the other hand, the indigenous social movements also gave continuity to collective action 'on the streets', beyond institutions and preventing the failure of the Constituent Assembly, refuting in that way any questions regarding their 'social movement' nature.

However, the centrality of the social movement in the political field is not only expressed in the prominence of indigenous and popular social movements. Perhaps more telling is the fact that the economic and political elite, faced with a scenario of losing power, also recurred to the social movement format to defend their interests. During the constituent process, based on topics such as the capital, regionalism and district autonomy, the opposition made use of 'mobilisation repertoires' traditionally characteristic of popular sectors. This plays down the organisation of the Constituent Assembly based on political parties, and emphasises that in the Bolivian political scenario the social movement positioned itself as the mechanism for political participation.

Thus, the analysis presented here shows how social movements have left their place on the fringes of politics to play a central role in them, assuming mediation between the state and society almost exclusively. In this process, the articulation and influence of 'political networks' in the 'state–society interface' stands out. As seen, this last concept suggests understanding democratisation processes in the sphere of the links, negotiation and transits between civil society and the state. In a context in which formal political institutions seem more and more incapable of representing social diversity, politics transcends formal channels through creating networks and agreements with changing social actors. The New Political Constitution of the State, approved in January 2009, was effectively the result of processes that occurred within and outside of institutional arenas, but it was also to a large extent the result of the 'political networks' that were articulated in this period, based on different topics: 'the construction of a constitution proposal from the indigenous movement', 'the two-thirds in the voting system of the Constituent Assembly', 'the capital' and 'district autonomy', for example.

This group of practices, understood as a 'state–society interface', allows for a greater connection between the political project of society and that of the state, and, for that reason, suggests thinking about a process of democratisation as defined by Tilly (see Chapter 1).

Indeed, despite the many negotiations and adjustments carried out, the new constitutional text showed its innovative and emancipatory potential. Throughout history, the expansion of citizen rights has been the result of specific political struggles, expressing social conquests. As Domingo explains, although 'recognition of new rights … talks of the re-accommodation of the structures of power in society', it is also necessary to play down their capacity for social transformation (Domingo 2009: 49). As seen in the discussion of 'new Latin American constitutionalism', one of its characteristics is the 'transitory nature' of these texts, expressing more a desire than a social reality. Thus, the new Bolivian political constitution is understood, above all, as a project in which it is still premature to say what the real impact of the 'refounding of the state' will be for the state–society relations.

Nevertheless, it must be highlighted that the 'Plurinational State' – as the result of the constituent process – represents an innovative state project, whose content is marked, to a great extent, by the Bolivian indigenous movement[23] making a substantial and real contribution, an aspect that deserves to be emphasised. At the same time, the new constitution is the result of many negotiations and political concessions between the economic elite and the emerging popular forces. Despite many difficulties and the fact that it almost failed, the constituent process was a shared one, with a high level of participation and influence – in particular through the social movement format and the articulation of 'political networks' – by, for better or worse, both the popular movements and the right-wing opposition forces. The position of the latter and the consensus reached with them cost the MAS government many supporters and earned him a lot of resentment, but it is exactly for these reasons that it is possible to consider the New Constitution a new social pact.

Notes

1. Due to the central role of indigenous movements in the political process analysed here, their appropriation of a discourse of rights is of particular importance. The international context also plays a significant role, since Agreement 169 from 1989 of the International Labour Organisation (ILO) has contributed considerably to the promotion and adoption of indigenous rights (Assies 1999).
2. 'Afterwards, part of this movement, in some way, created a kind of alliance or pact that was a little more stable, which ended up being the Unity Pact that assumes representation of the social movements.' Interview with Fernando Garcés, professor at the Universidad Mayor in San Simón. Cochabamba, 11 November 2010.

3. A variety of ideological currents can be identified within the MAS, such as an intellectual left-wing, more radical indigenous positions and a peasant trade unionism, for example.

4. The Social Democratic Power (PODEMOS), created in 2005, was a group of right-wing citizens aiming to unite opposition forces to fight Morales and the Movement towards Socialism in the 2005 elections and afterwards during the whole constituent process. It was led by former president Jorge Quiroga of the Nationalist Democratic Action (ADN) political party founded by the deceased Hugo Banzer.

5. This form of participation is also registered by Sarela Paz Patiño: 'As well as the deliberative work of the commissions, the assembly members were receptive to public audiences to listen to citizens, institutions and social organisations, in order to integrate their proposals and initiatives into the debates in their commissions. Another important deliberative opportunity was local meetings in the country's interior, with assembly members travelling to different districts to meet sectors of civil society and listen to their demands on the new Political Constitution of the State. Proposals, demands and requests were integrated and ordered by subject, based on the commissions, establishing the basis for possible articles for the new constitutional text' (Paz Patiño 2007: 169).

6. Support institutions will be discussed in the following chapters.

7. In a period marked by the uncertainty of political changes and the practical standstill the constituent process had come to, the then-prefect of the Cochabamba district, Manfred Reyes Villa, from the political opposition, called for an autonomous referendum in December 2006. The summons caused social uprising in the form of marches, both supporting and opposing the need for a referendum. On 11 January, the clashes finally led to a violent confrontation that killed three people and left dozens injured.

8. Vice-Presidency of the Plurinational State – Presidency of the Plurinational Legislative Assembly (2009), 'REPAC Report': http://www.vicepresidencia.gob.bo.

9. For more detailed information on the many disruptions to the Constituent Assembly, see the work of Inés Valeria Carrasco Alarrude and Xavier Albó (2008).

10. The PODEMOS party proposed that the assembly discuss returning the seat of government to Sucre, and this was supported by the regionalised opposition in the form of 'Civic Committees' from districts from the so-called 'Media Luna' (Beni, Pando, Santa Cruz and Tarija).

11. Here, the emergence of the 'social movement' format can be seen in the political opposition. As Salman indicates, it is necessary to make this development explicit, since when one talks about 'social movements' in Bolivia, it always seems to be perfectly understood that these are in favour of the government, making opposition 'movements' invisible (Salman 2011: 33). The importance of the existence of 'opposition movements' with an effective political impact is a point that will be made later on.

12. At this point, it is worth noting that the regional discourse of the 'autonomous movement' is not new in Bolivian history. On the contrary, one of the main characteristics of the creation of the Bolivian State is the struggle between regions. As the historian Rossana Barragán explains, current regional antagonism is armed with ethnic opposition and a definition of 'region' that changes constantly according to the political dispute. The frequent episodes of regionalism in Bolivia are related to the process of the construction of the Bolivian State, in which traditional state weakness does not allow for integration, and in which the ethnic opposition does not show sufficient solidarity to push through the construction of a federal government (Barragán 2009). In this way, regionalism refers to colonial events, which explains why it is a common phenomenon in the Latin American region, emerging when the status quo of power relations is in crisis. This, without a doubt, is the case with regionalism, which covered the dispute over the 'capital' during the constituent process, looking to transfer the centre of political power to the domain of the economic elite. In a

similar way, the autonomous movement tried to reduce the central government's power in favour of more regional power that would allow for greater and more direct control of the benefits of natural resources in the different regions.

13. The referendum question was the following: 'In the framework of national unity, do you agree with giving the Constituent Assembly the binding mandate to establish a regime of *district* autonomy, applicable immediately after the passing of the new Political Constitution of the State in the districts where this referendum wins a majority, so that the authorities be elected directly by citizens and receive executive powers, regulatory attributes and economic and financial resources from the national state that the new Political Constitution of the State and the law assigns them?' (italics are mine; Bolivia: Ley de convocatoria a Referéndum Nacional Vinculante a la Asamblea Constituyente para las Autonomías Departamentales, 6 March 2006). The fact that the topic of autonomy is explicitly understood as 'district autonomy' in the national arena is indicative of the opposition's skill to take the – originally indigenous – topic as a means of defending very different interests.

14. The prefect of the district of Chuquisaca was not eligible for the recall referendum, since he had only recently been elected.

15. Hugo Moldíz explains that the opposition was in reality led by an agro-exporter bourgeoisie settled in the district of Santa Cruz, and by a small number of families (around forty) who together concentrated more than three-quarters of the productive land in this district. Thus, the supporters of autonomy looked to confer national power onto the regional level with the aim of returning political power to the dominant classes, which they had partially lost since Morales came to power (Moldíz 2009: 123–25).

16. The government projected a reformulation of the pension system with the use of these resources, which meant a cut to the districts' budgets.

17. At the request of President Morales, the pro tempore president of UNASUR, the Chilean president, Michelle Bachelet, set up a commission to investigate the facts. In this respect, the final report said: 'It is worth assigning particular seriousness, among the events that occurred in Pando, to a racial, discriminatory element or component for ethnic reasons' (UNASUR 2008b: 34).

18. United Nations General Assembly (2009).

19. Ibid., p. 11.

20. Here is not the place to recount the atrocities carried out. For more detailed information on the events, please refer to the final UNASUR report previously quoted.

21. Article 168 of the New Political Constitution of the State.

22. The Plurinational Constitutional Court, a body which, in April 2013, ruled the constitutionality of Morales' candidature: Article 4. Re-election of the State's President and Vice-President.

   'In conformity with what was established in Article 168 of the Political Constitution of the State, the president and vice-president elected for the first time after the constitution came into effect are able to stand for re-election only once continuously. II. The time limit contained in paragraph II of the First Transitory Regulation of the Political Constitution of the State applies to the authorities who, after January 22nd 2010, continued to hold public positions, without new elections, designations or appointments.'

23. Representatives of both the Unity Pact and support institutions that cooperated in the process of drawing up the proposal agreed that between 60 and 90 per cent of the new constitutional text agreed with the original Unity Pact proposal.

4 'Political Networks' in the Post-Constituent Period, 2010–2016

This chapter begins by stating that the content of the relationship between the MAS government and social movements from 2010 onwards is diverse, varies over time and is frequently contradictory. These observations thus make a more conventional analysis difficult, that is to say, an analysis that assesses the relation between the state and the social movements in terms of autonomy and co-optation. This chapter proposes a different conceptualisation of the state–social movement relations as political networks that embody the state–society interface. The aim is to move beyond conceptualisations that pose social movements as either being in line with or against the state, by drawing more complex scenario with sets of changing alliances and oppositions that also involve other civil society actors.

The first section illustrates the dynamics of 'political networks' in the relationship between the MAS government and social movements, discussing the most important socio-political conflicts of the 2010–2016 period. The network analysis makes it possible to observe the incidence of other actors on the relationship by their involvement in the political networks. The most important ones for the case of Bolivia are the so-called 'support institutions' (national NGOs) and the media, whose role is dealt with in the second section. This analysis focuses on these two actors, who stood out during my research, but it must be emphasised that they are not the only ones. Other actors connecting through the political network arguably influence the relation. When observed, the discussion points to them but does not discuss them in detail as they fall outside the scope of this study. The last part of the chapter suggests defining the Movement towards Socialism as a 'political network', placing it at the intersection between state and society, using the justification that descriptions such as 'party' or 'social movements', or even hybrid ones, are insufficient.

'Political Networks' in the Plurinational State: '*El Gasolinazo*', TIPNIS, Health and Justice Conflicts and the Relationship with the Bolivian Workers' Centre

In the state-society relationship during the post-constitutional period, certain conflicts between the MAS government and social movements stand out, illustrating the 'political networks' dynamic and offering a glimpse into the relative autonomy that exists in both areas of the relationship analysed: state and society. Next, the most salient conflicts of the 2010–2016 period are analysed, as well as a supplementary analysis of the relationship between Morales' government and the Bolivian Workers' Centre trade union organisation (COB).

'*El Gasolinazo*'

The *El gasolinazo* conflict refers to Decree 780, through which the government would revoke the subsidising of the cost of liquid fuels,[1] leading to prices more than doubling. This measure, announced at the end of 2010, directly affected the whole population, but, more poignantly, popular sectors. Widespread rejection of this measure was quickly reflected in an increased number of protests and demonstrations.

The position taken in this conflict by the social organisations that constituted the Unity Pact is worth noting, since it demonstrates the nature of the Unity Pact as a 'political network'. From 2010 onwards, the cohesion of the Unity Pact was eroded. My research at the end of that year shows that its representatives were already making distinctions between 'militants' and 'affiliates': the first group was made up of more peasant organisations (such as the CSUTCB) while the second group were of a more indigenous origin (such as the CIDOB). As a CONAMAQ leader explained (Cochi Villca 2010, personal interview):

> There were differences. I think that there are three stages to be considered since the creation of the Unity Pact. The first: to go ahead with the whole Constituent Assembly process right up to the end, basically as a response to the October Agenda. The second: the times when the internal differences of the Unity Pact become obvious; these differences emerged through agreement, through the respect there was at the beginning of the Unity Pact, up to the moment prior to the constitutional referendum. The third stage: after the constitutional referendum up to the moment I think that the Unity Pact became weak, when there was no coordination or internal coordination.

In the same way, the CIDOB carried out an analysis of the differences that distanced the social organisations from the Pact:

In this group of confederations nationally, the MAS party and those who are part of the three national confederations that are direct MAS militants. The CIDOB, which unites thirty-four peoples in the lowlands, are not MAS militants, but allies. The CONAMAQ represents the Quechua and the Aymara from the highlands and are not militants either; they are like the allied CIDOB. This is important to be able to see how this situation emerged in Morales' second term. Right now, social movements are beginning to cause disruption. There's been a difference between the government's first term and all we have achieved with the confederations, and the second term of government. There has been a reaction from the CIDOB and the CONAMAQ. Not from others, who, being MAS militants, are obviously not going to revolt against themselves. We as allies are the critics that make the good and the bad visible. (Taco 2010, personal interview)

This interpretation is shared by the institutions that traditionally supported and worked with social organisations (national NGOs):

At least that's how I perceived it when I talked to some of the organisations, when the electoral circumstances we lived in for the last few years occurred, and in April when they ended. From then onwards, the organisations felt distanced from the government or felt that only some of them – CSUTCB, the 'interculturals' and the 'Bartolinas' – were convened. These are organic bodies for the government; we can say that they have founded the MAS, the IPSP, that they are closer. However, this was not the case for CONAMAQ, the CIDOB, the MST and many eastern organizations that consider the government an ally in the process. The others say 'it's my government', 'I am the government through the good times and the bad'; so sometimes they lose their capacity to be more critical, more assertive. On the other hand, these others – who are many – say we're not organic, we keep our agenda but we're in the process of change. It's with this sector that there has been a certain distancing. (Núñez 2010, personal interview)

The militant organisations showed apparently unconditional support for the MAS government, considering it 'their own' government, while organisations such as CONAMAQ and the CIDOB adopted a more critical position, arguing that the MAS had lost sight of its political north and that the 'process of change' needed to be 'rerouted' through the critical and coercive participation of social movements and civil society. It is here that particular reference to the five Organic Laws that the government aimed to pass to shape the new plurinational state is made. These laws were passed in a record time of four months, and this speed led to conflicts, in particular with the CIDOB. It is thus that 2010 was marked by distance and deterioration within the Unity Pact, which divided the social movements into 'militants' and 'affiliates'.

In this context, these same organisations came together without problems in the protests, strikes and blockades to oppose during the '*El gasolinazo*' conflict. In spite of Morales' efforts to explain and justify the decree,[2] social pressure finally forced the reversal of this measure. On this specific topic, social movements – 'militants' and 'affiliates' – once again found common ground, but this time in opposition to the government.

On this matter, in particular from a political network perspective, a decision was made by the upper echelons of government – emanating from the state – but with the absence of a 'political network' that included social organisations as central political actors. In this way, the absence of support from socio-political actors meant the government's aim did not have the support or legitimacy needed to be implemented. Rather, the effect was the rapid articulation of a political network that opposed the measure, which was sufficiently widespread and had sufficient political resources to make the government backpedal. In retrospect, the common interpretation made by the social organisations was that 'Evo was wrong' and that it had been an error to not 'consult the social organisations first'. Such declarations account for why the social organisation movements were not so much opposed to the government as to government *policy* – that is to say, the specific matter that this disagreement entailed.

The TIPNIS Conflict

The TIPNIS conflict appears critical to the discussion as it constituted perhaps the largest state–society conflict under the Morales administrations, and as it was successful in damaging the image of Morales and his government as pro-indigenous and pro-social movement, while also showing the vulnerability of the unity of the Bolivian indigenous movement. Perhaps exactly for these reasons, the conflict appears quite illustrative of the network dynamics characterising the state–society relation in Bolivia, with a central role for social movements. So the aim of this analysis is to show how the political network dynamics played out in the conflict, embodying the state–society interface.

The conflict was unleashed by the government's plan to build a road that would strategically connect the Cochabamba and the Beni regions – also achieving a more direct connection with Brazil – within a general framework of development and national integration. Of a total of three, the second part of the road ran through the middle of a protected area – the Isiboro Sécure National Park and Indigenous Territory (TIPNIS), making it considerably controversial in relation to issues of indigenous autonomy and the protection of the environment (the rights of Mother Earth), both of which have been vehemently promoted (at least discursively) by Morales' government. In that way, the governmental plan quickly began to be resisted by an indigenous social movement. Led by Fernando Vargas of the CIDOB (one of the social movement organisations that made up the Unity Pact), the indigenous people that occupied part of the TIPNIS area staged a march towards the capital, La Paz, demanding the abandonment of the plan. The VIII Indigenous March to Defend TIPNIS and the Dignity of the Indigenous People of the Amazon, the East and Chaco started in the northern province of the Beni in August 2011, and during its course received increasing media coverage, being renamed the March for Life and Dignity. The march was the scene of violent confrontations with the government, causing much indignation among the wider public and mounting support from urban sectors and civil society organizations.

Indeed, the initial movement of the indigenous populations of the TIPNIS area soon articulated into a wider political network, including a variety of actors. As Rivera Cusicanqui explains: 'During the march and when they arrived in La Paz, the indigenous marchers managed to bring together a large number of groups of youngsters, ecologists, feminists, Indianists and cultural activists, as well as a considerable group of anarchists, who marched with their own flags and placards' (Rivera Cusicanqui 2015: 46). Among these supporters, the participation of national NGOs such as CEJIS and the Earth Foundation stands out as they constituted former allies of the Movement towards Socialism. The political opposition also quickly joined the network, including Juan del Granado from the Movement Without Fear (another former ally of MAS) and Manfred Reyes Villa from the Cochabamba government, making use of the opportunity to criticise and delegitimise the government.

This expansion secured the success of the political network led by Fernando Vargas, forcing the government into negotiations and pressing the Law 180 for the Protection of the Isiboro Sécure National Park and Indigenous Territory, which would be finally approved in October 2011. This law declared the TIPNIS territory as 'intangible',[3] as well as explicitly renouncing construction of the controversial second part of the road project. This success turned out to be temporary, as the newly 'intangible' character of the territory instigated resistance and mobilisation among another group of indigenous populations within the TIPNIS area, serving as the base of articulation for an alternative indigenous movement demanding the construction of the road as initially planned. Under the leadership of the social movement organisation Confederation of the Indigenous Peoples to the South of TIPNIS (CONISUR), representing the Aymaran and Quechuan colonisers who had migrated to the region from the 1980s onwards,[4] a new march departed for La Paz. Other indigenous social movement organizations such as the CSUTCB and the 'Bartolinas' (both of which belonged to the

Unity Pact), as well as the important Federation of Neighbourhood Councils (FEJUVE),[5] moved to support this claim, but this 'contra-marcha' received much less media coverage and citizen support.

At this point, Morales' administration took the opportunity to propose an institutional get-out clause in the form of a 'Prior Consultation', but instead of deflating the conflict, the proposal seemed to aggravate the situation. The CONISUR march was accused of having been promoted by the government as a means to introduce the prior-consultation mechanisms as a legitimate solution, constituting a deceiving strategy to secure the construction of the road. This relates to the fact that CONISUR represented the people to the south of the park comprised mostly of coca farmers – providing an important link to Morales as a national leader of the *cocalero* movement – and counting approximately twenty thousand families. This number stood in contrast to the indigenous population of approximately two thousand in the rest of the area. Considering this data, the consultation proposed by the government arguably presented a manoeuvre to move forward with the project. There was also serious questioning of its 'prior' nature, since both the project's financing and the road's construction were already in progress before the conflict started. In this way, much resistance in the form of collective action was enacted, opposing once again a governmental plan – the realisation of a 'prior' consultation to the inhabitants of the area. The IX March began in April 2012 under the leadership of Fernando Vargas, who this time was joined by Adolfo Chávez, both from the CIDOB. This created a very odd situation in which indigenous people mobilised in opposition to one another, some in favour and others against the indigenous right to 'prior-consultation'. In other words, opposing political networks were coordinated around the issue of the consultation and its nature, effectively cutting through the indigenous movements' organisations.

The political networks appeared not only outside of state institutions. Effectively delegitimising the 'indigenous' government, an offensive was carried out by the parliamentary opposition against the road, siding with the congruent indigenous movements. The latter intensified as the conflict progressed. In January 2012, the most important leader of the CIDOB, Adolfo Chávez, signed a pact with the governor of Santa Cruz, Rubén Costas, one of the main leaders of the opposition to Evo Morales. As a result of this pact, the government of the Santa Cruz region created an Indigenous Ministry with the appointment of indigenous Ronald Gómez. This decision caused a lot of surprise: in a turbulent 2008, Rubén Costas had supported an autonomous referendum in the province of Santa Cruz with an extremely racist content. (*Bolpress*, 5 May 2008).

Perhaps more revealing than such unexpected alliances is the fact that the political network created to oppose the road expanded its links among the MAS' parliamentary benches, effectively destabilising the government. The indigenous congressmen Bienvenido Zacu and Pedro Nuni formed an 'indigenous backbench' to defend TIPNIS, an important division because it put at stake the two-thirds majority that up until then had been under MAS control (*Andean Information Network*, 24 January 2012; *La Razón*, 19 January 2012). In the ministerial cabinet, the minister of defence pronounced himself openly against the road. Once more, discussion and political struggle emerged both in the area of social movements (the indigenous movement organisations and the collective action in the form of marches), as well as inside the institutional spaces of politics. From a network perspective, conflict and discussion took place during the confrontation, a confrontation not between the state and social movements, or between the indigenous and non-indigenous sector, but between 'political networks' of socio-political actors that were articulated according to their position vis-à-vis a *specific matter*: the road's construction.

Among much resistance and conflict, the 'consultation' was finally carried out in November and December 2012, with sixty-nine TIPNIS communities participating. The official report indicates that this consultation process was accepted by fifty-eight communities, with 80 per cent saying 'yes' to the building of the road and 82 per cent rejecting the 'intangible' nature of the territory (Ministry of Public Works, Services and Housing 2012: 265–96). The official report was accompanied by another, elaborated by the Interinstitutional Commission of the Catholic Church and the Permanent Assembly of Human Rights of Bolivia, which had opposing conclusions, establishing that the consultation had not been carried out independently or in good faith (FIDH/APDHB-Bolivia 2013: 21). Upon these results, the government announced its decision to postpone anything related to the building of the road through TIPNIS until 2015. Given the general elections planned for October 2014, this was understood as a way for the government to put on hold an issue that had been highly politicised by the opposition (see, for example, Argirakis 2012 and Morales 2013).

The 2014 general elections saw an attempt to capitalise electorally on the erosion of and damage to the image of the MAS and Morales as a result of this conflict, with the creation of a political network led by the Green Party. Fernando Vargas was asked to be this party's presidential candidate because of his ideological alignment in the struggle to defend nature (*La Razón*, 4 June 2014). The Green Party also included international bodies in its network, being supported by institutions and non-governmental organisations from Europe and the United States, in linking to Global Greens, an international network grouping together ecological parties from all over the world.[6] Next to the 'indigenous' alliance with Fernando Vargas, the Green Party signed a political agreement with CONAMAQ (*La Razón*, 28 November

2013), involving this social organization's support in the upcoming elections. This alliance was particularly important because it brought about the 'break-up' of the Unity Pact.

Despite the fact that CONAMAQ and the CIDOB had been allies against the government in the conflict over TIPNIS, the CIDOB did not endorse their alliance with the Green Party (*El Día*, 29 June 2014). The TIPNIS conflict led to a time of weakness and disassociation for this organisation. In July 2012, the Beni leader, Melva Hurtado, was chosen as president of the organisation by the General Assembly, immediately declaring her support for Morales' government (*La Razón*, 2 August 2012). With this, she openly showed she did not recognise the presidency of Adolfo Chávez, who, at that time, was in the city of La Paz, leading the IX Indigenous March against the government's proposed consultation. Thus, parallel leaderships emerged, disputing the genuine representation of the eastern Amazon's indigenous people.

At least in the public's opinion, the TIPNIS conflict was understood to have caused divisions within the indigenous movement. The context of the 2014 general elections presented indications of that. Indigenous leader Fernando Vargas allied with the opposition in the form of the Green Party to stand in the elections as a presidential candidate. The indigenous congressmen Bienvenido Zacu and Lazaro Taco of the MAS, who had formed the indigenous backbench in defence of TIPNIS, sided with Adolfo Chávez to support the Social Democratic Movement (MDS), founded by Rúben Costas. Rafael Quispe, one of the most representative figures of the CONAMAQ, allied with the National Unity Front led by Samuel Doria Medina.[7] CIDOB, under the presidency of Melva Hurtado, declared its complete support for the MAS Morales–García Linera binomial ticket. In this way, the general elections paved the way for the articulation of new political networks, based on the alliances and disagreements caused by the TIPNIS conflict.

It is worth noting that, despite the high-profile image erosion and instability the conflict caused to the Morales' administration, the electoral opposition did not succeed in turning it into an advantage at the polls. As one of the conflict's main figures, Fernando Vargas won only 2.71 per cent of the vote and Samuel Doria Medina 24.23 per cent, as opposed to 62.36 per cent for the MAS. In my opinion, this was due to the fact that the building of the road through TIPNIS was a too particularistic and specific matter to create a political agenda with a national reach. The opposition undoubtedly used the situation to criticise and destabilise the government but, judging by the results of the election, it was unable to complement this strategy with a convincing alternative national policy proposal.

When analysing the conflict, it can be seen that, as in the case of '*El gasolinazo*', once again it concerns a government decision that lacked the support of a 'political network' that grouped key political actors, particularly the social (indigenous) organisations. At the same time, this led to the articulation of another 'political network' against the government plan, with sufficient political resources to make the government take a step back, at least in 2011. From 2012 onwards, the articulation of a 'political network' in favour of the road occurred, also led by indigenous organisations, which allowed the government to take an apparently neutral position from which to play the role of 'arbitrator' (Salman 2011: 35) and, in this way, lower the political tone of the discussion. The consultation emerged as a conflict resolution strategy, but quickly became itself an issue articulating opposite political networks, affecting its legitimacy. This is the reason that, despite the positive result, the government opted to postpone any steps ahead of the project of the road until after the elections. The electoral period and 2015 were effectively dominated by other topics that eclipsed the TIPNIS matter. In the context of the constitutional referendum on 21 February 2016, Fernando Vargas was involved in a campaign against Morales' re-election in TIPNIS territory (*Página Siete*, 5 January 2016). There were also reports of the construction of another two sections of the road – sections I and III – that did not go through the park (*Agencia Boliviana de Información*, 30 May 2016), although work on the controversial section of the road has remained on hold.

The public image of the Morales government as pro-indigenous and pro-social movement was severely damaged by the conflict, and public opinion seemed to agree that the conflict had had a dividing effect on the Bolivian indigenous movement. The entangled evolution of the conflict gave way to endless discussions about who represented the 'real' indigenous position. At this point it is necessary to reflect on this issue.

The analysis presented above shows that the 'indigenous' character of a movement, organisation and/or leader was not defining for its position towards the construction of the road or its relation to the MAS government. This was seen clearly in the organisations that made up the Unity Pact, where both the CIDOB and the CONAMAQ opposed the road, while the CSUTCB, the 'Bartolinas' and the 'Interculturales' supported the government's plan. The TIPNIS conflict appeared to create an 'inter-indigenous' dispute (Morales 2013: 85) that was more heterogeneous than normal. The apparent contradictions observed at the level of the government as well as within the indigenous movement have led to a series of insightful academic analyses about the meaning of 'indigenous' and 'indigeneity' in Bolivia.

In this regard, a very comprehensive study by Nancy Postero concluded that 'who counts as "indigenous" is a fundamentally political question, emerging from struggles over particular social, cultural, environmental and economic matters during particular moments' (2017: 183). Looking at the Ayllus Rojos movement and the lowland autonomy movement in Bolivia,

Perrault and Green (2013) have argued more generally that indigenous identity is subject to political uses and that understandings of indigeneity are continuously changing. They characterised these movements as territorial projects that mobilise 'essentialised understandings of indigenous identity' in order to attain legitimacy for historical claims to territory and political rights. Similar arguments have been made to understand the TIPNIS conflict. Laing (2015) analysed the differences in the framing of the issues that allowed for alliances, concluding that essentialised understandings of an indigenous identity linked to the environment have been instrumentalised both by the state and the lowland indigenous movement to legitimise competing claims on resource sovereignty.

Nicole Fabricant (2012) has pointed to the mutability of indigeneity as a language for political transformation and legitimisation. Analysing the current Bolivian scenario, she concludes that indigeneity has offered a new language for negotiating new relationships with the state. This new language, however, is not unequivocal. The TIPNIS conflict can be understood as the clashing of two emergent projects of '*lo indigena*' in Bolivia (Burman 2014). In a similar vein, Canessa (2014) speaks of a conceptual distinction between an 'inclusive national indigeneity for the majority which seeks to co-opt the state' and 'a concept of indigeneity for a minority which needs protection from the state'. According to the author, the TIPNIS conflict illustrated how a national indigenous culture has the strong potential for excluding marginal indigenous groups. Looking at the conflict, in a more recent publication Fabricant and Postero (2015) concluded that both the government and the lowland elite claimed to defend the interests of the indigenous populations, but in different ways, and that, in shaping their arguments, actors both in favour and against, denied indigenous agency and the structured effects of the economic system.[8]

The fundamental issue seems to be the one observed by Canessa (2014: 156): 'There is an inherent tension between the universality of indigeneity as a powerful and enabling globalised concept and the fact that the discourse of indigeneity is one that lays claim to a cultural and temporal specificity'. Indeed, as pointed out by Lucero (2008), the weakness of the literature on the indigenous movement is precisely its tendency to speak of the movement as one. The studies on the TIPNIS (reviewed above) support that view, as they show how the conflict has been important in materialising the often contradictory dynamics of indigeneity in Bolivia (McNeish 2013), pointing to the 'ever shifting semantics and semiotics of the concept of the "indigena"' (Burman 2014).

My analysis of political networks appears complementary to these studies. My aim is to show how the TIPNIS conflict can be understood as the articulation of different political networks that embody the state–society interface, in which the indigenous movements take up a central role in different constellations of alliances: the structures and processes of the conflict. The studies mentioned above are about the content of the conflict and its deeper origins, about how those alliances and relations are shaped and informed: 'indigeneity' as a language of negotiation, and the establishment of alliances based on the framing of issues by conflicting meanings of the 'indigenous'.

From the perspective of a political network analysis, it seems that the specific matter – in this case the construction of a road – acts as the trigger that sets all that content in motion. Through various and conflicting meanings of 'the indigenous', oppositions and alliances emerge that shape and articulate the political networks.[9] Seen from a political network analysis that acknowledges the 'shifting semantics and semiotics' of 'the indigenous', it seems inaccurate to speak of the 'incoherence' and 'contradictions' of the Morales government, the indigenous movement organisations and/or the opposition (governmental plans and discourse, unexpected alliances, co-optations, etc.), as the 'content' does not seem to be *fundamental* to conflict, but *instrumental* to very concrete issues – in this case, the construction of a road.

Health and Justice Sector Conflict

A third example of the importance of the specific issue in the relationship between state and social movements is the conflict with the medical sector that occurred in April and May 2012, following the government's plan to extend the doctors' working day from six to eight hours.[10] This idea was firmly rejected by the sector, with measures immediately organised to exert pressure, paralysing the public health service for fifty-three days through hunger strikes and marches. The strike was supported by the Bolivian Workers' Centre (the oldest trade union organisation in the country) and, once again, was given wide media coverage. The repeated failure of negotiations forced the government to 'suspend' the decree. The conflict continued then about the specific content of the term 'suspension' (the term is not a legal one), and mobilisations demanded it be repealed.

To resolve the conflict, the government created a summons for a National Social Summit of Health, in which not only the health sector and state agents but also social organisations were to participate. This event aimed to design a new health system and to solve the sector's problems, including the duration of the doctors' working day and the implementation of a universal health system, a plan that had been blocked by a majority opposition in the Senate during the 2006–2009 mandate. The summit would be organised by the Ministry of Health and Sport, assisted by the Bolivian Workers' Centre, the Bolivian Public University System and the National Health Council. The summit's organisation then suffered a series of delays related to disagreements over who should participate and how, as well as because of the decision to organise provincial summits that would end in a National Summit. In May 2013, the summit's organisation was seriously affected by a confrontation between the government and the COB over the new Pensions Law. With the delay also caused by the holding of provincial summits, the National Summit ended up being officially postponed until 2014 (*Página Siete*, 27 December 2013).[11] However, at the time of writing (August 2016), the summit has still not been held for reasons that are unclear.

As a result, in January 2015, the president announced the implementation of a single health system, but there is little clarity about how this plan is actually being implemented (*La Razón*, 23 January 2015). In 2013, after the conflict around the medical sector's working day, the government did introduce a primary health care plan called 'My Health'. This initiative, carried out on the advice of Cuban specialists, has been relatively successful. Thus, in June 2016, the International Meeting about Primary Health Care Experiences was held in the city of Cochabamba, Bolivia. During the event, the Pan-American Health Organisation (OPS) praised the advances made by Bolivia, naming it as one of the most advanced countries as far as bridging gaps was concerned. In the same way, the OPS celebrated the fact that, in its five-year plan for 2016–2020, the government was aligning its aims with the strategies and resolutions proposed by the OPS Executive Council. Although, as far as health is concerned, the plan makes allusions to consolidating social cross-sector participation with the involvement of social organisations, there is no specific mention about holding a national summit as was initially envisaged.[12] It is worth noting that the previous development plan (2010–2015) had made no reference to social organisations' participation in the area of health.

The government's call to hold a summit once again shows the need for projected reforms to be defined and maintained by a wide social base, made up not only of specialists but also – and above all – by (popular) social organisations. The success of the health workers' social movement in bombarding the government plan with questions should be understood in relation to its capacity, as a political network, to bring together important socio-political actors (with sufficient political resources) with a specific demand: to maintain the six-hour working day. In this case, the support the social movement received from the COB, one of the most important and legitimate popular organisations in the country, should also be highlighted, as well as the media coverage, which revived citizens' fondness for the movement, thus creating pressure on the government.

In this conflict, the absence of indigenous organisations from the Unity Pact is noted. This is partly explained by the overlap between this and the TIPNIS conflict, at a time when the health service was not considered a priority by the indigenous sector. At the end of 2013, when conflict around

TIPNIS had calmed down, the CSUTCB and the 'Bartolinas' rural organisations – normally considered government allies – gave their opinion on the matter. These organisations made plans to autonomously organise a National Health Congress to replace the government's summit, with the aim to prevent further delay on universal attention. Both the COB and the health professionals' sector reacted by defending the government idea of carrying out the summit, arguing that otherwise 'it would show contempt for the president's commitment' (*La Razón*, 24 October 2013).

The slightly confusing image that emerges from the possible alliances in this conflict is partly due to the fact that, as opposed to at the beginning of the conflict, this was no longer about a specific matter – the number of hours in a working day – that put the government up against a certain social sector. Rather, the government was proposing that reforms to the health system, with its integral problems, be discussed at the summit with the whole of society (represented by its organisations), and to thus redesign the health system according to a universal scope that would stand the test of time. In this way, the government managed to leave behind the bipolar and sectorial nature of the matter, and made it less likely to become politicised. At the same time, it became a much more complex problem for socio-political actors, who hoped to form a 'political network' wide enough to maintain and also *define* the level of reform that they wanted to achieve. In this way, there was an easing in the social conflict, which allowed the government to advance with other non-controversial programmes and health projects while it waited for the social summit.

Something similar occurred in the area of justice, with the justice reform being perhaps the most urgent and complex topic that the reformative MAS government faced. During the constituent process (2006–2009), the judicial power experienced one of its greatest legitimacy crises. The resignation of several magistrates due to pressure from the Executive paralysed the Constitutional Court for almost three years, at the same time as significant reforms to its very basis were being proposed. With the approval of the new Constitution in 2009, it was decided that the power to impart justice should come from the people (Art. 178), which translated into the appointment of the highest authorities through elections and universal suffrage. In the same way, the new Constitution recognised indigenous justice as having the same hierarchy as ordinary justice. Since then, a series of laws have been approved with the aim of reforming the justice system,[13] which, up to now, has been weakened. These laws include special faculties awarded to the president to designate interim authorities during the transition and adjustments to the new constitutional text.

Given the topic's complexity, it can be argued that social conflict has not been expressed through social protests as such, but rather in high levels of citizen distrust and constant complaints of weakness and a lack of autonomy in the judicial system. This social rejection saw a clear expression concerning the process of electing the highest judicial authorities, which involved many objections from the political opposition and citizens, in particular in relation to the preselection of candidates in charge of the Legislative Assembly. The result was a campaign in favour of a null or empty vote, with these effectively overtaking the number of valid votes at the polls (Pásara 2014).

At this point, the government recognised the need to count on the backing of civil society organisations to generate legitimacy and a capacity for reform in the judicial arena. After the Constitution's approval, and counting as well on a majority in the Senate following the 2009 general elections, Morales' administration went ahead with a series of reforms by passing laws and decrees that have not particularly helped to improve the workings (or image) of the judicial system because they have not been supported by the relevant actors in either the judicial system or the civil society organisations. Thus, on assuming his third mandate as president in January 2015, Morales announced: 'We are going to hold a summit to cause a revolution in Bolivian justice. All sectors of society are invited to take part in this profound transformation of Bolivian justice' (*La Razón*, 22 January 2015). The need for such a summit demonstrates again the relative character of the autonomous capacity of the state, as this plan anticipated and thus acknowledged that reforms were doomed to fail if not supported by a 'political network' that included a considerable number of social organisations.

The National Justice Summit was held on 10–11 June 2016 in Sucre. 'Pre-summits' had been held in the regions in May to compile a list of the most important citizen proposals. Members of the executive, legislative and judiciary branches took part in the summit, as well as representatives from different civil society organisations, basing their work on the following topics: redesigning the profile of law students, incorporating life sentences, preventing and fighting against corruption, the delaying of justice, refounding the system using indigenous justice and selecting magistrates by public vote.

Up until now, information on and results of the summit have not been gathered systematically beyond what the press has been able to do. For example, there is no list of the actors who participated in the summit, making it difficult to evaluate how representative the event was, fuelling accusations by politicians that the majority of those who participated had come from sectors linked to the government. The fact that the event concluded with resolutions on each issue suggests a certain level of consensus, but it is too soon to say whether political networks were forged effectively to unite state and society actors and allow for the reforms needed to be sustained. It was soon clear that the implementation of the summit's conclusions would be a long process. Only with the actual implementation of reforms will it be possible to assess if the proposed plans allow for the articulation of political networks that sustain and provide legitimacy for such changes.

Relationship with the COB

The relationship between Evo Morales' government and the Bolivian Workers' Centre is particularly relevant for two reasons. On the one hand, as seen in Chapter 2, the Bolivian Workers' Centre is the oldest social organisation in the country, with notable participation in politics in the twentieth century and with experience of 'co-governing' during the transition to democracy under President Hernán Siles Zuazo (1982–85). On the other, the COB is a traditionally left-wing popular movement that has been a reference for the organisation and political articulation of the Bolivian indigenous movement, as observed in social organisations with roots in trade unions such as the CSUTCB and the 'Bartolina Sisa' indigenous-peasant organisations. In that sense, the COB can be understood as a natural ally of Evo Morales' government. However, their relationship has been marked by tension, which once again highlights the 'political networks' dynamic in the state–society relationship in Bolivia today.

As indicated in Chapter 2, from the 1980s onwards the Bolivian Workers' Centre saw its position and political influence diminish, which was in contrast to the rise of the *cocalero* movement and then the indigenous movement. This was clearly expressed during the Gas War in 2003, when the COB's attempts to play a main role in the protests against Sánchez de Lozada's government failed.[14] Sánchez de Lozada fled due to social protests, leaving the political stage open to an alternative force. The fact that it was eventually Vice-President Carlos Mesa who took charge made it clear that the COB did not have a political instrument – a political party – that could assume political power. By contrast, the *cocalero*/indigenous movement was already convincingly aligning itself with the MAS under Morales' leadership, resulting in the electoral victory of December 2005.

The COB did not openly participate in the Constituent Assembly period. Their relative absence during the cycle of demonstrations between 2000 and 2005 greatly diminished their legitimacy, pushing them into a more marginal position and one that was critical of the MAS government. The COB's inflexible classist approach towards the proposal of interculturality and complementarity of indigenous culture meant that the organisation was mainly opposed to the MAS government during this period. However, although there were no COB miners' leaders among the constituents, a classist approach was still adopted by various MAS constituents, as well as by other left-wing constituents with a Marxist background. Thus, at the decisive moment – when there was more confrontation with opposing regional right-wing forces – the COB did move to support the government. This approach took the form of a more stable alliance from 2008 onwards, formally announced in the press and formalised by the inclusion of the COB into the National Coordinating Body for Change (CONALCAM).[15] The COB's support endured until December 2009, when the New Political Constitution of the State was approved and Morales was re-elected.

In December 2009, '*El gasolinazo*' brought the COB face to face with the MAS government, when again the specific matter at hand was defining for the nature of the relationship. The COB joined in with the protests of organisations and social movements, which finally ended up with the decree being repealed. Despite not completely breaking up the alliance that had been established in 2008, from this time on the distance between the two increased. In April 2011, the COB was already in conflict with the government, demanding through a series of demonstrations a 15 per cent wage increase, which was 5 per cent more than that proposed by the official plan. After the government made an initial concession – an increase of 1–2 per cent for tradesmen and health workers – the COB was unable to unify the affiliated sectors and was also prevented from going back to its fluid relationship with the government.

The conflict surrounding TIPNIS made the breakdowns within the COB more visible. In 2012, the Bolivian Workers' Centre General Assembly decided to support the march defending TIPNIS, openly contradicting what had been previously announced by the organisation's leaders. During this period, the coca farmers and peasants in favour of the road's construction looked to reinforce their position within the COB and bring it closer to the government's position. The new COB leadership under Juan Carlos Trujillo at first adopted a more conciliatory approach to relations with the government. However, when elections were held at the General Assembly in January 2012, the COB made its independence in relation to the MAS government explicit through the creation of a Workers' Party. In short, the COB was in a difficult-to-define position in relation to the MAS government.

The idea of a political instrument in the labour sector had been discussed within the COB for a while, in particular among the more radical segments. At the beginning of 2013, the Workers' Party was founded, holding its first congress and even presenting a political agenda, but it dissolved quickly. The truncation of the Workers' Party has two explanations. On the one hand, it was blamed on co-optation strategies and government repression of the MAS. On the other, it was related to government decisions in favour of the workers' sector, such as the concessions in the Pensions Law, the nationalisation of the silver mines in Mallku Khota (July 2012), the nationalisation of airport services (February 2013), the nationalisation of the Colquiri mine (June 2013) and the approval of a double bonus for workers (November 2013). In this way, during this period, the COB's position was never particularly clear and was characterised by ambiguity and splits, with these being perhaps the main reasons for the failed attempt at a Workers' Party.

At the end of 2013, the COB once again aligned with the Morales government, in the context of the upcoming presidential elections in October 2014 – in other words, it was a time to confront the 'common enemy'. This alliance was supported with union candidates for the elections, a 10 per cent wage increase, the reopening of mines, and housing being provided to the sectors affiliated with the COB. For its part, the union organisation decided to suspend the elections for union leaders and leaders of other affiliated sectors. In this way, a relative alliance was once again established between the COB and the government. The validity of this pact was expressed at the beginning of 2016, when the COB's National Congress renewed its leadership and decided to support the deepening of the 'process of change'. Reinforcing the pact in this way can once again be understood in relation to another moment of confrontation with the political opposition, namely the Constitutional Referendum on 21 February 2016, whose aim was the re-election of Morales in the 2019 general elections. Thus, on 17 February, the COB made the following announcement:

> Because of its historical responsibility, the Executive Committee of the Bolivian Workers' Centre makes known nationally and internationally the firm decision of Bolivian workers regarding (cob.org. bo):
>
> (1) Their support for the modification of Art. 168 of the state's Political Constitution in the 21 February referendum, to guarantee the reapplication of our colleague Evo Morales Ayma as president, and our colleague Álvaro García Linera as vice-president, as representatives of our class and the people, with the responsibility of taking a closer look at the *Process of Change* until the goal of the socialist state has been reached.
>
> (2) The COB, whether its head office or affiliates, is responsible for and promises to take a closer look at, developing, consolidating and projecting the *Process of Change*, because the liberation of the poor and exploited is their very job.
>
> (3) The COB in the framework of union independence will fight to consolidate the economic, social, political and labour rights of all Bolivian workers and workers worldwide.[16]

In this sense, the congressional resolution made in January to look for empowerment for workers within the so-called 'process of change' was put into acts by association with the MAS government. Despite this, in mid-2016, there was once again a serious confrontation between the COB and Morales' government because of the government's decision to close the state company ENATEX, created in 2012 to save the last great Bolivian textile company. Despite the economic resources available, this government initiative failed, forcing eight hundred workers to be fired, which was highly criticised by the COB and led to demonstrations. The conflict considerably deteriorated the relationship with the government, and a possible rupture of the alliance was announced.

Despite this, the events show how confrontation occurred regarding this specific matter without leading to a complete rupture. As a leader of the Bolivian Workers' Centre expressed in July 2016 at the peak of the conflict (Quispe, J. 2016, personal interview):

> Although we support Evo, we don't accept absolutely everything. The COB maintains its principles and makes complaints to ensure workers are respected … Evo Morales talks of 'living well' but does the opposite. The COB and the government are opposed. This distances us but does not break us, because they have constructed [strong ties with us]. The Workers' Party was not created as we wanted. The aim was very diehard; there was no vision to get ahead, so we preferred to follow the October Agenda with Evo Morales.

Therefore, the relationship between the COB and the MAS government could be described as a love–hate one, and understood in terms of the division/weakening of the social organisation and of more or less successful strategies of co-optation by the government; but this creates a confusing picture of very ambiguous positions. The relationship is better described as a network dynamic, bringing the actors in question closer together or distancing them. In general terms, it can be said that at decisive political moments – of confrontation with the political opposition – the COB is shown as part of the political network articulated by the MAS, in alliance with other socio-political actors and social organisations. In the periods when the MAS government faces fewer threats, opportunities arise so that conflicts and confrontations based around specific matters like sectorial demands flourish.

As in the conflicts analysed, the relationship with the COB shows that the specific nature of the matter in question is the more defining element for the content of the relationship between the state and social movements. This partly coincides with Salman's interpretation that the 'ambivalence of MAS makes several movements oscillate between being allies and the opposition. Their position depends on specific topics and facts, and tactical uncertainty' (Salman 2011: 38). However, whereas Salman talks of three circles of social movements built around the MAS in a kind of gradient of 'affinity' moving towards greater autonomy (Salman 2011, 2013), the network analysis presented here shows a more dynamic (changing) and complex relationship. This analysis explains the observations made by Walter Q. Morales on whether social movements are 'autonomous actors' or rather 'subject to manipulation and official control'. 'The answer to this question is complicated because both situations can and do exist' (own translation, Salman 2013: 87). In effect, verifying the number of positions that the same social movement can take on regarding the government (sometimes in agreement, sometimes in conflict and sometimes rather ambivalent) arguably makes giving unequivocal answers to conventional questions about the autonomy of such actors impossible.

Describing relationships as 'political networks' shows the relative political power the government enjoys, even when it has a majority of members of Congress as well as in the Senate. The most salient conflicts of the 2010–2016 period show that whether a 'political network' – made up above all of social movements (with a capacity for mobilisation) and other socio-political actors with sufficient political resources to maintain and legitimise the proposed plans – exists or not is considerably more decisive. In the conflicts concerning '*El gasolinazo*', the construction of the road through TIPNIS and the length of the health workers' working day, it has been observed that any government decision without this kind of foundation is inevitably cut short.

In other words, in the current political scenario of Bolivia, the institutional structures for the formulation and execution of policies are not sufficient to actually carry out public policies. Such structures need to have corresponding arenas occupied by social movements and other socio-political actors. From a network perspective, it can be argued that, to carry out public policies, a 'political network' constituted of sufficient socio-political actors – i.e. both 'political' and 'social' – is needed. Thus, the Bolivian political scenario coincides considerably with the theory of Chalmers et al. (1997) in the sense that popular representation becomes more and more dependent on the participation of social and state actors in a changing group of 'associative networks' that fuse or blur the limits between activities of 'interest articulation', 'interest aggregation', 'formulation of demands' and 'formulation of public policies'. In this way, the position of Goldstone et al. (2003) that it is necessary to question the divide between 'institutionalised politics' and 'non-institutionalised' ones is supported.

In this part of the analysis, the different social movements' position regarding Morales' government has been looked at from a network perspective, making use of the concept of 'political networks'. This focus also allows us to visualise the participation of other types of socio-political actors who, in this way, also influence the state–social movements relationship. In the following section, we will discuss their role.

Other Actors in Political Networks: 'Support Institutions' and the Media

In the current Bolivian political scenario, two types of actor who take part in 'political networks' particularly stand out, since they have a significant influence on political processes: non-governmental organisations and the media.

In the case of non-governmental organisations, their importance stems from the time of authoritarian regimes, a stage in which they played an important role in resistance. Afterwards, with democracy restored and the simultaneous implementation of the neoliberal model, the contraction of the state apparatus created an opening in society for them to carry out a series of functions. Later, the legitimacy crisis of conventional political institutions (such as political parties) and the political importance of 'social' actors (such as social movements) created a scenario in which politics was no longer only practised at the institutional level.

In the same way, the expansion of politics into areas previously conceived as 'social' has created a context in which the media has acquired a more explicit and decisive role. As will be seen, both the media and non-governmental organisations form part of the 'political networks' that mark the content of the relationship between the state and society as a whole, and the state–social movements relationship in particular. From this perspective, they effectively influence political processes.

Non-Governmental Organisations: Support Institutions (National NGOs)

Non-governmental organisations have played an important part in the state–society relationship for decades in Bolivia, assuming different roles. In a comprehensive look at the role of external help in Bolivia, Rodríguez-Carmona observes the different functions of this type of organisation. During the dictatorship, NGOs served as a 'link between the people and public management', working to represent root organisations and training new ranks of leaders to replace the ones being continuously taken by the authoritarian regime. Later, with the return to democracy, NGOs turned into being 'places and channels for social participation', with their predominantly political function being highlighted. As popular organisations started to demand the right to talk with their own voice, NGOs found themselves occupying a different position, directing their efforts towards more direct types of intervention, in particular regarding rural development (Rodríguez-Carmona 2009: 34–36). With the implementation of structural adjustment policies and the subsequent halt in new hires by the state from the second half of the 1980s onwards, NGOs took on a series of traditionally state functions. The substantial increase in poverty together with the explosive increase in international cooperation funds caused NGOs in Bolivia to multiply and become more professional (Arellano-López and Petras 1994: 558–59).

NGOs played an important role in legitimising and implementing the neoliberal project but, at the same time, they also had an important effect – sometimes intentional and sometimes unintentional – concerning politically empowering of root organisations. Although it is true that neoliberal decentralisation and the expansion of NGOs in civil society caused popular demands to be sectorialised, and, in this way, undermined popular organisations at a national level (as was the case with the labour organizations) (Petras 1997), at the same time it created common ground and training opportunities that significantly contributed to a greater degree of organisational and political coordination (Loayza Bueno and Datta 2011: v).

As far as non-governmental organisations are concerned, the effect of empowering the political coordination of social movements who played an important role in the political scenario in the last few years must be mainly attributed to the so-called 'support institutions'. These entities can be understood as 'southern NGOs' as opposed 'northern NGOs', characterised by their greater sense of responsibility towards the groups they work with (their 'clients') (Malavisi 2010: 54).

In my interviews with representatives from different social organisations, references to 'support institutions' were recurring, indicating a common understanding of who belongs to them and who does not. Such designation is also used in the (scarce) literature that specifically refers to the role of this type of entity.[17] Among the most renowned ones are the Centre for Legal and Social Studies (CEJIS), the Centre for the Development of Labour and Agricultural Studies (CEDLA), the Centre of Andean Communication and Development (CENDA), the Episcopal Pastoral Social Commission (CEPAS-CARITAS), the Indigenous Fund, the NINA programme, and the Centre for the Promotion of and Research into Peasantry (CIPCA). These institutions are characterised by a long trajectory of developing both knowledge and different kinds of activities in favour of the indigenous and rural populations.

These national NGOs have played an important role in articulating an ethno-political identity and providing root organisations with knowledge and political resources to allow for a more effective coordination of demands to the state (Loayza 2010: 15–16). Eulogio Nuñes, director of CIPCA-Santa Cruz, who has worked in this institution for more than twenty years, explained in a personal interview on 5 November 2010:

> CIPCA is going to turn forty. I think it's one of the oldest NGOs. It was created during the dictatorships and I think that it always chose peasants, the indigenous, helping them organise themselves well and produce sustainable and productive economic initiatives ... Also helping these organisations to lobby so that their ideas become public policy, including at a local, regional and national level.[18]

Along the same lines, Walter Limache, national director of the NINA Programme, indicated in a personal interview on 11 October 2010: 'Empowerment has always been the aim of the NINA programme, and empowerment means occupying decision-making spaces and participating in those management spaces from the organisation itself.'[19] It is worth noting that the role these institutions have played in the training and education of social leaders for the political articulation of many social movements took on a greater importance in politics from 2000 onwards. In a personal interview on 16 November 2010 Iván Bascopé of CEJIS in La Paz said the following in this respect: 'We told them they needed to be prepared. They needed to strengthen their organization organically, they had to look after it, improve their administrative capacities and empower themselves with their demands, as other leaders have done in their time, to prepare their processes'. The long trajectory of accompanying and empowering organisations has produced across-the-board relationships and ones in which trust has been established. Walter Limache explained in a personal interview (10 November 2010):

At NINA, we contribute to and work on opportunities for organisations to come together. The space the NINA programme occupies is one in which organisations come together and leaders come with their problems, finding an identity based on the similarities between their programmes and those of other organisations, coordinating them to become a common force... This is the reason why we are so close to the organisations and why there is so much trust. We have been working for twenty-one years and I dare to say with a lot of objectivity about what these very organisations are feeling.

This political coordination and close relationship can also be observed in the work of CIPCA. According to Eulogio Nuñez (personal interview, 5 November 2010):

Our relationship with the organisations is really fluid. CIPCA is an organisation that has seen the APG, the CIDOB, and the Confederations born. With the regional ones, for example, we have supported them quite a lot at the beginning, helping them to become legal. I think that we have a relationship of respect with the organisations, involving open, across-the-board and sincere talks.

Marcelo Ortega, from CEPAS-CARITAS, indicated during a personal interview on 21 October 2010 that the training of leaders is the basis for a relationship of trust: 'Also considering that several leaders have emerged from the training CARITAS Social Pastoral has provided in different regions, if there is a relationship, it is perhaps a more personal one because of the relationship that already existed'.[20]

The relevance and influence of these institutions can be seen in the role they played during the constituent process. At a preparatory meeting of the organisations that composed the Unity Pact in September 2004, it had already been decided that the support institutions would provide a technical team in charge of making the construction of the Unity Pact proposal more systematic. At a meeting of indigenous organisations in May 2006, it was decided that such a 'Technical Commission' would be formed in the following way: 'Two leaders and one consultant from each organisation (CSUTCB, CSCB, FNMCB-BS, CIDOB and MST-B), one technical expert from each Indigenous Educational Block, and one technical expert from each one of the support institutions (CEJIS, CENDA, the NINA programme, CEPAS and CESA)' (Garcés et al. 2010: 44).

My interviews with those who made up part of the technical team are a testimony to the impact these institutions and their participation in the 'Technical Commission' had on the successful elaboration of a single, integral proposal for the Unity Pact. Their proposal would have an impact on the Assembly and finally form the basis for the current constitutional text. In the previously cited personal interview Mr Nuñez of CIPCA observed:

> I had the chance to be part of the technical team ... an invisible technical team. What was visible was not important, but we did quite a lot of intense work on events at a local, borough, county and national level. In the end, we were able to present a proposal for the Unity Pact. And there were many people linked to NGOs, technical experts from organisations, involved in creating this proposal ... it is an opportunity that I value a lot. Many things are thought of by people – that is, using their logic.

These institutions were not only in charge of making the input of the different organisations more systematic for the construction of a single proposal. Before and after the Constituent Assembly period, they provided opportunities and (logistical, organisational and financial) resources for the organisations to come together and be able to work. During a personal interview on 11 October 2010 Walter Limache from the NINA programme explained:

> The creation of the proposal for the constitution took a lot of time. First, each person worked on their own little proposals. When the process from May to August [2006] began, the law announcing the Assembly had come out in March and the date to submit the proposal was 6 August, because that was when the assembly would start. We held six national events, with thousands of hours of technical work between leaders and technical experts, thousands of hours of discussion and revision. We fought with the new people who arrived and suggested things that had already been dealt with. Once the proposal had been presented, we found certain contradictions,

weaknesses in some things and a lack of others during the Assembly itself, until a new one was presented that was more official, coordinated, much more coherent, and that was submitted during the Assembly itself.

Iván Bascopé from CEJIS, who also belonged to the 'Technical Commission', explained in this regard during a personal interview on 16 November 2010s: 'Our technical friends and consultants from other institutions know that at that time we made up the technical team, we really were – I tell you openly – the people who drew up the constitution. We were the first to draw it up, when demands were being made; we drew it up between February and March 2007.'[21]

On this same topic, during a personal interview on 30 May 2010, Sergio Velásquez of CENDA underpins the specific relationship between the technical experts and the organisations, and the intense work of the commission:

> The organisations themselves with the technical team from the institutions had their own dynamic after 2007, when the text in detail was approved. According to the law of August 2007, the constitutional text had to be submitted. They made us work through the night to produce this text, because the assembly members were afraid that they would be accused of not complying with their duties. In the plenary sessions, there was no way of making progress. The MAS, trying to comply with its role at least partially, had to have at least a rough draft. In parliament, they did not want to extend the timeframe, which is why it was fast-tracked – because, if not, there would have been duties not complied with.

The following testimony from Walter Limache (personal interview on 10 November 2010) also shows that there were moments in which the technical experts from these institutions left their supporting positions to take on a more decisive role, beyond the will of the Unity Pact organisations:

> At one point, the organisations were disintegrating. The Unity Pact was disintegrating and all the efforts of the proposal were being diluted. And so we managed to coordinate again, holding an event for five days that ended up being ten, and a very detailed proposal emerged that could not be published because there were four points of disagreement. I decided to publish the text anyway. I took out a run of fifty thousand copies. To the leaders who complained, I was responsible, they should come after me. We sent it by plane to Sucre because there were road blocks. The leaders' initial reaction was focused on finding out on whose authorisation I had published this. And I said to them, 'I'm tired of making photocopies, but let's meet, I want you to tell me what your problem is'. It was distributed in the assembly and caused waves. It fell like a bomb on the whole of the right-wing: the Unity Pact proposal. The next day, the leaders called me back to ask me for more copies.

These testimonies coincide with the literature that made the constituent process more systematic, establishing that, although the content of the Unity Pact's proposal used the same resources and the innovative work of different organisations together, the creation of the Unity Pact proposal could not have occurred without the technical, logistical and financial support of the support institutions. Thus, Loayza concludes that think tanks such as CEJIS, CEDLA, CENDA, CEPAS-CARITAS, CESA, Agua Sustentable, the Indigenous Fund, the NINA programme and CEFREC were crucial to bringing together the different indigenous organisations that, to top it off, formed the Political Instrument for the Sovereignty of the People (afterwards adopting the name MAS), as well as producing a set of knowledge that was used by the social movements to argue their demands and improve their political and negotiating position (Loayza 2010: 15).

Beyond the constituent process, the importance of the links between social movements and the support institutions is reflected in how these opportunities served as a kind of basis for recruiting important MAS and then government figures, among which the NINA programme particularly stands out. David Choquehuanca, chancellor of Bolivia from 2006, was national director of the NINA programme between 1998 and 2005, after being a CSUTCB leader. Evo Morales himself also took part in this leadership training programme (Limache 2010, personal interview, 11 October).[22]

The Centre for Legal and Social Studies produced a considerable number of important government figures, such as Alfredo Rada (who was a government minister, Deputy Minister of Institutional Management and Consular Affairs and then Deputy Minister for Coordination with Social Movements and Civil Society Organisations), Susana Rivero (Minister of Rural Development), Javier Escalente (Deputy Minister of Rural and Farm Development) and Guillermo Dalence (Minister of Mining). Vice-President Álvaro García Linera, who was president of the board of the assembly of associates of this institution,[23] is also on this list, as well as Alejandro Almaraz, Deputy Minister of Territory. The latter summarised his journey from accompanying the organisations to political coordination and finally to becoming part of the Executive body thus (Almaraz 2010, personal interview):

> I was one of the MAS strongman in 1998–99. I was one of the first political leaders of MAS, there were eleven or twelve of us. There was no 'non-peasant' organisation or one made up of consultants. In reality, that's what we were, a group of consultants for the organisations who, accompanying their activities, also led to a level of political projection for the social organisation. We were three lawyers who mostly dealt with agricultural processes. We were Carlos Romero, current Minister of Autonomous Regions, Hugo Salvatierra who was Minister of Rural Development and me. They didn't want to continue so I took on the role [as Deputy Minister of Land].

It should be noted that the presence of these figures in the government did not imply the co-optation of support institutions, as demonstrated by the open confrontations between these types of institution and Morales' government (*Página Siete*, 19 September 2011). Alejandro Almaraz is one of the people who has frequently criticised Morales' administration. In June 2011, a confrontation occurred because of a publication by a group of intellectuals and MAS dissidents called *Manifiesto del 22 de Junio: Por la recuperación del proceso de cambio con el pueblo. Manifiesto de la Coordinadora Plurinacional de la Reconducción* (The June 22 Manifesto: To Recuperate the Process of Change with the People. Manifest by the Plurinational Coordinator for Redirection) (Almaraz et al. 2011). This publication unleashed a controversy that Vice-President Álvaro García Linera responded to the following month with the publication *El 'oenegismo', enfermedad infantil del derechismo (O como la 'reconducción' del Proceso de Cambio es la restauración neoliberal)* ('NGO-ism': A Puerile Right-Wing Illness [Or How the 'Redirection' of the Process of Change is the Neoliberal Restauration]) (García Linera 2011), in which he branded those who had signed the manifesto as 'politically resentful', arguing that their criticism derived from their links to NGOs and foundations that, according to him, had created a 'cushy relationship and neoliberalised mentality towards social organisations' (García Linera 2011: 10). The response was in the form of another publication called *La MAScarada del Poder* (The MASquerade of Power) (Almaraz et al. 2012).

This controversy shows that the presence of NGO actors in state structures and their support for or criticism of the government is a real and delicate matter. This controversy is based around the true sense of the 'process of change' that, at least discursively, should be defined by social organisations inasmuch as it was these groups who both encouraged and took a leading role in the process. However, the fact that the ensuing discussion occurred between high levels of government executives and intellectuals with links to this kind of institution makes it clear that social organisations were never alone. There was an important process that involved accompanying and advising, as well as talks and discussions, in which the social organisations and movements undoubtedly played a main but not exclusive role. The importance and relevance of social organisations and movements is reflected in the contest of who understands best their 'process of change': either the current government or the highly legitimate group of dissidents with their work in support institutions and who have been around for a long time (some for more than thirty years).

Along these same lines, it is easier to understand the subsequent attack by the government on four national NGOs: the Centre for Labour and Agricultural Development Studies (CEDLA), the Centre for Documentation and Information Bolivia (CEDIB), the Earth Foundation and the Millennium

Foundation, some of them with more than twenty-five years activity in the country. In 2015, these bodies were accused of political meddling and were even threatened with expulsion from the country by Vice-President García Linera. The attack was a response to their activism on environmental issues, which, since the TIPNIS conflict, had been the MAS government's Achilles' heel.

The confrontations between the government and support institutions have not had significant consequences,[24] and the fact they occur at the higher levels of leadership is worthy of attention. At lower levels, a work of collaboration and coordination can still be observed, not only between support institutions and social organisations but also with the government. Personal connections from the past are vitally important, as Marcelo Ortega of CEPES-CARITAS explained (personal interview on 21 October 2010):

> Several leaders have taken part in the training that the CARITAS Social Pastoral has carried out in different counties with whom there may be a relationship, perhaps a more personal one because of the previous relationship, but not officially. Institutionally, we have an agreement with the INRA,[25] with whom we carry out sanitation work at a county level. There are programmes in CARITAS that have signed agreements with the relevant government body, although a direct understanding does not exist. Agreements are reached by people who have left here because of their history and tradition of working together, not necessarily because the government's wants to do it. Despite the Church having so much involvement in the terms of health and education, we have subsidised works beyond the reach of previous governments and beyond the reach of this one. We are always looking for new agreements in these areas. (Ortega 2010, personal interview)

From a disaggregated perspective of the state, relations are indeed maintained between government bodies, support institutions and social organisations, based on specific work topics. This is consistent with the observations from a study of NGOs in Bolivia in the 1990s. As far as their relationship with the government is concerned, this study concluded that 'the quality and intensity of these relationships is more or less correlated to the NGO's general capacity … in their sector or regarding their specific matter' (Wils 1995: 276). This shows certain continuity in the way NGOs and the state relate to each other, even when there has been a substantial change to the political elite.

Perhaps even more important, however, is the role that support institutions play together with other NGOs in creating spaces for different types of actors to come together, including state agents and representatives from social organisations. During my research at the end of 2010, the political debate was based around interpreting the regulations and implementation of the new political constitution. This debate was taking place on a range of 'non-institutional' arenas in the form of forums, seminars, meetings and workshops. Examples of the ones I had the opportunity to participate in are the International Forum for Applying the Law to the Previous Consultation (La Paz, 28 September), the *Pensando el Mundo desde Bolivia: 'Refundación del Estado en Bolivia'* International Conference (La Paz, 5 October), the II Post Constituent Seminar in Bolivia on Indigenous Rights in the Plurinational State (La Paz, 18–20 October), the Autonomous Forum and the new CPE, an Interdisciplinary Opportunity for Reflection (Santa Cruz, 4 November) and the Conference on 'Decolonisation and the Plurinational State' (Cochabamba, 10 November).

These kinds of event were organised by NGOs – or rather by institutions financed by them – to provide opportunities for international cooperation. It is noteworthy that the events not only provided an opportunity for meetings between representatives from social organisations and state agents on specific topics but also between other kinds of actors such as intellectuals, academics and political analysts (both national and international). The main aim was communication and information, but mostly *dialogue*, which emphasises the across-the-board and reciprocal nature of this interaction. In these areas, both government agents and the representatives of social organisations were, in effect, equally able to participate in the exchange of information and nego- tiations from their relative positions.

The fact that the organisers did not participate in the talks or negotiations also stood out, as they limited their role to the orchestration of the encounter. This contrasted with their more 'classic' type of help in the form of training, consultancy and unilateral technical assistance, as well as their traditional role representing and speaking in the name of the marginalised sectors. Thus, the international cooperation agencies, NGOs and support institutions appear to have left behind their role as spokespeople or mediators for the indigenous, the poor, and such like, where these actors themselves present their own analyses and initiate talks and negotiations directly with state employees. This coincides with the interpretation of sociologist Jorge Komadina (personal interview on 10 November 2010):

> In the past, there were also events with representatives from the state and from different civil society organisations. The difference is that, prior to these events, the aim was to open up a new political opportunity, whereas now that this has occurred, it is all about participation. Since the channels or participation mechanisms still do not exist, these forums provide an oppor- tunity for deliberation where visions come face to face. There is an import- ant process of politicisation in civil society, always very popular and strong in terms of the discourse's hostility, questions, assuming positions, the other person's way of looking at things, political adversaries, strong vocabulary.

Conventional analysis has allocated the role of mediator between the state and society to this kind of arenas.[26] However, an alternative and perhaps more correct interpretation is that the different types of NGO are one more actor in the 'political networks' that frame relations between the state and social movements, and which therefore influence the content of this relationship.[27] Since these NGOs have the capacity to produce knowledge on specific topics, to provide political and financial resources and create opportunities for encounters between the state and social movements, NGOs are important in creating links based on specific topics. At the same time, because they have political resources, NGOs in the current Bolivian scenario appear to have a role that goes beyond mediation, based on a position in which they effectively participate in defining topics and articulating 'political networks'.

Specific examples of their influence on the political articulation of the indigenous movement can be seen not only when they promote opportunities for encounters but also when they provide knowledge and language to formulate a common political discourse based on an ethnic identity. In the same way, during the constituent process, support institutions formed part of the 'political network' articulated around the specific matter of the formulation of a constitutional proposal based on the indigenous discourse. Although it could be said that the main actors in this network were the indigenous movements and organisations that made up the Unity Pact, together with MAS congressmen and agents in state structures and other social movements, that process would not have achieved the same results without the role played by the support institutions, academics and intellectuals.

In other words, the specific matter of the formulation and approval of a constitutional text – using as its basis the discourse and resources of the indigenous movement – was successful to the extent that it managed to articulate key socio-political actors (for example, social, political, intellectual and NGO movements and organisations) with sufficient political resources into a 'political network'. In the same way, the TIPNIS conflict affected the government's position and legitimacy because a 'political network' was formed around it, made up of movements and social organisations, state agents, NGOs and intellectuals, all with sufficient political resources to enter into conflict with the 'political network' that emerged in favour of the government plan.

This also explains the fact that one of the highest state structures, the vice-presidency, was concerned both about responding to and undermining the criticism of the government party's dissidents with a history in support institutions. It is about actors who enjoy great legitimacy, and their opinion is therefore a threat inasmuch as they criticise the current government. However, this also explains the fact that academic and intellectual actors will never be lacking in the events previously described. Such (national and international) actors have important political resources – knowledge, expertise, prestige in the eyes of other bodies – which is why a 'political network' coordinated around a particular topic benefits from their participation.[28]

This interpretation coincides with the analysis of Haug (2013) on the importance of social movements having opportunities to meet and deliberate, as well opportunities to meet with other actors. Making specific reference to the coordination of networks, Haug explains that the creation of a collective identity is not the only way that a network can become a group actor. According to Haug, meeting opportunities are part of the social movements' infrastructure. Thus, the author suggests that social organisations' decision making not only involves that within the organisational structure of a certain social movement. Rather, decision making and the construction of a social movement infrastructure is part of the same process (ibid.: 719–25). From a network perspective, the 'political network' made up of a series of actors based on a specific matter is redefined according to the position of each different actor, at the same time as the individual position of each actor is redefined through their network participation, all with the aim of achieving the organisation's goal.

As can be seen in the following section, my analysis from a network perspective differs slightly to Haug's position in the sense that I believe a social movement's infrastructure cannot be limited to the physical space in which different types of actors meet. Other actors may be involved in the 'political network' without necessarily holding physical meetings or sharing the organisation's aim, and they can have an impact when responding to other interests. This is indeed the case of the media in the current political context in Bolivia.

The Media

The importance of the role played by the media in the country's current political field can be seen by the reference made to them by Evo Morales in his first speech as president. On that occasion, the president said (*Bolpress*, 23 January 2006):

> Thank you. I would like to acknowledge some of the media, professionals who have always recommended us to learn. However, some journalists, both male and female, always demonised our social struggle and permanently condemned us using lies. Some journalists and media have submitted us to a kind of media terrorism, as if we were animals, as if we were savages.

From that moment on, it can be said that there was a tense relationship between the media and the current government. Clear signs of this can be seen, for example, in January 2010 when the government announced the reformulating of a law to regulate the media, which was resisted by part of this sector. A second confrontation occurred in October 2010 based on two controversial articles of the Law against Racism and all Kinds of Discrimination that, according to the sector, infringed their freedom of expression. In this sense, Torrico Villanueva indicates that the conflict so characteristic of the first years of Morales' government was reproduced in the information and media sector, with the media reconfigured around a struggle for political control, causing a bipolar kind of division (Torrico Villanueva 2011b: 257–59). In summary, when referring to the Laws of Communication, polarisation was created between the media and the state.[29]

The tension partly responds to the growing influence of the media in the current political climate in Bolivia (Exeni 2010: 7; Equipo ONADEM 2011: 7), and their influence on defining the agenda and even marking out political boundaries. On the other hand – and perhaps more importantly – said opposition responds to the politicisation of the media. As will be seen later on, the confrontation between the state and the media reflects more an opposition between political positions than a structural one. Therefore, given its proven influence, the media can be understood as a political actor that participates in the political game. Using a network analysis, the media is understood as a political actor that participates in 'political networks' and therefore also influences the relationship between the state and social movements.[30]

There seems to be consensus in academia that the media's actions are not only limited to transmitting information, but that they have a real effect on the political environment (see, for example, Street 2001; Axford and Huggins 2001). Dalghren even maintains that the media are in the process of transforming the practice of democracy in modern societies by becoming the institution that dominates the public arena and the centre of gravity for political practices (Dalghren 2001: 85). However, the fact that the term 'media' involves a range of actors allows for its definition as a 'political actor' to be objected to, since the latter implies observing a deliberate and sufficiently unified action (Page 1996: 20).

At this point, Cook's argument is relevant, since he defends the fact that the media are more than a 'political actor' and, in fact, constitute a true 'political institution' (Cook 2005). According to the author, the different media organisations create a set of systemised principles of action that last over time, and they supervise a key area of political and social life. The pressure of uncertainty and an increasing degree of professionalisation make the different means of communication seem similar. Their close relationship to government processes must also be added to this definition. These processes provide the scenarios, actors and common thread between the stories reported on. However, journalists enjoy a considerable field of action, copying and pasting these elements according to their own interests, which may be different to political ones. This creates an intrinsic source of tension for journalists and politicians that is difficult to resolve and is in a constant state of renegotiation (ibid.: 15). The author observes that there is a sufficient degree of unification, orientation and consistency to thus talk about a 'political institution'.

It is not necessary to consider it as a political institution to acknowledge that the media acts as mediator of the public debate and influences the creation of the political agenda (Chavero et al. 2013). The media becomes the channel that makes conflicts visible and also influences the course of events. On the one hand, this influence is visible by favouring certain groups; on the other, it is also visible in the characteristically sensationalist coverage of violence and conflict over negotiation and talks (Macassi 2010: 10). Inasmuch as many political decisions are based on media coverage, it cannot be denied that the media go beyond an informative function and become of much consequence in the political field.

When checking the political nature of the media, the clash between the current Bolivian government and the media has not been a phenomenon that is exclusive to Bolivia. Kitzberger (2010) has indicated that the wave of left-wing governments in Latin America is characterised by the emergence of conflict and a polarisation between the media and the government, responding to the common legacy of neoliberalism (ibid.: 5–6). According to the author, the media landscape underwent a notorious change with the market reforms of the 1990s, in which 'expansion, concentration and commercialisation gave a new relevance to media institutions in social and political life' (ibid.: 7). Reacting to neoliberal politics, the link between these institutions and the economic and social elite – together with the absence of an autonomous discourse – exposed the media as 'instruments of the powerful', and revitalised criticism of the region's reformist traditions (ibid.).

The confrontation between this type of government and the media has also been linked to a loss of legitimacy among political parties, with whom the media conglomerates maintain a close relationship. As well as often sharing the same social origin, the link between these actors is based on reciprocal agreements that defend specific interests. The author indicates that, in this context, the media's weak autonomy disappears as its owners use the media to defend their position. By replacing the political elites, the new governments block access to political power, explaining the aggressiveness and 'cartelisation' that are characteristic of media reactions (Kitzberger 2010: 14).[31]

In effect, the region's specific historical context has influenced the media becoming an actor closely linked to the political elite. As Elizabeth Fox (1988) shows, there were attempts at a regional level to reform and regulate the media in the 1970s, which culminated in the Inter-Governmental Conference on Communication Policies in Latin America and the Caribbean, San José, 1976. Its reform proposals and critical analysis identified the monopoly of national media empires as an obstacle towards a more representative democracy. However, in the transition governments, media reform proposals were a matter that was difficult to agree upon on the agenda, mostly because of the lack of society support and strong resistance from private businesses. All this occurred at a time when the new regimes were in a vulnerable position, struggling to stay in power and to implement far-reaching structural changes (ibid.: 180–81).

To a certain extent, the Bolivian experience also responds to the characteristics of regional historical development. In his analysis on the need to reform the media in Bolivia, the sociologist and social communicator José Luis Exeni explains that one of the greatest difficulties lies in the validity of the Print Law, considered as part of the sector's 'heritage'.[32] The problem lies in the fact that the norm is ineffective, having been passed more than eighty years ago and not updated since (it does not take into consideration the work of the 'new' media), and is not sufficiently well known. Thus, it serves more as a kind of licence for impunity, especially in a scenario in which the media sector is dominated by private-commercial actors and where the biggest absentee is the public media (Exeni 2010: 46–50).

The ineffectiveness and lack of validity of the Print Law is partly explained by the fact that Bolivia went through a long period of military regimes (between the 1960s and the 1980s), which involved harsh media repression. For example, television was exclusively in state hands from 1969 onwards. This long period of authoritarian rule caused the deterioration of the media, since it was subject to fear, self-censorship and co-optation. As a result of the fall of the regime of Hugo Bánzer in 1978, the media became more independent. By 1987, three years after the creation of the first independent television channel, the media was already being dominated by the private sector.

With the return to democracy, the urgency of other reforms, together with the state's lack of legitimacy as an actor in the field of communications, coincided with a larger field of action for the private sector. However, as Rivadeneira Prada explains, 'the cure for the government's poor handling and manipulation of the situation was worse than the original disease' (Rivadeneira Prada 1988: 166; own translation). Following regional tendencies, the majority of television channels became an instrument of consumerism, serving the interests of the (neoliberal) national and economic political system, closely linked to transnational and industrial corporations (ibid.). Thus, the media did not develop any service of interest to the national community, resulting in superficial news coverage characterised by banality and sensationalism (Gómez Mallea 2005: 29).

With the coming to power of the MAS government and the subsequent changes to the political elite, superficiality and commercial orientation – typical characteristics of the media in Bolivia – have given way to a scenario of political polarisation, expressed through opposition between private media and the public sector media recently created under the Morales' administration. Both reports from the National Observatory for Media were highly critical of the quality of the information provided by different media, and voiced concern about the polarisation in the sector.

Studies carried out in 2009 show that, in different episodes and in a bipolar political scenario, the media favoured either one political position or the other. In addition to a prevalent focus on sensationalism and violence, the media's partial coverage meant an absence of pluralism, analysis and depth in the topics tackled. These different studies concluded that the role of the media not only reproduced political hostility but also contributed to radicalising positions, impeding understanding and talks.

Therefore, before the presidential elections in 2009, for example, a private television network was sponsor and then promoter of the main opposition candidate (Torrico Villanueva 2011a: 18). The coverage of the elections for governors and mayors in April 2010 was characterised by 'the confrontation between political forces', in which the media's focus 'was mainly centred on the confrontation between Evo Morales/the MAS and the political and regional opposition' (Equipo ONADEM 2011: 127). A study on new public media concluded that their journalism was not sufficiently diverse in terms of sources or topics. The sources of information dominating these media are linked to the government or related sectors, and prioritise political topics to the detriment of other topics of public interest (Villegas Taborga 2011: 93). Among the 'potential topics of conflict', another report on the TIPNIS conflict identified a 'communicational distortion between the actors and the media, a focus that accentuates the disagreements and incompatibility between the parts' (UNIR 2011: 19).

Therefore, Exeni concludes that, in the current scenario, the media are not only polarised but also polarising, with a clear streak of political activism. By not covering and expressing the social and political change, the media are understood to contest the current government, notoriously affecting their credibility (Exeni 2010: 68–71).[33] In this way, the media's traditional alliance with the elites has been reverted so that, in cases such as TIPNIS, popular causes receive a lot of coverage, encoded as government opposition.

This leads us to consider the relationship between social movements and the media.[34] From the 1970s onwards, the study of social movements has seen the media as key to political content, and literature has signalled how these actors make strategic use of the media with different aims (Carroll and Ratner 1999: 2). Social movements need the media to achieve a greater mobilisation and validation, and to expand the scope of their demands. With news of a conflict reaching a greater public, the movement manages to improve its relative position of power. In this sense, not only is the amount of coverage that a social movement receives important but also its content, since this allows it to win the sympathy of third-party actors and provides possibilities for strategic alliances. For this reason, social movements depend on the media to a great extent (Gamson and Wolsfeld 1993: 116).

More recently, and having greater relevance to this analysis, is the proposal of Ruud Koopmans (2004). This author argues that the decisive part of interaction between social movements and political authorities no longer occurs in direct physical confrontation in specific places but rather in mediated encounters on disputes in the public arena of the press. According to him,

> media discourse is a crucial source of strategic information on which the activists from different movements base their decisions, as well as a way of voicing and evaluating strategies ... What is true for social movements is also applied to the actors they interact with, whether authorities, counter-movements or allies. All of these use the media as a crucial source of information from their different points of view and behaviour, and evaluate and adapt their own strategies as a result of the interactions produced in the public sphere. (Koopmans 2004: 370)

In this sense, the role of the media appears to be central to the relationship between the state and social movements, not only due to its great capacity for action in selecting both the topics and the content of the information (*framing*), but also because those practices are dependent of the relationships of power outside of the media (ibid.: 376). This last point appears most relevant to the Bolivian context, where the media is highly politicised. Thus, the media not only serve as a source of information. They arguably influence the state–social movements relationship and participate actively in the political game, constantly negotiating with different actors and defending their own interests by deciding what to cover and how.

From this it can be deduced that the media have a real effect on the practices of social movements. One important effect is that social movements, interested in reaching a wider public, jeopardise their demands by wanting to present them in a more attractive language. In the same way, while the media put greater emphasis on entertainment (as opposed to journalism itself), the decisions and strategic leadership are bent towards commercial demands to achieve coverage. Lastly, in as much as the media prioritises the visual aspect of their news, social movements are encouraged to adopt strategies that emphasise spectacle, drama and confrontation (Gamson and Wolsfeld 1993: 123–24).

As previously indicated, what applies to the social movements–media relationship can also be applied to the media in relation to any other actor in the political game. This means that the media influences state authorities in the same way – an aspect that is particularly appropriate in the Bolivian case for two reasons. Firstly, given the political partialism of the media, the government feels pressure to maintain and/or re-establish its legitimacy by opposing them more explicitly. Secondly, social movements have become one of the main actors on the current Bolivian political scene. Faced with a legitimacy crisis of the formal political institutions, the practices of social movements have emerged as one more – and perhaps the most legitimate – way for political participation. In the last decade, decision making has occurred both within formal political institutions and beyond them, and – more importantly – in the arena of social movements. For that reason, the influence of the media on social movements is a determining factor in political decision making.

Certainly, in the wide media coverage the TIPNIS conflict received, a large part of the media formed part of the 'political network' opposed to the road's construction. Therefore, the media was not only effective at inciting conflict with the government but also at exercising a great deal of pressure by influencing public opinion, forcing the government to reframe and reformulate their plan. At the same time, that pressure caused a reaction in other social sectors in favour of the road, taking the same format as the action against it: marches, social movements and conflict. In this way the media had great influence on this particular conflict's development.

The relevance of the media can be observed both for social movements and formal political actors, and for how this sector has influenced the state–social movements relationship. The dynamic of interrelationship, conceptualised as a network dynamic, coincides with the criticism made on the *political agenda setting* function the media exercises. That line of argument indicates that the news is not chosen but rather constructed as a result of the joint action between journalists and sources. The concept of *political agenda building* has been suggested to describe a collective process of elaboration that implies reciprocity between the media, actors with decision-making power and the general public (Charron 1995: 79).

If it is understood that the media have an explicit political role, it is worth asking what role they should play in deepening democracy and creating governability. Two positions can be identified. The first involves the negative effect of the media on democratic governability because of its tendency towards commercial interests and sensationalism that ultimately distorts, exaggerates and/or manipulates information. From a more positive point of view, the media creates an opportunity for citizens to show their acceptance or rejection of governors, obliging the latter to act as a result of these reactions, while the media serves also to point citizens to dysfunctional political actions. In this way, the relationship between media and governability is complex, particularly if dysfunctional practices are not exclusive to the government body but are also found in the media sector itself (Trelles Cruz 2006: 6).

Even so, in Bolivia there seems to be no doubt that a democratic government needs to guarantee citizen rights to information and communication,
respecting both freedom of expression and of the press (Exeni 2010: 7;
Equipo ONADEM 2011). In the same way, in the Latin American context,
the PNUD indicates that an agenda of democratic governability should at
least contemplate the democratisation of the public media, guaranteeing
equal access (PNUD 2008: 49). This is indicative of the acknowledgement
of the political role played by the media. As Mastrini and de Charras (2005)
explain, the struggle for the right to communication and information is political, since it is based on a dispute about economic and symbolic resources.
This explains why the need to democratise communicational resources causes
tension between the left-wing government and the owners of the media.

From a network perspective, the media are valuable political resources,
which is why any political aim looks to include such actors in its 'political
network'. In the case of Bolivia, inasmuch as the media acts as a political actor
of the opposition, the government looks to redistribute and/or appropriate
their political resources, in order to articulate them in the 'political network'
that favours their position. On the other hand, the topics or demands that do
not follow the government line find an important ally for political resources
in the media as a political actor of the opposition. At the same time, the
media also look to align themselves with other important actors to favour
their interests. This highlights a complex dynamic in the articulation of
'political networks', based on different political aims that can also coincide.
Shown through the example of TIPNIS, the indigenous social movements
who opposed the government plan created a kind of alliance with the media,
since the latter contributed to the 'political network' the valuable resource of
being able to influence public opinion and thus validate their demands. For
their part, by giving wide and partial coverage of the conflict, the media – as
government opposition – integrated an actor with great political resources
(namely an indigenous social movement – in other words, a highly legitimate political actor) into a 'political network' articulated to oppose and
delegitimise the government.

Characterisation of the Political Network 'Movement towards Socialism'

As the 'political instrument for social movements' and the current government party, the Movement towards Socialism (MAS) will now be analysed as
an entity located at the intersection between state and society. The difficulty
of conceptualising the MAS as a social movement or as a political party serves
to justify its alternative description as a 'political network'. Along the same

lines as the analysis presented, it is proposed to conceptualise the MAS as one more of the 'political networks' that characterises the state–society relationship in today's Bolivia.

The 'Movement towards Socialism': Social Movement or Political Party?

As seen in Chapter 2, at the beginning the Movement towards Socialism was created as the political representative of an indigenous-peasant bloc, whose leadership was assumed by the *cocalero* movement – in the person of Evo Morales – to then give way to a clearer rise of the indigenous bloc itself. The MAS was born as the 'political instrument' of different indigenous and peasant organisations, the latter with a definite trajectory in unions, with the aim of accessing political power at a local level through the recently created Law of Popular Participation in 1994. The combination of a series of factors, particularly the electoral success in the coca farming regions of Chapare and the legitimacy crisis of political parties, catapulted the MAS into national politics.

Its origins in the social movements have provided the Movement towards Socialism with an internal organisation that distinguishes it from traditional political parties, and made it the object of study by different authors. Literature widely agrees that the MAS cannot be understood as a political party in the traditional sense, although there is no agreement on how the MAS should be conceptualised either. In a comparative study, Van Cott conceptualised the MAS as an 'ethnic party', looking to identify the conditions that fostered the 'strategic' change from movement to party. In this way, her study centred on the socio-political institutional environment that allowed an 'ethnic party' to enter a country's party system, gaining relevance in the political environment and being 'successful', with the latter understood as electoral success (Van Cott 2005).

Van Cott's study is complemented by other studies that have actually concentrated on internal dynamics, in which the organisational functioning of the Movement towards Socialism is characterised by tension (Salman 2013). Hervé do Alto and Pablo Stefanoni identify tension between the MAS's social base of support and the incursion of an 'alien' social group as the result of the transition from the 'political instrument of the social movements' to 'an opposition party' and finally to 'a government party'. According to the authors, the 'real centre of power' has been displaced towards more institutional bodies dominated by professionals, the middle class, and former militants from the traditional left (Do Alto and Stefanoni 2010b: 2–3). Another source of tension emerges in the MAS as a 'peasant party', in which electoral success has been accompanied by the growing heterogeneity of its social foundations, combined with an 'internal hierarchy characterised by a peasant valuation', which becomes even more complex if the role of the arbitrator developed by Morales is taken into account (Do Alto 2011: 109).

Other authors attribute tension within the MAS organisation to its 'hybrid' character. Hugo Moldíz indicates that tension exists within the MAS when trying to combine the 'party form' that is appropriate for urban sectors with the 'community form', more in line with rural social organisations (Moldíz 2009: 89). Using a similar line of analysis, Anria (2013) maintains that the MAS is a hybrid organisation that operates with different organisational dynamics and logic, which mainly depend on the geographical space in which they operate. In rural areas, the functioning of the MAS is better understood as a social movement since it reflects its basis of social mobilisation, while in urban areas it is better described as a populist machine in which the main dynamic consists of conquering existing organisations and social networks. Therefore, it has been proposed that the MAS be conceptualised as a 'movement party' (Molina 2011).

According to Herbert Kitschelt, the 'movement party' presents a figure for the transition between social movement and political party. Movement parties are, in reality, coalitions of political activists who emerge from social movements and who try to apply the organisational practices and strategies of social movements in the arena of party competition. Thus they are characterised by a combination of formal politician activities with extrainstitutional mobilisations, and by the absence of an intense internal organisation (Kitschelt 2006: 280–81).

Kitschelt's description of 'movement parties' is particularly apt when describing the MAS from its creation up to 2004; that is to say, from its conception as a 'political instrument' to its emergence as an 'opposition party', by maintaining the informality and lack of organisational intensity characteristic of social movements, and by enacting politics both through institutional bodies and on the streets.[35] At this time, the MAS combined two other characteristics of the 'movement party': charismatic leadership and participative coordination from the grass roots (Kitschelt 2006: 280–81). According to Harten, in the period prior to 2004, the internal functioning of the MAS was characterised by a culture of participation in which contributions in decision making from the grass roots up were structurally guaranteed (Harten 2011a: 76), at the same time as Morales' leadership grew in importance in coordinating the MAS.

However, the description as 'an ethnic party', 'rural party' or 'movement party' turns problematic when studying the period after Morales became president and the MAS had been inserted into the state structure as the government party.[36] Although its indigenous-peasant origin and indigenous discourse to a large extent created the MAS identity, it is true that from 2005 onwards, the Movement towards Socialism aimed to attract every social sector that was discontented with the political and economic system, especially in a context of electoral competition. Among these, subaltern urban sectors stand out, as well as a middle-class segment that could sympathise with a more moderate 'left'.

To appeal to wider sectors of society, different strategies were used. In urban areas of La Paz, the MAS searched to expand its network of alliances with popular urban organisations (Anria 2010). At the same time, faced with the elections, the MAS attracted candidates with a different basis of social support, in particular in the middle classes, exercising little control and thus aligning a wider basis of support (Lazarte 2010; Do Alto 2011; Zegada et al. 2011; Molina 2011). The clearest example of this strategy was observed in the 2009 and 2010 elections, when the MAS openly looked for alliances with former candidates from the opposition (Harten 2011a: 79).

In relation to the party's 'ethnic' or 'indigenous' identity, the development of the MAS as a government party makes such descriptions problematic. Postero maintains that the MAS, by moving between group activism and parliamentary political practice, has known how to group together its 'heterogeneous' basis of support under a banner of 'indigenous nationalism' (Postero 2010a: 19). In a similar way, Albro argues that the MAS is not a separatist party that promotes an ethnic-national project. On the contrary, it makes use of the construction of coalitions at a regional, national and international level to compare indigenous matters with non-indigenous ones, and in this way coordinates popular discontent with the status quo through an indigenist discourse (Albro 2005). This is consistent with what Harten observes as the combination of a 'logic of equivalents' and a 'logic of differentiation' of social demands, in which the term 'indigenous people' becomes an 'empty signifier' capable of integrating a diversity of identities, even those of the 'white' middle class. Thus, 'indigenous' has been described as the 'essence of the plurinational state' (Harten 2011b: 87).

The definition of a 'movement party' is also problematic. In the first place, Kitschelt defines a 'movement party' as a *transnational* and *unstable* phenomenon (2006: 288). Certainly, in the context of recent Bolivian party history, the almost twenty years of the Movement towards Socialism are, at the very least, noteworthy. At the same time, the MAS continues to challenge Michelsian bureaucratic processes or institutionalisation, as well as its absorption into conventional party political practice. Thus, it does not appear to lead to either of the two ends that Kitschelt prescribes: its disappearance or its transformation into a formal political party (2006: 282–84).[37] In the same way, although the MAS has been described internally as a 'unstable coalition' (Mayorga 2007) under the leadership of Evo Morales, this actor has been the only constant and lasting figure on the Bolivian political scene in the last ten years.

A more appropriate description is that of Roberts regarding the concept of an 'organic party', in which the division between the party and social organisations are intentionally diluted, with the aim of maintaining a direct link with the social struggles beyond the institutional environment. In this way, the 'organic party' aims to avoid subordinating itself to the logic of political power, although this also leads to sources of tension (Roberts 1998: 75). Such trajectory coincides with the MAS period as an opposition party and even Evo Morales' first government, when it was indeed very difficult to draw a line between the party and the social movements and when the majority of the party's leaders were directly recruited from social movements. This was especially notorious in Morales' first cabinet, in which the majority of his ministers came directly from social leadership, and continued into the cabinet created in January 2010, in which eight of the twenty ministers chosen came from social movements.[38] In this same way, the party has been described as 'not very institutionalised' and 'having political offices with little experience in public management', as well as political performance that has been closely linked with 'an increasing number of protests and social movements' (Do Alto 2008: 40).

However, in the last few years, the concept of an 'organic party' has not been able to completely capture the MAS dynamic. Roberts explains that organic parties have difficulties in expanding their electoral foundations beyond their social roots, since their form of participation limits their power to attract activist circles. The high margin of votes obtained by the MAS – 20.9 per cent of the vote in the polls of 2002, 53.7 per cent in 2005, 64.2 per cent in the 2009 elections and 61.3 per cent in 2014[39]– shows that the MAS has been one of the most electorally successful political parties in Bolivian history. Roberts maintains that this 'exception' only occurs when an organisation's social roots are linked to charismatic leaders who are more attractive to a wide range of voters, thus leading to a hybrid between an 'organic party' and a 'populist electoral' model (Roberts 1998: 77). This is exactly what seems to occur in the MAS as a result of their rise to power. As Crabtree argues, the role of their political leader Evo Morales has been 'extremely important' in explaining the growth of the party and their capacity to appeal to the majority of the electorate (Crabtree 2011: 141). This is why the topic of Evo Morales' political leadership will be dealt with in the next chapter.

Agreeing with Do Alto, it can be concluded that the MAS allows for the limit between collective action and party action to be questioned, since it 'highlights the number of "walkways" and the continuity that exists between both scenarios of action' (Do Alto 2008: 42). Along the same lines, the Bolivian Movement towards Socialism shows an empirical weakness concerning the theoretical distinction between 'institutional politics' and 'noninstitutional politics', reinforcing the argument of Goldstone et al. (2003)

that both the social movement and the political party belong to the same field of action, with no fundamental differences between one and the other.

The Movement towards Socialism as a Political Network

As previously explained, the social mobilisations and political instability of the period between 2000 and 2005 were the expression of a legitimacy crisis within the political system, specifically concerning the political party system, state institutions and the model of neoliberal development. The relationship between the state and the social movements during this period was marked by confrontation and hostility. Social movements made their distrust and rejection of state institutionality explicit by exercising strong social pressure. For its part, the state could not reconcile social demands with the current political model, opting to repress the social demands, which explains the serious confrontations that occurred.

During Morales' government, the relationship between the different social movements has been characterised by the variety of its contents, which makes the use of more conventional descriptions such as 'co-optation' or 'autonomy' problematic. It has been possible to see that the same social movement can at one time be 'co-opted' in relation to the government and at another highly 'autonomous'. From a network perspective, it is not about contradictions or incoherence, but rather the 'political networks' dynamic.

The 2006–2009 period was marked by the constituent process developed in the context of a strong polarisation between the traditional elite that had not yet resigned itself to the loss of political power and the new popular political force. The Constituent Assembly was one of the most important demands of the 'October Agenda' that, as has been seen in previous chapters, contained a series of demands from different sectors. During this period, there were regular meetings between representatives from social organisations, MAS congressmen and with Morales himself, to not only discuss the proposals but to defend the constituent process from the alleged sabotage by the opposition. The 'specific matter' of the Constituent Assembly – a popular political project that was opposed to the traditional elite – gave way to strong cohesion between different social movements, the MAS and the government, to the point that it was particularly difficult to distinguish between different actors. At the same time, the 'political network' in favour of the popular project – and more importantly, the 'political network' opposed to it – was clearly defined.

As was seen in the previous chapter, the 'political network' included the MAS and social movements during the Constituent Assembly but, despite their relative cohesion, it did not form a homogenous or united body. The instrumental role and relative autonomy of the indigenous movement and the important role of the support institutions was clearly observed in the practices of the Unity Pact, but also through the creation of a body such as the REPAC by the MAS, MAS alliances with other adept parties such as the Movimiento sin Miedo and the participation of other social sectors (urban, manufacturing and labourers). As Chalmers et al. (1997) explain, a 'political network' can be made up of a changing group of 'political networks'. The Unity Pact is the clearest example of this. Understood as a 'political network' based around 'indigenous' matters, this pact brings together the relevant actors to analyse, debate and insist on the specificities of the common aims of the Constituent Assembly, linking itself to the MAS and the support institutions, for example.

The changing nature of the 'political networks' can also be observed through the approval of the new constitutional text. Between 2007 and 2008, and still in a bipolar political context, a campaign directed at promoting the 'No' vote through which the new Carta Magna was going to be approved was launched from the city of Santa Cruz. Based on this 'specific matter', the MAS once again looked to coordinate a political network in the form of the National Coordinating Body for Change (CONALCAM). According to the government discourse, this body should form part of a kind of 'supra-state power' that would coordinate the social power of the social movements with that of the legislative and executive powers, taking the lead in the 'process of change'. In my opinion, it is more accurate to describe CONALCAM as a 'political network' – bringing together social movements and the state structure to eclipse differences and conflicts – that is capable of deciding the result of the referendum in the same way as the Unity Pact was decisive for the draft drawn up by the Constituent Assembly. This also explains the fact that, once the 'specific matter' (approval of the constitutional text) was resolved, the CONALCAM 'political network' lost importance. The Unity Pact's loss of influence and action in the post-constituent period can be explained in the same way.

The overwhelming electoral victory of the MAS in the national elections at the end of 2009 meant the defeat of the opposition, and started a period that has been described as MAS 'hegemony' (Errejón Galván 2011; Zegada et al. 2011; Uharte Pozas 2013). Having obtained 64 per cent of the votes, the MAS gained a majority both in the Chamber of Deputies and the Senate, convincingly consolidating their political power. At the time of defeating the 'common enemy' and of gaining political power, unlimited possibilities were projected for the MAS government as a 'political instrument' or 'government for the social movements'. This marked a new stage for the relationship between the state and social movements, in which the absence of the 'common enemy' weakened the MAS's 'political network' internally, making way for more sectorial and, therefore, more conflictive demands to be made, in a kind of 'intra-hegemonic conflict' (Quiroz and Sandoval 2012).

The erosion of the 'political network' was notorious from 2010 onwards. My research, carried out at the end of that year, into the five social movements that made up the Unity Pact shows that its representatives were already making a distinction between 'militants' and 'affiliates': the first group comprised more rural organisations (such as the CSUTCB) and the second more indigenous ones (such as the CIDOB). The militant organisations showed their apparently unconditional support for the MAS government, considering it their 'own', while organisations such as CONAMAQ and the CIDOB were more critical, arguing that the MAS had lost sight of its political north and that the 'process of change' needed to be 'refocused' through the critical and coercive participation of social movements and civil society.

In reality, these fissures responded to diverging interests. Up to 2010, it could be said that the most important points in the common 'October Agenda' – namely the Constituent Assembly and the nationalisation of hydrocarbons – had been carried out, and that the common enemy from the political opposition had been defeated. Therefore, the political arena was opened up for a series of demands of a more specific nature, which until that moment had been eclipsed by the larger common aims and which could not all be satisfied at the same time. Faced with this scenario, the government opted for a strategy of prioritising and selection, producing a weakening of its links with (some) social movements (Harten 2011b: 87).

However, this interpretation has given rise to the consideration of certain consistent structural changes over time. Looking at the organisations that made up the Unity Pact, it can be argued that the MAS government, by prioritising the demands of the rural/peasant bloc, maintained stronger links with 'militant' organisations while it weakened its links with 'affiliated' organisations (something similar can be observed in other sectors of society, who saw in government policies how some of their aims were being carried out and others not). However, as stated earlier, the scenario is less static, since the quality of the relationship between the social movement and the state is defined according to 'specific matters'.

The state–social movements relationship in today's Bolivia thus has a complex dynamic, which at first seems contradictory or incoherent: the same social movement can seem highly 'autonomous' at one point and very 'co-opted' at another. Such interpretation presumes a clear division between state and society actors, which – from the empiric Bolivian experience, particularly the MAS phenomenon – seems problematic. From this perspective, it can be seen that the topic that brings the MAS and the social movements together is the one that defines the content of the relationship, explaining why conflict and agreements may both occur – even simultaneously. This has to do with how 'political networks' are coordinated around 'specific matters', dependent on the creation of common aims. Therefore, as long as the aim pursued by the MAS can be identified as coherent or in agreement or compatible with the specific interest, the social movement looks to coordinate itself through this network. Although this may be – and sometimes is – interpreted as 'co-optation', the analysis presented here has shown how this same social movement, on a different topic, can have greater 'autonomy' when faced with the opposition presented by the government.

Thus, following this analysis, the MAS can be understood as a great 'political network' in which indigenous social movements firstly managed to formulate common interests and aims that, through the 'instrument', they could pursue in an institutional political environment. Secondly, this process of formulation and articulation went through a process of reinforcement and extension, involving a series of popular actors, partly because of Morales' leadership and partly to oppose or resist a kind of common enemy, discursively located among the civic committees, the 'right', the economic elite, neoliberalism, imperialism and colonialism. This formulation of common interests and aims had its maximum expression in the demand for a Constituent Assembly, in which the political project acquired a national dimension. This explains the high level of approval and votes obtained by the 'political network' in the constitutional referendum in 2009 and the subsequent general elections (2009, 2014), both greater than the rate of approval that had been achieved in the elections at the end of 2005.

As has been seen in the different political episodes, the existence of a great 'political network' in the form of the MAS has not prevented different actors from joining other networks based around specific topics. This explains why, in the highly polarised and politicised discourse in today's Bolivia, accusations of betrayal are frequent between the state and social movements (for example, the role of the CIDOB during the TIPNIS conflict and their love–hate relationship with the COB). In other words, there are large themes underlying the political network MAS, but this does not seem to prevent some of its members (social movements, social leaders, civil society organizations, etc.) from joining alternative and even opposing, smaller, political networks on specific issues. Thus, political networks embodying the state–society interface entail a highly dynamic relationship, varying according to specific policies and interests, and making the impact of other socio-political actors visible. These are coordinated in different 'political networks' depending on specific interests, and affecting the relationship between the state and social movements. This chapter has discussed the two actors that stood out: the support institutions and the media.

These actors have valuable political resources, which is why they are important allies when carrying out political aims through the coordination of 'political networks'. Thus, the creation of the MAS cannot be understood as separate from the role that support institutions played in the formulation of politics and of a common political discourse, as well as when facilitating opportunities for meetings and talks. In the same way, despite the undeniably key role of social movements, the constituent process would not have been the same without the participation of the respective 'technicians' from the support institutions. Similarly, because of its capacity to influence public opinion and – in part – to construct the political agenda, the media has had an impact on the political environment that can be better appreciated using a network analysis. In a context like the Bolivian one, in which media actors are highly politicised – and where there does not seem to be a midpoint between the media in state hands and the media that answers to the now replaced political-economic elite – the impact of their active participation in the coordination of 'political networks' should be considered.

This scenario coincides with that described by Kahler et al. (2009) in relation to modern societies. The diversity and complexity of society 'overloads' the state, and spreads political resources between 'public' and 'private' actors.[40] In the case of Bolivia, this diversity and complexity is expressed through the coordination of different types of social movements, while this 'overload' is observed through the State's inability to contain and channel the demands from society. Kahler et al. explain that, as a result of this, 'public political networks' emerge that have the capacity to mobilise the necessary political resources, both in and beyond the state sphere, by facilitating more across-the-board interaction between the different interests. This, in effect, seems to be the role the Movement towards Socialism plays in the relationship between social movements and the state.

At this point, the concept of 'network governance' – understood as a response to the modern need to collaborate with a range of actors outside political institutions to formulate and implement public policies – seems extremely appropriate for the outline of the relationship between state and social movements under the MAS government in the period between 2010 and 2016. This concept is even more relevant if the traditional institutional weakness and the legitimacy crisis of the political parties and the institutional system in general is considered, as well as the preponderance of social movements in the political arena. In this scenario, the political processes – that is to say, the coordination of 'political networks' that involve a range of socio-political actors in the state–society interface – have the same or even greater importance than what occurs in the confines of institutional politics. The emergence of 'network governance' reinforces Goldstone's proposal that an analytical differentiation between movement and party, or institutional politics and non-institutional politics, lacks an empirical basis.

This chapter has suggested a conceptualisation of the relationship between the state and social movements from a network perspective. The content of this relationship is mainly defined based on specific topics and specific political aims in the articulation of 'political networks' that embody the 'state–society interface'. This type of analysis makes visible the role of other socio-political actors that also influence the relationship, among which support institutions and the media stand out. These observations make it hard to carry out a more conventional analysis that aims to characterise the state–social movement relationship in terms of 'autonomy/conflict' and/or 'co-optation', since this terminology assumes a division between the state and society, and it is exactly this conceptualisation that has been called insufficient when analysing the Bolivian reality (Tapia 2009). Using the concept of 'political networks', it has been shown that the conflictive nature of collaboration or co-optation of the relationship cannot be fixed, but rather it changes depending on the topic that brings the state actor closer to or up against the social movement. It is therefore the articulation of 'political networks', either in favour of or against certain policies, that defines the state–social movement relation.

Notes

1. This subsidy was established by supreme decree in December 1997 in the neoliberal government of Hugo Bánzer Suárez. The considerable difference in prices encouraged fuel smuggling to a value of 150 million dollars, providing a de facto subsidy for consumers in bordering countries. With growth in the national economy expected, it was hoped that these figures would increase, which the government described as an 'unsustainable' economic 'bleeding out'.
2. The government suggested redistributing the recuperated funds, an amount equivalent to USD $380 million.
3. The term 'intangible' would afterwards be discussed in depth, since it could also be interpreted as prohibiting any type of productive or extractive activity in the park, putting at risk the normal activities of the indigenous population living in the territory.
4. This refers to the coca-growing population to the south of the TIPNIS, both Aymaran and Quechuan indigenous populations, but not native to the territory of the TIPNIS. However, CONISUR also represents the three indigenous populations that originally belonged to TIPNIS: Oromono, Puerto Pancho and Santo Domingo. 'Conisur is a subdivision within TIPNIS ... financed by the government'. *La Razón*, 4 February 2012.
5. As explained in Chapter 2, FEJUVE played a central role in the 'Gas War', positioning itself since then as one of the most important and legitimate social organisations.
6. Federation of Green Parties of the Americas (FPVA), www.globalgreens.org.
7. Finally, in the 2014 elections, the Social Democratic Movement and the National Unity Front allied with the National Unity Front, with Samuel Doria Medina as presidential candidate.
8. According to Fabricant and Postero (2015), the TIPNIS conflict was but one example of the larger struggle over land in Bolivia, in which the global economic system needs to be taken in consideration. The authors argue that, among other examples, the TIPNIS conflict shows how little power the Morales government has against multinationals and global interests, as national laws are not stronger than transcorporations or multinational conglomerates.
9. Sánchez-López (2015) argues that the plurality of interests and understandings of citizenships are the main factors explaining the TIPNIS conflict.

10. The measure was a result of social demands to improve the deficient health service.
11. The confrontation between the government and the COB meant that at one point the government decided to dissolve the summit's organising committee. At the end of 2013, the government and the COB restarted negotiations, including putting the topic of the Health Summit on their agenda. To date, the government has held provincial summits in Santa Cruz, Beni and Chuquisaca. (*El Diario*, 20 August 2013; *La Patria*, 13 September 2013).
12. Ministry of Development Planning (2016). 'Economic and Social Development Plan in the Framework of Integral Development to Live Well, 2016–2020'.
13. For a more detailed discussion, see Orias Arredondo 2015.
14. Many leaders and affiliated unions opted to not respect the COB's summons, waiting for a decision on the matter from the CSUTCB. Neither the MAS nor the Gas Umbrella Organisation supported the COB at this time.
15. CONALCAM was founded in January 2007 with the aim of mobilising social organisations in support of the 'process of change', directly connecting a wide coalition of organisations and social movements with the state's high command (the president and vice-president), as well as with the MAS.
16. Source: cob.org.bo.
17. For example, Gianotten 2006; Garcés et al. 2010; Viaña 2011.
18. Interview in Santa Cruz, 5 November 2010.
19. Interview in La Paz, 11 October 2010.
20. Interview in La Paz, 21 October 2010.
21. This seems to agree with Loayza's interpretation that it was CEJIS who, carrying out intense research into constitutionalism, human rights, the nation-state, ethnic relations, etc., produced twenty-four essays that made up a national constitution. These had never been formally considered by the Constituent Assembly or its commissions, but they were the basis of the constitution approved in Oruro. According to the author, the fact that the assembly did not produce sufficient advances coincided with Morales' urgent need for political success, which is why the twenty-four proposals were eventually approved without further delay (Loayza 2010: 15–16).
22. Interview with Walter Limache, national director of the NINA Programme. La Paz, 11 October 2010.
23. 'The Vice-President and Chancellor held important positions in NGOs'. *Página Siete*, 19 September 2011.
24. As has been the case in other international experiences. In 2008, Morales' government expelled the US ambassador and the Drug Enforcement Administration (DEA), accusing them of conspiring against the government. In May 2013, the Bolivian government ordered USAID (the US Agency for International Development) to leave the country, also because of supposed meddling and conspiring against the government. Using the same argument, the Danish NGO IBIS was expelled from the country in December 2013. See 'Chancellor makes IBIS expulsion official through written order', *Página Siete*, 27 December 2013; and 'Danish NGO IBIS voices its surprise at its expulsion from Bolivia, and seeks talks', *La Razón*, 20 December 2013.
25. Instituto Nacional de la Reforma Agraria, a public office on land reform.
26. See, for example, Bebbington et al. 1993; Macdonald 1997; Fernando and Heston 1997.
27. On this topic, a study carried out on the relationship between social movements and the NGOs in Bolivia is interesting (Von Freyberg 2012), as the author observes how, from the 1960s onwards, different actors have connected more and more directly, creating relationships that allow for network structures to be seen. See, in particular, the table on p. 97.
28. At this point, it is worth noting that, during these events, the position of these actors was considered as slightly less important than that of, for example, the representatives from

social organisations and/or state actors who had no technical or academic training. This is indicative of a change in political culture, in which science and reason have lost their privileged position as the only source of knowledge. In these events, the interpretation of the organisation's representative or the untrained executive had as much or more legitimacy as that of an expert on the topic.

29. Interview with Antonio Aramayo, director of the UNIR Foundation to which the National Media Observatory (ONADEM) belongs. La Paz, 15 May 2012.

30. The idea of the media as one more actor in state–society relations is also supported by the notion of 'political communication', described as 'an opportunity for mediation between the state and society, which allows for public discussion in common recognition of the power of reason and the richness of exchanging the ideas and opinions illustrated' (Mattelart 1997: 57, quoted in Trelles Cruz 2006: 2).

31. Also see Philip Kitzberger 2012. For a more detailed analysis of the different experiences, see, for example, Trelles Cruz (2006) on Peru and Trejo Delarbre (1994) on Mexico.

32. This occurred during a union meeting of media journalists and workers, held along principle lines and given the norm's historical nature dating from 1925.

33. For a more detailed description of how the media were a clear force of opposition during governments in Bolivia and Venezuela, see Pascal Lupien (2013).

34. It is worth noting that the exponential growth of the private media in the neoliberal period is partly due to the role of social movements during authoritarian regimes. As Fox explains, at the beginning of the 1960s, the church in Latin America supported popular organisations in their demands for structural changes, identifying themselves more and more with popular movements. In this context, the church offered up its radio stations and other means of communication as an alternative media source for rural and marginalised groups. It was this development that caught the attention of political leaders, who recognised a key role for the media in their countries' economies, culture and politics. Therefore, social movements, political parties and organisations led by the church included media reforms among their demands (Fox 1988: 177).

35. A clear example of this is the role MAS played during the Gas War, as well as in the conflicts between the government and the coca farmers in the period 2000–2005 (see Chapter 2).

36. See also Salman (2011) on the difficulties that exist when defining the MAS as a movement party.

37. It is also worth mentioning that in his discussion of 'movement parties', Kitschelt does not appear to include the possibility that this type of actor adopts the role of 'government party'. Before getting to this, and when already an opposition party, the 'movement party' adheres to one of the two alternatives described here. Thus, the strong presence of the MAS in state structures, as well as the political power that it has, are factors that make describing it as a 'movement party' problematic.

38. Regarding the ministries of Foreign Relations (David Choquehuanca), Productive Development and Plural Economy (Antonia Rodríguez), Public Works and Housing (Walter J. Delgadillo), Mining and Metals (José Pimentel), Justice (Nilda Copa Condori), Environment and Water (María Esther Udaeta), Rural Development and Land (Nemesia Achacollo) and Cultures (Zulma Yugar), it is worth noting that social leaders were excluded from key ministries (such as those of the Presidency, the Government, the Economy, Hydrocarbons and Autonomous Regions).

39. Data obtained from the National Electoral Board.

40. It is worth noting that the distinction between 'public' and 'private' actors also comes from the state–society dichotomy and, therefore, becomes problematic as a result of an analysis from the network perspective.

5 Political Leadership and 'Political Networks'

This chapter analyses the role of political leadership in a scenario constituted by political networks that affect the state–society relationship. In the state–social movements relationship, social leadership emerges as an important factor. As mediators between the two, social leaders occupy a complex position full of contradictions. Frequent criticism of the leader's performance, whether because of their inability to represent the interests of their social base (co-optation) or because of their particularistic vision, shows the difficulty of juggling the state vision – necessary for national government – with active participation from political actors who, by definition, have particularistic or corporate in terests. The importance of these actors is best illustrated by the preponderance of Evo Morales' political leadership, who combines the roles of the highest social leadership position and leadership of the state in his person. This is explained by his capacity to articulate a variety of actors in political networks in support of the governmental plans.

With the following analysis, this chapter aims to make three points. First, the difficult character of the leadership of social movements when they occupy government offices is perhaps more the result of a traditional analysis in terms of 'autonomy' and 'co-optation'. The political network analysis solves many of the contradictions and contributes to filling the gap of leadership in the social movement literature. Second, the analysis presented in the previous chapter may create the impression that the state–society interface, embodied in political networks, results in a rather horizontal relation between equally influential socio-political actors. The salient role of leadership, particularly that of Evo Morales, demonstrates that this is not the case, and that the state and society are indeed marked by asymmetric relations, as suggested by the literature (see Chapter 1). So despite the dialectical structures and processes, individual actors retain much influence. Lastly, by looking at the polemic issue of the re-election of Morales, the chapter reflects on the impact of political leadership for the democratic practice in a context of network governance.

The Role of Political Leadership in 'Political Networks'

Often, discussion of the relationship between Morales' government and social movements in Bolivia strongly criticises social leadership's alleged practices of co-optation involving practices of corruption, stating that said practices are negative and undermine social organisations' autonomy, thus causing the so-called 'process of change' to relapse. At the same time, the centrality of the figure of Evo Morales, first as a leader of social movements and then as a head of state, forces an analysis of the role of political leadership, both regarding the relationship between the state and social movements, and concerning how the political process of the last decade is understood.

In an interesting article on the emergence of radical movements among the masses, Pappas indicates that, by studying social movements as 'contentious politics' (McAdam, Tarrow and Tilly 2001) and assuming that action is always collective, a large vacuum is created regarding the role of individual political leaders. The author maintains that political leaders are considered intermediaries and tacticians of events, but are not independent actors who are by themselves capable of defining the course and results of the social struggle (Pappas 2007: 1121). On the other hand, from a political network perspective, the topic of political leadership has been a subject of reflection for several authors (Newman 2005; Christopoulos 2016; Balkundi and Kilduff 2006; Silvia 2011). During my fieldwork, the topic of social and political leadership was frequently touched upon in interviews with different actors, particularly in regard to the period when the Constitutional Referendum in February 2016 was voted on.[1]

Social Leadership: Between a Rock and a Hard Place

The position of social leadership should be considered first, since it emerges as both problematic and contradictory in a process in which social movements emerge as the main actors in the political arena. As previously mentioned, the MAS coming to power in 2006 meant that a series of leaders from social movements assumed positions of political power and were recognised as legitimate actors in the political arena. Salman (2009) has characterised the leadership of social movements as a new political elite that has taken the place of the traditional one. It is characterised by its mestizo and indigenous origins, with an emphasis on its humble roots – which gives it an almost exclusive legitimacy to communicate with popular sectors – and its manifest rejection of protocol and political pomposity.

The insertion of social movements into state structures has occurred through their inclusion on MAS lists, whether as delegates for the grassroots, forming part of the Movement towards Socialism itself, or by invitation. According to Fernando Molina, there are two ways to participate in this kind of political representation. Firstly, the candidate is invited to take part because of his/her electoral potential, and secondly, because of the need to redistribute political power between movements through conformity or political obedience, thus ensuring the support of the grassroots (Molina 2010).[2] Given their roots in social movements and their access to political power, social leadership is located at the crossroads of the integral state vision and social movements' sectorial demands. This tension creates contradictions that apparently have no solution, and so the leadership's performance is subject to a continuous stream of criticism from different sides.

My interviews with representatives from different social organisations show that the role of social leadership is a controversial subject. Complaints about co-optation and the bad practices adopted by these actors are recurrent, although there are greater differences concerning understanding who is co-opted by whom, and who is not.

Social organisations have shown themselves to be more critical of the governmental line in the last few years, which has distanced them from it and even led to open confrontations. There are indications of government co-optation of the social leadership of the closest organisations. Thus, for example, a leader of the FEJUVE maintains that, 'The FEJUVE are co-opted by the government. That is to say, the government manages them. Its leaders have no vision; they're only looking for personal benefit' (Berrera 2012, personal interview). These social organisations recognise that there is a very direct relation with the government, but that this is limited to the national leadership of social organisations that – from their perspective – are seriously misrepresented:

> The other CONAMAQ sector, at Apu-Mallku level, is directly related to the government but there is no consensus within the CONAMAQ itself about its institutional structure. Typically, what occurs is the same as what happens with the Interculturals who have connections at a leadership level ... Apparently, social movements are only represented at a leadership level and without consent from the whole organisation from the bottom up. This can be seen throughout the conflicts ... leaders are not carrying out their job as leaders or as communicators effectively; there's a line between the grassroots and the top dogs. The leaders are more concerned about their jobs in government coordination and have become project consultants, but they're still projects that come from above. There's a public offer from the state – a package of projects – and the leaders keep an eye on them and want to hold on to them. There's no consensus at the lowest level, since the demands are different there. That's why I think that there's a rupture ... The leaders' perception has a whole history of accumulating social capital, but when they're already at those levels there's a tendency to be co-opted by the state. (Kochi 2010, personal interview)

This tendency towards co-optation and a lack of representation is mainly linked to social organisations that the Movement towards Socialism identifies as 'militants'; that is to say, the CSUTCB, the 'Bartolinas' and the 'Interculturals':

> We're represented in the discourse; we're represented in theory. In practice though, it's not like that at all. There's a difference between militancy, their affiliation with the party. They have more opportunities for representation. The can't talk against the government. For them, it's akin to death to say that this government isn't looking after us. We've said that if the president makes a mistake, we have to tell him. That's our duty as an organisation. When we hold an assembly, we invite him and say, 'Mr. President, why?' That's what we're there for, to look and see what's being done. We have to be on duty and follow the social movement's mandate. (Faldín 2010, personal interview)

Along these same critical lines, the Jilir Apu Mallku (highest authority) of the CONAMAQ maintained (personal interview, 19 April 2012):

> Between 2010 and 2011, we saw that there were three organizations (the CSUTCB, the Colonisers and the Bartolinas) more connected to the government. The CIDOB and the CONAMAQ were no longer so connected, because they were more critical. The other three occupy a place in government, they've beaten us. So, being part of the Unity Pact is no longer an advantage for the CONAMAQ ... Since last year [2011], the other three organizations have occupied every position, they think they're the government. We don't even have a 1 per cent stake in the government.

Effectively, at the beginning of the post-constituent period, this distribution distanced some of the social organisations, both from the Unity Pact structure and the Movement towards Socialism. Favouring the representation of social movements with a peasant union profile, such as the CSUTCB, rather than organisations that identified as more 'indigenous', such as the CONAMAQ and the CIDOB, responded to the need to redistribute political power at the same time as guaranteeing social support from the grassroots. It must be remembered that the 'political instrument' was born from peasant union organisations and was only supported by 'indigenous' organisations afterwards, with President Morales himself coming from a more 'unionist' than an 'indigenous' profile.[3] The result is that this distinction restricts indigenous organisations' political influence, such as CIDOB and CONOMAQ, explaining their more critical position towards the MAS government.

In the same way, the problem of the co-optation of social leadership stands out and is identified in social organisations that are more affiliated with the government. The following observations from the social leader of the

'Bartolinas' show how the problem exists at the very heart of the organisation (Quispe 2010, personal interview, 24 April):

> Another weakness is internal fighting, between heads, leaders, authorities. This restricts growth in our very organisations. Let's say a colleague doesn't want anyone else to do better than them ... The organisation is weakened by a struggle for positions. There's been a lot of confusion over what is organic and what is political ... Now everyone goes their own way, looking to be a leader, wanting to be at the head, wanting to be a minister. They're already thinking about the next election, creating little groups. That's not the instrument's aim. We've become like any other political party. People from the right have infiltrated our organisations easily and have gained positions. And our leaders, who are invested and more than capable, haven't got them.

Along the same lines, a leader of the CSUTCB indicates (Belmonte 2012, personal interview):

> Sometimes, leaders don't consult the grassroots. When their term at the CSUTCB ends and they don't get a position, they deviate, they join the right ... A lot forget about the organisations for many different reasons and want to pursue their own interests. But the majority comply. We've seven commissions that coordinate with their areas. In the MAS itself, they've joined without consulting the grassroots. Some representatives opt for favouritism, more politicians. These are the weaknesses that need to be improved ... In the majority of cases, they take us into account. The ministers don't listen to us sometimes ... Organisations should be consulted more. Intermediaries are needed to make information worthwhile.

Social leadership's lack of autonomy and representation in positions of political power is thus also recognised by those social organisations that, being more aligned with the government, effectively qualify as 'co-opted'. However, it is interesting that these organisations' perception is that co-optation and lack of representation are not limited to their very structures, but rather are also extremely present in organisations and social movements that, in general, are more critical of the current government. In other words, the criticism or opposition shown by these social movements does not respond to a more autonomous position in their relationship with the government, but rather to unrepresentativeness and co-optation in social leadership. Lorenza Quispe of the 'Bartolinas' explains (personal interview on 18 July 2016):

> There are some very opportunistic people. Some leaders do things in the name of the organisations [but] they have not been agreed upon with the grassroots. This causes weakness. For example, the leaders of the

CIDOB say that the Unity Pact no longer exists, but the grassroots do. The CONAMAQ, the leaders don't want it anymore but the regions, the affiliates, the majority [do]. The grassroots agree with the process of change, with the political instrument. So, they have to move ahead ... I think that the CIDOB and the CONAMAQ are managed by NGOs. Social organisations have NGOs that they support, so do we, but they can't say anything or impose their will. Support has to be unconditional. The CONAMAQ has let itself be managed. Before Evo, there were leaders who were against it and who, when they saw that Evo was winning, supported him, but their support wasn't heartfelt. Now they've done a U-turn. On the other hand, the CSUTCB, the Bartolinas and the Colonisers have always been strongly opposed. The CONAMAQ has representatives in government, but that doesn't mean ... Now the problem is TIPNIS, but those who are opposed [to the construction of a highway that crosses through this national park] don't even know. I think it's really political. They say that the president has risen through the ranks in the name of the indigenous people and that he's not fulfilling his role. Those leaders want to take over the presidency, that's why there's opposition. They're managed, for example, by Fondo Verde [an international organisation dedicated to the environment and which is coordinated by Fondo Verde Internacional, located in Peru]. There are other intentions, they're taking money, they're managed. They're well fed, travelling in cars all over the place, killing animals. The marches aren't like that. The problem is that they want to overthrow the president, but not cleanly ... The problem is that when people give them things, they want more. They do not conform, like the CIDOB and the CONAMAQ, and they want more, when they've had so many projects, they've received so much. This makes the others resentful. As the grassroots, they are with us, leaders convince them with money. People, for money, do U-turns. They have to be strong and safe to lead the process. There has always been betrayal, and there always will be.

Similarly, a CSUTCB leader mentions the following on the TIPNIS conflict (Belmonte 2012, personal interview):

It's very political. Everything's twisted. They take the wood. The forest isn't virgin anymore. There's a lot of looting and corruption. There's a lot of business done within the parks. Documents are signed, selling or awarding concessions. The people who live there beg, and the leaders take advantage. They're financed by NGOs to wear down the government. They'll get tired. If there's money, they're going to continue, if not, they'll get tired. I think they're going to publish documents that show the leader's bad business deals.

This interpretation is also the same as that of the 'Interculturals' (Alarcón 2012, personal interview): '[They're] leaders paid for by NGOs who, in the name of the community, bring in money from other countries. The people who live there want a highway. It's a political game I don't want to get involved in it. Lots of leaders are like that. You have to draw your own conclusions.' In this way, buying off social leaders seems to be common in how social organisations, as well as other actors, are perceived. Thus, in my interviews with different support institutions and political analysts, the government's use of benefits or bribery of social leadership, as well as that by other actors (such as NGOs and other social organisations described as 'the opposition') is frequently labelled as a persistent problem.

From this point of view, the impact of social leaders in positions of political power is played down, with no real participation from these types of actor. Rather, they fulfil an instrumental function, legitimising and validating decisions taken in other arenas (personal interviews with Limache 2010 and 2012; Ortega 2010; Lamas 2012; Mariaca 2010). In the words of the political analyst Jorge Komadina (2010, personal interview): 'Some leaders form part of the government or the government party, so they do not enjoy the critical distance needed to evaluate how their own demands are fulfilled; therefore, they are completely neutralised … They have no discourse or autonomous identity regarding this government. They are slightly subordinated to the government. From my point of view, there's an instrumental, long-term relationship, but this isn't relevant.'[4]

All these testimonies insinuate that buying off leaders and sharing out 'jobs' are the order of the day, as one of the common practices that defines the relationship between the state and social movements. However, this observation should be put into perspective. As Do Alto explains, the 'tendency to take advantage of benefits' is not only an expression of the 'survival of political patronage, but is widespread in indigenous and popular sectors as part of "de-colonization" and the construction of equal opportunities' (Do Alto 2011: 104). Therefore, the corporate relationship also responds to the rationale of justice and to a time when the popular class benefits from the resources of power that had arrived (Zegada 2010, personal interview).

It can therefore be concluded that social organizations (those most affiliated and most critical of the government) and external observers are both considerably more critical of the role that social leadership plays in the mediation between the state and social movements. Social leaders, submerged in client-orientated practices, do not have sufficient capacity or autonomy to coordinate and assert the demands of their bases of representation to the state.

Their difficult position becomes even more obvious if the perception of state authorities of how these actors function is taken into account. In an interview, the deputy minister of the Coordination of Social Movements and Organisations of Civil Society talks of the 'failed role of social leaders as a connection'. The Movement towards Socialism's taking of power and the defeat of the political opposition when the New Constitution was approved created high expectations among social organisations, which translated into an explosion of demands. According to the deputy minister, given the impossibility of satisfying everyone at the same time, social leaders in government positions have a duty to communicate with the grassroots and make them understand exactly what will be done during their time in power – but currently they are not fulfilling this role, which is attributed to a lack of training, orientation and political vision (Navarro 2010, personal interview). Along the same lines, the minister of employment indicated in a personal interview on 25 May 2012 that not all leaders understand what it means to be a popular government, due to a lack of political training and the inability to modulate from activism and demands to a modus operandi based on proposals and construction.[5]

Among these different and sometimes contradictory perceptions of social leadership, a common interpretation refers to generational differences. Social leadership in state structures is currently undergoing a transition – a situation in which the 'old' leadership has still not gone, but the 'new' teams have not yet finished taking power. The former leaders are older and so have more political experience, especially in union leadership and social movements. Many of them have personally experienced the dictatorship and its consequences, and they still have vivid memories of it all. Even more importantly, this group generally responds to 'on the job' training; in other words, they have consolidated their leadership in the resistance and social mobilisation of the 1990s and played a leading role in the social unrest that led to the current government taking power.

This history is in great contrast to that of the new generation. The new leaders are, in comparison, much younger and have therefore had a considerably more limited political career. Added to this is the fact that these young leaders received their political training in the 'Evo era'; in other words, in a context in which social movements played a main – and not marginal – role in politics from within state structures. In their training period, these young leaders lived through a time of 'unlimited possibilities' that redefined social leadership, replacing its struggle for recognition with new political opportunities. This development was mentioned in several of my interviews, both with representatives of social organisations and with the institutions that accompany them, as well as with state authorities.[6] In general, it can be said that the new teams conceive social leadership as a 'springboard' to state positions. This should be understood as a significant economic jump, particularly for the popular low-income social groups. The recurring practices of benefits and the buying off of leaders should also be understood in relation to this.

My interviews with representatives from social movements also show that these developments have led to fierce competition for leadership positions within the social movement, creating power struggles as well as a lack of commitment and loyalty to the social mandate once positions of power have been won. This is reinforced by the large call made on social leaders by the new government to occupy governmental positions. According to Walter Limache (2012, personal interview), this demand has divested the organisations and social movements of their strongest leaders, which has weakened them in relation to the government. At the same time, the need to fill the new vacancies has encouraged the rise of leaders with less experience in politics, less commitment to social matters, and less legitimacy within their organisations.

Therefore, the characteristics of the new generation of leaders have had repercussions on the state–social movement relationship in two different ways. On the one hand, they have weakened the movement's position by showing that they are less committed to their social mandate and by creating internal struggles. On the other, they have affected the government since, although they are more inclined to accept benefits in exchange for support of the government, they lack solid support from the grass roots to secure the substantial social backing the government requires.

Analysis reveals the complexity of social leadership's position in the state–social movement in Evo Morales' government. The different critical perceptions – contradictory among themselves – force the question of whether the current political scenario really allows these actors to function 'positively' or 'optimally'. From a network perspective, there appears to be no agreement among the different actors on what a good social leader is. In the same way, the general accusation of 'co-optation' acquires different meanings depending on the actor. In this, social organisations see a lack of commitment and loyalty towards their social base; from the state's perspective, too strong a defence of the sectorial demand is indicative of the lack of vision and political training needed to construct a new type of state. In the same way, the most critical positions towards the government are often understood – by the government and by social organisations and external actors (support institutions and political analysts) – as a form co-optation too, but this time by the political opposition (see the analysis of conflict in the previous chapter).

Social leadership, at the crossroads of the state–social movement relationship, is thus characterised by a series of strains and contradictions that apparently cannot be resolved. This is characteristic of the diversity of conflictive principles, identities and interests in modern Bolivian society. At the same time, the complexity of the leadership position is indicative of a political culture that does not allow – or in which there is no space for – 'neutral' or 'autonomous' positions, since every position is automatically politicised.

Thus, to understand what it means when a social leader or social movement is described as 'co-opted', 'autonomous' or 'critical', it is necessary to consider above all who emits this opinion. In the current Bolivian political scenario, these terms seem to refer more to political positions than to analytical categories.

The position of the social leader as mediator is thus understood as someone who is 'between a rock and a hard place', since they are at the midpoint between the state's integral vision and the social organization's sectorial demands. Here, it is particularly interesting to analyse the role played by President Evo Morales, the most important 'social leader' of the last decade, who currently holds the most important position of institutional political power.

Evo Morales' Political Leadership

The apparently immense and unresolved contradictions and tension that social leaders experience when they occupy a political office, as outlined in the previous section, seem to have been somewhat resolved in the figure of Evo Morales. It is worth remembering that Morales came to power in 2005 having won an unprecedented 52 per cent of the vote, and was then re-elected in 2009 with 64 per cent. This substantial increase in votes for Morales was historic (Oviedo Obarrio 2010), and went down only slightly to 61 per cent in the 2014 general elections. In general, he garners more admiration than disapproval, as shown again and again in the opinion polls, which, even at their lowest, have still been better than his predecessors' and the current opposition's best results. A Constitutional Referendum held on 21 February 2016 voted against subsequent candidature of Morales in the 2019 general elections. By a slim margin of 2.6 per cent, the leadership of Morales was given an expiration date. However, this impediment was short lived. In November 2017, the Constitutional Court ruled that the limits on re-election were in breach of the individual political rights availed by the San José of Costa Rica international pact. The controversial ruling intensified the political campaign that had already been started, making the possibility of Morales remaining in power for over twenty years quite feasible.

Considering the above, and a 41 per cent approval rating[7] over his more than ten years in power, speaks of the importance of Morales' political leadership. Evo Morales has been frequently associated with other Latin American leaders such as Correa and Chávez in different frameworks, whether in the emergence of 'the new left' (Barret et al. 2008; Cameron and Hershberg 2010; Levitsky and Roberts 2011), as 'the socialism of the twenty-first century' (Burbach et al. 2013), as a 'usurper of power at work' (Diamint and

Tedesco 2014), and, more frequently, as a populist leader (Seligson 2007; Del Tronco 2013; de la Torre 2013; Collins 2014).

Describing Morales' leadership as populist certainly offers some guidelines on how to understand his strong presence on the current political scene. The emergence of populist leaders in the last few years has been connected to the absence of results in both public policies and efficient accountability. These factors cause citizen distrust of the representative institutions, which is resolved by a popular leader who presents the most direct kind of symbolic accountability (Del Tronco 2013). As seen in Chapter 2, the political institutions' legitimacy crisis and the economic development model were effectively determining factors in the creation of the Movement towards Socialism and in Morales coming to power.

In a regional study, Seligson also adjudicates the populist tendency in the Latin American region to its characteristic low level of trust in liberal democracy institutions. Stressing the opinion polls, the author warns that there is a regional tendency to permit populist measures that have possible negative effects for liberal democracy (Seligson 2007). Thus, a predominant interpretation identifies charismatic authority, the tendency to concentrate power in the executive, and the exploitation of the opposition's discourse, which creates a hostile division between 'the people' and the supportive traditional elite, as traces of populism. The same are generally understood as being negative for the practice of democracy. From this perspective, the emergence of a populist leader is understood as dysfunctional for democratic consolidation or intensification.

However, the populist definition does show some issues when looking at Bolivia. Analysing the cases of Bolivia and Ecuador, Jennifer Collins (2014) indicates that the fact that Morales and Correa have emerged from strong social movements contradicts the common understanding that the emergence of populism is typical of a weak and disorganised civil society. The author shows that, in the case of these two countries, the identity of 'the people' around whom the populist discourse is forged was not formulated by the charismatic leader as theory prescribes, but was constructed through the activism of strong social movements. The role of the leader comes second, with their capacity to appeal to a wider audience, thus ensuring they can take power through elections.

In line with my analysis, Collins maintains that in the Bolivian case in particular, the presence of strong and active social movements forces the autonomy of the political leader's actions, in a complex relationship with social movements that is characterised by heterogeneity and conflict (ibid.: 85). According to her, the cases of Ecuador and Bolivia challenge the populist model that puts the role of the charismatic leader at its centre, proposing Laclau's vision as a better evaluation. As a result, the essence of populism emerges as the construction of an identity that cannot be assigned to a single person or as a transformative political project. Thus, the determining role of social movements in the construction of the populist project implies that the discourse is not only a vehicle for the election of charismatic leaders but also has the potential to be the means through which radical changes are imposed, beyond the status quo but within democratic confines (Collins 2014).

Van Cott (2008) presents another, more positive view on strong leadership. The author has studied the roles of mayors from 'indigenous' political parties in Ecuador and Bolivia (the MAS) and their effect on institutional innovation and democratic intensification. The study concludes that political leadership is a decisive factor for democratic innovation in the Andean region, in particular in contexts of little or weak institutionality, such as Bolivia and Ecuador (ibid.: 59). The author identifies a series of characteristics that allow for positive effect which, although based on the observations of local leaders, can be applied surprisingly well to an analysis of Morales' leadership. These include charisma; a continuous and visible presence in the community with frequent interaction with constituents; support for civil society groups; a degree of autonomy in relation to organisational benefactors; the capacity and desire to negotiate effectively beyond ethnic divisions and with external actors; and the capacity to be re-elected (ibid.: 63). All of these characteristics would contribute to the consolidation of democratic institutional reforms.

In a specific article on his leadership, Morales is described as a 'situational charismatic', allowing him to move through the sphere of civil society towards that of the state, using complex negotiations and situations (Mayorga 2009). This interpretation is consistent with Van Cott's observations that the leader's charisma makes it possible for the ambiguities and complexities of the institutional prerogatives of the new democratic institutions, which are characteristically weak, to be negotiated (Van Cott 2008: 66). In the same way, Van Cott indicates that the leader's practice of involving himself directly with his basis of support beyond institutional opportunities, thus creating relationships of confidence at a personal level (67), has been identified as one of Morales' strategies to consolidate his leadership (Harten 2010b: 81; Zegada et al. 2011: 286).

Van Cott further maintains that leadership is effective at making institutions innovate and at intensifying democracy, to the extent that it is capable of dealing effectively with a series of actors. The author signals that it is highly important to have alliances with civil society actors with pro-democratic visions in order to produce 'synergy' (Evans et al. 1997) between the state and society, allowing for fewer obstacles when implementing reforms or institutional innovations. At the same time, since the leader must use his position to pursue aims that go beyond a specific vision, he must be able to maintain a certain distance (autonomy) from the grassroots that support him, in order to present himself as a credible option in negotiations with other actors in different contexts.

These aspects can be recognised in Morales' leadership. As has been shown in previous chapters, social movements – particularly indigenous social movements – have emerged as the principal political actors of the last decade as creators and carriers of a new political project, with a high level of legitimacy. If Morales' figure was crucial to leading the coalition of social movements – the MAS – to victory in the elections, the agency and support of social movements was essential to implementing large-scale reforms. Among the most emblematic cases were the formulation and approval of a new constitutional text (because it had the support of social movements); the government's unsuccessful attempt to remove fuel subsidies; and the construction of the motorway through the TIPNIS National Park (because of fierce opposition from social movements).

On the other hand, the recurring complaint from indigenous social movements has been that the president has not dealt with their demands and that he often makes decisions in an authoritarian way or even promotes policies that are against their interests (interviews). This allows the president to enjoy a considerable field of action beyond (indigenous) social movements and to appeal to – and negotiate with – other types of actor, who do not generally or necessarily respond to an 'indigenous' identity or interests, such as other popular sectors or, even more importantly, actors from the economic elite.[8] A clear example of this is the government's initiative to regain access to the sea. Morales called upon the participation of the country's former presidents, even naming Carlos D. Mesa as an official spokesman and Eduardo Rodríguez Veltzé as an agent for Bolivia in the lawsuit against Chile over their obligation to negotiate sovereign access to the sea in the Hague International Court of Justice.

Leadership in Political Networks

In reality, the qualities described by Van Cott coincide with the characteristics projected by literature regarding network governance political leadership. In other words, the success of Morales' political leadership can be understood as his capacity to function as a coordinator of political networks in the context of network governance.

In specific relation to political leadership, network governance is understood as the result of the erosion of the power of the nation-state, with the processes of governance being characterised by interaction at multiple levels, both within and outside the nation-state. Such forms of network coordination replace hierarchies and the market as the dominant forms of interaction (Newman 2005: 719). The political networks thus emerge 'as a specific form of the complex relationship between state and civil society (between political institutions and social organisations), responding both to pressure from civil society (who, with their demonstrations, promote the development of public institutions) as well as the state's capacity to react to social pressures and modify their relationship with civil society organisations' (Licha 2001: 2).

The emerging interdependence of government actors and civil society organisations when creating public policies makes political leadership more complex, since the leader is obliged to regulate between traditional hierarchical leadership (typical of political institutions) and 'collaborative' leadership, coordinating networks. In the same way, the leader plays an important role in network coordination, defining which actors are included and which excluded (according to the necessary resources), as well as in the formulation of the aim (*framing*) of the network (Silvia 2011: 66–69).

From a network leadership perspective, many of the contradictions that emerge in the different interpretations of Morales' political leadership are resolved. The need to modulate between different roles according to the opportunities available for action and to formulate discourse that appeals to the relevant socio-political actors for their inclusion in a political network explains why Morales is sometimes perceived as an authoritarian leader. He takes his main and other decisions (interviews) as a leader with the capacity for consensus (Molina 2013: 12), operating in an institutional context that 'demands political agreement' (Laserna 2007: 115).[9] In a similar interpretation, Anria observes that, in the absence of formal channels of accountability, the MAS's ultimate decision-making power lies in Evo Morales but, at the same time, this does not mean that he has complete autonomy to govern. The absence of formal channels of participation does not imply that these do not exist informally, creating a margin of influence for social organisations that limits the actions of the president (Anria 2010: 112–13).

In the same way, Morales plays an important role in the coordination of a common identity based on the 'people', allowing for alliances to be created or support from diverse social actors to be counted on. This is the common interpretation emerging from an analysis of Morales' leadership as an expression of populism, in which the opposition's discourse is a source of cohesion in the shared identity against the 'common enemy' (Harten 2011b: 154–73; de la Torre 2013; Collins 2014), which is identified discursively in 'imperialism' and 'neoliberalism' (Gomez Bruera 2006; Postero 2010b).

However, this same interpretation becomes more complicated when the 'contradictions' and criticisms of the MAS and Morales from different sectors are taken into account. The traditional left, in particular the COB, has not implemented the necessary radical changes, even making pacts with right-wing sectors to the detriment of their own interests. This, in part, is also the position of some academic analysts and leftist intellectuals once related to the

MAS but who now argue that the 'process of change' has been diverted.[10] The political opposition, in particular the right in the Media Luna regions, have placed Morales together with Chávez as extremist leaders determined to finish off democracy and capitalism (Postero 2010a: 30). The CONAMAQ and the CIDOB social organisations, representing indigenous people from both the highlands and lowlands, have criticised Morales' government for repeatedly jeopardising the interests of their grass roots. This shows that although an opposition discourse exists based on a popular/indigenous identity – which serves to coordinate different actors based around Morales and the MAS – this is, by itself, neither foolproof nor sufficient.

In my opinion, more than 'inconsistencies' (Zegada et al. 2011: 294) in government administration or the lack of a coherent ideology/political project (interviews), contradictions are apparent and actually reflect a way of doing politics in which diverse actors are coordinated and re-coordinated around specific, changing aims. The severe institutional legitimacy crisis in the country between 2000 and 2005, together with the political empower-ment of strong social movements, created a very feasible political scenario for Bolivia, in which the state apparatus is dependent on constant interaction and collaboration with actors from civil society to formulate and implement politics – in other words, a 'network governance' scenario. Morales emerged as a key player in political network coordination through his capacity to unite the different MAS tendencies (Laserna 2007: 101) and also because he could coordinate actors beyond the confines of the 'instrument'. As Do Alto and Stefanoni explain, Morales consolidated his position at the same time as 'he prevailed as an essential figure to the extent that … he becomes a coordina-tor between these new, more and more diverse and heterogeneous sectors and the social groups that are the basis of the "instrument"' (Do Alto and Stefanoni 2010b: 4).

According to Gray Molina, the dynamic within the MAS revolves around the 'conciliatory' figure of the president, containing the tension between dif-ferent parties (Gray Molina 2010: 74).[11] It could be argued that the role of the president is useful to the social movements' 'instrument'. As previously observed, the 'instrument' has had, in the figure of Morales, a successful electoral strategy, from the first time he stood for the presidency to the last general elections in 2014.

However, the role of Morales is not limited to his success in the elections. My interviews with representatives from different social organisations, polit-ical analysts and government representatives – even those most critical of his government – assign Evo Morales' leadership a central role. This shows that Morales is a highly influential political figure in different sectors of society, to the point that he is understood to be the backbone of the current political process. In the words of the former deputy minister of the Coordination with

Social Movements and Civil Society Organisations, Cesar Navarro (2010, personal interview):

> Nowadays, politics revolves around the president. One of President Evo's opinions or actions is the most important political act of all. You're not going to see a decisive political article in the news if the president doesn't have an opinion on it ... I think we're living in a time in which the president poses questions to society – ethical questions (with his work ethos), cultural questions because of his origins, and ideological ones for the left because he's an anti-imperialist. So nowadays, politics revolves around the president and conflict evolves around his constitutional support, the MAS.

Putting this more into context, Jorge Dulón, from the Foundation for Multiparty Democracy, also observes the strength of Morales' leadership (2010, personal interview):

> Today he is the political leader that sustains the process – an unorganised and sometimes inefficient one – but his leadership on an international level makes everything legitimate and sustainable. He still has a lot of muscle, a lot of presence. He's the reflection of the leader that history has needed to generate changes from the social class that has always been in the background. Symbolic changes first, before anything else.

Similarly, sociologist Jorge Komadina explains (2010, personal interview):

> The figure of Morales is absolutely central, because of his symbolism, his political role, his capacity to coordinate these organisations. He is a symbol, a strategist, a central figure, in such a way that, were he to disappear from the political scene, the MAS would be undermined because none of its other leaders have the capacity to coordinate or unite such diverse social groups with such diverse demands, regions, leaderships and different political sensibilities. Thus, Morales' role is key because it's the role that coordinates these movements, these groups and leaderships. He is above these organisations and, accompanied by the bureaucratic upper echelons, he is somehow able to make strategic decisions that the networks of social organisations that support the government and party comply with.

This shows that Morales has a notorious capacity to coordinate diverse actors, defining and moving forward according to common aims. Given the political context, in which popular social and indigenous movements acquire greater legitimacy, it is not surprising that this capacity emanates partly from his ethnic and popular origins. The pro-indigenous discourse is encapsulated in the figure of the president (Mayorga 2009: 122) and Morales has seen the benefits of cultivating his image as a popular and indigenous leader (Postero 2010a: 26). This ethnic component is crucial to generating strong adhesion from social organisations. Fernando Garcés explained during a personal interview on 11 November 2010: 'Another important element is Evo's play on double identity, which works well with a temporary discourse. Why do we say that Evo Morales is the first indigenous president? In Villarroel's time he wasn't, but Villarroel spoke Quechua and came from the Quechua community, etc. The discursive icon was not "indigenous" at that time.'

Since under the Morales administration 'the indigenous' has become the political subject for a national political project, the ethnic link between organisations and the president becomes important: '[The social movements] see this humble, simple, sincere person, who has emerged from the social movements, as their last hope. They think that he could be the one with all the answers. We've already believed in men who've had many opportunities and haven't done anything for the country. Here's a new leader who, coming from the people, understands people's needs and is capable of responding to them' (Ortega 2010, personal interview). Pamela Cartagena from the CIPCA interprets things in the same way, observing that Evo Morales ethnicity has a lot of influence in indigenous organizations, with them able to say that 'Evo is the same as me'(2012, personal interview).

Ethnic identification appeared in all my interviews with social organisation representatives, demonstrating that his indigenous origins alone inspire a high level of confidence: 'Only a leader with our roots can make changes' (Belmonte 2012, personal interview). At the same time, on sharing the same roots, there is the opportunity for a direct relationship: 'Before, it was a privilege to sit with the president or a minister; it was no more than a photo opportunity and then it was over. Now we have the privilege of sitting and talking, face to face' (Faldín 2010, personal interview).

In terms of the organisations' autonomy, the high degree of identification with and confidence in Morales has the negative effect of not allowing anyone to criticise him: 'We also make mistakes. With the president, we don't want to make a bad impression, we never say he's wrong' (Quispe, L. 2012, personal interview). Also: 'We can't betray him, because Evo is a fellow member' (Belmonte 2012, personal interview). Morales' rise within the social movements has also been noted by the support institutions, who observe that it is impossible to criticise Morales, since they can't fight against themselves (Bascopé 2010, personal interview). In the words of the National Coordinator of the NINA programme:

> Nowadays, leaders do not directly question the model or the president. In their hearts, they still relate to an identity in which 'the Indian is my president and it doesn't matter if he doesn't pay attention to us, he's still an Indian and we're going to defend him'. (Limache 2012, personal interview)

The fact that there is generally no direct criticism of Morales does not mean that his government's performance is not reviewed negatively. In several of my interviews, representatives expressed their discontent and disagreement with the government line, though always leaving Morales free of blame. In general, government errors or diversions are blamed on those surrounding the president. Porfirio Kochi, former leader of the CONAMAQ, explains (2010, personal interview): 'Nobody doubts Evo Morales' honesty, transparency and commitment, but those who surround him, the agents of national politics, impede the implementation of the New CPE'. In particular, criticism is aimed at government policies involving the vice-president and the body of ministers. In the words of Lázaro Taco of the CIDOB (2010, personal interview):

> When the president arrives, matters are resolved in meetings ... Ministers and those under the vice-president initiate confrontations, when the president as leader could easily go and talk to them directly and solve the problem. These are the people who surround the president and won't let him come and meet his people.

This criticism only deepens when such actors are not recognised as carriers of an indigenous identity, once again pointing to the centrality of indigenous discourse and symbolic representation in Morales' person. Thus, Octavio Alarcón, from an ally organisation, indicated (2012, personal interview):

> We've worked to consolidate the position of the first indigenous president, Evo Morales Ayma, but the ministers haven't. We don't speak the same language, they don't have the same sentiments, they don't know our needs. They still don't have all the power, but just a representative, that's why it's weakened.

My interpretation is that leadership in relation to social movements' political power has a more complex interaction in a changing dynamic of mutual interdependence, materialised through specific events and topics. In this dynamic modus operandi, Morales functions as a constant figure through whom it is possible to appeal to different sectors, despite the contradictions and conflicts emerging between specific interests and government lines. Locating the errors at the team that surrounds Morales allows him to keep acting as the coordinator around whom everything revolves and, at the same time, gives civil society organisations an opportunity to channel their discontent. In this respect, César Navarro maintains (2012, personal interview):

> This leads to conflict. It's not a conflict that causes a crisis, but a conflict that causes social uneasiness. A crisis understood as the loss of the state authority's legitimacy. The leaders say, 'If the ministers won't listen to us,

we'll talk to the president'. Thus, implicitly, they recognise that there's an authority that resolves things. Before it was 'go away' and their authority was not recognised.

In effect, any criticism does not question the government's legitimacy in general as much as its performance regarding specific topics. In my interview with the CONAMAQ's highest leaders at a time when it was being most critical of the government about TIPNIS, they still maintained that: 'We didn't say "Let's topple the government". The change goes on; we're in a process of change'. This shows that, in reality, criticism and conflict form part of a political model in which the social movement – as the main political actor – creates the format of political participation. Through them, the aim is to capture the president's attention because of a perceived affinity of interests (the identity relationship) and, above all, because of his capacity to coordinate political networks around a specific topic in order to fulfil certain aims. This is where political vision makes the difference, transcending the role of 'mediator', 'moderator' or 'arbitrator'.

In this vein, Morales can be understood as the 'visionary leader' in the typology developed by John and Cole (2008). In their article on political leadership in a context of network governance, the authors identify the challenges facing the political authority and the need to encapsulate and unify diverse actors, with the potential for conflict among themselves, in a political environment characterised by institutional fragmentation, the participation of new actors and a more open and flexible pattern of decision making (ibid.: 99). In their typology, the visionary leader is characterised by their capacity to bring leaders together, unite some of the most obstinate, divided positions and establish creative policies and effective coordination. The complexity of the political scenario is placed face to face with the will of the leader, who is capable of forcing strong, though unequal, coalitions (ibid.: 102–3).

Political experience, understood as the capacity to hold on to one's political position, is another important quality for leadership in a network governance scenario, since it allows for the mechanisms used to form coalitions to be improved and/or consolidated (Kjaer 2013: 267). In the specific context of the Andean region and 'organic' political parties, Van Cott also indicates that the impact of political leadership on innovation and democratic consolidation benefits from the leader's capability to extend their term in power for a prolonged period of time: 'In the absence of strong institutions, re-election allows mayors to visualise projects to be carried out and to use their personal political capital to institutionalise participatory processes, since people have more time to get involved and generate a sense of appropriation' (Van Cott 2008: 69). Thus, Morales' leadership is explained through the traditional institutional weakness that characterises Bolivia, but also the complex political reforms that the MAS government set into motion, beginning with a new social pact. This context makes formal participation mechanisms and political execution secondary to less formal processes or ones in the process of being formalised.

Along these lines, Silvia (2011) affirms that one of the network leader's most important activities is to generate support from both internal and external actors. At this point, trust is the glue that holds the network together.[12] Emerging from different organisational and cultural contexts, the operational processes and different perspectives that come together may obstruct network coordination. In addition, actors such as social (indigenous) movements have assumed a central role in political tasks, in which more personal relationships of identification and/or trust take precedence. The trust that the leader can inspire both in their persona and between different network actors is highly important to appease dividing tendencies (ibid: 70). Thus, the capacity to evoke trust in different social organisations, in particular indigenous movements, explains why Morales is described as the most influential political leader in the current political scene.

Direct Democracy and the Media: The Constitutional Referendum on Re-election on 21 February 2016

Trust is identified as one of the leader's most important qualities, explaining the superiority of Evo Morales' political leadership, in particular from the political network analysis perspective. The element of trust also helps us to understand the events and effects of the Constitutional Referendum of 21 February 2016, the so called '21F', which put Morales' leadership to the test. At that very political moment, Morales' integrity and transparency were cast into doubt, severely damaging the previously mentioned image of trust, causing Morales to 'lose' the referendum.

Direct Democracy and the Topic of the Re-election

The National Coordinating Body for Change (CONALCAM)[13] presented the legal initiative for the referendum. The referendum's aim was to obtain a constitutional reform that allowed the second consecutive re-election of both the president and the vice-president. Article 168 is the article in question and establishes that re-election can only occur consecutively once. The proposal for constitutional reform was approved in a combined session of the Legislative Assembly by 112 votes to 41 on 26 September 2015. Law 757, which convened the referendum, was approved by 113 votes to 43 on 5 December of the same year.

In academia, the referendum has been discussed as an instrument of 'direct democracy'. The concept refers, for example, to the practices of referendums, plebiscites and citizen consultation as a set of political tools through which citizens use the private and universal suffrage of the polls, which is not part of the regular electoral process, to make decisions or give opinions (Altman 2011). According to Altman, mainstream definitions of democracy focus mainly on the electoral connection between voters and representatives, disregarding the democratic practice of citizens' direct involvement in policy issues. In this way, 'direct democracy' debates point to discontent with more formal or technical definitions of democracy, and argue in favour of the complementary potential of direct democracy. For the Latin American region, these instruments have been mainly associated with recent left-wing regimes and debates on 'participatory democracy'.

Literature on the topic is divided between those who defend and those who criticise direct democracy (Welp 2010). On the one hand, it has been argued that mechanisms of direct democracy do indeed have a 'progressive' effect (Lissidini 2015), and could be an effective tool in countering the representative systems' legitimacy crisis (so characteristic of Latin American political scenarios) (Welp 2010); they may even be a necessary complement to the representative democracy model in order to enhance democracy definitions and indicators (Altman 2013). On the other hand, direct democracy critics see the risk of undermining representative democracy institutions and of them becoming mere instruments for citizen manipulation. Looking at the Latin American region, critics have emphatically pointed to the fact that most referendums have been initiated by presidents aiming to concentrate power and weaken democratic controls (Durán-Martínez 2012).

The use of 'direct democracy' instruments show statistical growth around the world, a trend that is very much present in the Latin American region (Altman 2011; Soto Barrientos 2012). The use of referendums in particular has increased over the last two decades, with almost every Latin American country undergoing some sort of institutional reform that includes referendums, plebiscites and citizen consultation (Durán-Martínez 2012; Lissidini 2015).

Bolivia has followed this regional tendency by implementing direct democracy instruments since 2004. In that year, the gas referendum was held as a direct result of the Gas War, giving way to the nationalisation of hydrocarbons. In 2008, at the peak of the inter-regional conflict, autonomous referendums were carried out in the regions of Santa Cruz, Beni, Pando and Tarija. The government declared those referendums illegal, although they received international support. In that same year, the political opposition, eventually with the support of pro-government political forces, held the recall referendum, with the positions of the president, vice-president and eight of the nine regional mayors put to the citizen vote. The new constitution was approved in 2009 via a constitutional referendum. Together with these national plebiscites, it is worth mentioning the prior consultation of 2012 in relation to the building of the highway through the TIPNIS National Park. Although the consultation was local, the destabilising political effect of the conflict reached national level. This explains why the consultation has been heavily discussed and politicised (see previous chapter).

The constitutional referendum on 21 February 2016 is thus the country's last example of direct democracy. The fact that the referendum dealt with the possible re-election of candidates to the highest government positions also reflects another regional tendency that has appeared over the last twenty years. With the return to democracy in the 1970s and 1980s, Latin American governments put heavy emphasis on limiting the Executive's power. The majority prohibited presidential re-election, or only allowed it consecutively once. From the 1990s onwards, the region saw a series of reforms passed to allow for consecutive re-elections: Peru in 1993 under Fujimori's government; Argentina in 1994 under Menem's government; and Brazil in 1997 under Cardoso's government. More recently, Venezuela (2009) and Nicaragua (2014) have implemented reforms that allow indefinite re-elections. Nicaragua eliminated any impediment to re-election in its constitution in January 2014. This is how Daniel Ortega was re-elected in 2016 with more than 70 per cent of the votes, extending his presidency from 2007 to 2022. In 2015, the Dominican Republic re-established immediate re-election, allowing Danilo Medina to stand and continue as president, winning a historical 61 per cent in the last elections in 2016. Finally, it is important to mention the case of Honduras, where re-election is forbidden by the constitution. In 2009, the coup d'état that ousted President Zelaya was justified because of his attempts to make re-election possible. In 2015, the country's Supreme Court declared the dubious article of the constitution that prohibits presidential re-election as inapplicable, allowing President Juan Orlando Hernández to follow in Zelaya's footsteps, without opposition or scandal, when announcing in November 2016 that he would stand in the upcoming elections in November 2017.

On the other hand, opposite tendencies can also be observed in the region. In June 2015, Colombia passed a constitutional reform that prohibited presidential re-election only a decade after this had been approved. In Brazil, a constitutional addendum was initially passed in 2015 to forbid re-election. In Paraguay, President Horacio Cartes was forced to publicly withdraw from standing for re-election as a result of constitutional reform after demonstrations, and in April 2017 Congress finally voted unanimously against it.

In summary, only four of the eighteen Latin American countries have completely prohibited re-election: Mexico, Guatemala, Colombia and Paraguay.

The other fourteen allow for re-election but under different (consecutive or non-consecutive) conditions.

The example of Ecuador is relevant to what is happening in Bolivia. In December 2016, a reform was approved to allow indefinite re-election. However, a transitory ruling preventing President Correa from running in the February 2017 elections was passed (with the new regulation only coming fully into effect in May 2017). This is how the controversy surrounding the candidature of Correa, who on several occasions had publicly confirmed that he would not look to prolong his stay in power, was alleviated and indefinite re-election approved, with the debate on presidential re-election being separated from Rafael Correa's political leadership.

This is (still) not the case in Bolivia. On the contrary, the topic of re-election in Bolivia has, from the very beginning, been closely linked to Morales' leadership. As discussed in Chapter 3, the Constituent Assembly presented a version of the constitution that was negotiated with the political opposition, before coming up with the version that was finally approved by the Constitutional Referendum in 2009. One of the most important concessions made by the government at that time was on re-election, agreeing that the ruling on 'only one consecutive' presidential re-election in the new constitution would take into account Morales' first mandate,[14] thus explicitly preventing him from standing in the 2014 elections. However, upon the electoral campaign, Morales expressed his intention to stand for re-election, and Congress (in which his party held a majority) decided to take the matter to the Plurinational Constitutional Court. That body ruled in April 2013 that Morales' candidature was constitutional:

Article 4. Re-election of the State's President and Vice-President.
I. In conformity with that established in Article 168 of the State's Political Constitution, the president and vice-president chosen for the first time under the valid Constitution are free to stand for re-election only once consecutively.
II. The prescription contained in the First Transitory Ruling, Paragraph II of the State's Political Constitution is applicable to authorities that after 22 January 2010 continued to hold public positions, without new elections, appointment or nomination.[15]

Morales won the elections in 2014, obtaining the support of 61.3 per cent of the population, only a few percentage points less than his result in the 2009 elections (64.2 per cent), once again consolidating his power in the government with his 'first' and therefore last re-election within the legal framework established by the new Political Constitution.

21F Morales' First Electoral Defeat: The Media in Political Networks

The fact that Morales and the MAS decided relatively far in advance to secure his standing in the upcoming elections should be understood in relation to the 2015 political climate. Morales ended 2014 with a 75 per cent approval rating, the highest in the region (*La Razón*, 9 January 2015). Even more noteworthy was the fact that Morales ended 2015 with a 65 per cent approval rating (*Página Siete*, 25 December 2015), after a year in which the drop in the prices of commodities on the international market, which had begun in 2014, made a downturn in the economy felt. The country's economic policies were described as 'cautious' by the World Bank, explaining that Bolivia was one of the few countries that was in conditions to face the international crisis head on (as opposed to, for example, Brazil).

The explosion of the corruption scandal in the Indigenous Fund – a body created in 2005 with the aim of supporting diverse projects from indigenous populations – was not enough to cause serious damage to the administration's image of success. Despite the fact that there were accusations of embezzlement directly involving members of the MAS party (*BBC Mundo*, 6 December 2015), President Morales settled the case by ordering an extensive investigation and the persecution of everyone involved, seemingly limiting political damage. In addition, as recently as September 2015, the International Court of The Hague accepted Bolivia's lawsuit in its dispute with Chile for sea access. The ruling was interpreted as an initial triumph for Bolivia and Morales' government (*BBC Mundo*, 24 September 2015), thus explaining the high approval rating with which the government closed the year. In summary, there were sufficient indications that Morales had the support of the population, and that this would pave the way to a candidature in the 2019 elections.

With the referendum ahead, by January 2016 the polls fluctuated between a tie and a marginal victory for the 'Yes', while political analysts indicated a victory for Morales as being highly possible. Undoubtedly, the president's first electoral defeat since 2002 could not be blamed on a single factor, and a series of elements of a more structural nature should be considered. The vivid belief that democracy is 'alternation of power', particularly among the middle class, plays a role, and the increasing rejection of long-term leftist leaders can also be observed as a regional trend. Examples of this have been the dismissal of President Rousseff in Brazil, Rafael Correa's handing over of political leadership in Ecuador, intense protests on the streets against Nicolás Maduro's government in Venezuela, and the election in Argentina of Macri, who put an end to ten years of the Kirchners' administration. The generational differences at the high ranks of leadership, as indicated in the previous section, are also reflected in the electorate. The new 'Evo generation' does not share the sense of urgency or social struggle that formed the basis of support of the MAS's 'process of change'. On the contrary, political discourse with a transformative agenda seems to have been replaced by one of pragmatism and stability, which has not been able to encapsulate young people's aspirations (Achtenberg 2016). To this is added the natural political fatigue of a decade of government and the imminent downturn in economic growth. From a strategic point of view, the political opposition's structural fragmentation has been vitally important to the MAS's electoral victories.

Despite their importance, all these elements already existed in the period prior to the referendum, when a victory for the government political forces was still expected. The relatively narrow margin in the polls leads one to think that events in the city of El Alto[16] in the weeks prior to the referendum, as well as the corruption scandal known as the 'Zapata case', helped to determine the result. In particular, the latter reflects the important role of the media as a highly influential political actor.

Days before the elections, it was revealed that the president's former lover, Gabriela Zapata, allegedly the mother of his child, held an important position in a Chinese company that had just won a multimillion contract with the state without having put in an official bid. This led to serious accusations of 'traffic of influence', directly involving the president. The timing could not have been better for the opposition. The scandal was immediately blown up by the media and social networks, and used to directly attack the president himself.[17] The speed and frenzy with which the attack occurred quickly constrained the space for reasonable criticism and investigation, giving free reign to accusations, misrepresentations, insinuations and ultimately outright lies. It is also worth noting that the scandal took the pro-government political forces by surprise, thus indicating their level of confidence in a YES victory. More importantly still, it showed the government's complete inability to defend and promote itself to a public opinion dominated by the media and social networks. Because of their blunders and inefficiency, the government showed their incapacity to deal with the avalanche of accusations and lies, and unable to prevent serious damage to the images of both the president and the government party at a crucial political moment.

As has been indicated, it is impossible to identify a single factor that explains Morales' first electoral defeat on 21 February 2016. However, from a political network perspective, clear indications of the decisive nature of the 'Zapata case' emerge.

Firstly, there was the damage caused to the 'trust' identified as crucial to understanding Morales' network leadership. During the MAS government's extensive term, this was not the first (or last) accusation of corruption, and perhaps not even the most serious. In fact, a survey carried out in mid-2017 revealed that 64 per cent thought that the level of corruption was the same or less than in previous administrations, compared with 33 per cent who thought it was greater under Morales (*Página Siete*, 5 June 2017). In February 2016, the MAS government survived the Indigenous Fund corruption scandal with relative ease. It can be argued that said scandal was more serious, not only because of the high cost it had for the state but also because it lasted a long time and involved prominent MAS figures of indigenous origin. The Indigenous Fund case manifestly broke with the government discourse that linked corruption and the looting of the state with 'the politics of the past' and the 'political elite', and that described indigenous politicians – mainly because of their humble, popular and marginalised nature – as naturally having impeccable morals. The issue with the 'Zapata case', as a way of denouncing corruption, resides in the fact that, for the first time, Evo's 'exceptionality' was questioned (Achtenberg 2016). Thus, doubts were sown about the president's integrity that precisely affected the backbone of his political leadership, at a time when the question was not so much about whether a possible re-election was democratic but rather about whether Evo Morales' political leadership should continue.

A second element refers to the accusation's timing. It was presented on 3 February, with the eighteen remaining days before the elections being enough time for the media to inflate and exploit this news, and for the political opposition to manipulate it as part of their NO campaign. However, it was not enough time to implement – and much less conclude – an investigation that would differentiate facts from speculation. The politicising of the previously described public arena got worse in the period prior to the referendum, making any reasonable reflections from even a timid neutral position impossible. On the contrary, the debate was unleashed in a public arena dominated by the media and social networks, where the media coverage was very uneven, and in favour of the NO campaign and the attacks against Morales. Attempts to deny these accusations, largely because of the ineptitude with which they were emitted, were easily ruled out or distorted in order to create new attacks.

The third element refers to the Zapata case's function as something 'specific' around which a political network was organised against the president's political leadership and against the YES campaign. As opposed to the 2014 elections, the 2016 referendum did not pitch Morales against the opposition who, divided among themselves, did not manage to close the gap between their candidates and Morales. From the beginning, the referendum allowed for opposing forces to create an alliance in the NO political campaign. Despite this, the last polls prior to the scandal showed that such an alliance would not manage to defeat Morales. In this sense, it can be understood that the 'Zapata case' was decisive. As an accusation of corruption – a strictly 'non-electoral' matter – the case allowed for the adhesion of actors, mainly the media, who would not otherwise have joined the NO political campaign so openly. On being presented as a matter of transparency, responsibility and justice, the 'Zapata case' made it possible for the media to be integrated into the NO campaign, maintaining their image as the 'fourth power' and 'investigative journalism', even though their aim was clearly to discredit by presenting unsubstantiated and impartial information. In this way, the political network was reinforced with what is perhaps the most valuable political resource at key political times: influence on public opinion.

More than a year after the referendum, little seems to remain of the scandal. The son's existence was never proved, which meant the accusation of influence peddling remained unfounded. Neither could other irregularities related to CAMC be proved, beyond the fact that Zapata was never an employee and that she had defrauded the company. The new twists and turns in the 'Zapata case' resonated in the media, but little was cared for evidence. In this sense, the truthfulness of the accusations became secondary (others would say 'irrelevant'), since thanks to the fortunate timing, their effect had already materialised: Morales and the MAS had already lost the referendum on 21 February 2016.

The fourth element that, in my opinion, is indicative of the decisive character of the 'Zapata case' and the central role the media had, relates to the reaction of the government to the results. Four days after the defeat, the president blamed social networks for his defeat and announced that the role of social media needed to be discussed in relation to misinformation (*El País*, 24 February 2016). In April 2016, the president opened his own Twitter account and created the General Office of Social Networks as part of the Ministry of Communications (*Los Tiempos*, 19 April 2016). This body's aim was to 'publicise, consult and interact' with 'cyber communities', as well as 'improve the platforms for information and communication of state administration through the use of social networks' and 'promoting the use of social networks within civil society' (Ministerio de Comunicación). In this same way, in September 2016, the minister of defence, Reymi Ferreira (2016), published his book *Caso Zapata: La Confabulación de la Mentira*. Lastly, the government ordered the filming of a documentary to Argentine journalist Andrés Sal.lari, titled 'El cartel de la mentira' [the lies cartel], an expression that, in May 2016, the then-minister of the presidency, Juan Ramón Quintana, used to refer to the four types of media that, in his opinion, played a key role in the 'treacherous attack' against the president in media coverage of the 'Zapata case'. The documentary was premiered in mid December 2016 and was shown for free in cinemas and on the internet.[18] Both the book and the documentary aimed to make short work of the media's manipulation of information, and of the opposition's interference in the scandal. These actions show that the government recognised the need to explicitly and efficiently make incursions into the public space that is mediated and constructed by the media and social networks, understood as an essential condition for successful political administration.[19]

My interviews with social leaders in July and August 2016 also explain the result of the referendum along these lines, highlighting the use of lies and manipulation by the opposition in combination with the MAS's inferior communication with the population and, in particular, with young people. The leader of CONAMAQ explains:

> the oligarch and imperialist right has created such a set up ... with the referendum, lots of lies have come to light ... in the past, they manipulated us with torture ... in the past it was the Condor Plan, now it's lies. It wasn't the time for the referendum; they needed more time to show the people their results. (Choque 2016, personal interview)

Referring to the media and social networks, the leader of the 'Bartolinas' said:

> February 21st was a complete lie planned by the right. The press did a good job with the Zapata case ... they invented things as part of a campaign of lies. The middle class were not particularly aware of what was going on. They believed the lies. (Mamani 2016, personal interview)

As a factor explaining the electoral defeat, the first secretary of the CSCIOB indigenous organisation, Victor Cabezas, in a personal interview on 25 July 2016 highlighted this lack of communication: 'Social organisations have not communicated their achievements. People believe that we're worse off than in neoliberal times.' Social organisations' interpretation of a lack of effective communication from the government to the 'people' and to 'organisations' made particular reference to young people. Gualberto Arispe, one of the highest leaders in the CSUTCB and president of MAS Youth, explained during a personal interview on 22 July 2016:

> There's been deceit, lies and slander on social networks, affecting a new generation that, for the first time, is voting ... Young people make up a high percentage of those who define the vote, more or less 22 per cent of the total. Afterwards, young people don't care if it was all lies. It's been analysed at every level of our grass-root organisations and the conclusion is that it's all lies and deceit. Now we have to deny everything and show the president's achievements. Our new fellow leaders have to be presented, down to a regional level, using social networks; making people aware and making them understand that the process was hard won.

Thus, in relation to young people, the representative of CONAMAQ indicated: 'We want to teach young people, young professional people, so that they don't forget their identity, so that they learn ... [to use] technology'

(Choque 2016, personal interview). In the same way, Edmundo J. Nogales, from the National School for Political Training, maintains that 'there's been no focus on forming critical young people. The improvement in the economy means better access to technological tools and this has helped the opposition, who use these tools to reach young people, young people without the capacity to be critical' (personal interview on 21 August 2016).

The incursion of the president into social networks, the creation of a government body focused on social networks and the informative material (the book and documentary), together with the interpretations of the MAS's base organisations, point to the importance of the media and social networks in the referendum's results. However, they also show that both the government and social organisations recognise that the lies and manipulation surrounding the 'Zapata case' were only successful because of internal faults and the lack of an effective and up-to-date communication: making use of new technology to both spread the administration's achievements and to offer a counter-narrative of the Zapata case specifically aimed at young people.

As indicated, academic debate is divided between those who see the positive effects on democracy in the use of 'direct democracy' and those who, above anything else, identify the risks. In his comprehensive work called *Direct Democracy Worldwide*, Altman (2011) concludes that, to understand the effect of direct democracy, it should be observed how the mechanism's design interacts with the institutional environment. Thus, in countries with low-intensity democracies in general, mechanisms of direct democracy are a result of weaknesses of representative institutions and of the political party system, and not the other way around. However, Altman indicates that not every country with weak representative institutions uses mechanisms of direct democracy, in the same way that not every country that uses such mechanisms systematically shows a weakening of the political party system. In specific reference to Bolivia, Altman says:

> Nonetheless, for the opposition, some mechanisms of direct democracy – those mandated plebiscites – sometimes open up a window of opportunity (despite all of their weaknesses) in these volatile democracies. Because of their very nature, mechanisms of direct democracy create at least two clearly differentiated positions, and if there is hope for free and fair elections, mechanisms of direct democracy should not be automatically rejected by the opposition. They could be considered a window of opportunity for challenging 'edgy' executive leaders (e.g. Venezuela 2007) or 'edgy' constitutional reforms (e.g. Guatemala 1999). (Altman 2011: 197)

This seems to have been the case with 21F in Bolivia, where, despite the referendum initiative emanating from pro-government political forces in a political scenario that was initially looking favourable (with high levels of approval for both President Morales and his administration), the mechanism of direct democracy served to put into check this 'edgy' executive leader and the 'edgy' constitutional reform it proposed. As Altman says, based on the result of the referendum, it could be concluded that despite criticism of Morales' administration regarding its democratic quality, the government clearly could not take advantage of their position of power to push through (or manipulate) the citizen vote in their favour. Therefore, the electoral process appears to have been 'free and just'. Exactly this conclusion turns the analysis contradictory.

As shown in the previous section, the way in which media coverage of the 'Zapata case' occurred, both in the traditional media and on social networks, and at a critical political moment, was decisive for the result. The media coverage, far from being investigative, critical and impartial, focused on deliberately attacking the foundation of Morales' network leadership: the trust inspired by his 'exceptional nature'. In my opinion, the extent of these accusations' falseness and the opportunistic timing of the same show how the 'Zapata case' allowed a 'political network' to emerge in support of the NO political campaign which, through the media and social networks, was successful in manipulating public opinion about the president, and thus in defining the referendum result. Therefore, the actions and effect of this particular 'political network' should be considered, since they compel us to question the 'free and just' description of the referendum's electoral process.

When trying to assess the democratic nature of the mechanisms of direct democracy implemented by the government, the 21F case shows that it is not sufficient to only consider the mechanism's design and that of the institutional environment. The Bolivian case shows that it is also necessary to contemplate the actions of other types of actor in the public arena that can damage the democratic quality of the process. Thus, paradoxically, the institutional weakness of the Bolivian state – lacking effective, regulated and current channels of information for civil society – allowed the NO campaign to coordinate its political network through the media and present distorted and partial information at a critical political moment. In the same way, 21F's process and result showed the active and effective participation of the media in politics, and thus, paradoxically, refutes the frequent accusations made about restrictions of the freedom of expression and the press under Morales' administration.

Political Leadership: The Issue of Re-election and Democracy

The government has been successful in enabling Morales' candidature at the 2019 elections, despite the result of the 21 February Constitutional

Referendum. In this way, his pivotal role in Bolivian politics has been secured and invigorated in the run up to the 2019 elections, and very probably after that too. For this reason, it is necessary to reflect on the role of his political leadership in the current Bolivian scenario. More specifically, this last section aims to reflect on the impact of re-election on the process of democratisation, in a context of network governance.

The manipulation of information, understood as a deficiency of the referendum process, calls into question the legitimacy of the result, at least from a theoretical point of view. The Morales administration was quick to undermine its outcome by announcing at the end of 2016 that it would seek a legal way to the re-election, either by a new referendum or through the president's resignation six months before the end of his term (*El País*, 23 January 2017). Morales was undoubtedly invigorated by some opinion polls that continued to show high levels of approval for his administration. In August 2016, the MORI survey company carried out a study on the ten years of the president's administration; the results showed a 62 per cent approval rating for his administration, and 77 per cent recognised the important role (56 per cent 'important' and 21 per cent 'very important') of his leadership for the nation's development (*Cambio*, 10 August 2016). The 'Muestras y Mercados' private company carried out a study in September of that year that showed that 52 per cent of the population thought that Evo Morales should continue as leader of the Movement towards Socialism (*El Periódico*, 22 September 2016). In January 2017, a survey showed that 58 per cent of the population approved the president's actions, although 63 per cent rejected his possible re-election (*El Deber*, 22 January 2017).

As far as political leadership is concerned, the surveys that were carried out on the referendum are significant. One survey asked: 'If Morales were to lose the referendum, which MAS leader should be his successor?' The results seen in the graph below show that the MAS's most prominent figures were far from having the same approval ratings as President Morales (who, in the last elections, won more than 60 per cent of the vote). Former chancellor David Choquehuanca, who has often been described as Morales' natural successor, did not even attain an approval rating of 10 per cent.

In June 2016, a similar survey on who should be the MAS candidate showed that the highest percentage (31 per cent) did not know or did not answer; Vice-President Álvaro García Linera obtained 21 per cent of the preference; and 17 per cent responded that 'nobody' was in a position to succeed Morales in leading the party. Once again, the rest of the MAS's most prominent figures did not obtain more than 7 per cent of support (*Página Siete*, 26 June 2016). This data illustrates the problem of Evo Morales' political leadership, as the then deputy minister of Coordination with the Social Movements and Civil Society pointed to me as early as 2010 (personal interview on 1 December):

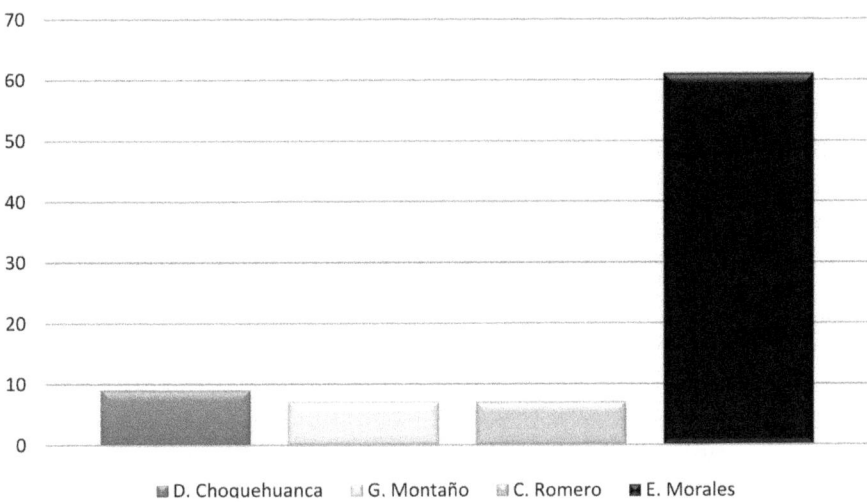

▪ D. Choquehuanca ▫ G. Montaño ▪ C. Romero ▪ E. Morales

Figure 5.1 Support for prominent MAS figures as possible successors of Evo Morales in percentages of voter intention. Source: Author elaboration, based on the survey data (*Página Siete*, 8 December 2015).

It's a leadership that isn't constructed in parallel with others, but rather by destroying them. This is also serious. It's gone beyond other popular leaderships … We haven't developed local, regional political leaderships. We're all under Evo's shadow, even those from the right … That's the challenge. We need to construct leaderships … If you don't have leadership, you're just an administrator trying to keep everybody happy.[20]

More than six years later, this observation is still relevant. The lack of political leadership within the Movement towards Socialism continues to be a concern. As previously indicated, social organisations have lost their best leaders to state administration, which has led to the internal weakening of their organisations. On the other hand, my interviews carried out in mid-2016 mention that leaders do exist:

'There are leaders-in-training'. (Mamani 2016)
'There are leaders in Bolivia, but they're much unfocused'. (Cabezas 2016Heads of the CSCIOB)
'About our leaders, there're many within the MAS … For example, there's a 24-year-old senator and a 22-year-old mayor in Potosí. We've elected authorities everywhere who are working and creating'. (Arispe 2016)

The MAS is the only party in Bolivia with a national presence in local politics. The regional and local elections in 2015 secured six of the nine governments for the party in office while gaining control of two-thirds of the 339 local authorities. This corroborates the opinions expressed in my interviews on the existence of multiple political leaderships. The problem seems to be not so much a lack of leaders, but rather a lack of leaders at national level. The creation of the National School for Political Training, aimed at young people ('the Evo generation'), can also be understood in this sense, and has the aim of raising awareness and providing political training, thus creating opportunities for debate and reflection that go beyond the local context, to build up new leaderships.[21]

The lack of political leadership at the national level is not exclusive to the MAS, but is also found in the political opposition. In 2016, a survey asked: 'If Evo Morales won the referendum, which opposition leader is best placed to stand against him in an election?'. In June and November of that year, surveys were carried out with a similar question regarding which opposition leader had the best chance of standing against Morales' possible candidature in the 2019 elections. The data from these surveys has been summarised in the following graph, limited to the opposition leaders who obtained the highest percentages.

This data is revealing in several ways. Firstly, it shows that no oppositional leader is alone able to capitalise on the resistance of different sectors of society to the Morales government. As previously indicated, the political opposition remains divided and, up to now, has not been able to present an alternative

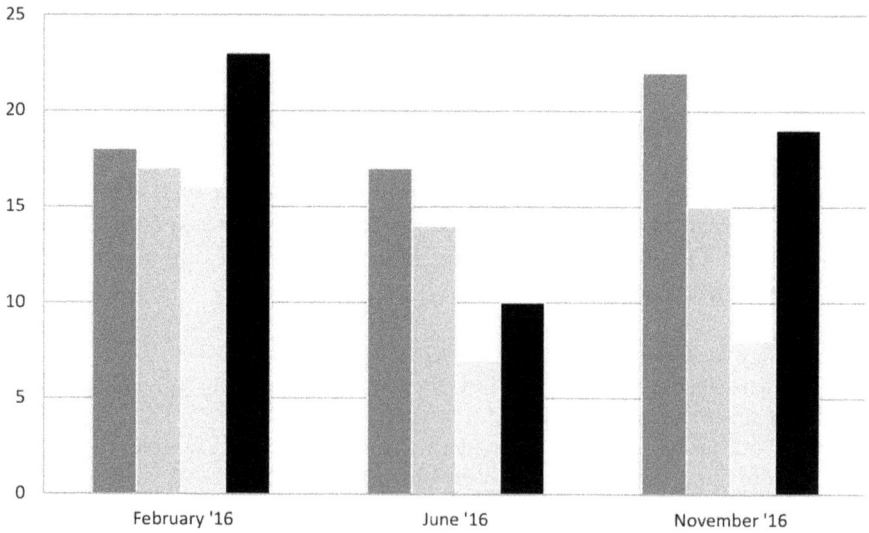

Figure 5.2 Support for opposition leaders standing against Evo Morales in percentages of voter intention. Source: Author elaboration, based on the survey data.

political project that, in the public's opinion, can measure up to the present government administration. This must also be understood in relation to the high levels of approval for Morales' administration (which fluctuates between 40–70 per cent, according to different surveys), given that a proportion of the population does not support Morales (in a new re-election) or the MAS, but does recognise the achievements of his administration and does not see the potential for continuity or improvement in the opposition. As seen in Chapter 4, the opposition looked for citizen support on very specific topics – such as security and protection of the environment – during the last elections; but these topics lacked relevance to vast sectors of society, and did not manage to garner attention on a national level. This can also be understood in relation to the hegemonic nature of the MAS's political discourse (Postero 2010a; Zegada et al. 2011; Farthing and Kohl 2014). At the time of writing, opposition leaders seem not have managed to move beyond their basis of local/regional support. The case of the governor of the Santa Cruz region, Rubén Costas, is illustrative, as his approval ratings are relatively constant because they are based on regional support.

The case of the opposition leader Samuel Doria Medina from the National Unity party should also be considered, since it reflects the nature of the political party system in Bolivia. Unidad Nacional is the only political party, apart from the MAS, that has participated in every national election over the past fifteen years. The following graph shows the fluctuations of the political party system. From 2002 onwards, each national election saw the incursion of new political parties, as well as their rapid disappearance. In this sense, the Unidad Nacional party's relative stability and its progress up to the last elections in 2014 – with 7.8 per cent in 2005, 5.7 per cent in 2009, and 24.2 per cent in 2014 – meant it had to be considered as a promising contender, even more so in a post-referendum scenario in which Morales' leadership was eclipsed. The preference levels obtained by Medina in the 2016 surveys are, in this sense, disappointing.

The third person to consider is Carlos Mesa, who is consistently placed second after Evo Morales. It is important to note that he is a rather 'apolitical' figure: Mesa owes his public recognition to his lengthy career as a journalist and historian and, more recently, as official spokesperson for the maritime cause. He has no party affiliation and has, on several occasions, stressed that he has no political ambitions and that he will not stand as a candidate in 2019. In this sense, voter preference can be understood as an indication of the persistent citizen distrust of political parties and, indeed, politics in general. After his short term as president between 2003 and 2005 (see Chapter 2), Mesa chose to keep a low political profile until 2014, when Evo Morales named him official spokesperson for the maritime cause. The relative success with which he has developed this campaign, and his role in

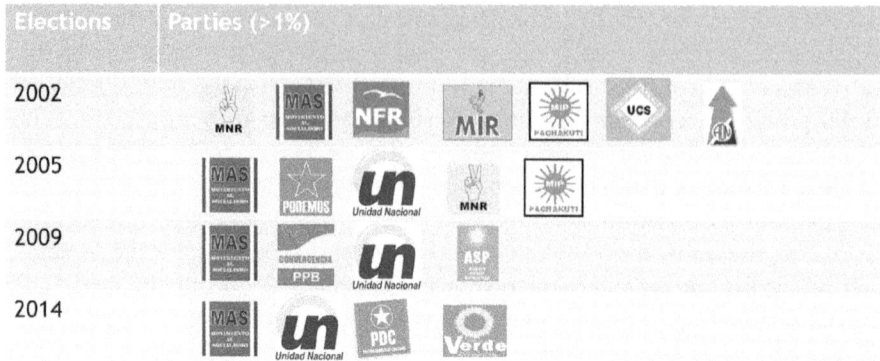

Figure 5.3 Fluctuations in the political party system at the general elections. Source: Author elaboration, based on data from the Electoral Supreme Court (www. oep.org.bo). The initials stand for: Revolutionary Nationalist Movement (MNR), Movement towards Socialism (MAS), New Republican Force (NFR), Revolutionary Left Movement (MIR), Pachakuti Indigenous Movement (MIP), Solidarity Civic Unity (UCS), Nationalist Democratic Action (ADN), Social Democratic Power (PODEMOS), National Unity (UN), Plan Progress for Bolivia – National Convergence (the Convergencia–PPB alliance), Assembly for the Sovereignty of the Peoples (ASP), Christian Democratic Party (PDC) and the Bolivian Green Party (Verde). Figure created by the author.

it, has undoubtedly helped to increase his political value, perhaps particularly so because he is dealing with a topic of national interest. To this must be added the fact that Mesa has known how to maintain his distance from pro-government political forces (and the opposition). In 2016, Mesa openly judged another re-election of Morales as constitutionally inappropriate, leading to a confrontation with the MAS (*La Razón*, 1 October 2015). In a political scenario that makes neutrality practically impossible, Mesa has projected himself as an independent figure, capable of transcending party interests and of standing 'beyond politics'. Paradoxically, this is exactly what has placed him in the middle of the political scene.

As the data in the graphs on the previous pages shows, the only real alternative to Mesa in the polls in 2016 was the 'Nobody' option. A large part of the population considered that neither the opposition's candidates nor the non-candidate Carlos Mesa were in any condition to compete with Morales' political leadership. This information underlines César Navarro's observation that Morales' leadership is constructed by 'destroying' other leaders, both in the MAS and in the opposition, patently pointing to a situation of a vacuum in leadership if Morales were to disappear from the political scene.

According to a survey carried out in March 2017, 66 per cent of citizens patently rejected voiding the referendum's result. However, the same survey showed that half the population considered that Morales would be a candidate in the 2019 elections anyway (*Página Siete*, 26 March 2017). The fact that the post-referendum surveys on the intention to vote, which took place before the ruling of the Constitutional Court in November 2017 and consistently included Morales as well as the non-candidate Carlos Mesa as options, show that the public debate was considering future scenarios that did not comply with the current institutional and 'reasonable' restrictions. As observed in previous chapters, Bolivian politics over the last ten years has revealed numerous examples in which the institutional framework or 'rationale' are not – on their own – determining factors but rather are subject to the creation of political networks that coordinate actors in society (such as social movements, NGOs and/or the media). Morales' candidature still being considered was in a sense a reflection of the likelihood of such a scenario despite institutional constraints, as well as indicative of the existence of a relatively large political network in support of that scenario. The ruling by the Constitutional Court in 2017 in a way sanctioned or legalised what was a virtual reality in the public sphere.

The result of the referendum had the important effect of strengthening and expanding the political network supporting the candidature of Morales. Firstly, the result constituted a wake-up call for the MAS, making it clear that the race is never over and that it must be fought right up to the end. Secondly, the government has recognised the necessity to strategically and consciously make incursions into the public arena through the media (both traditional media and new social media), and has acted accordingly. Thirdly, the negative result of the referendum has caused the strengthening of the coalition of the movements and social organisations that back Morales and the MAS. In comparison to previous years, my interviews with social leaders in mid-2016 showed a much more positive valuation of the connection with the government, both with ministers and the president, as well as of the connection to and cohesion of the Unity Pact and CONALCAM. The following quote illustrates this point:

> The Unity Pact has met with the president in order to become strong again … Proposals emerge from the Unity Pact and CONALCAM for the president to translate into viable laws and regulations … There's a lot of stability and a fluid communication … We have a close relationship with the deputy minister [from the Coordination with Social Movements and Civil Society Organisations] and also a direct relationship with other ministers. We don't need to request an audience; everything's done by mobile and we get a quick response. (Cabezas 2016, personal interview)

Another event that illustrated the growing cohesion of the indigenous movements behind Morales was the celebration of the National Rural, Productive and Community Day, held on 2 August 2016. It was Morales' first official public event in two months, after a knee operation forced him out of the public eye. The event had been announced and promoted by the Unity Pact organisations, with the president participating in the promulgation of decrees in favour of the productive rural sector. A lot more people arrived than expected, converting it into something large scale that, after Morales arrival, took a different turn. The president was warmly received by the organisations who ratified and backed him. The leader of the CSUTCB, Feliciano Vegamonte, declared:

> Nowadays, like never before in Bolivia's history, we're side by side with our brother and president Evo Morales, to tell you that the native indigenous and Bolivian people are never going to abandon him and we're going to carry on fighting by his side, because he's always been the only indisputable leader. (*Agencia Boliviana de Información*, 2 August 2016)

A few weeks later, a member of the National School for Political Training confirmed to me that it was the first important meeting of the Unity Pact after the corruption scandal of the Indigenous Fund and the referendum on 21 February. The number of people who attended, far more than had been expected, took the organisation by surprise, meaning that many people could not get into the theatre where the event was being held because of a lack of space: 'Everyone wanted to see the president. People, all kinds of people, ended up outside. It was really emotional' (Nogales 14 August 2016, personal interview). A little later, at an event held in Cochabamba, the Unity Pact formally declared: 'All of us have agreed to give our backing to our brother the president, Evo Morales, so that he can continue with the process of change' (*Página Siete*, 20 August 2016).

The wake-up call of 21 February has meant that both the MAS and Morales are facing the political campaign for the 2019 election more aware and alert. Entering the media-dominated public arena, in particular that of social networks, has been a strategic move in this direction, aimed at articulating this valuable actor within the MAS's political network and with its sympathisers. In the same way, there were clear indications of a renewal of the support from the networks of organisations and indigenous social movements, which intensified as the government moved forward with its strategy to enable the re-election. This is illustrated by the series of events in which large portions of the population were mobilised before and after the court's rulings in support of Morales' candidature.

This could be clearly observed in February 2018. Two years after the referendum and months after the ruling of the Constitutional Court, different sectors of the population prepared mobilisations both against and in favour of Morales' candidature. Just as during the constituent process

(2006–2009), it again seemed to be a competition about which band was able to mobilise the largest number of people. A massive concentration to announce Morales' candidature at the statue of the indigenous 'El Chiriguano' in the city of Santa Cruz on 20 February 2018 largely surpassed the size of the one organised against it the following day at the statue of 'El Cristo'. This was significant, as the city of Santa Cruz had been considered to be the stronghold of the political opposition in previous years. At least at the level of the numbers and impacts of the mobilisations, the Morales band seems to have won the arm wrestling (*La Razón*, 19 February 2018), pointing to the strength and expansion of the political network behind his political leadership.

On the other hand, the rejection of a possible re-election of Morales has been articulating a political network, led by members of the political opposition and supported by citizen movements under banners such as 'Bolivia dijo No', 'Esto no es Venezuela' and 'A mí me gusta la democracia', which had been recurrent during mobilisations as well as in social media. Activism started almost immediately after the constitutional ruling of November 2017, with a campaign for the null vote on the elections of judiciary officials in December of that year, and it was very successful. The null vote constituted over 50 per cent of the total, and although the announced clashes and violence did not take place, the result was effective in ousting a sense of rejection of Morales leadership. This was reinforced by the fact that social media was flooded with pictures of ballots containing messages allusive to the issue of re-election, such as 'Bolivia dijo NO'.

Unlike the political network in support of Morales' re-election, which links predominantly domestic actors, the political network against it has derived its strength from international actors. At the end of March 2018 the Venice Commission, at the request of the Organisation of American States OAS issued a report in which it concluded that re-election in presidential and semi-presidential systems is not a human right, and it openly declared to be in favour of term limits (*La Razón*, 10 April 2018). This was used to reinforce the demand that had been presented at the Inter-American Court of Human Rights by former ombudsmen Rolando Villena and Waldo Albarracín, together with the Permanent Assembly for Human Rights in Bolivia (APDHB), against a new candidature by President Morales. The demand was also accompanied by an official declaration by the electoral court about the binding character of the February 2016 referendum (*El Deber*, 13 April 2018). The admission of the demand by the court was celebrated by the opposition in February 2018, as it was announced that a decision from this organ would overrule the decision by the Bolivian Constitutional Court (*La Razón*, 11 February 2018; *Página Siete*, 10 February 2018). However, later in 2018 the Court rejected the demand (*Los Tiempos*, 17 August 2018).

On the basis of the analysis presented, it can be argued that Morales' 2019 candidature depends as much on the institutional/legal framework as on the political networks that are being articulated to garner support from other important actors, such as social movements, the media and international organisations. This ongoing arm wrestling is expected to continue until the very end of the electoral campaign.

How must such obstinate actions to secure and prevent the candidature of Morales be understood, beyond the common explanations of individual political ambitions? And what does the possible re-election mean for the process of democratisation?

As explained in the first sections of this chapter, political leadership in the last ten years – particularly that of Morales – has been a crucial factor, which is why the idea of an absence of leadership is, at the very least, concerning. As shown by the surveys on possible successors from within his own party and from the opposition, his disappearance from the political scene would translate in a leadership vacuum, which raises concerns. The preoccupation has been reinforced by Venezuela's experience, where its 'Bolivarian' political project was largely defined by the leader. The Venezuelan case reinforces the Weberian affirmation that the leader's charisma cannot be institutionalised or transferred (Hellinger and Spanakos 2017), and that the strategy of moulding Maduro's leadership to the image and under the shadow of Chávez does not seem to have been successful in ensuring a 'Chavismo without Chávez' (Arenas 2016). Thus, the legitimacy of and support for Maduro's government has deteriorated to such a point that a political crisis has occurred which, together with the economic downturn, has also placed the country in a very uncertain scenario.

It must be noted that the tragic death of Hugo Chávez turned him into a kind of martyr, resulting in a kind of hero worship around him (Michelutti 2016) and at the same time making it difficult to consolidate his successor's leadership (Joffres 2015). But despite this important difference, Bolivians may consider the developments in Venezuela and the stability promised by a subsequent term of Morales, in the run up to the 2019 elections. Even more so because, although both countries have suffered drops in the prices of raw materials, Bolivia's economic policies are solid, and resistant to the unfavourable economic climate, as the country closed 2017 with the leading economic growth in the region (*La Razón*, 14 December 2017; *América Economía*, 6 February 2018).

The experience of Ecuador is deemed to be worthy of consideration as well, presenting a political scenario marked by an equally charismatic leader. Correa's government also flirted with the idea of re-election, but he personally abstained at the end of 2016. This should be understood in relation to harsh criticism of re-election as being 'anti-democratic', as well as to the downfall of the Latin American left, which occurred that year. His appointed successor, Lenin Moreno, who was supposed to secure continuity of the Correista political project and even serve as just an interim pending Correa's return, has turned out to be quite a surprise. Almost immediately after assuming power, the Moreno government started to move in an opposite direction, resulting in a failed attempt by his own political party to remove him from his position. This has escalated into open confrontations with his predecessor, who returned to Ecuador to prepare his candidature in opposition to Moreno, effectively dividing the Correista party.

In regard to the effects of re-election for the democratic practice, it is interesting to consider the study carried out by De Ferrari (2015). Analysing fifty-one years of elections in the Latin American region, the study contains a series of important conclusions that refute the dominant idea that the electorate holds the government party collectively responsible when studying what type of candidate influences government accountability in the elections. Considering the fact that political parties have different factions (Sartori 1976), De Ferrari divides the presidential candidates into three categories: presidents who seek re-election; successors (political allies of the outgoing president); and non-successors (intra-supporting opponents of the president). This division is constructed on two elements: the degree to which the electorate identifies the presidential candidate with the performance of the outgoing government, and the electorate's perception of the continuity of two administrations from the same party (ibid.: 200). This analysis generates significant differences between the three categories; in particular, between 'successors' and 'non-successors', showing that the electorate does not hold the political party responsible as a whole for the past administration. The exiting president's reputation is not transferred automatically to presidential candidates emerging from the party, and the electorate does take into account the candidate's closeness to the outgoing president when casting their votes. This explains, for example, the slim margin by which Moreno won the election in Ecuador. As far as economic performance is concerned, the study shows that evaluation in the elections varies considerably: the electorate punishes all three types of candidate for a downturn in the economy and only rewards 'successors' and 'presidents who seek re-election' when the economy is positively evaluated.

In combination with the Bolivarian experiences, the study points to the complexity of the decision to stand again or to designate a successor, since a series of factors must be considered when choosing a presidential candidate. In the case of Bolivia specifically, it can be said that the current popularity of the president and the high level of approval for his administration are not in themselves sufficient to conclude that Morales is the MAS's best option, now his candidature has been enabled. As the political campaign advances, it is expected that the MAS and the president's administration will be subject to more and more severe criticism in the (social) media-dominated public arena, with the already visible pressure from the international community, and where the possibility of another 'Zapata case' cannot be excluded. In this sense, the candidature of Morales is not certain and, as stated before, depends much more on the political networks in favour and against it than on the legal constraints and opportunities.

After a total of thirteen years in power, it is reasonable to assume that an alternative candidate would spare the MAS from difficulties in the electoral campaign: such an alternative candidate would allow the party to present itself as being receptive to criticism by enacting change within the party at the most important level (its leadership), while capitalising electorally on the achievements of the previous administration. However, as has been demonstrated throughout this chapter, Morales' leadership has been key to government administration and the MAS's electoral success, converting it into something almost 'indispensable' for the 'process of change'. It is still necessary to consider the extenuation that Morales' leadership was closely linked to social demonstrations and movements, particularly the indigenous, as pointed out in Chapter 2. In the words of Balderacchi (2017: 151): 'If Correa and Chávez's election should be primarily ascribed, along with other contextual factors, to their personal abilities to convince the electorate, in Bolivia the 2005 election of Morales is instead unequivocally linked to the constant rapid strengthening of the indigenous/popular social movement'. This explains why 'Evo-ism' is not referred to like 'Chavism'. Even so, Morales' leadership has been 'overwhelming' for other leaders in the party (and for the opposition). In other words, Morales' current thirteen years in power have practically blocked the path for a successor. In this sense, it is worth asking whether, if the decision was taken today, the remaining time would be enough for the deconstruction of his leadership and the construction of an alternative one.

Considering the above, the Morales' candidature for the 2019 elections has rationale, which will inevitably add to the debate that became more heated at the time of the referendum on the rotation of power as a fundamental trait of democracy (for example: *Página Siete*, 16 September 2015; *El Diario*, 6 October 2016; 2017), and which will recur in the run up to the 2019 elections. De Ferrari's study sheds some light on this when he concludes:

> The results of this article also have direct implications for the debate on the advantages of allowing presidents to run for consecutive terms (Carey 2003). I show that the re-election rule is an important tool for enhancing electoral sanctioning. As long as elections are not conducted on an 'uneven playing field' (Levitsky and Way 2010), the advantages of allowing

presidents to run for re-election seem to be clear on normative grounds. Thus, if the re-election provision enhances accountability when used in the right context, we should start thinking about the stage in the process of democratic consolidation at which a country can start contemplating its introduction. (De Ferarri 2015: 223)

De Ferrari thus sustains that in an advanced stadium of democratic consolidation, which guarantees fair elections, re-election increases accountability towards the electorate and brings with it advantages for the strengthening of democracy. In other words, the alternation of power is not fundamental per se for democracy to be fully practised. In fact, it seems to be more about having a real 'expectation' that elections often result in a rotation of power, rather than whether rotation actually occurs at every election.

Another study maintains that it is not possible to theorise on 'state building' and democracy separately, but rather that the dual construction of democratic states, from which a contradictory relationship emerges, should be considered. On the one hand, a concentration of power is needed to build state institutions; on the other, this concentration of power needs to be restricted to guarantee the norms of liberal democracy. On this basis, the author maintains that a stable democracy is based on three pillars: effective state institutions; the autonomy of these institutions from other actors; and the existence of significant mechanisms of accountability (Bowen 2015).

In this sense, when considering the state of democracy in a regime, the rotation of power should not be overestimated. The above studies effectively show that the democratic practice is complex, marked by tension and contradictory relations. Guaranteeing the 'expectation' of rotation in a free and just context is one element, among others, that contributes to strengthening democracy. For example, the lack of rotation of power in the Russian regime is seen as seriously questioning the quality of democracy by basing itself on practices that undermine state institutions and accountability mechanisms. On the other hand, Germany's Angela Merkel assumed power in November 2005, a few months before Evo Morales, and has just recently started her fourth term. Her continuity is not perceived as problematic (although she suffered a loss, her party again won the majority of votes), considering that her leadership is based on effective and strong institutions. If these two examples are understood as the two extremes of the continuum of building democratic states, locating the position of Evo Morales' Bolivian regime on that continuum would allow for a greater basis on which to assert the democratic or anti-democratic nature of a possible re-election.

The support of indigenous organisations and movements is the *sine qua non* condition, which should be recognised as one of the greatest achievements of the 'process of change'. At this time, this support is found behind Morales: Morales' leadership continues to be the axis around which the state articulates with social movements and civil society organisations, which is of vital importance to political decisions. This is exactly the problem. Beyond the legal framework that makes it possible, Morales' candidature is not unequivocally the best option, as he will face serious difficulties in the political campaign. These difficulties could well be mitigated by opting for a successor. However, the support by the social (indigenous) organisations has proven crucial, and social organisations are very conscious of this. Their backing alone is not capable of guaranteeing the MAS electoral victory – but, on the basis of this study, no political option has any chance without this backing. That is perhaps the greatest achievement of 'process of change'. The identity, emotional and personal relationship of the indigenous social organisations with Morales' leadership has always been maintained and, in the current scenario, has been cemented. That political network, which forms the basis of the MAS, is, in my opinion, enough to explain the MAS party strategy to continue with Morales' leadership and candidature.

Still it is important not to overestimate the 'emotional' and 'identifying' nature of the connection to Morales. Indigenous organisations have shown their relative autonomy from the president at key moments ('*el gasolinazo*'; the TIPNIS conflict) and greater political maturity in the country's decisive moments: the vision of the nation reflected in the Unity Pact proposal for the Constituent Assembly. Undoubtedly, the identity relationship has a lot of weight when it comes to choosing Morales, but perhaps more important still are the cold political calculations of the masses when they do not see a viable alternative that represents their interests in the opposition. In the same way, it must be considered that new juvenile contingents have emerged in the electorate who did not live through the struggles against neoliberalism enacted by Morales, and whose discursive reiterations no longer generate a similar impact as at that particular moment in history. Although the opposition has not shown the capacity to renew leaderships that win over citizens who will always consider the improvements to their quality of life insufficient, this is not a guarantee that new generations will unconditionally support a process that has not renovated its discourse with sufficient political speed.

Notes

1. In both the 2014 general elections and the Constitutional Referendum in February 2016, the topic under discussion was extending Evo Morales' political leadership. Therefore, these touched on the most important matter – the indispensability of the leader and his possible successors (from both the MAS as well as from the political opposition). This topic will be dealt with in more detail later on in this chapter.
2. The lists of candidates were drawn up by social leaders invited to do so by the upper echelons of the party (Molina 2010).

3. The content of these categories deserves an analysis that reflects their complexity, which will not be gone into here. Simplifying, one of the most notable differences is highlighted: the Earth's creation. The peasants see the Earth as land that must produce – an economic resource. The indigenous conceive it more as 'territory', Mother Earth, of which they are an integral part. This causes a conflict of interests between 'the peasant' and the 'indigenous' (Pino Jordán 2010).

4. Interview with Jorge Komadina, researcher from the Centre for Applied Studies on Economic, Social and Cultural Rights (CEADESC). Cochabamba, 10 November 2010.

5. Interview with Daniel Santalla Torres, minister of Work, Employment and Social Security, former leader of the Bolivian Workers' Centre (COB). La Paz, 25 May 2012.

6. Here, I would like to highlight an interview with the director of the NINA programme on the creation of social leaderships. La Paz, 24 April 2012.

7. IPSOS survey, carried out in April 2017 (http://www.ipsos.com.bo/).

8. It must be mentioned that Morales has managed to negotiate and make pacts with economic powers initially opposed to his regime; for example, with the Confederation of Private Business Owners of Bolivia: 'Comunicado de Prensa. Presidente Evo Morales destaca reunión "histórica" con el sector privado', La Paz, 23 August 2012; 'Empresarios privados aceptan pagar el doble aguinaldo; falta definir modalidad', *Página Siete*, 26 November 2013; 'Empresarios se suman al plan para traer al G77', *La Razón*, 16 December 2013; 'Bolivia pone en vigor una nueva ley de promoción de inversiones', *El País*, 4 April 2014; 'Morales cita a empresarios para enfrentar juntos la caída del crudo', *La Razón*, 5 January 2015; 'Gobierno y empresarios construirán agenda "público-privada" para el desarrollo de Bolivia', *Correo del Sur*, 1 June 2016; 'Las "recetas" Empresarios-Gobierno reportan un avance de 30%', *Los Tiempos*, 29 March 2017; 'Gobierno y empresarios decidieron instalar mesas de trabajo', *El Deber*, 8 May 2017.

9. In his article, Roberto Laserna explains how the Bolivian state, under the presidency of Evo Morales, goes through its period of greatest institutional decentralisation, which in practice means that Morales, with an absolute majority in the polls, has less power than any president elected in the second round in the 1980s. The country's regional autonomies and mayors, who manage important fiscal resources, were not designated by the government, but rather by votes. Lastly, state companies now have administrative autonomy (Laserna 2007: 114). Together with the considerable political impact of the social movements, all this outlines a scenario of complex constraints for the national executive power.

10. See, for example, the highly critical article by Pablo Regalsky (2010) that concludes that social movements have been co-opted, and the system of party political representation has been reinforced, while the favourable economic climate has allowed the incorporation of the business sector. In this way, the initial demand for a Constituent Assembly that really democratised property and control of natural resources as demanded by indigenous social movements, did not occur.

11. Pablo Stefanoni makes a similar interpretation, observing Morales' arbitrary role, which serves to maintain the 'complex and unstable platform' that is the MAS (Stefanoni 2010: 158–59).

12. See also the article by Hidle and Normann (2013) on the importance of trust in network governance leadership.

13. CONALCAM was founded in January 2007 with the aim of mobilising social organisations in support of the 'process of change', directly connecting a broad coalition of organisations and social movements to the highest levels of the state (president and vice-president) as well as the MAS.

14. At that time, it was agreed that re-election should consider the period in government prior to the new constitution. Morales shortened his constitutional period to stand in

the December 2009 elections, thus obtaining what should be understood as consecutive re-election, which was the reason he was ineligible as a candidate in the 2014 elections.

15. Source: http://www.tcpbolivia.bo/tcp/

16. Only days before the referendum, El Alto was the scene of a march led by prominent members of the MAS protesting against the local government, leading to violent confrontations. During the incident, the council premises were set on fire, killing six and injuring 256. In 2015, Soledad Chapetón was elected mayoress of the MAS, which represented the loss of the city of El Alto as a bastion of MAS support. The incident occurred only a few days after the mayoress had declared her support for the NO campaign.

17. Therefore, it could be said that it is possible to observe in society what Benkler has called 'the networked Fourth Estate' (Benkler 2011). Benkler has described this phenomenon as a group of practices, organisational models and technology that are associated with the freedom of speech that gives the public control over the government. However, it is different to traditional media. Since it has no limits, the networked Fourth Estate includes a diverse group of actors (profit-making and non-profit media, academic centres and individual networks distributed within the media, together with traditional press organisations). Its emergence is related to the internet freedom that allows individuals and cooperative network associations to give their opinions and organise themselves in favour of specific causes. Because of its character, the networked Fourth State combines elements of both traditional and new forms of media (news media), and 'professionalism' and 'responsibility' – as well as 'unprofessionalism' and 'irresponsibility' – can be found on both sides (ibid.). See also Benkler 2011: 311–97.

18. The documentary is available on youtube.com (https://www.youtube.com/watch?v=GbFv WnGU72U).

19. Likewise, a survey carried out by MORI in June 2016 showed that 70 per cent of the population thought the media manipulated information about the Zapata case, and more than half thought that this had influenced the referendum's end result.

20. Interview with César Navarro, deputy minister of the Social Movements and Civil Society Organisations Body. La Paz, 1 December 2010.

21. This body has a school in each of the country's regions (except Pando); each has around twenty active members. The school organises activities focused on organisations and social movements, with the aim of formulating critical positions that allow for the advance of the 'change process'. MAS members as well as other members of the left participate, thus creating an opportunity for sevearl groups to be coordinated. In particular, it is directed at the 'Evo generation', and aims to be an opportunity for training far removed from and independent of the MAS. (Skype interview with Edmundo J. Nogales from the National School for Political Training, 21 August 2016). See also: http://escuelanacionaldeformacion.blogspot.nl/0.

Conclusion

The academic debate on social movements in Latin America has tended to emphasise their manifest opposition vis-à-vis the state. Considering the region's socio-historic context, this antagonism may be a result of the tension between two political positions. As opposed to the new social movements in Europe, Latin American social movements initially emerged to recover democracy, and only in second instance to strengthen it. Apart from this, the more general academic literature has placed social movements in the arena of what is social and/or non-institutional politics, where two positions can be distinguished on the effect of social movements' actions on the practice of democracy. On the one hand, by pressuring the state structure through social activism, social movements undermine the position of the institutions in charge of representing and channelling social interests towards the state – the political party system – thus infringing on democratic consolidation. On the other, social movements embody the emancipation of groups marginalised by the dominant system that, by means of alternative ways of and spaces of participation, are able to assert their interests within the institutional political system, making it more responsive to their needs. In that way, they contribute to the strengthening of democracy. Despite their differences, in both theoretical perceptions the opposition between the state and the social movement is characteristic.

The Bolivian political scenario over the last few decades has been considerably different to the hypothetical ones in these models. Following the regional tendency, the impact of social movements in the political arena became much more explicit in Bolivia towards the turn of the millennium, reaching its peak in the electoral victory of the Movement towards Socialism (MAS) in December 2005. As seen in Chapter 2, in a 'dialectal' relationship between the state and society after the return to democracy, social movements gradually organised in opposition to the state, with clear examples of this in the development of a strong indigenous movement and the urban social movements that managed to halt government plans during the 'Water' (2000) and 'Gas' (2003) Wars, among others. The political–social configuration in which the social movement becomes the most important actor in politics and takes on the role as the mediator of society's interests towards the state is suggested as a result of 'dialectical' state–society interaction, more specifically related to the legitimacy crisis affecting the political party system. This refers back to the debate presented in Chapter 1 that problematises the oppositional 'institutionalised politics' versus 'non-institutionalised politics', which poses that social movements and political parties actually belong to the same system. In the face of a weakened channel (the political party system's loss of legitimacy because of co-optation), other channels (social movements) began intensifying their activity, with the limits between 'institutional' and 'non-institutional' politics being 'blurred'. In this way, the political system's inability to represent the interests of vast sectors of society became a deter- mining factor in the social movements' growing political articulation. Their political nature is made explicit through the creation of the 'political instru- ment' in the 1990s, which would later penetrate state institutions in the form of the MAS, and which would make its leader, Evo Morales, head of state.

From this moment onwards, the social movement's central role in state– society mediation takes on a more definite form. The MAS coming to power meant that social movements entered state structures and social leaders joined the executive. As shown in the Chapter 3, social movements came to play a leading role in politics during the constituent process. During this period, the 'dialectical' relationship of state–social movements started to be observed in the scenario of a 'state–society interface'. As a response to the struggle of social movements, the state–society interface was understood as an opportu- nity for state and society to come together and interact in an arena character- ised by conflict, negotiations, unequal relations and the impact of 'informal networks'. As the concept suggests, democratisation processes occur through the links, coordination and movement between civil society and the state. Thus, considering the debates related to the 'judicialisation' of politics and the 'new Latin American constitutionalism', it is suggested that the constitu- ent process was a crossroads between state and society that continued aligning visions and political projects that were conflictive among themselves in the framework of a limited timeframe to produce a tangible result (a new consti- tutional text). Likewise, the constituent process was an opportunity to bring up proposals, negotiate and form consensus in a more definite way, with the impact of social movements observed through their articulation in political networks, connecting state actors in the scenario of a state–society interface.

This example of a 'state–society interface' has three important aspects. Firstly, social movements demonstrate their capacity to effectively transcend their belligerent character to move from protest towards proposals, making a qualitative leap in their repertoire of action. Particularly indicative of this is the fact that indigenous movement – through the Unity Pact – was the only sector of society to present a full proposal for the constitutional text that incorporated an integral vision of the state. This 'qualitative leap' thus refers not only to their capacity for dialogue, negotiation and consensus, but also to their ability to transcend a particularistic vision – supposedly so characteristic of social movements – to accept a vision of the 'common good'. Social movements' importance at this time is also reflected in the fact that the Unity Pact's draft formed the basis of the constitutional text that was eventually approved.

Equally indicative of the central role of the social movement in politics during the constituent process is the fact that the traditional political and economic elite – who saw themselves lose their privileged position – resorted to the social movement format to defend their interests. The collective action of the civic and autonomous movement against the MAS government and the Constituent Assembly had a significant impact on this political process. Therefore, between 2006 and 2009, a social struggle occurred within the institution of the Constituent Assembly, as well as beyond it – with the same or greater impact – in confrontations between strong social movements in the non-institutional spaces of the streets. Although the indigenous and popular movements acted creatively in workshops and through task forces, they also remained mobilised in order to defend the constituent process. Therefore, the previously mentioned qualitative leap did not end up defusing the demonstrations or deactivating the movements, which otherwise could have questioned their nature as 'social movements', but remained agitating, reinforcing the argument that the 'social movement' actually played the main role in this 'state–society interface'.

The second aspect that stands out during this period is the result of the constituent process: the new Political Constitution of the state. In reflecting to a great extent the Unity Pact proposal, and as a result of intense negotiations and consensus – once again within institutions as well as outside of them – a new kind of 'social pact' emerged. Taking into account the debate on 'new Latin American constitutionalism', this document suggests a series of social victories in a process that established a new equilibrium between the different political and social forces. The debate underlines the 'transitory nature' of the new constitutional text by describing a kind of desire or project more than a reality. According to this interpretation, this book conceives the new Political Constitution of the Bolivian state, in effect since January 2009, as a project, first and foremost as an attempt to redefine state–society relations.

The third aspect that should be highlighted is the influence of social movements through their articulation in political networks. During the constituent process, the Unity Pact was a clear example of how indigenous social movements coordinated into a political network with state actors (for example, the REPAC) as well as actors in society (national NGOs) and other popular movements. The connection between this group of actors is what solidified their considerable ability to determine the Constituent Assembly's final results. Likewise, it was seen how the political opposition also opted for the same dynamic, organised social movements (the civic and autonomous movements), and sought alliances with other actors, namely the media.

The network dynamic, which assigned social movements a central role, is observed more clearly in the post-constituent period, after Evo Morales' second re-election. Chapter 4 analysed the most noteworthy socio-political conflicts between 2010 and 2016, showing the MAS's relative political power, even when it enjoyed absolute majorities in both the Chamber of Deputies and the Senate. The analysis showed that the existence or lack of a political network is a considerably more determining factor. In effect, social movements (because of their capacity for demonstrations) and the media are presented as actors with valuable political resources to either maintain and legitimise a political project or discredit it. The conflicts analysed showed that the lack of support of a political network was the reason why policies projected by the MAS were inevitably cut short, such as the so-called '*gasolinazo*' and the TIPNIS conflict. Thus, in a scenario characterised by 'network governance', institutional opportunities to formulate and carry out policies are not enough to ensure public policies are carried out. As was observed, such opportunities need to be correspondingly supported by social movements and other socio-political actors in order to effectively implement public policies. In other words, in the current 'network governance' observed in Bolivia, political decisions are considerably dependent on 'political networks' made up of sufficient socio-political actors, both 'political' and 'social'. In this regard, as Chalmers et al. (1997) propose, popular representation becomes more and more dependent on the participation of social and state actors in a changing group of 'associative networks', whose limits between activities that 'articulate interests', 'add interests', 'formulate demands' and 'create public policies' are fused or blurred.

As Kahler et al. (2009) indicate, modern societies are characterised by a diversification and complexity that 'overloads' the state, and by the distribution of political resources between 'public' and 'private' actors. In the case of Bolivia, this diversity and complexity is expressed through the coordination of different types of social movement, while an 'overload' is observed through the state's inability to contain and channel society's demands. As a result, Kahler et al. explain that 'public policy networks' emerge with the capacity to mobilise the necessary political resources, both in the state sphere and beyond it, by facilitating horizontal interaction between different interests. In this analysis, the Movement towards Socialism emerges as an example of a political network, mediating the state–society relationship and bringing together the political resources necessary, such as financing and legitimacy for decision making.

This book has conceptualised the Movement towards Socialism as an important 'political network' organised as a result of the alignment of a group of interests as well as around opposition to a 'common enemy' discursively located in civic committees, the 'right', the economic elite, neoliberalism and colonialism. This conceptualisation is able to explain with more precision why the political network's internal cohesion decreased once most of the common aims had been achieved and the 'defeat' of the 'common enemy' had occurred – that is to say, after the passing of the new constitution and the second re-election of Evo Morales in 2009. The weakened cohesion is observed in the frequent and mutual accusations of betrayal from the government and social movements. Likewise, the analysis of political episodes between 2010 and 2016 shows that the existence of a strong 'political network' like the MAS does not prevent different actors from forming alternative and parallel groups or (smaller) networks based on specific matters, sometimes in line with and at other times against the government position, and even cutting through the MAS political network itself. In effect, a changing group of alliances and collaborations between state actors and social actors is one of the characteristics of 'network governance'.

The apparent contradiction or inconsistencies in the fact that the very social movement that appears to be 'co-opted' by the government at a certain point appears highly 'autonomous' in another is perfectly logical in the 'network governance' framework. The specific topic that brings together the state actor and the social movement defines the content of this relationship, to the extent that it either allows or prevents a 'political network' from articulating. In other words, as long as the aim pursued by the government is identified as being either coherent, agreeing or compatible with the specific interest, the relation with the social movement is qualified as one of 'collaboration' or 'co-optation'. When interests are not sufficiently aligned, the relationship is described as 'conflictive' or 'autonomous'. Therefore, the specific level of 'autonomy' or 'co-optation' that a movement maintains in relation to the government denotes a more specific position and moment in time rather than a particular mechanism or pervasive characteristic of the relationship between the state and social movements.

The analysis of political networks and network governance makes the actions and influence of other socio-political actors who effectively affect the state–society relationship more visible, as the specific topic that brings together the state actor and the social movement also articulates other actors with a significant impact on the political project's development. Two stand out in the results of my fieldwork: support institutions (national NGOs) and the media (including social networks). Their importance lies in the fact that they have valuable and different types of political resources that provide important support for the 'political networks'. Thus, without undermining the importance of (indigenous) social movements, neither the creation of the MAS nor the result of the constituent process can be fully appreciated without considering the role of the support institutions. In the same way, the media (including social networks) continue to influence the political process because of their capacity to make an impact on public opinion and the political agenda, as shown by the conflict surrounding the construction of the highway through the TIPNIS National Park and the results of the Constitutional Referendum on 21 February 2016. The important impact of media actors is also a result of the relative weakness of political institutions (the state and the political party system), which permit a more influential participation of alternative actors in the political networks. Therefore, considering traditional institutional weakness, the 'network governance' description is even more appropriate, since it can be understood in relation to the legitimacy crisis of political parties and of the institutional system in general, as well as in relation to the importance social movements adopt in the political arena. This scenario explains why political processes – the articulation of 'political networks' that involve a range of socio-political actors in the state–society interface – have the same or greater importance than those in the confines of institutional politics.

The network analysis could create the impression that the interconnections between socio-political actors are rather horizontal, but the salient role of political leadership shows they are not. The characterisation of the current political scenario in Bolivia as 'network governance' also contributes to explaining the importance of social leadership. Standing at a crossroads between the state and social movements, the social leader's position intensifies the tension and contradictions that emerge when attempting to draw up common aims among sectorial interests, articulating political networks. Under Morales' government, social leadership has to respond to the dual and contradictory actions of defending the specific interests of its social base at the same time as moving forward with the country's political project and the vision of the state. In other words, in network analysis, social leadership faces the complicated task of both articulating 'political networks', and formulating and implementing public policies that are of common/national interest but that promote and carry out the interests or concessions of their social basis of support. The complexity and difficulty of this job is expressed through the fact that the majority of social leaders are severely criticised by state actors, their social basis of support and other actors in society.

In effect, the variety of actors interrelated through social leadership do not seem to share the same understanding of what an optimal performance in this position entails. This explains why the frequent accusations of co-optation and practices of clientelism have different meanings depending on the actor that makes them. Therefore, social organisations identify 'manipulation', 'co-optation' or 'bribes' as interests that are not being represented effectively to the state apparatus and that show a lack of commitment and loyalty to the base of support. From the state's point of view, however, an unwillingness or inability to compromise on social demands is interpreted as a lack of vision and political instruction, both of which are needed to build a new type of state. In the same way, when an actor is critical of the government line on a specific topic – when showing itself as 'autonomous' for some – the government and social organisations (who, at this point, share the pro-government line) also accuse them of submitting to co-optation and manipulation by the political opposition. Thus, the relativity of social movements' 'autonomy' and 'co-optation' is also valid for the position of social leadership.

Such terminology responds to a dichotomist conceptualisation of state and society, in which the social movement that belongs to the social arena is conceived as independent of the state structure. As has been discussed throughout this book, this separation is problematic in the Bolivian context. The network approach used to analyse relations between Evo Morales' government and society in Bolivia makes a more dynamic and interconnected relationship visible, in which the limits between the political and social arena are blurred to the point that such categories complicate more than clarify the analysis. The interaction between different types of actor in 'political networks' – embodying the state–society interface – shows that, in a mutual and continuous process of transformation, the 'autonomy' or 'co-optation' of a specific actor is relative to or dependent on the interests and aims of the actors involved in a specific subject in the political network. This explains the contradictions that characterise the position of social leadership and that inevitably lead it to be qualified as a failure in the majority of cases.

The great exception is undoubtedly Evo Morales. His perseverance for more than ten years in the ambiguous position of being the most important social leader and the head of state demonstrates his capacity to deal relatively successfully with the complexities of his position. It also offers an explanation of why his figure appears to be so essential to the 'process of change', as I was told repeatedly during my fieldwork. A network leadership analysis attributes a series of qualities or capabilities to the figure of the 'visionary leader' Morales, allowing him to contain and channel conflicts and contradictions, and articulate a range of disparate actors in 'political networks'. His capabilities are understood as critical to the advancement of the MAS government's political agenda in conflictive and polarising scenarios, and where carrying out that agenda – precisely because it seeks to implement institutional reforms – cannot count on institutional support to facilitate the political process.

His leadership, however, has not been exempt from criticism or accusations. This is not surprising, given the position he is in, but there are elements of his leadership that are a cause for concern. In a scenario of institutional weakness, it is easier to highlight the authoritarian features of strong political leaders. In the same way, it is worth asking exactly how democratising and emancipating a political project can be when it becomes so intimately connected to individual peculiarities. In this sense, the rotation of power seems to acquire importance as a means of preventing the concentration of power on the one hand, and promoting a political project's continuity beyond the leader himself on the other. As Bowen (2015) explains, the 'dual' construction of democratic states – which is based on effective state institutions, the autonomy of these institutions and the existence of accountability mechanisms (see Chapter 5) – must be considered. Supporting this, this book maintains that it is a mistake to overvalue the rotation of power when assessing a regime's democratic nature – even though when faced with strong and prolonged leaderships this may appear logical. Undoubtedly, guaranteeing the *expectation* of a rotation of power in a free and just context is an important element for building democracy, but it is only one of several contributing factors, particularly considering the complexity and historical determinations that mark state building in Bolivia specifically and Latin America in general.

Apart from the theoretical debate, it is not possible to conclude from the results of this study that prolonging Morales' time in power is detrimental to building democracy. What is true is that, up until now, none of the political opposition's projects have really presented a viable alternative, and nor has a successor been identified who is capable of 'filling his shoes' in such a complex and demanding scenario as the one depicted in this book. Likewise, following Van Cott's argument (2008), the very resolve and strength of the political leader is vitally important to the implementation and consolidation of reforms in a context of institutional weakness and innovation. In this sense, the question that emerges is 'How long is just enough?'. This is certainly a question that risks being answered too late, but is one that I must leave unanswered.

Morales' coming to political power is the result of the 'dialectical' relationship between the state and society, understood as a constant process of mutual transformation. Therefore, the institutional reforms that the MAS government has been implementing are both the result and cause of a redefinition of state–society relations. As far as their impact on the building or strengthening of democracy, this book maintains that there is room for optimism. Bolivian social movements in general embody a democratising project, by creating opportunities for participation and political influence for social sectors excluded from the formal political system. In Bolivia, the reforms under Morales' administration – accompanied by considerable economic growth – have undoubtedly led to great improvements in the position of indigenous people and popular sectors, and have established an innovative legal framework that allows for advances to be made in this respect. As a result of a 'state–society interface', the impact of the indigenous movement on the new 'social pact' (the new constitution), whose aim is to build a new type of state, suggests a greater connection between existing political projects and the one embodied by the state. In Tilly's terms, the new constitution reflects the 'will of the people' to a greater extent, and so arguably it reflects a process of democratisation.

Regarding the focus of this research – the state–social movement relationship – this study suggests understanding the relationship between state and society in Bolivia as being redefined and moving towards 'network governance', where social movements assume a leading role. This form of governance responds to the demands of modern societies, which are typified as diverse and complex. The networks that are articulated to formulate and implement public policies have the virtue of bringing together socio-political actors with knowledge of and a relevant degree of involvement in decision making, capable of identifying problems and producing negotiated, flexible and operative responses. Equally, the fact that the decision-making process involves the affected actors has a positive effect in reducing the risk of resistance to the implementation of policies, thus contributing to their legitimacy and efficiency.

According to literature, it is this exact combination of institutional and non-institutional opportunities that makes it possible to avoid greater dangers that may threaten network governance. Like any position of power, there is the risk that, from this privileged position, the system is manipulated to give priority to specific interests. To this is added the possibility that the proliferation of political networks could make governing less transparent, and atomise and fragment public governance. For this reason, it is important that state agents participate in the networks to really guarantee the creation of a 'state–society interface', characterised by conflict, negotiation and consensus, and guaranteeing its nature as a bearer of democratising potential. From a democracy model perspective, it is not about substituting a representative model with a participatory one. The network governance observed in Bolivia is shown as a rather complex model that combines new forms of more direct participation and representation, by means of social movement, with the more conventional institutions of democracy.

Complementing representative channels with ones for citizen participation is not exclusive to the political regime in Bolivia, but has been observed in other regional contexts, showing that their results are not necessarily positive. In a comparative study, Balderacchi (2015) maintains that the new institutional opportunities for citizen participation in Ecuador and Venezuela have favoured concentrating power in the executive, undermining the representative institutions and the separation of powers. The study indicates that, by contrast, in Bolivia the informal nature of participation mechanisms, such as CONALCAM, imperfectly favour popular autonomous participation in political decision making. Thus, the informality of political networks in the state–society relationship, often in the form of personal connections, paradoxically generates a more democratic practice in political decision-making instead of making co-optation or corruption easier (as is usually thought) – at least on the basis of the Bolivian case.

At this point, it must be highlighted that such a combination – going from a representative model to a participatory one, and from institutional opportunities to informal ones – is not the result of brilliant or pre-designed state engineering. Rather, it is the sum of the intentional and unintentional effects of socio-political actors' interaction in a process understood as involving the continuous and mutual transformations to which state and society – as parts of the same system – are submitted. As Baldaracchi (2015: 153) explains, the indigenous organisations' firm intention to participate in important political decisions, together with the government's vulnerability to their possible desertion or mobilisation, has drastically reduced the government's room for manoeuvre as far as the creation of participatory mechanisms is concerned, thereby producing greater participation in democracy. In this sense, the figure of the plurinational state that reflects these processes is also understood as not having reached its culmination. As Tilly explains, building democracy is characterised by constant democratisation and 'de-democratisation' processes that are condemned to an uncertain end. According to this, the degree or scope of democratisation can only be decided upon in comparison to specific past moments and possible future scenarios. Along this line of analysis, I conclude that, in relation to the 'pacted democracy' and the neoliberal model, the reforms and redefinition of state–society relations under Morales' government have led to politics being opened up to historically excluded sectors, reflecting a greater connection between the will of the people and public policies – that is to say, democratisation.

However, the same line of analysis means it is essential to consider the setbacks or parallel processes of 'de-democratisation', as well as risks and possible improvements. Emerging from a more integrated idea of state and society like the one shown in this book, by including a regulatory component, the concept of governability is useful for outlining a possible future scenario and therefore visualising the current process's defects. Governability is understood as a state of dynamic equilibrium between the level of societal demands and the political system's capacity to deal with them legitimately and efficiently. Governability is not then the quality of a certain government but rather a quality of the system in which the state–society relationship is embedded. It refers to the group of mechanisms and processes through which citizens and social organisations organise, advance their interests and measure their differences. It is particularly important to consider both sides of the relationship at a time when 'social' actors acquire a more explicit political role, such as the case of social movements in Bolivia.

The Bolivian case shows that the incursion of social movements into the political arena has led to the effective participation of groups of society previously excluded by the dominant political system. The legal reforms aimed at providing institutional opportunities for this development made it possible to think about better mechanisms for organising and addressing interests. 'Political networks' entail a more direct participation and the actors' involvement in the production of public policies that are more in tune with the social demands and needs, and that have a greater degree of legitimacy. In other words, the 'network governance' system complies to a great extent with the second part of governability's definition: a system capable of attending to demands efficiently and legitimately.

Reservations arise when considering the 'dynamic equilibrium' between social demands and the capacity to deal with them. Such equilibrium underpins the importance of the system's stability, in which short- and long-term aims inevitably clash – in other words, the tension between a necessary, integral long-term vision (embodied by the state) and the need to satisfy particularistic demands quickly for societal actors. Although it is true that the Bolivian case reflects important examples in which social movements – in particular indigenous movements – have been able to act beyond their sectorial interests by adopting a vision of the nation, it is also true that demonstrations and social protests as a means of advancing sectorial demands continue to be a characteristic of Morales' government, resulting in the high levels of conflict observed in the country. The social movement format is essentially extremist and combative, and therefore encourages political polarisation and exacerbation. In this way, it does not quite contribute to a climate of dialogue and consensus. The institutional reforms aimed at providing an institutional framework to the social movement as a channel of participation and political representation can help to appease these tendencies, although the proved effectiveness of social pressure will not allow for dissolving them altogether. Economic growth and (partial) satisfaction are still not a guarantee of fewer social demonstrations. In this sense, the student movement in Chile from 2010 onwards demonstrates that even the best levels of economic and social development do not prevent social unrest. Equally illustrative is the case of Brazil, which, in the last decade, has experienced extraordinary economic growth under the progressive governments of Lula and Rousseff. During this period, Brazil has managed to lower its levels of poverty with the emergence of a large middle class. Paradoxically, it was exactly this middle class that played a starring role in the protests against Rousseff's government, contributing to her removal and the installation of a right-wing government. Something similar occurred in Argentina, with Macri's election marking the end of a decade of Kirchneirsm. Thus, social movements are being consolidated as key players because of their effectiveness, inciting hostility within the political process, despite the satisfaction of social demands. Although this translates into a state that is more alert and responsive to the demands of society, it also poses a risk to the regime's durability, and to the dynamic equilibrium.

In effect, in a 'network governance' system – which also implies the emergence of a diversity of actors in the coordination and implementation of public policies (see chapters 3, 4 and 5) – there is the imminent risk of the weakening of the state as a coordinating centre of socio-political life, particularly in a context of traditional weakness and institutional innovation like in Bolivia. The political conflicts between 2010 and 2016 show the limited margins of the state's decision making and political action when this does not find embeddedness in or connection to the state–society interface – a political network that involves sufficient relevant actors outside the state arena. The events of the referendum on 21 February 2016 show that the political project that pro-government forces saw as practically accomplished was easily overruled by a political network, even when that network's base of legitimacy was questionable. In this way, concern for the excesses of power – regarding other Latin American contexts with which the MAS government has frequently been associated in the academic debate on democratisation in Latin America, as well as in the public debate on Morales prolongation in power amidst his candidature in the 2019 elections – in the light of results of this book and in terms of governability, give way to concerns about how to increase it.

Along these lines, it is worth considering the argument of Bowen (2015), who proposes considering the dual building of democratic states, combining state building with strengthening democracy. In effect, the author describes the contradictory relationship that exists between the concentration of power, necessary for building state institutions, and the limits and controls of state power, as dictated by the regulations of liberal democracy. According to Bowen, a stable democracy should be able to support itself based on three pillars. Together with capable state institutions and the existence of effective accountability mechanisms, the democratic regime requires that powerful state institutions be autonomous both within and beyond the state. Considering the case of Ecuador under Rafael Correa, the author observes that citizen groups have served as 'veto players' because of their capacity to overthrow government plans, showing parallels with what is observed in the Bolivian case. The question that therefore emerges is how the state can reinforce its autonomy in relation to different interest groups at the same time as maintaining significant accountability mechanisms. In other words, how can real participation and citizen control – identified as essential for the practice of a strong democracy – prevent the state becoming the prisoner of specific groups? A delicate balance – one that is difficult to build let alone assess – is necessary.

Network governance, as currently observed in Bolivia, entails a disaggregated view of the state, which, when infiltrated by sectorial interest groups, is undermined as the crux of political power. In the worst scenarios, its greater capacity for reflecting social interests and conflicts could result in the state institution being distilled into social conflicts distorted by internal discord. Therefore, the reflection on modern 'network governance' in terms of 'governability' reintroduces the old European problem of the '*raison d'État*'. It is worth noting that this question has been posed again in the most recent academic discussions as a result of globalisation processes that pose serious difficulties for the traditional state position (e.g. discussions on the sovereignty of the nation-state). In other words, the possible risk of a weakened state or one that is overly dependent on external actors (at a national and international level) is not specific to the Bolivian context with its strong social movements, but is a general problem.

As a result of globalisation, Castells has introduced the concept of 'the Network State' (2008) to describe the states that undergo a series of transformations to adapt to the modern lack of sovereignty in a global framework, and decentralisation in the national context. In this way, the state can be re-enforced, to the extent that it gains legitimacy as the body that coordinates constant and interactive negotiations between national governments, co-national governments, supranational entities, international institutions, regional governments, local governments, social movements and NGOs. Decision making and representation occur throughout this chain, and do not necessarily follow a prescribed hierarchy. The state functions as a network, in which every point interacts with others, and all are equally necessary for state functions to be carried out.

Given that this book has concentrated on state–social movement relations, there is not enough evidence to say that the plurinational state of Bolivia is effectively a kind of 'Network State', although it is suggested that the concern for state autonomy makes it necessary to think about a context that is wider than the national one, suggesting also a network analysis and conceptualisations of interconnected and integrated systems. Thus, in line with this book, Castells maintains that the 'networks of power' that govern the network society are not fused together but rather are part of a constant strategy of alliances and rivalries, forming ad hoc networks based on specific projects (Castells 2015: 8). In this scenario, Castells also identifies the emergence of 'networked social movements' as part of a worldwide tendency, also responding to deficiencies in political representation systems and, as a result, the lack of legitimacy. 'Networked social movements' are alternative channels of representation and political participation that look to coordinate alternative networks of resistance and social change as forms of 'counter-power'. According to the author, these movements are characterised by a network dynamic that has multiple forms, including online and offline social networks. These networks are found either within the movement, connected to other world movements, in the world blogosphere, in the internet blogosphere, in the media or in society in general (ibid.: 249). In the case of Bolivia, social movements' connection to state actors could also be included.

Castells also indicates that network technology is important since it provides a platform for the networking practice to continue and expand. In effect, the events analysed in this book have demonstrated the growing importance of the media and – more recently – of online social networks in politics. The government's decision to enter the world of online social networks using special state institutional accounts demonstrates their political importance. On the other hand, the use of social networks such as Twitter and Facebook by indigenous social movements in Bolivia is still limited. The network dynamic is rather observed aside online social networks, where other types of connections (that may also include online social networks) articulate 'political networks'. At this point, it is worth noting that these kinds of connections have become easier through communication networks of a more private nature, such as mobile phones and private messaging systems such as WhatsApp, which allow Bolivian social movements' evolution to be described as 'networked social movements'.

Therefore, the 'network governance' that gives social movements a leading role, and that characterises the state–society relation in the plurinational state, does not so much present the singularity (or anomaly) of the Bolivian case but rather expresses its very own version of a much more general phenomenon. It also indicates the need to follow up on the development and impact of the Bolivian political system's transformation, not only as far as the possibilities and risks for building and strengthening democracy in that country are concerned, but also because of the relevance of these experiences for other contexts.

References

Newspaper Sources
Cambio
Correo del Sur
El Deber
El Día
El Diario
El Mundo
El País
El Periódico
La Patria
La Razón
Los Tiempos
Página Siete

Electronic Media Sources
Agence France Presse
Agencia Boliviana de Información
Agencia Mexicana de Noticias NOTIMEX
América Economía
Andean Information Network
BBC Mundo
Bolpress
Europa Press – Servicio Latinoamericano
NACLA

Personal Interviews
Alarcón, Octavio. 2012. Secretary of the Syndicalist Confederation of Native Intercultural Communities of Bolivia. 22 May. La Paz, Bolivia.
Almaraz, Alejandro. 2010. Former Vice-Minister of Land. 12 November. Cochabamba, Bolivia.
Arispe, Gualberto. 2016. Leader and Court Clerk of the CSUTCB, President of MAS Youth. 22 July. La Paz, Bolivia.
Bascopé, Iván. 2010. Research at Centro de Estudios Jurídicos e Investigación Social CEJIS. 16 November. La Paz, Bolivia.
Becerra, Felix. 2012. Jiliri Apu Mallku of the CONAMAQ. 19 April. La Paz, Bolivia.
Belmonte, Leandro. 2012. Leader of the Unified Syndical Confederation of Peasant Workers of Bolivia (CSUTCB). 24 March. La Paz, Bolivia.
Berrera, Carlos. 2012. Leader of the El Alto FEJUVE, President of FEJUVE in 2003. 9 May. La Paz, Bolivia.
Cabezas, Victor. 2016. First Secretary of the CSCIOB. 25 July. La Paz, Bolivia.

Cartagena, Pamela. 2012. Researcher at CIPCA. 23 May. La Paz, Bolivia.

Choque, Gregorio. 2016. 'Tata', second-highest authority of the National Council of Ayllus and Markas of Qullasuyu of Bolivia (CONAMAQ). 19 July. La Paz, Bolivia.

Cochi Villca, Elías. 2010. Leader of the National Council of Ayllus and Markas (CONAMAQ). 18 November. La Paz, Bolivia.

Dulón, Jorge. 2010. Researcher for the Foundation for Multiparty Democracy. 23 September. La Paz, Bolivia.

Faldín, Diego. 2010. President of the Umbrella Organisation of Native People of Santa Cruz (CPESC). 5 November. Santa Cruz de la Sierra, Bolivia.

Garcés, Fernando. 2010. Professor at the Universidad Mayor of San Simón. 11 November. Cochabamba, Bolivia.

Kochi, Porfirio. 2010. Leader of the CONAMAQ during the period of the Constituent Assembly. 19 November. La Paz, Bolivia.

Komadina, Jorge. 2010. Researcher at the Centre for Applied Studies on Economic, Social and Cultural Rights (CEADESC). 10 November. Cochabamba, Bolivia.

Lamas, Miguel. 2012. Journalist and Researcher at Somossur. 4 May. Cochabamba, Bolivia.

Limache, Walter. 2010. National Director of the NINA Programme. 10 November. Cochabamba, Bolivia.

———. 2010. National Director of the NINA Programme. 11 October. Cochabamba, Bolivia.

———. 2012. National Director of the NINA Programme. 27 April. La Paz, Bolivia.

Mamani, Maribel Santa María. 2016. Secretary of the CNMCIOB-BS. 25 July. La Paz, Bolivia.

Mariaca, Karina. 2010. Consultant for the Unity Pact. 30 September. La Paz, Bolivia.

Navarro, César. 2010. Deputy Minister of Coordination with the Social Movements and Civil Society Organizations. 1 December. La Paz, Bolivia.

———. 2012. Deputy Minister of Coordination with the Social Movements and Civil Society Organizations. 26 April. La Paz, Bolivia.

Nogales, Edmundo J. 2016. Representative from the National School for Political Training. 14 August (Skype interview).

———. 2016. Representative from the National School for Political Training. 21 August (Skype interview).

Núñez, Eulogio. 2010. Director of CIPCA-Santa Cruz. 5 November. Santa Cruz de la Sierra, Bolivia.

Ortega, Marcelo. 2010. Project Manager at CEPAS-CARITAS. 21 October. La Paz, Bolivia.

Quispe, Jaime. 2016. Leader of the Bolivian Workers' Centre and Secretary of Foreign Affairs. 18 July. La Paz, Bolivia.

Quispe, Lorenza. 2012. Leader of the Potosí region's 'Bartolina Sisa' National Confederation of Working-Class and Native Women of Bolivia. 24 April. La Paz, Bolivia.

Santalla Torres, Daniel. 2012. Minister of Work, Employment and Social Security, former leader of the Bolivian Workers' Centre (COB). 25 May. La Paz, Bolivia.

Taco, Lázaro. 2010. Leader of the Confederation of Indigenous Peoples of Bolivia. 4 November. Santa Cruz de la Sierra, Bolivia.

Velásquez, Sergio. 2012. Secretary and Researcher at Centro de Comunicación y Desarrollo Andino CENDA, consultant to Unity Pact. 30 May. Cochabamba, Bolivia.

Zacu, Bienvenido. 2010. Congressman of Guarayan origin, President of the Commission for Nation and Indigenous Native Rural People (C.E.I.). 16 November. La Paz, Bolivia.

Zegada, María Teresa. 2010. Lecturer and Researcher at the Faculty of Social Sciences at the Universidad Mayor de San Simón and the Universidad Católica Boliviana. 13 November. Cochabamba, Bolivia.

Books and Journals

Achtenberg, E. 2016. 'After the Referendum, What's Next for Bolivia's Progressive Left?' NACLA, 15 April.

Albó, X. 2008a. 'El perfil de los constituyentes'. *T'inkazos, Revista Boliviana de Ciencias Sociales* 23/24: 49–63.

———. 2008b. *Movimientos y poder indígena en Bolivia, Ecuador y Perú*. La Paz, Bolivia: CIPCA, Garza Azul 'Impresores & Editores'.

Albro, R. 2005. 'The Indigenous in the Plural in Bolivian Oppositional Politics'. *Bulletin of Latin American Research* 24(4): 433–53.

Almaraz, A., et al. 2011. *Manifiesto del 22 de Junio: Por la recuperación del proceso de cambio con el pueblo. Manifiesto de la Coordinadora Plurinacional de la Reconducción*. Retrieved 10 January 2019 from https://vientosur.info/spip.php?article5583.

———. 2012. *La MAScarada del Poder*. Cochabamba, Bolivia: Textos Rebeldes.

Altman, D. 2011. *Direct Democracy Worldwide*. Cambridge: Cambridge University Press.

———. 2013. 'Bringing Direct Democracy Back In: Toward a Three-Dimensional Measure of Democracy'. *Democratization* 20(4): 615–641.

Alvarez, S., et al. 1998a. *Cultures of Politics and Politics of Cultures*. Boulder, CO: Westview Press.

———. 1998b. 'Introduction: The Cultural and the Political in Latin American Social Movements', in idem, *Cultures of Politics and Politics of Cultures*. Boulder, CO: Westview Press, pp. 1–29.

Aminzade, R. 1995. 'Between Movement and Party: The Transformation of Min-Nineteenth-Century French Republicanism', in J. Craig Jenkins and B. Klandermans (eds), *The Politics of Social Protest*. Minneapolis: University of Minnesota Press, pp. 39–62.

Anria, S. 2010. 'Bolivia's MAS: Between Party and Movement', in M.A. Cameron and E. Hershberg (eds), *Latin America's Left Turns: Politics, Policies and Trajectories of Change*. Boulder, CO: Lynne Rienner Publishers, pp. 101–26.

———. 2013. 'Social Movements, Party Organization and Populism: Insights from the Bolivian MAS'. *Latin American Politics and Society* 55(3): 19–46.

Arellano-López, S., and J.F. Petras. 1994. 'Non-governmental Organizations and Poverty Alleviation in Bolivia'. *Devolopment and Change* 25: 555–68.

Arenas, N. 2016. 'El chavismo sin Chávez: la deriva de un populismo sin carisma'. *Nueva Sociedad* 261: 13–22.

Argirakis, H. 2012. *La Conflictividad Social como Epistemología del Poder*. La Paz: Programa de las Naciones Unidas para el Desarrollo.

Assies, W. 1999. 'Multi-Ethnicity, the State and the Law in Latin America'. *The Journal of Legal Pluralism and Unofficial Law* 31(43): 145–158.

———. 2003. 'David versus Goliath in Cochabamba: Water Rights, Neoliberalism, and the Revival of Social Protest in Bolivia'. *Latin American Perspectives* (Popular Participation against Neoliberalism) 30(3): 14–36.

———. 2005. 'Some Notes on Citizenship, Civil Society and Social Movements', in W. Assies et al., *Citizenship, Political Culture and State Transformation in Latin America*. Amsterdam: Dutch University Press, pp. 93–110.

———. 2011. 'Bolivia's New Constitution and its Implications', in A.J. Pierce et al., *Evo Morales and the Movimiento al Socialismo in Bolivia: The First Term in Context, 2006–2010*. London: Institute of the Studies of the Americas, School of Advanced Study, University of London, pp. 93–116.

Assies, W., et al. 2005. 'Citizenship, Political Culture and State Transformation in Latin America', in W. Assies et al., *Citizenship, Political Culture and State Transformation in Latin America*. Amsterdam: Dutch University Press, pp. 3–26.

Atkinson, M.M., and W.D. Coleman. 1989. 'Strong States and Weak States: Sectoral Policy Networks in Advanced Capitalist Economies'. *British Journal of Political Science* 19(1): 47–67.

Axford, B., and R. Huggins (eds). 2001. *New Media and Politics.* London: Sage Publications.

Bacallao-Pino, L.M. 2016. 'Redes sociales, acción colectiva y elecciones: los usos de Facebook por el movimiento estudiantil chileno durante la campaña electoral de 2013'. *Palabra Clave – Revista de Comunicación* 19(3): 810–837.

Balderacchi, C. 2017. 'Participatory Mechanisms in Bolivia, Ecuador and Venezuela: Deepening or Undermining Democracy'. *Government and Opposition* 52(1): 131–61.

Balkundi, P., and M. Kildfuf. 2006. 'The Ties That Lead: A Social Network Approach to Leadership'. *The Leadership Quarterly* 17: 419–439.

Barragán, R. 2009. 'Hegemonías y "Ejemonías": las relaciones entre el Estado Central y las Regiones (Bolivia, 1825–1952)'. *Íconos* 34: 39–51.

Barret, P., et al. 2008. *The New Latin American Left: Utopia Reborn.* London: Pluto Press.

Bebbington, A., et al. 1993. *Non-governmental Organization and the State in Latin America: Rethinking Roles in Sustainable Agricultural Development.* London: Routledge.

Benkler, Y. 2011. 'A Free Irresponsible Press: Wikileaks and the Battle of the Soul of the Networked Fourth Estate'. *Harvard Civil Rights–Civil Liberties Law Review* 46: 31–97.

Berger, S. 1979. 'Politics and Anti-Politics in Western Europe in the Seventies'. *Daedalus* 108: 27–50.

Berg-Schlosser, D. 2004. 'Concepts, Measurements and Sub-Types in Democratization Research', in D. Berg-Schlosser (ed.), *Democratization: The State of the Art.* The World of Political Science: The Development of the Discipline Book Series. Volume 1, Mayo. Wiesbaden: VS Verlag für Sozialwissenschaften/GWV Fachverlage GmbH, pp. 53–64

Bigs, S., and H. Matsaert. 1999. 'An Actor-Oriented Approach for Strengthening Research and Development Capabilities in Natural Resource Systems'. *Public Administration and Development* 19(3): 231–62.

Bogason, P., and J.A. Musso. 2006. 'The Democratic Prospects of Network Governance'. *American Review of Public Administration* 36(1): 3–18.

Boggs, C. 1986. *Social Movements and Political Power.* Philadelphia, PA: Temple University Press.

Böhm, S., et al. 2010. 'Impossibilities of Autonomy: Social Movements in and beyond Capital, the State and Development'. *Social Movement Studies* 9(1): 17–32.

Booth, J.A., and M.A. Seligson. 2009. *The Legitimacy Puzzle in Latin America Political Support and Democracy in Eight Nations.* Cambridge: Cambridge University Press.

Börzel, T.A. 1997. 'What's So Special About Policy Networks? – An Exploration of the Concept and Its Usefulness in Studying European Governance'. *European Integration online Papers (EIoP)* 1(016); http//eiop.or.at/eiop/texte/1997-016a.htm.

Bowen, J.D. 2015. 'Rethinking Democratic Governance: State Building, Autonomy, and Accountability in Correa's Ecuador'. *Journal of Politics in Latin America* 7(1): 83–110.

Brandt, K.W. 1986. 'New Social Movements as a Metapolitical Challenge: The Social and Political Impact of a New Historical Type of Protest'. *Thesis Eleven* 15: 60–68.

Burbach, R., et al. 2013. *Latin America's Turbulent Transitions: The Future of Twenty-First-Century Socialism.* London: Zed Books.

Burman, A. 2014. 'Now We Are Indígenas': Hegemony and Indigeneity in the Bolivian Andes'. *Latin American and Caribbean Ethnic Studies* 9(3): 247–71.

Burstein, P., and A. Linton. 2002. 'The Impact of Political Parties, Interest Groups and Social Movement Organizations on Public Policy: Some Recent Evidence and Theoretical Concerns'. *Social Forces* 81(2): 381–408.

Calderón, F., A. Piscitelli and J.L. Reyna. 1992. 'Social Movements: Actors, Theories, Expectations', in A. Escobar et al., *The Making of Social Movements in Latin America: Identity, Strategy and Democracy*. Boulder, CO: Westview Press, pp. 19–36.

Calla, R. 2008. 'Indigenous Peoples, the Law of Popular Participation and Changes in Government: Bolivia 1994–1998', in W. Assies et al., *The Challenges of Diversity: Indigenous Peoples and Reform of the State in Latin America*. Amsterdam: Thela Thesis, pp. 77–94.

Cameron, M.A., and E. Hershberg (eds). 2010. *Latin America's Left Turns*. London: Lynne Rienner Publishers.

Camou, A. 2000. 'La múltiple (in)gobernabilidad: elementos para un análisis conceptual'. *Revista Mexicana de Sociología* 62(4): 159–88.

Camou, A., and J.E. Castro (eds). 1997. *La sociedad compleja: Ensayos en torno a la obra de Niklas Luhmann*. Mexico: Facultad Latinoamericana de Ciencias Sociales/Triana Editores.

Canessa, A. 2014. 'Conflict, Claim and Contradiction in the New Indigenous State of Bolivia'. *Critique of Anthropology* 34(2): 151–71.

Cannon, B., and P. Kirby (eds). 2012. *Civil Society and the State in Left-Led Latin America: Challenges and Limitations to Democratization*. London: Zed Books.

Carnoy, M., and M. Castells. 2001. 'Globalization, the Knowledge Society, and the Network State: Poulantzas at the Millennium'. *Global Networks* 1(1): 1–18.

Carrasco Alarrude, I.V., and X. Albó. 2008. 'Cronología de la Asamblea Constituyente'. *Tinkazos* 11(23–24): 101–28.

Carreras, M. 2012. 'The Rise of Outsiders in Latin America, 1980–2010: An Institutionalist Perspective'. *Comparative Political Studies* 45(12): 1451–82.

Carroll, W.K., and R.S. Ratner. 1999. 'Media Strategies and Political Projects: A Comparative Study of Social Movements'. *Canadian Journal of Sociology* 24(1): 1–34.

Castells, M. (1996) 2000. *The Rise of the Network Society*. Oxford: Blackwell Publishing.

———. 2008. 'Hacia el Estado Red? Globalización económica e instituciones políticas en la era de la información'. Ponencia presentada en el Seminario sobre "Sociedad y reforma del Estado", organizado por el Ministerio de Administracao Federal e Reforma Do Estado, República Federativa do Brasil, Sao Paulo, 26–28 March 1998.

Castillo Gallardo, M. 2004. 'Movimiento cocalero en Bolivia: Violencia, discurso y hegemonía'. *Gaceta de Antropología* 20: 20–35.

Cavarozzi, M. 1992. 'Beyond Transitions to Democracy in Latin America'. *Journal of Latin American Studies* 24: 661–84.

CEPAL. 2003. *Hacia el objetivo del milenio de reducir la pobreza en América Latina y el Caribe*. Santiago: Publicación de las Naciones Unidas.

Chalmers, D.A., et al. 1997. *The New Politics of Inequality in Latin America: Rethinking Participation and Representation*. New York: Oxford University Press.

Charron, J. 1995. 'Les médias et lessources: Les limites deu modèle de l'*agenda-setting*'. *Hermès* 17–18: 73–92.

Chavero, P., et al. 2013. 'La mediatización de la agenda política: la discusión del pacto social como conflicto de agendas, 2009–2011'. *Revista Latina de Comunicación Social* 68: 639–55.

Christopoulos, D.C. 2016. 'The Impact of Social Networks on Leadership Behaviour'. *Methodological Innovations* 9: 1–15,

Collins, J.N. 2014. 'New Left Experiences in Bolivia and Ecuador, and the Challenge to Theories of Populism'. *Journal of Latin American Studies* 46: 59–86.

Cook, T.E. 2005. *Governing with the News: The News Media as a Political Institution*. London: The University of Chicago Press.

Costain, N., and McFarland, A.S. (eds). 1998. *Social Movements and American Political Institutions*. Lanham, MD: Rowman & Littlefield, Inc.

Couso, J. 2004. 'Consolidación democrática y poder judicial: los riesgos de la judicialización de la política'. *Revista de Ciencia Política* XXIV(2): 29–48.

Coy, P.G., and T. Hedeen. 2005. 'A Stage Model of Social Movement Co-optation: Community Mediation in the United States'. *The Sociological Quarterly* 46: 405–35.

Crabtree, J. 2011. 'Electoral Validation for Morales and the MAS (1999–2010)', in A.J. Pearce (ed.), *Evo Morales and the Movimiento al Socialismo in Bolivia*. London: Institute for the Study of the Americas, pp. 93–142.

Craig Jenkins, J. 1995. 'Social Movements, Political Representation and the State: An Agenda and Comparative Framework', in J. Craig Jenkins and B. Klandermans, *The Politics of Social Protest*. Minneapolis: University of Minnesota Press, pp. 14–35.

Dagnino, E. 1998. 'Culture, Citizenship and Democracy: Changing Discourses and Practices of the Latin American Left', in S. Alvarez et al., *Cultures of Politics and Politics of Cultures*. Boulder, CO: Westview Press, pp. 33–63.

Dagnino, E., et al. 2006. *La disputa por la construcción democrática en América Latina*. Mexico: Programa Interinstitucional de Investigación-Acción sobre Democracia, Sociedad Civil y Derechos Humanos, Centro de Investigaciones y Estudios Superiores en Antropología Social (CIESAS).

Dahl, R. 1989. *Democracy and its Critics*. New Haven, CT: Yale University Press.

Dahlgren, P. 2001. 'The Transformation of Democracy?', in R. Huggins (ed.), *New Media and Politics*. London: Sage Publications, pp. 64–88.

De Bakker, F.G.A., F. den Hond and M. Laarmanen. 2017. 'Social Movements: Organziations and Organizing', in C. Roggeband and B. Klandermans (eds), *Handbook of Social Movements across Disciplines*. New York: Springer, pp. 203–231.

De Ferrari, I. 2015. 'The Successor Factor: Electoral Accountability in Presidential Democracies'. *Comparative Political Studies* 48(2): 193–230.

Deheza, G.I. 2008. 'Bolivia: es posible la construcción de un nuevo Estado? La Asamblea Constituyente y las autonomías departamentales'. *Revista de Ciencia Política* 28(1): 61–79. Pontificia Universidad Católica de Chile.

Del Tronco, J. 2013. 'Desconfianza y *Accountability*: Las causas del populismo en América Latina'. *Latin American Research Review* 48(2): 55–78.

Deonandan, K., and D. Close (eds) 2007. *From Revolutionary Movements to Political Parties*. New York: Palgrave Macmillan.

Desai, M. 2003. 'From Movement to Party to Government: Why Social Policies in Kerala and West Bengal are so Different', in J.A. Goldstone (ed.), *State, Parties and Social Movements*. Cambridge: Cambridge University Press, pp. 170–96.

Diamint, R., and L. Tedesco. 2014. 'El liderazgo político sudamericano en perspectiva comparada'. *Nueva Sociedad* 249: 34–48.

Díaz, A. 1997. 'New Developments in Economic and Social Restructuring in Latin America', in W.C. Smith et al., *Politics, Social Change and Economic Restructuring in Latin America*. Miami: North–South Center Press, University of Miami, pp. 37–56.

Do Alto, H. 2008. 'El MAS-IPSP boliviano, entre movimiento social y partido político'. *Análisis Político* 62: 25–43.

———. 2011. 'Un partido campesino en el poder: Una mirada sociológica del MAS boliviano'. *Nueva Sociedad* 234: 95–111.

Do Alto, H., and P. Stefanoni. 2010a. 'El MAS, las ambivalencias de la democracia corporativa'. *Coloquio de Análisis y estudios políticos: 'El MAS, un partido en tiempo heterogéneo'*. PNUD – Idea Internacional.

———. 2010b. 'El MAS: las ambivalencias de la democracia corporativa'. Documento de trabajo, Segundo Coloquio PNUD: Democracia interna en la elección de candidatos del Movimiento al Socialismo, La Paz, 23 February.

Domike, A. (ed.). 2008. *Civil Society and Social Movements: Building Sustainable Democracies in Latin America*. Inter-American Development Bank.

Domingo, P. 2009. 'Ciudadanía, derechos y justicia en América Latina. *Ciudadanización-judicialización* de la política'. *Revista CIDOB d'Afers Internacionals* 85/86: 33–52.

Doowon, S. 2006. 'Civil Society in Political Democratization: Social Movement Impacts and Institutional Politics'. *Development and Society* 35(2): 173–95.

Drake, P.W. and Hershberg, E. 2006. *State and Society in Conflict: Comparative Perspectives on the Andean Crises*. Pittsburgh, PA: University of Pittsburgh Press.

Dufuour, P. 2008. 'From Protest to Partisan Politics: When and How Collective Actors Cross the Line. Sociologica Perspective on Québec Solidaire'. *Canadian Journal of Sociology* 34(1): 55–81.

Durán-Martínez, A. 2012. 'Presidents, Parties, and Referena in Latin America'. *Comparative Political Studies* 45(9): 1159–1187.

Earle, L. 2013. 'Drawing the Line between State and Society: Social Movements, Participation and Autonomy in Brazil'. *The Journal of Development Studies* 49(1): 56–71

Eckstein, S., and Garretón, M.A. 1989. *Power and Popular Protest: Latin American Social Movements*. Berkeley: University of California Press..

Equipo ONADEM. 2011. 'Las elecciones del 4 de abril de 2010: Lo hecho y lo dicho en diarios y TV', in ONADEM *Medios a la Vista 2: Análisis sobre el Derecho a la Información y la Comunicación y el Periodismo en Bolivia 2009–2011*. La Paz: Fundación Unir Bolivia, Observatorio Nacional de Medios ONADEM, pp. 119–30.

Errejón Galván, I. 2011. '*Evo Pueblo*: La construcción hegemónica del MAS en Bolivia', in I. Errejón Galván and A. Serrano (eds), *Del asalto a la transformación del Estado en Bolivia*. Barcelona: Viejo Topo, pp. 111–41.

Escárzaga, F. 2012. 'El Ejército Guerrillero Tupak Katari (EGTK), la insurgencia aymara en Bolivia'. *Pacarina del Sur* [online], year 3, no. 11 (April–June). ISSN: 2007-2309. {module 61}. Disponible en Internet: www.pacarinadelsur.com/ nuestra-america/ oleajes/441-el-ejercito-guerrillero-tupakkatari-egtk-la-insurgencia-aymara-en-bolivia[/ div2].

Escobar, A. 1992. 'Culture, Economics and Politics in Latin American Social Movements Theory and Research', in A. Escobar et al., *The Making of Social Movements in Latin America: Identity, Strategy and Democracy*. Boulder, CO: Westview Press, pp. 62–88.

Escobar, A., and Alvarez, S.E. 1992. *The Making of Social Movements in Latin America: Identity, Strategy and Democracy*. Boulder, CO: Westview Press.

European Union. 2006. *Bolivia: Elecciones a la Asamblea Constituyente y Referéndum sobre las Autonomías Departamentales. 2 de julio de 2006. Informe Final*. La Paz: Misión de Observación Electoral de la Unión Europea. Retrieved 28 January 2013 from http://ace-project.org.

Evans, P., et al. 1985. *Bringing the State Back In*. New York: Cambridge University Press.

Evans, P. (ed.). 1997. *State-Society Synergy: Government and Social Capital in Development*. Berkeley: University of California.

Exeni, J.L. 2010. *Mediocracia de alta intensidad. Bolivia: Medios de comunicación y democracia en contextos de cambio*. La Paz, Bolivia: Instituto Internacional para la Democracia y la Asistencia Electoral IDEA.

Fabricant, N. 2012. *Mobilizing Bolivia's Displaced: Indigenous Politics and the Struggle over Land*. Chapel Hill: University of North Carolina Press.

Fabricant, N., and N. Postero. 2015. 'Sacrificing Indigenous Bodies and Lands: The Political–Economic History of Lowland Bolivia in Light of the Recent TIPNIS Debate'. *Journal of Latin American and Caribbean Anthropology* 20(3): 452–474.

Fals Borda, O. 1992. 'Social Movements and Political Power in Latin America', in A. Escobar et al., *The Making of Social Movements in Latin America: Identity, Strategy and Democracy.* Boulder, CO: Westview Press, pp. 303–16.

Farthing, L., and B. Kohl. 2014. *Evo's Bolivia: Continuity and Change.* Austin: University of Texas Press.

Fernando, J.L., and A.W. Heston. 1997. 'NGOs between States, Markets, and Civil Society'. *The Annals of the American Academy of Political and Social Science* 554: 46–65.

Ferreira, R. 2016. *Caso Zapata: La Confabulación de la Mentira.* La Paz: Editorial El País.

FIDH/APDHB-Bolivia. 2013. *Bolivia: Informe de Verificación de la Consulta realizada en el Territorio Indígena Parque Nacional Isiboro-Secure.* La Paz, Bolivia.

Fleury, S. 2002. 'El desafío de la gestión de las redes de políticas'. *Revista Instituciones y Desarrollo* 12–13: 221–47. Barcelona, Spain: Institut Internacional de Governabilitat de Catalunya. http://www.iigov.org.

Foweraker, J. 1995. *Theorizing Social Movements.* London: Pluto Press.

Fox, E. (ed). 1988. *Media and Politics in Latin America: The Struggle for Democracy.* London: Sage Publications.

Fuente Jeria, J. de la. 2010. 'El difícil parto de otra democracia: La Asamblea Constituyente de Bolivia'. *Latin American Research Review* 45: 5–26.

Fuentes-Nieva, R., and Nelli Feroci, G. 2017. 'The Evolving Role and Influence and Growing Strength of Social Movements in Latin America and the Caribbean'. *International Development Policy* (October): 323–338.

Gago, V., and Mezzadra, S. 2017. 'A Critique of the Extractive Operations of Capital: Toward an Expanded Concept of Extractivism 1'. *Rethinking Marxism* 29(4): 574–591.

Gamboa Rocabado, F. 2010. 'Transformaciones constitucionales en Bolivia: Estado indígena y conflictos regionales'. *Colombia Internacional* 71: 151–88.

Gamson, W.A., and G. Wolfsfeld. 1993. 'Movement and Media as Interacting Systems'. *Annals of the American Academy of Political and Social Science* 528: 114–25.

Garcés, F. 2007. 'Ordenamiento territorial, recursos naturales y Asamblea Constituyente en Bolivia: hacia un Estado plurinacional?'. *Comentario Internacional* 7 (II semestre 2006 / I semestre 2007): 229–39.

Garcés, F., et al. 2010. *El Pacto de Unidad y el Proceso de Construcción de una Propuesta de Constitución Política del Estado.* La Paz, Bolivia: Preview Gráfica.

García Linera, A. 2011. *El 'oenegismo', enfermedad infantil del derechismo (O como la 'reconducción' del Proceso de Cambio es la restauración neoliberal).* La Paz, Bolivia: Vicepresidencia del Estado Plurinacional, Presidencial de la Asamblea Legislativa Plurinacional.

García Linera, A., et al. 2010. *Sociología de los Movimientos Sociales en Bolivia.* La Paz, Bolivia: Plural Editores/AGRUCO/NCCR Norte-Sur. Cuarta Edición.

Gargarella, R., and C. Courtins. 2009. *El Nuevo constitucionalismo latinoamericano: promesas e interrogantes.* Santiago de Chile: CEPAL.

Garretón, M.A. 1989. 'Popular Mobilization and the Military Regime in Chile: The Complexities of the Invisible Transition', in S. Eckstein (ed.), *Power and Popular Protest: Latin American Social Movements.* Berkeley: University of California Press, pp. 259–77.

Gianotten, V. 2006. *CIPCA y poder campesino indígena: 35 años de historia.* La Paz: Plural Editores.

Gibbs, T. 2004. 'Democracy's Crisis of Legitimacy in Latin America'. *NACLA Report on the Americas,* 1 July 2004.

Glenn, J.K. 2003. 'Parties out of Movements: Party Emergence in Postcommunist Eastern Europe', in Goldstone, J.A. (ed.), *States, Parties, and Social Movements.* Cambridge: Cambridge University Press, pp. 147–169.

Goldstone, J.A. (ed.). 2003. *States, Parties, and Social Movements*. Cambridge: Cambridge University Press.

Gomez Bruera, H. 2006. 'Evolandia no es Hugolandia'. *Nexos: Sociedad, Ciencia y Literatura* 28(346): 41–52.

Gómez Mallea, A. 2005. 'Comunicación y conflictos culturales en Bolivia. El papel de los comunicadores en la reconstrucción de la hegemonía'. *Punto Cero* 10(11): 23–32.

Gray Molina, G. 2004. 'Comentario de George Gray Molina', in PNUD-Bolivia, *Crisis y Reforma de los Partidos en Bolivia*. La Paz, Bolivia: Cuaderno del Futuro, No. 19, Informe del Desarrollo Humano, pp. 45–56.

———. 2010. 'The Challenge of Progressive Change under Evo Morales', in K. Weyland et al., *Leftist Governments in Latin America: Successes and Shortcomings*. New York: Cambridge University Press, pp. 57–76.

Gurza Lavalle, A., and E. Insunza Vera. 2010. '1. Precisiones conceptuales para el debate contemporáneo sobre la innovación democrática: participación, controles sociales y representación', in idem (eds), *La innovación democrática en América Latina: tramas y nudos de la representación, la participación y el control social*. Mexico D.F.: CIESAS and Universidad Veracruzana, pp. 17–80.

———. 2015. 'El control democrático del Estado en Latinoamérica'. *Desacatos* 49: 6–7.

Gustafson, B. 2002. 'The Paradoxes of Liberal Indigenism: Indigenous Movements, State Processes, and Intercultural Reform in Bolivia', in D. Maybury-Lewis et al., *The Politics of Ethnicity: Indigenous Peoples in Latin American States*. Cambridge, MA: Harvard University Press, pp. 267–306.

Gutiérrez Aguilar, R. 2008. *Los ritmos del Pachakuti: Movilización y levantamiento indígena-popular en Bolivia*. Buenos Aires: Tinta Limón.

Gutmann, A., and Thompson, D.F. (eds). 2004. *Why Deliberative Democracy?* Princeton: Princeton University Press.

Hagopian, F., and S. Mainwaring (eds). 2005. *The Third Wave of Democractization in Latin America: Advances and Setbacks*. Cambridge: Cambridge University Press.

Hahn, D.R. 1996. 'The Use and Abuse of Ethnicity: The Case of the Bolivian CSUTCB'. *Latin American Perspectives* 23(2): 91–106.

Handler, J.F. 1992. 'Postmodernism, Protest, and the New Social Movements'. *Law and Society Review* 26(4): 697–731.

Harten, S. 2011a. 'Towards a "Traditional Party"? Internal Organization and Change in the MAS in Bolivia', in A.J. Pearce (ed.), *Evo Morales and the Movimiento al Socialismo in Bolivia*. London: Institute for the Study of the Americas, pp. 63–91.

———. 2011b. *The Rise of Evo Morales and the MAS*. London: Zed Books.

Haug, C. 2013. 'Organizing Spaces: Meeting Arenas as a Social Movement Infrastructure between Organization, Network and Institution'. *Organization Studies* 34(5–6): 705–732.

Healy, K. 1991. 'Political Ascent of Bolivia's Peasant Coca Leaf Producers'. *Journal of Interamerican Studies and World Affairs* 33(1): 87–121.

Held, D. 2006. *Models of Democracy*. Cambridge: Polity Press.

Hellinger, D., and A.P. Spanakos. 2017. 'The Legacy of Hugo Chávez'. *Latin American Perspectives*, Issue 212, 44(1): 4–16.

Hidle, K., and R.H. Normann. 2013. 'Who Can Govern? Comparing Network Governance Leadership in Two Norwegian City Regions'. *European Planning Studies* 21(2): 115–30.

Holloway, J. 2002. *Change the World without Taking Power: The Meaning of Revolution Today*. London: Pluto Press.

Hurtado, J. 1986. *El Katarismo*. La Paz, Bolivia: Instituto de Historia Social Bolivia ISBOL.

Ibáñez Rojo, E. 2000. 'The UDP Government and the Crisis of the Bolivian Left (1982–1985)'. *Journal of Latin American Studies* 32: 175–205.

Isuani, F. 2005. 'Los desafíos de la gestión intergubernamental en la implementación de programas sociales'. Tucumán, Argentina: Trabajo preparado para el Tercer Congreso Nacional de Administración Pública.

Insunza Vera, E. 2005. 'Interfaces socioestatales y proyectos políticos: La disputa entre rendición de cuentas y participación ciudadana desde la perspectiva de la igualdad compleja', in A. Monsiváis-Carrillo (ed.), *Políticas de transparencia: ciudadanía y rendición de cuentas.* Mexico: Instituto Federal de Acceso a la Información Pública, pp. 17–30.

———. 2006a. 'Capítulo 9. Para analizar los procesos de democratización: interfaces socioestatales, proyectos políticos y rendición de cuentas', in E. Insunza Vera and A.J. Olvera (eds), *Democratización, rendición de cuentas y sociedad civil: participación ciudadana y control social.* México: CIESAS-UV-Miguel Angel Porrúa, pp. 265–91.

———. 2006b. 'El reto de la confluencia: Las interfaces socioestatales en el contexto de la transición política mexicana (dos casos para la reflexión)', in E. Dagnino et al., *La disputa por la construcción democrática en América Latina.* México: Programa Interinstitucional de Investigación-Acción sobre Democracia, Sociedad Civil y Derechos Humanos, Centro de Investigaciones y Estudios Superiores en Antropología Social (CIESAS), pp. 275–329.

Jelin, E. 1997. 'Emergent Citizenship or Exclusion? Social Movements and Non-Governmental Organizations in the 1990s', in W.C. Smith et al., *Politics, Social Change and Economic Restructuring in Latin America.* Miami: North–South Center Press, University of Miami, pp. 79–104.

———. 1998. 'Toward a Culture of Participation and Citizenship: Challenges for a More Equitable World', in S. Alvarez et al., *Cultures of Politics and Politics of Cultures.* Boulder, CO: Westview Press, pp. 405–14.

Jiménez, M.C. 2012. 'La importancia del accountability social para la consolidación de la democracia en América Latina'. *Revista de Relaciones Internacionales, Estrategia y Seguridad* 7(2): 97–130.

Joffres, A. 2015. 'Le Venezuela dans l'ere post- Chávez: quelques éléments de compréhension d'une géopolitique multiniveau'. *Outre-Terre* 2(43): 148–67.

John, P., and A. Cole. 2008. 'Political Leadership in the New Urban Governance: Britain and France Compared'. *Local Government Studies* 25(4): 98–115.

Johnston, H. 2011. *States and Social Movements.* Cambridge: Polity Press.

Joppke, C. 1991. 'Social Movements during Cycles of Issue Attention: The Decline of the Anti-Nuclear Energy Movements in West Germany and the USA'. *The British Journal of Sociology* 42(1): 43–60.

Jordan, G., and C. Weedon. 1995. *Cultural Politics: Class, Gender, Race and the Post-Modern World.* Oxford: Blackwell.

Kahler, M., et al. 2009. *Networked Politics: Agency, Power and Governance.* New York: Cornell University Press.

Kauffman, L.A. 1990. 'The Anti-Politics of Identity'. *Socialist Review* 20: 67–80.

Kenis, P., and V. Schneider. 1991. 'Policy Networks and Policy Analysis: Scrutinizing a New Analytical Toolbox', in B. Marin and R. Mayntz (eds), *Policy Networks: Empirical Evidence and Theoretical Considerations.* Frankfurt a.M.: Campus, pp. 25–59.

Kitschelt, H. 2006. 'Party Movements', in R.S. Katz and W. Crotty (eds), *Handbook of Party Politics.* London: Sage Publications, pp. 278–91.

Kitzberger, P. 2010. 'The Media Activism of Latin America's Leftist Governments: Does Ideology Matter?'. GIGA Research Unit, Institute of Latin American Studies, No. 151.

———. 2012. 'The Media Politics of Latin America's Leftist Governments'. *Journal of Politics in Latin America* 3: 123–39.

Kjaer, U. 2013. 'Local Political Leadership: The Art of Circulating Political Capital'. *Local Government Studies* 39(2): 253–72.

Klandermans, B., and C. van Stralen (eds). 2015. *Movements in Times of Democratic Transition.* Philadelphia, PA: Temple University Press.

Kliksberg, B. 1998. 'Repensando el Estado para el desarrollo social: más allá de dogmas y convencionalismos'. *Reforma y Democracia* 8. Documento incluido dentro de la Biblioteca Digital de la Iniciativa Interamericana de Capital Social, Ética y Desarrollo – www.iadb.org/etica.

Kohl, B., and L. Farthing. 2007. *El bumerán Boliviano.* La Paz, Bolivia: Plural Editores.

Kriese, H. 1989. 'New Social Movements and the New Class in the Netherlands'. *American Journal of Sociology* 94(5): 1078–1116.

Kriese, H., et al. 1995. *New Social Movements in Western Europe: A Comparative Analysis.* Minneapolis: University of Minnesota.

Kooiman, J. 2008. 'Exploring the Concept of Governability'. *Journal of Comparative Policy Analysis* 10(2): 171–90.

Kymlicka, W. 2001. *Politics of the Vernacular: Nationalism, Multiculturalism and Citizenship.* Oxford: Oxford University Press.

Kymlicka, W., and C. Straehle. 2001. 'Cosmopolitanism, Nation-States, and Minority Nationalism', in W. Kymlilcka et al., *Politics of the Vernacular: Nationalism, Multiculturalism and Citizenship.* Oxford: Oxford University Press, pp. 221–23.

Lagos, M. 2001. 'Between Stability and Crisis in Latin America'. *Journal of Democracy* 12(1): 137–45.

Laing, A. 2015. 'Resource Sovereignties in Bolivia: Re-Conceptualising the Relationship between Indigenous Identities and the Environment during the TIPNIS Conflict'. *Bulletin of Latin American Research* 34(2): 149–66.

Larraín, J. 2000. *Identity and Modernity in Latin America.* Cambridge: Polity Press.

Laserna, R. 1993. 'Integración y gobernabilidad: Los nuevos desafíos de la democracia en Bolivia'. *Nueva Sociedad* 128: 120–31.

———. 2007. 'El caudillismo fragmentado'. *Nueva Sociedad* 209: 100–17.

Lazarte, J. 2010. *Nuevos códigos de poder en Bolivia.* La Paz, Bolivia: Plural Editores.

Levitsky, S., and K.M. Roberts (eds). 2011. *The Resurgence for the Latin American Left.* Baltimore, MD: Johns Hopkins University Press.

Licha, I. 2001. 'Las redes políticas sociales: un desafío de la gerencia social'. Paper presented at the CLAS VI International Congress on the Reform of the State and Public Administration, Bueno Aires, Argentina. 5–9 November 2001. Retrieved 11 January 2019 from http://www.unap.cl/p4_unap/docs/curso_sociologia/gerencia_redes_politicas_sociales.pdf.

Lievesley, G. 2009. *Reclaiming Latin Amerca Experiments in Radical Social Democracy.* London: Zed.

Lissidini. A. 2015. 'Democracia directa en América Latina: avances, contradicciones y desafíos. *Nueva Sociedad,* Documentos: Democracia, Julio 2015. Retrieved 11 January 2019 from http://nuso.org/documento/democracia-directa-en-america-latina-avances-contradicciones-y-desafios/?page=9.

Loayza Bueno, R. 2010. *Racismo y Etnicidad en Bolivia.* La Paz: Konrad Adenauer Stiftung.

Loayza Bueno, R., and A. Datta. 2011. *The Politics of Evo Morales' Rise to Power in Bolivia: The Role of Social Movements and Think Tanks.* London: Overseas Development Institute.

Lofland, J. 1996. *Social Movement Organizations: Guide to Research on Insurgent Realities.* Berlin: Aldine de Gruyter.

Long, N. 1990. 'From Paradigm Lost to Paradigm Regained? The Case of an Actor-Oriented Sociology of Development'. *European Review of Latin American and Caribbean Studies / Revista Europea de Estudios Latinoamericanos y del Caribe* 49: 3–24.

———. 1999. 'The Multiple Optic of Interface Analysis'. Background paper on Interface Analysis, UNESCO, s.l.

———. 2001. *Development Sociology: Actor Perspectives*. London: Routledge.

Lopes De Souza, M. 2016. 'Lessons from Praxis: Autonomy and Spatiality in Comtemporary Latin American Social Movements'. *Antipode* 85(5): 1292–1316.

López Pacheco, J., and S. Hicapié Jiménez. 2014. 'La rendición social de cuentas en la calidad de la democracia: Una discusión sobre aportes y retos de la política comparada'. *Reflexión Política* 16(31): 7–17.

Lucero, J.A. 2008. *Struggles of Voice: The Politics of Indigenous Representation in the Andes*. Pittsburgh, PA: University of Pittsburgh Press.

Lupien, P. 2013. 'The Media in Venezuela and Bolivia: Attacking the "Bad Left" form Below'. *Latin American Perspectives* 40: 226–46.

Macassi, S. 2010. 'Medios y conflictos sociales entre el rating y el activismo'. *Diálogos de la Comunicación* 78: 1–11.

Macdonald, L. 1997. *Supporting Civil Society: The Political Role of Non-Governmental Organizations in Central America*. London: Macmillan.

Madrid, R.L. 2008. 'The Rise of Ethnopopulism in Latin America'. *World Politics* 60(3): 475–508.

Mainwaring, S., and T.R. Scully. 1995. *Building Democratic Institutions: Party Systems in Latin America*. Stanford, CA: Stanford University Press.

Makaran-Kubis, G. 2009. 'El nacionalismo étnico en los Andes: El caso de los aymaras bolivianos'. *Latinoamérica. Revista de Estudios Latinoamericanos* 49: 35–78.

Malavisi, A. 2010. 'A Critical Analysis of the Relationship between Southern Non-governmental Organizations and Northern Non-governmental Organizations in Bolivia'. *Journal of Global Ethics* 6(1): 45–56.

Martínez Dalmau, R. 2008. 'La integración en el nuevo constitucionalismo latinoamericano', in E. Tremolada Álvarez, *Crisis y perspectiva comparada de los procesos de integración*. Bogotá: Universidad Externado de Colombia, pp. 73–93.

Martínez Escamilla, V.H. 1996. 'Las políticas públicas desde la perspectiva de las redes sociales: un nuevo enfoque metodológico'. *Política y Cultura* 7: 37–60. Universidad Autónoma Metropolitana – Xochimilco Distrito Federal, Mexico.

Mastrini, G., and D. de Charras. 2005. 'Twenty Years Mean Nothing'. *Global Media and Communication* 1: 273–88.

Mayorga, F. 2007. 'Movimientos Sociales, Política y Estado'. *Opinión y Análisis* 1(84): 1–17. La Paz: Fundemos/Hans Seidel Stiftung.

———. 2009. 'Evo: Liderazgo sin fronteras?'. *Umbrales* 19: 119–33.

Mayorga, R.A. 2004. 'La crisis el sistema de partidos políticos en Bolivia: causas y consecuencias'. *Cuadernos del CENDES* 21(57): 83–114.

Mazzuca, S.L. 2007. 'Reconceptualizing Democratization: Access to Power versus Exercise of Power', in G.L. Munck et al., *Regimes and Democracy in Latin America: Theories and Methods*. Oxford: Oxford University Press, pp. 39–50.

McAdam, D. 1982. *Political Process and the Development of the Black Insurgency, 1930–1970*. Chicago: University of Chicago Press.

McAdam, D., J.D. McCarthy and M.N. Zald (eds). 1996. *Comparative Perspectives on Social Movements:Political Opportunities, Mobilizing Structures and Cultural Framing*. Cambridge: Cambridge University Press.

McAdam, D., Tarrow, S.G. and Tilly, C. 2001. *Dynamics of Contention*. New York: Cambridge University Press.

McNeish, J.-A. 2006. 'Stones on the Road: The Politics of Participation and the Generation of Crisis in Bolivia'. *Bulletin of Latin American Research* 25(2): 220–40.

———. 2013. 'Extraction, Protest and Indigeneity in Bolivia: The TIPNIS Effect'. *Latin American and Caribbean Ethnic Studies* 8(2): 221–42.

Medeiros, C. 2001. 'Civilizing the Popular?: The Law of Popular Participation and the Design of a New Civil Society in 1990s Bolivia'. *Critique of Anthropology* 21(104): 401–25.

Melucci, A. 1980. 'The New Social Movements: A Theoretical Approach'. *Social Science Information* 19: 199–226.

Mesa de Concertación. nd. 'Experiencia Boliviana Participación y Control Social'. Retrieved from www.mesadeconcertacion.org.

Michels, R. 1911. *Zur Soziologie des Parteiwesens in der modernen Demokratie; Untersuchungen über die oligarchischen Tendenzen des Gruppenlebens.* Leipzig: Werner Klinkhardt.

Michelutti, L. 2016. '"We Are All Chávez": Charisma as an Embodied Experience'. *Latin American Perspectives* 44(1): 232–50.

Migdal, J.S. 2001. *State in Society.* New York: Cambridge University Press.

Ministry of Public Works, Services and Housing. 2012. *Informe Final del proceso de Consulta Previa, Libre e Informada a las pueblos Moxeño-Trinitario, Yuracaré y Chimane del Territorio Indígenas y Parque Nacional Isiboro Securé (TIPNIS) 2012.* La Paz: Iskra Editores.

Moldíz, H. 2009. *Bolivia en los tiempos de Evo: Claves para entender el proceso boliviano.* Mexico, D.F.: Ocean Press and Ocean Sur.

Molina, F. 2010. 'El MAS en el centro de la política boliviana', in PNUD-Bolivia, *Mutaciones del Campo Político en Bolivia.* La Paz, Bolivia: Impresiones Gráficas 'Virgo', pp. 241–302.

———. 2011. 'El modelo de resolución política del MAS', in R. Cortéz Hurtado (ed.), *Cuaderno de Futuro 26: Claves de la transición del poder.* La Paz: PNUD, EDOBOL, pp. 251–300.

———. 2013. 'Por qué Evo Morales sigue siendo popular? Las fortalezas del MAS en la construcción de un nuevo orden'. *Nueva Sociedad* 245: 4–14.

Morales, W.Q. 2010. *A Brief History of Bolivia.* New York: Facts on Life.

———. 2013. 'The TIPNIS Crisis and the Meaning of Bolivian Democracy under Evo Morales'. *The Latin Americanist* 57(1): 79–90.

Moura, S. 1996. 'Redes de acción pública en la gestión local: tendencias actuales'. *América Latina Hoy* 14: 61–67. Salamanca, Spain.

Munck, G.L. 2004. 'Democracy Studies: Agendas, Findings, Challenges', in D. Berg-Schlosser (ed.), *Democratization: The State of the Art.* Wiesbaden: The World of Political Science: The Development of the Discipline Book Series, Volume 1, Mayo. VS Verlag für Sozialwissenschaften/GWV Fachverlage GmbH, pp. 80–94.

Newman, J. 2005. 'Enter the Transformational Leader: Network Governance and the Micro-politics of Modernization'. *Sociology* 39: 717–34.

Nolte, D., and A. Schilling-Vacaflor (eds). 2012. *New Constitutionalism in Latin America.* German Institute for Global and Area Studies (GIGA). Aldershot, UK: Ashgate.

O'Donnell, G. 1992. 'Transitions, Continuities and Paradoxes', in S. Mainwaring et al., *Issues in Democratic Consolidation: The New South American Democracies in Comparative Perspective.* Notre Dame, IN: University of Notre Dame Press, pp. 17–56.

———. 1993. 'Acerca del Estado, la democratización y algunos problemas conceptuales: Una perspectiva latinoamericana con referencia a países poscomunistas'. *Desarrollo Económico* 130: 163–84.

———. 1999. *Counterpoints: Selected Essays on Authoritarianism and Democratization.* Notre Dame, IN: University of Notre Dame Press.

O'Donnell, G., and P.C. Schmitter. 1986. 'Resurrecting Civil Society (and Restructuring the Political Space)', in G. O'Donnell et al., *Transitions from Authoritarian Rule: Prospects for Democracy.* London: Johns Hopkins University Press, pp. 48–56.

O'Donnell, G., et al. 1986. *Transitions from Authoritarian Rule: Prospects for Democracy.* London: Johns Hopkins University Press.

Offe, C. 1985. 'New Social Movements: Challenging the Boundaries of Institutional Politics'. *Social Research* 52(4): 817–68.

Orellana Halkyer, R. 2008. 'Municipalization and Indigenous Peoples in Bolivia: Impacts and Perspectives', in W. Assies et al., *The Challenges of Diversity: Indigenous Peoples and Reform of the State in Latin America*. Amsterdam: Thela Thesis, pp. 181–94.

Orias Arredondo, R. 2015. *Reformal judicial en Bolivia: elementos para el diagnóstico y desafíos*. La Paz: Friedrich Ebert Stiftung.

Our Water Commons. nd. 'Water Solutions. Case 5: "Social Control" and Public-Collective Partnerships with Community-Run Systems in Cochabamba, Bolivia'. www.ourwatercommos.org/water-solutions.

Oviedo Obarrio, F. 2010. 'Evo Morales and the Altiplano: Notes for an Electoral Geography of the Movimiento al Socialismo, 2002–2008'. *Latin American Perspectives* 37: 91–106.

Pacto de Unidad. 2010. *El Pacto de Unidad y el Proceso de Construcción de una Propuesta de Constitución Política de Estado*. La Paz, Bolivia: Programa NINA.

Page, B.I. 1996. 'The Mass Media as Political Actors'. *PS: Political Science and Politics* 29(1): 20–24.

Pappas, T.S. 2007. 'Political Leadership and the Emergence of Radical Mass Movements in Democracy'. *Comparative Political Studies* 41: 1117–40.

Pásara, L. 2014. *Elecciones judiciales en Bolivia: Una experiencia inédita*. Fundación para el Debido Proceso. Retrieved 10 January 2019 from https://dplfblog.com/2017/07/07/elecciones-judiciales-en-bolivia-segundo-intento/.

Patzi Paco, .F. 1999. *Insurgencia y sumisión: Movimientos indígeno-campesinos, 1983–1998*. La Paz, Bolivia: Muela del Diablo Editores.

Paz Patiño, S. 2007. 'Una mirada retrospectiva sobre la Asamblea Constituyente en Bolivia'. *RIPS. Revista de Investigaciones Políticas y Sociológicas* 6(002): 161–76. Universidad de Santiago de Compostela.

Pelletier, R., and D. Guérin. 1998. 'Les nouveaux mouvements sociaux constituent-ils un défi por les partis politques? Le cas du Québec'. *Canadian Journal of Political Science* 31(2): 311–38.

Peña, A., and Davies, T. 2017. 'Responding to the Street: Government Responses to Mass Protests in Democracies'. *Mobilization* 22(2): 177–200.

Perreault, T. 2006. 'From the *Guerra del Agua* to the *Guerra del Gas*: Resource Governance, Neoliberalism and Popular Protest in Bolivia'. *Antipode* 38(1): 150–72.

Perreault, T., and B. Green. 2013. 'Reworking the Spaces of Indigeneity: The Bolivian Ayllu and Lowland Autonomy Movements Compared'. *Environment and Planning D: Society and Space* 31: 43–60.

Petras, J. 1997. 'Imperialism and NGOs in Latin America'. *Monthly Review* 49(7): 10–27.

Philip, G. 2003. *Democracy in Latin America: Surviving Conflict and Crisis*. Cambridge: Polity Press.

Pichardo, N.A. 1997. 'New Social Movements: A Critical Review'. *Annual Review of Sociology* 23: 411–30.

Pino Jordán, A.M. 2010. '¿Qué es lo indígena y qué lo campesino?'. Dissertation at the Forum of the Presentation of the UN Declarion of Indigenous Peoples Rights. Puno, Peru. February 2010. Retrieved 11 January 2019 from http://servindi.org/actualidad/31111.

PNUD. 2008. *Una brújula para la democracia: Aportes para una agenda de gobernabilidad en América Latina*. Buenos Aires: Siglo XXI editores.

Postero, N. 2005. 'Movimientos indígenas bolivianos: articulaciones y fragmentaciones en la búsqueda del multiculturalismo', in N. Postero et al., *La Lucha por los Derechos Indígenas en América Latina*. Quito: Ediciones Abya-Yala, pp. 265–310.

———. 2010a. 'Morales's MAS Government: Building Indigenous Popular Hegemony in Bolivia'. *Latin American Perspectives* 37(3): 18–34.

———. 2010b. 'The Struggle to Create a Radical Democracy in Bolivia'. *Latin American Research Review* 45: 59–78.

———. 2017. *The Indigenous State: Race, Politics and Performance in Plurinational Bolivia.* Oakland: University of California Press.

Prada, R. 2008. *Subversiones indígenas.* La Paz, Bolivia: Muela del Diablo Editores, Comuna y Consejo Latinoamericano de Ciencias Sociales.

Prats, J. 2001. 'Gobernabilidad democrática para el desarrollo humano: Marco conceptual y analítico'. *Instituciones y desarrollo* 10. IIG/PNUD/Generalitat de Catalunya.

Proietto, R. 1995. 'New Social Movements: Issues for Sociology'. *Social Science Information* 34: 355–88.

Proyecto de Ley de Convocatoria a la Asamblea Constituyente presentada por el Pacto de Unidad. http://www.gobernabilidad.org.bo/images/stories/documentos/PIOCs/ Docsh istoricos/8_prop_ley_conv_ac_pactounidad.pdf.

Przeworski, A. 1992. 'The Games of Transition', in S. Mainwaring et al., *Issues in Democratic Consolidation: The New South American Democracies in Comparative Perspective.* Notre Dame, IN: University of Notre Dame Press, pp. 105–52.

Quiroz, M., and L. Sandoval. 2012. 'Conflicto intrahegemónico en Bolivia en el bloque en el poder MAS/movimientos sociales'. *Anuario del Conflicto 2011.* Barcelona: Universidad de Barcelona, pp. 341–66.

Regalsky, P. 2010. 'Political Processes and the Reconfiguration of the State in Bolivia'. *Latin American Perspectives* 36: 35–50.

Revilla, M. 1994. 'Gobernabilidad y Movimientos Sociales, una Relación difícil'. *América Latina Hoy* 8: 21–25.

Rivadeneira Prada, R. 1988. 'Bolivian Television: When Reality Surpasses Fiction', in E. Fox (ed.), *Media and Politics in Latin America: The Struggle for Democracy.* London: Sage Publications, pp. 164–70.

Rivera Cusicanqui, S. 1986. *Oprimidos pero no vencidos: luchas del campesinado aymara y qhechwa de Bolivia, 1900–1980.* Geneva: Instituto de Investigaciones de las Naciones Unidas para el Desarrollo Social.

———1993 'Democracia liberal y democracia de ayllu', in M. Pacheco et al., *Bolivia en la hora de su modernización.* Mexico: Universidad Autónoma de México, pp. 257–84.

———2015. 'Strategic Ethnicity, Nation, and (Neo)colonialism in Latin America. *Alternautas* 2(2): 10–20.

Roberts, B.R. 2001. 'Las nuevas políticas sociales en América Latina y el desarrollo de ciudadanía: una perspectiva de interfaz'. Document presented at the workshop 'Agency, Knowledge and Power: New Directions'. University of Wageningen, Netherlands.

Roberts, K.M. 1998. *Deepening Democracy? The Modern Left and Social Movements in Chile and Peru.* Stanford, CA: Stanford University Press.

Rodríguez-Carmona, A. 2009. *El proyectorado. Bolivia tras 20 años de ayuda externa.* La Paz: Plural Editores. Primera edición: Intermón Oxfam, 2008.

Romero Ballivián, S. 2003. 'CONDEPA y UCS: El declive del neopopulismo boliviano'. *Revista de Ciencia Política* XXIII(001): 67–98. Pontificia Universidad Católica de Chile.

Rossi, F.M., and D. della Porta. 2015. 'Mobilizing for Democracy: Social Movements in Democratizations Processes', in B. Klandermans and C. Van Stralen (eds), *Movements in Times of Democratic Transition.* Philadelphia, PA: Temple University Press, pp. 9–33.

Rustow, D.A. 1970. 'Transitions to Democracy: Toward a Dynamic Model'. *Comparative Politics* 2(3): 337–363.

Roxborough, I. 1997. 'Citizenship and Social Movements under Neoliberalism', in W.C. Smith et al., *Politics, Social Change and Economic Restructuring in Latin America.* Miami: North–South Center Press, University of Miami, pp. 57–75.

Rubin, J.W., and V. Bennet (eds). 2015. *Enduring Reform: Progressive Activism and Private Sector Responses in Latin America's Democracies*. Pittsburgh: University of Pittsburgh Press.

Salman, T. 2009. 'Searching for Status: New Elites in the New Bolivia'. *European Review of Latin American and Caribbean Studies* 86: 97–105.

———. 2011. 'Entre protestar y gobernar: Movimientos sociales en Bolivia en tiempos del MAS'. *Tinkazos* 29: 21–43.

———. 2013. 'El Estado, los movimientos sociales y el ciudadano de a pie: exploraciones en Bolivia entre 2006 y 2011'. *América Latina Hoy* 65: 141–60.

Sánchez-López, D. 2015. 'Reshaping Notions of Citizenship: The TIPNIS Indigenous Movement in Bolivia'. *Development Studies Research* 2(1): 20–32.

Sartori, G. 1976. *Parties and Party Systems: A Framework for Analysis*. New York: Cambridge University Press.

Scholte, J.A. 2005. 'The Sources of Neoliberal Globalization'. United Nations Research Institute for Social Development, Overarching Concerns, Programme Paper Number 8.

Schönwälder, G. 1997. 'New Democratic Spaces at the Grassroots? Popular Participation in Latin American Local Governments'. *Development and Change* 28(4): 753–770.

Schultz, J. 2005. *Lecciones de Sangre y Fuego: El Fondo Monetario Internacional y el 'Febrero Negro Boliviano'*. La Paz, Bolivia: Centro para la Democracia.

Schumpeter, J. 1943. *Capitalism, Socialism and Democracy*. London: George Allen & Unwin.

Scott, A. 1990. *Ideology and the New Social Movements*. London: Routledge.

Seferiades, S., and H. Johnston. 2012. *Violent Protest, Contentious Politics and the Neoliberal State*. Farnham, UK: Ashgate Publishing.

Seligson, M.A. 2007. 'The Rise of Populism and the Left in Latin America'. *Journal of Democracy* 18(3): 81–95.

Shugart, M., and S. Mainwaring. 1997. *Presidentialism in Latin America*. Cambridge: Cambridge University Press.

Silva, P. 1999. 'The New Political Order in Latin America: Towards Technocratic Democracies?', in R. Gwynne and C. Kay (eds), *Latin America Transformed: Globalization and Modernity*. New York: Oxford University Press, pp. 157–70.

———. 2006. 'The Politics of Neo-liberalism in Latin America: Depoliticization and Technocratic Rule in Chile', in R. Robinson (ed.), *The Neoliberal Revolution: Forging the Market State*. London: Palgrave, pp. 39–57.

Silva, P., and F. Rojas Aravena (eds). 2013. *Gobernabilidad y Convivencia Democrática en América Latina: Las Dimensiones regionales, nacionales y locales*. Costa Rica: FLACSO.

Silvia, C. 2011. 'Collaborative Governance Concepts for Successful Network Leadership'. *State and Local Government Review* 43(1): 66–71.

Slater, D. 1985. 'Social Movements and a Recasting of the Political', in D. Slater et al., *New Social Movements and the State in Latin America*. Amsterdam: CEDLA, pp. 1–21.

Slater, D., et al. 1985. *New Social Movements and the State in Latin America*. Amsterdam: CEDLA.

Smith, P.H. 2005. *Democracy in Latin America: Political Change in Comparative Perspective*. New York: Oxford University Press.

Solheim, H. 2013. 'Legitimidad, eficacia y relación interinstitucional entre autoridades civiles y Policiales en Bogotá, 1995–2012', in P. Silva and F. Rojas Aravena (eds), *Gobernabilidad y Convivencia Democrática en América Latina: Las Dimensiones regionales, nacionales y locales*. Costa Rica: FLACSO, pp. 127–56.

Sørensen, E. 2002. 'Democratic Theory and Network Governance'. *Administrative Theory & Praxis* 24(4): 693–720.

Sørensen, E., and J. Torfing. 2005a. 'Network Governance and Post-Liberal Democracy'. *Administrative Theory & Praxis* 27(2): 197–237.

———. 2005b. 'The Democratic Anchorage of Governance Networks'. *Scandinavian Political Studies* 28(3): 195–218.

Sørensen, G. 2008. *Democracy and Democratization: Processes and Prospect in a Changing World*. Boulder, CO: Westview Press.

Soto Barrientos, F. 2012. 'La Democracia como forma de Estado: análisis de los mecanismos de participación directa en la constitución Suiza'. *Estudios constitucionales – Revista Semestral del Centro de Estudios Constitucionales de Chile* 10(1): 373–402.

Souto Maior Fontes, B.A., et al. 2008. 'Redes, gobernanza urbana y prácticas asociativas: el ejemplo del Programa de Salud de la Familia'. *Estudios Sociológicos* XXVI(1): 33–63.

Stahler-Sholk, R., H.E. Vanden and , G.D. Kuecker (eds). 2008. *Latin American Social Movements in the Twenty-First Century. Resistance, Power, and Democracy*. Lanham, MD: Rowman & Littlefield Publishers, Inc.

Stefanoni, P. 2010. *'Qué hacer con los indios...' Y con otros traumas irresueltos de la colonialidad*. La Paz, Bolivia: Plural Editores.

Stepan, A. 1978. *State and Society: Peru in Comparative Perspective*. Princeton, NJ: Princeton University Press.

———. 1986. 'Paths toward Redemocratization: Theoretical and Comparative Considerations', in G. O'Donnell et al., *Transitions from Authoritarian Rule: Prospects for Democracy*. London: The Johns Hopkins University Press, pp. 64–84.

Steyn, I. 2012. 'The State and Social Movements: Autonomy and its Pitfalls'. *Politikon: South African Journal of Political Studies* 39(3): 331–51.

Street, J. 2001. *Mass Media, Politics and Democracy*. New York: Palgrave.

Ströbele-Gregor, J. 1994. 'From Indio to Mestizo... to Indio: New Indianist Movements in Bolivia'. *Latin American Perspectives* 21(2): 106–23.

Svampa, M., and P. Stefanoni (eds). 2007. *Bolivia: Memoria, insurgencia y movimientos sociales*. Buenos Aires: CLACSO.

Tapia, L. 2009. *La coyuntura de la autonomía relativa del estado*. La Paz, Bolivia: CLACSO, Muela del Diablo Editores.

Tarrow, S. 1983. *Struggling to Reform: Social Movements and Policy Change during Cycles of Protest*. Ithaca, New York: Cornell University.

———. 1998. *Power in Movement: Social Movements and Contentious Politics*. Cambridge Studies in Comparative Politics. Cambridge: Cambridge University Press.

Taylor, L. 2005. 'Citizenship and Political Culture: The Political Agent and the Natural Hierarchy', in W. Assies et al., *Citizenship, Political Culture and State Transformation in Latin America*. Amsterdam: Dutch University Press, pp. 241–55.

Thompson, L., and C. Tapscott (eds). 2010. *Citizenship and Social Movements: Perspectives from the Global South*. London: Zed Books.

Tilly, C. 1978. *From Mobilization to Revolution*. Reading, MA: Addison-Wesley.

———. 2004. *Social Movements, 1768–2004*. Boulder, CO: Paradigm.

———. 2007. *Democracy*. New York: Cambridge University Press.

Tilly, C., and S. Tarrow. 2007. *Contentious Politics*. Boulder, CO: Paradigm.

Torre, C. de la. 2013. 'In the Name of the People: Democratization, Popular Organizations and Populism in Venezuela, Bolivia and Ecuador'. *European Review of Latin American and Caribbean Studies* 95: 27–48.

Torre, J.C. 1997. 'The Politics of Transformation in Historical Perspective', in W.C. Smith et al., *Politics, Social Change and Economic Restructuring in Latin America*. Miami: North–South Center Press, University of Miami, pp. 21–36.

Torres-Rivas, E. 1993. 'América Latina: Gobernabilidad y democracia en sociedades en crisis'. *Nueva Sociedad* 128: 88–101.

Torrico Villanueva, E.R. 2011a. 'La Información y la Comunicación como derechos fundamentales en la transición política boliviana', in ONADEM *Medios a la Vista 2: Análisis sobre el Derecho a la Información y la Comunicación y el Periodismo en Bolivia 2009–2011*. La Paz: Fundación Unir Bolivia, Observatorio Nacional de Medios ONADEM, pp. 17–20.

———. 2011b. 'La reconfiguración del campo mediático boliviano desde la política (2006–2011)', in ONADEM *Medios a la Vista 2: Análisis sobre el Derecho a la Información y la Comunicación y el Periodismo en Bolivia 2009–2011*. La Paz: Fundación Unir Bolivia, Observatorio Nacional de Medios ONADEM, pp. 251–60.

Trejo Delarbre, R. 1994. '¿Videopolítica vs. Mediocracia? Los medios y la cultura democrática'. *Revista Mexicana de Sociología* 56(3): 23–58.

Trelles Cruz, M.E. 2006. 'Medios de comunicación y gobernabilidad: Escenarios de interdependencia en la comunicación política'. *UNIrevista* 1(3): 1–9.

Uharte Pozas, L.M. 2013. 'La disputa política por la hegemonía democrática en Bolivia'. *Intersticios* 7(2): 149–66.

UNASUR. 2008a. *Declaración de la Moneda: Santiago de Chile, septiembre 2008*. Retrieved 7 March 2013 from: http://www.unasursg.org/index.php?option=com_content&view= arti cle&id=446:declaracion-de-la-moneda-santiago-de-chile-septiembre-de-2008&catid=96:- declaraciones.

———. 2008b. *Informe de la Comisión de UNASUR sobre los sucesos de Pando: Hacia un alba de justicia para Bolivia*. November 2008.

UNIR. 2011. 'Análisis de la conflictividad del TIPNI y potenciales de paz' [Analysis of the TIPNIS conflict and the potential for peace]. Digital resource consulted 11 January 2019 through www.unirbolivia.org: http://www.unirbolivia.org/nueva3/images/stories/cabec era/21oct2011_Anlisis_conflictividad_TIPNIS__y_potenciales_de_paz_links.pdf.

United Nations General Assembly. 2009. 'Informe Público de la Oficina del Alto Mando Comisionado de las Naciones Unidas para los Derechos Humanos en Bolivia sobre los Hechos de Violencia ocurridos en Pando en Septiembre de 2008'. La Paz, Bolivia: Oficina del Alto Comisionado para los Derechos Humanos de Bolivia, March 2009.

Van Cott, D.L. 2000. 'Party System Development and Indigenous Populations in Latin America: The Bolivian Case'. *Party Politics* 6(2): 155–74.

———. 2005. *From Movements to Parties in Latin America: The Evolution of Ethnic Politics*. Cambridge: Cambridge University Press.

———. 2008. *Radical Democracy in the Andes*. Cambridge: Cambridge University Press.

Van Dyke, V. 1995. 'The Individual, the State, and Ethnic Communities in Political Theory', in W. Kymlicka et al., *The Rights of Minority Cultures*. Oxford: Oxford University Press, pp. 31–56.

Viaña, J. 2011. 'La compleja trama de permanente interlocución/ruptura entre movimientos sociales y el gobierno del MAS en Bolivia 2006–2009', in R. Cortéz Hurtado (ed.), *Cuaderno del futuro N° 26: Claves de la Transición del Poder*. La Paz: PNUD, EDOBOL.

Vicepresidencia del Estado Plurinacional. 2009. *Memoria REPAC*. Retrieved 8 January 2019 from https://www.vicepresidencia.gob.bo/IMG/pdf/repac.pdf.

Viciano Pastor, R., and R. Martínez Dalmau. 2010. '¿Se puede hablar de un nuevo constitucionalismo latinoamericano como corriente doctrinal sistematizada?'. Valencia: University of Valencia, pp. 4–5. Paper presented at the VII World Congress of International Law Association, 6–10 December 2010. Retrieved 15 January 2012 from http://www.juridicas. unam.mx/wccl/ponencias/13/245.pdf.

Villegas Taborga, S. 2011. 'Fuentes oficiales y temática política prevalecen en los medios gubernamentales', in ONADEM *Medios a la Vista 2: Análisis sobre el Derecho a la Información y la Comunicación y el Periodismo en Bolivia 2009–2011*. La Paz, Bolivia: Fundación Unir Bolivia, Observatorio Nacional de Medios ONADEM, pp. 93–98.

Von Freyberg, D. 2012. 'Movimientos sociales y ONG locales e internacionales: Historia de un desencuentro', in S. Piris Lekuiona (ed.), *Movimientos Sociales y Cooperación: Ideas para el debate*. Spain: Universidad del País Vasco, Instituto de Estudios sobre Desarrollo y Cooperación Internacional, pp. 81–106.

Webber, J.R. 2011. *From Rebellion to Reform in Bolivia: Class Struggle, Indigenous Liberation and the Politics of Evo Morales*. Chicago, IL: Haymarket Books.

Welp, Y. 2010. 'El referendo en América Latina: Diseños institucionales y equilibrios de poder'. *Nueva Sociedad* 228: 26–44.

Weyland, K. 2004. 'Neoliberalism and Democracy in Latin America: A Mixed Record'. *Latin American Politics and Society* 46(1): 135–57.

Whitehead, L. 2002. *Democracy: Theory and Experience*. New York: Oxford University Press.

Wickham-Crowley, T.P., and S. Eckstein. 2015. 'The Persisting Relevance of Political Economy and Poltical Sociology in Latin American Social Movements Studies'. *Latin American Research Review* 50(4): 3–25.

Wils, F. 1995. 'Las ONGs y sus redes en Bolivia: hacia una síntesis. Conclusiones y Recomendaciones', in F. Wils et al., *Organizaciones No Gubernamentales y sus Redes en Bolivia*. La Paz: Gemeenschappelijk Overleg Medefinanciering GOM, Centro de Estudios y Proyectos CEP, pp. 268–96.

Wolford, W. 2015. 'Rethinking the Revolution: Latin American Social Movements and the State in the 21st Century', in J.W. Rubin and V. Bennett (eds), *Enduring Reform: Progressive Activism and Private Sector Responses in Latin America's Democracies*. Pittsburgh, PA: University of Pittsburgh Press, pp. 53–80.

Yúdice, G. 1998. 'The Globalization of Culture and the New Civil Society', in S. Alvarez et al., *Cultures of Politics and Politics of Cultures*. Boulder, CO: Westview Press, pp. 325–52.

Zaremberg, G., V. Guarneros-Meza and A. Gurza Lavalle (eds). 2017. *Intermediation and Representation in Latin America*. New York: Palgrave Macmillan.

Zegada, M.T., et al. 2011. *La democracia desde los márgenes: transformaciones en el campo político boliviano*. La Paz, Bolivia: Muela del Diablo Editores, CLACSO.

Zuazo, M. 2009. *Cómo nació el MAS? La ruralización de la política en Bolivia*. La Paz, Bolivia: Fundación Ebert.

Zurbriggen, C. 2003. 'Las redes de políticas públicas: Una revisión teórica'. Instituto de Ciencia Política, Montevideo, Uruguay; Institut internacional de Gobernabilitat de Catalunya. Retrieved 11 January 2019 from: ttp://saludpublicavirtual.udea.edu.co/cvsp/politicaspub licas/0015.zurbriggen_redes_politicas_publicas.pdf.

Index